Limerick County Library

80012 006 3149 9

D0265418

'eabhar' 'OF M'
LIMI CK

The Economical Environmentalist

WITHDRAWN FROM STOCK

The Economical Environmentalist

My Attempt to Live a Low-Carbon Life and What it Cost

333.72

Prashant Vaze

LIMERICK
0063 3149
COUNTY LIBRARY

earthscan

publishing for a sustainable future

London • Sterling, VA

First published by Earthscan in the UK and USA in 2009

Copyright © Prashant Vaze, 2009

All rights reserved

ISBN: 978-1-84407-807-3   hardback
        978-1-84407-808-0   paperback

Typeset by Safehouse Creative
Cover design by Rob Watts

All calculations in this book can be replicated using the greenhouse gas calculator at www.economicalenvironmentalist.co.uk

For a full list of publications please contact:

Earthscan
Dunstan House
14a St Cross St
London, EC1N 8XA, UK
Tel: +44 (0)20 7841 1930
Fax: +44 (0)20 7242 1474
Email: earthinfo@earthscan.co.uk
Web: www.earthscan.co.uk

22883 Quicksilver Drive, Sterling, VA 20166-2012, USA

Earthscan publishes in association with the International Institute for Environment and Development

A catalogue record for this book is available from the British Library

Library of Congress Cataloging-in-Publication Data
Vaze, Prashant.
  The economical environmentalist : my attempt to live a low-carbon life and what it cost / Prashant Vaze.
     p. cm.
  Includes index.
  ISBN 978-1-84407-807-3 (hbk.) -- ISBN 978-1-84407-808-0 (pbk.) 1. Sustainable living--Economic aspects. 2. Environmentalism--Economic aspects. 3. Carbon offsetting--Social aspects. 4. Green movement--Economic aspects. I. Title.
  GE196.V39 2009
  333.72092--dc22

                                                          2009018126

At Earthscan we strive to minimize our environmental impacts and carbon footprint through reducing waste, recycling and offsetting our CO_2 emissions, including those created through publication of this book. For more details of our environmental policy, see www.earthscan.co.uk

This book was printed in the UK by MPG Books, an ISO 14001 accredited company. The paper used is FSC certified.

Mixed Sources
Product group from well-managed forests and other controlled sources
www.fsc.org Cert no. SA-COC-1565
© 1996 Forest Stewardship Council
FSC

I dedicate this book to Ayeisha and Satish.
You so often see with disarming clarity what needs to be done.
Sorry about the state we're leaving the place in;
please don't hold it against us when you pay for our pensions.

Contents

List of Figures, Tables and Boxes

Figures

The Economical Environmentalist

Tables

Boxes

Preface

The working title of this book was The One Tonne Challenge. It should become evident by Chapter 3 why that title never made it to the final cut. For most of my life I have been a committed environmentalist, but just not a very good one. I knew that I needed to reduce my emissions; I just never got around to it.

So the book's title became *The Economical Environmentalist* instead. And the last four weeks have been an important period of time for both the economy and the environment.

Three weeks ago the world's climate scientists gathered in Copenhagen presaging the climate conference which the city will host in December. The three days of presentations were sombre even by climate scientists' funereal standards. The Congress concluded that the worst-case IPCC scenarios were being realized. Climate change wasn't something for the future; the climate system was already moving beyond the normal patterns of variability. Over the past six years, 35,000 people died in the 2003 European heatwave; 1 million lost their homes from the 2005 Mumbai floods and 100,000 died in the Myanmar cyclones of 2008. This body-bag count isn't mine. It is that of Rajendra Pachauri, who leads the international panel of climate scientists. If climate change was the villain in a James Bond movie – a Hugo Drax or Auric Goldfinger – he could put his feet up and content himself with what a good job he'd done in bringing society to its knees. Yet *The War on Terror* is more likely to add to the cost and inconvenience of your flight than the rhetoric on climate change.

Yesterday I had dinner in central London. Less than half a mile away, Jamie Oliver was serving dinner to 29 of the world's most powerful people. If the press speculation is correct, the G20 leaders argued, over their Scottish salmon, about whether and how to tighten the rules on tax havens, by the time the roast lamb was served they might have debated how much the IMF need be given to prop up ailing economies. There was already unanimity that banks need to be more tightly regulated. All the leaders would have been conscious of the scale of the challenge that faced them domestically: tens of thousands out of work, thousands of previously viable businesses now closed and the collapse in public finances. The overriding political imperative for the next two years would be to restore the world's economy to its usual trends, but hopefully taking out the bad bits.

But perhaps a more interesting report, *Prosperity Without Growth*, was published on the eve of the summit by Tim Jackson of the UK's Sustainable Development Commission. It asked UK politicians to embrace a different vision. It argued that our finance industry's problems, the inequalities within and between countries and the disappointing trends in human well-being are not isolated problems arising from rogue bankers, incompetent regulators or lax lending policies, but the systemic result of society and businesses setting themselves the wrong goals. Instead of striving for growth, our aim should be for a steady-state economy, living within the constraints of community hopes, material resources, physical locations and sustainable energy flows.

The contrast between the two agendas is stark. In December the world's leaders will congregate in Copenhagen in what is already being trumpeted as the 'green growth conference'. They will unveil their plans to ramp up international climate commitments and deliver clean, green growth. Signing bits of paper is easy; developing and deploying the policies to make them happen is not. And while top-down policies are necessary, they will not deliver change fast enough to prevent the continuance of climate chaos. Our leaders have already signed many agreements which we are on track to fail: European emissions reduction targets for 2020, fuel poverty targets for 2010, renewable energy targets for 2020. Ink is cheap; the political capital to effect meaningful change is dear and cannot be quantitatively eased into existence.

I will argue in Chapter 2 that the world needs to start reducing greenhouse gas emissions within ten years. Changing our consumption habits is the only show in town which can act fast enough to do this. But the conventional political process is unlikely to deliver this. It is for individual people to take responsibility for their impacts on the environment and make whatever changes they can in their lives.

There is no unique trajectory a person must follow to reduce his or her own emissions. While writing this book I have met several people who already live low-carbon lives, either through their poverty or their bloody-mindedness. But this 5 per cent of the population are not the appropriate role model for the majority of people. This book is written for people like me who *get it* intellectually, but are looking for pragmatic advice on how to reduce their impacts on the environment cost-effectively. I am still amazed by how quickly and easily I have managed to make substantial reductions in my own emissions. While many of the changes will also save money, not all of them are cost free.

This book is a personalized account of my last year. The science and numbers are, to the best of my knowledge, pukka. If you've got any better data or alternative data, do let me know and I'll sort it out for the accompanying website. The book is also a work of fiction, for while I do really have a wife and two kids, and we really did get married in 2007, I have taken some liberties with what occurred to spare blushes. So I doubt they'll vouch for the episodes or conversations documented in this book.

Prashant Vaze
Camden, London
April 2009

Acknowledgements

Any list of thanks has to start with my wife Maya de Souza who persuaded me to give up my job and give writing a go. My brother Prabhat commented at length on the transport chapter and we've probably spoken about pretty much every idea and datum in the book. Alex Macgillivray persuaded me to persevere with the book and make it more personal, late one evening, even after my stable-mate Chris Goodall issued *How to Live a Low-Carbon Life*.

I'd also like to thank my former colleagues from Defra, Office of Climate Change and the secretariat of the Committee on Climate Change who seeded many of the book's ideas through their analysis, conversation and disagreement. Thanks in particular are due to Dave Cawley and Neil Witney for their comments on early drafts; Jonathan Brearley, Tony Grayling, Tony Pike, Richard Price, Jill Rutter, Michael Feliks, Kate Levick, Katharine Thoday, Tom Luff, Michelle Pittini, David Joffe, Hunter Danskin, Dimitri Zenghelis, Nafees Meah, Jan Kiso, Paul Johnson and David Kennedy for the many debates we've had on a low-carbon society. I've had many largely fruitless conversations with friends and family about energy, environment and life. Sometimes these have plugged gaps in my knowledge; sometimes they merely underline how weird and inventive a species we are. People who fall into in this category include Asha and Bhaskar Vaze, David MacKay, Tanny Liverpool, Mark de Souza, Roy de Souza, Adam Deacock, Alexis Rowell, Justin Bere, David Towns, Julian Morgan, Frances Harris, Fergus Lyon, Ramesh Kumar, Nick Mabey, Natasha Warikoo, Sunil Vaze, Shrikant Vaze, Janette Vaze, Stephen Tindale and Edwin Lloyd. Thanks also to the many staff at Earthscan who've helped bring this book to fruition; this has included Rob West, Hamish Ironside, Claire Lamont and Gudrun Freese in particular.

Over the year I wrote this book I've learnt a lot from my 'community' in Camden, including the idea that community isn't just a geographic place but also a shared way of looking at things. Thanks to the not so serious book club, especially Edward Milford, Richard Walker, Godfrey Spickernell, Victoria Green, Ed Ross and Natalie Bennett; other local environmental activists, including John Doggett and Chit Chong from Camden eco-home; and Gill and Robert Aitken, who amply, and so unlike me, demonstrate it is possible to be a mandarin and still be handy with the sheep's wool. Thanks to Mark Ridsdill-Smith, Ro Randall, Andy Brown, Shilpa Shah and Chris Baker from Cambridge Carbon Footprint. The CamdenCAN email list has been the source of occasional insight and not just about hemp; thanks also for useful titbits from Rob Cartwright.

I have had to check numerous facts and figures with friends, businesses, trade associations and academics. Many who have not known me from Adam have contributed their time. Thanks to Ben Lane, staff at Good Energy, staff at Abel and Cole, Louise Boom, Tadj Oreszczyn, Gundula Azeez, Tara Garnett and the brilliant food climate research network she runs, Chris Parkin, Peter Melchett, Peter Kaufman, Sigrid Stagl, Richard Dibley, Matt Prescott, Lilli Matson, Paul Dickinson, staff at the Green Concierge, staff at Scout Moor wind farm, Guy Robinson, Craig Jones, Keith James, Mark Lumsden, Steve Biddle, Ben Smith, Lynn Sloman, Paul Watkiss, Chris Penn, Sîan Berry, Tom Rye, Nick Eyre, Gavin Killip, and staff at Knauf insulation.

Thanks finally to Defra and the Environment Agency whose monies I misappropriated to finance my year of trying to live a lower carbon life.

Introduction

Introduction

Most Englishmen would rather die than think, and many of them do.
(Dorothy Sayers)

It is no use saying, 'We are doing our best'. You have got to succeed in doing what is necessary. (Winston Churchill)

Why Read this Book?

Have you ever asked yourself whether it's better for the environment to scrap your old gas guzzler and buy a more energy-efficient model, knowing that it takes energy to make the new car? Or whether cycling to work really reduces greenhouse gas emissions, if you're left so hungry at the other end you wolf down a bacon sandwich? Whether offsetting of carbon really reduces emissions or just makes you feel better?

I hope Dorothy Sayers is wrong in her reading of the English psyche; this book assumes so. It sets out to help you sort through the mountains of advice to identify the changes you need to make that will make a *real* difference. Using science, economics and real-life experiences it addresses the questions that you might encounter if you're sincerely trying to cut back on your emissions.

If we are to avoid runaway climate change we don't have much time. Winston Churchill was speaking about the Second World War in the quote reproduced above. But his point *what we do now has to count* is as valid today as it was then. In war there is immediacy between action and gain, inaction and slaughter. Confusingly for us, the feedback between today's emissions and runaway climate change in the future is just as inexorable as the feedback loop in war, but the effect is lagged by many decades. In hindsight our children may well blame us for failing to act sufficiently when the threat was so clearly evident.

The book is also being published during a time of economic downturn. As I write, the biggest recession my generation has experienced is unfolding. Day after day the headlines have spoken about lay-offs and industry bailouts. People are understandably nervous about losing their jobs. We need to reduce our emissions over the next few years with this backdrop. The advice needs to make sense from a carbon point of view and, just as importantly, from the financial point of view too.

Climate change is too close, too big and too urgent to wait for someone else to take the lead. We cannot blame the Americans, the Chinese, government or big business, and leave it to them to get their house in order before we act. People as consumers, voters and workers are the real motive force. Ultimately the world's emissions will fall only if people change what they buy, how they wield their political muscle and how they run their working lives.

Any good bookshop has at least half a dozen books listing tips to reduce your emissions. There are also many websites and carbon calculators that help you convert your fuel readings and transport bills into carbon dioxide emissions. Many are good. But most contain long lists of possible actions with little evaluation of their effectiveness, cost or feasibility. There is something to be said for switching off your mobile phone charger when it's not being used – I have reduced my emissions by 4 kilograms of carbon dioxide ($kgCO_2$) a year by doing so. But I'd be deluding myself if I pretended this absolved me for my carbon emissions from flying to the US last year, which gave rise to over two tonnes of carbon dioxide (tCO_2).

This book evaluates the types of options available to individuals in a rigorous fashion. It considers many of the choices we make including big-ticket items like buying cars; and also the day-to-day decisions about what food to eat. A large part of our emissions are hidden – they take place on our behalf by the businesses that produce, transport and dispose of the goods we buy. The connection between purchasing these goods and carbon dioxide emissions is less apparent than when we pay the electricity or gas bill, or put fuel in our cars, but it is just as real. Our purchase decisions determine the size of the market for these goods and hence the scale of indirect emissions. Much more greenhouse gas emissions arise from producing a kilogram of beef than from producing a kilogram of chicken but this won't be evident on the label. The book considers, where possible, the greenhouse gas emissions from the entire life cycle of the good.

Characters in this Book

A little about myself: I have worked as an economic analyst for the UK government for most of my career. I have spent about half my career working on energy and climate change policy and have been lucky enough to meet executives in the major energy companies, banks and construction companies, and also the nascent low-carbon businesses too. I have fed into and seen at close quarters some of the environment and climate debates over the past decade. I have no doubt that the senior officials and ministers are largely sincere in their desire to address climate change. But there is a huge gulf in wanting to do something in government, and actually making it happen. Instead there is another bout of displacement behaviour: reviews, consultation documents, strategies, commissions led by the great and the good, and then nothing. Without the necessary political consensus and ministerial colleagues' support, things don't happen. It's much easier to halt progress than initiate it.

I made a conscious attempt to decarbonize my life last year. This book is a diary cum annotated map of my journey. It was a year in which I got married, organized a weekend away for 15 friends, maintained my car-dependent, long-distance relationship with my children who live with my ex-wife, and rediscovered that while being vegetarian might well be healthier it's not as much fun as being carnivorous. The book also describes the experiences of other people I have met over the last year. Box 1.1 gives pen portraits of Angie and Duncan.

Box 1.1 *Characters in the book*

Duncan works in an advice centre helping local people manage their debt problems. He lives in a modern purpose-built flat in North London. He's committed to reducing his energy use and is quietly getting on with the task, motivated by a desire to help the world and because he has no great material ambitions himself. You wouldn't see him dead in a protest or at a rally, and he's never joined any of the environmental NGOs. Though he is well paid he doesn't own a car, nor does he foresee needing one. He owns a laptop and a CD player, but these are pretty much his only consumer goods; he doesn't even have a mobile phone. He lives in a flat-share with two others and has lived there for over a year since he got back from teaching for two years in South America. He feels lucky to be working in the local authority in the economic downturn, since the job is secure. Duncan's ambition is to do a master's degree and then work overseas again. He'd like to find a partner and settle down someday, but there's still time: he's only 25 years old.

I met Angie one hot summer's weekend in North London when I was manning a stall using a laptop to calculate people's carbon footprints. I had spoken to several people who used two or three times more energy than the average Briton. I saw Angie and assumed she was more of the same; she was a well-spoken elderly lady and I took her to be a retired doctor or lecturer. She is a widow and her son passed away. She lives with a tenant, in the ground floor flat of an aged and slightly decrepit Victorian home. But poverty has restricted her opportunities to use energy. She hasn't holidayed in years, catches the bus to work, and has never driven a car. She eats meat just once a week, and heats the room she is sitting in with a mobile electric heater. It seemed odd to find her shopping in the genteel suburbs of London. She lives off the state pension and with a few hours' work as a receptionist at an osteopath practice. The pay is rotten, and it takes her half an hour by bus to get to the job. Unfortunately, she became indebted when her son fell ill and subsequently died. Her husband passed away over 30 years ago. Her home is sparsely furnished and pretty much everything needs replacing or mending. The pride of place on her mantelpiece is a photograph of the Pope. She has been a devoted Catholic all her life, and was even a nun for a few years. Yes, she cares about the environment but her first priority was to get out of debt.

My lifestyle, while not exactly environmentally profligate, has not been conspicuously low carbon either. Many of the bad climate choices I have made, I have sleepwalked into: leaving the central heating on full blast when on holiday, of holidaying far further away than necessary because of the glamour of being able to report back to friends, of equipping the kitchen with racks of spotlights because I didn't have the energy to argue against the business who simply wanted to sell me more kit. Others make similar decisions, and in the aggregate they can have a dramatic impact on the country's total emissions.

Some of the changes proposed in this book will be difficult, at least in the short term. Maybe replacing dairy milk with soya milk is not for you. But humans are adaptable animals and hopefully this book will help you understand the most effective and palatable changes you can make. This sense of what really works and what doesn't – this carbon consciousness – becomes instinctive after a while. Soon it feels wrong to leave devices on unnecessarily. The idea of purchasing a non-energy-efficient car feels abhorrent.

The Gap between Caring about Climate Change and Doing Something

Bringing the UK's emissions down to sustainable levels needs actions by individuals, businesses and companies

Why is this book being directed at individuals, why not at government or businesses? There is whole book to be written about the issue of what can be done by government and business to hasten these processes; but not this book.

The UK government has made a commitment to reduce the country's emissions by 80 per cent within a generation. This is a target our children must deliver, but for which we have to set the foundations. Decarbonization to this scale is nothing like our previous environmental problems. There is no off-the-shelf substitute for fossil fuels, no carbon-free sources of energy that we can switch to tomorrow – renewables, carbon capture and nuclear will take decades to implement and we have barely started. Unlike the reduction of sulphur dioxides from power stations, there is no easy end-of-pipe fix. The sources of greenhouse gases – cars, planes, factory chimneys, central heating boilers and cattle – are too diffuse to find a single solution.

The scale of the challenge is so huge that government, business and individuals each need to play their parts. Government needs to use its powers of regulating, planning, taxing, licensing and grant-giving. Businesses need to provide clear and reliable information to consumers, bring innovative low-carbon products to the market and reduce energy use in their own production processes.

But individuals, I would argue, have the most important role to play within this compact. We have take responsibility for our decisions about how to equip and insulate our homes, where to holiday and about our personal mobility. As voters, we decide whether to punish through the ballot box any political party that dares support a local wind farm, or threatens to introduce an energy tax. The final chapter of this book has more to say about what government and businesses might do to help individuals decarbonize.

Climate change is one of the most serious threats facing us

Don't take my word for it. Look what our leaders are saying and doing.

A number of people say that the threat of climate change is exaggerated, or that scientists with a vested interest are skewing the discussion for reasons of self-interest. The trouble with this argument is the sheer number of prominent people with no axe to grind – senior figures from government and business, as well as religious leaders – who speak as passionately as any environmentalist.

Senior former public figures have been exposed to unequivocal evidence of climate change, and recognize it as being one of the biggest long-term challenges facing our society. Some of them are making climate change a large part of their 'retirement' careers. This list includes former world leaders, Al Gore and Tony Blair; Nick Stern, a former chief economist at the World Bank and the UK Treasury; two former government chief scientists, Robert May (a population zoologist) and David King (a physical chemist); and Adair Turner, a former head of the Confederation of British Industry (CBI). Successful chief executives from business, like John Browne from BP and Stuart Rose from Marks and Spencer, also speak eloquently and passionately on the issue. These neutral observers are convinced that climate change is an existential threat to society. This has gone well beyond being a concern to scientists and environmentalists.

But there is a gulf between our concern for climate change and concrete actions being taken

This book is about what individuals can do. The fact that you've read this far probably means you're already convinced about the need to act. It is worth reminding yourself you are not alone. The majority of people in the UK are concerned and wish to act to stop climate change.

People are broadly persuaded that climate change is happening and is a threat. In their most recent social research report, Ipsos MORI[1] found that 46 per cent of people thought that climate change was mainly caused by people and a further 41 per cent thought climate change was caused by both people and natural processes. A large majority of people (70 per cent) believe that if there is no change the world will soon experience a major environmental disaster.

But this widespread belief that disaster looms around the corner and that we are responsible through our actions does not translate into changes in behaviour. When asked about what they had done over the past year to reduce climate change, most people said 'nothing'. The Ipsos MORI results are reproduced in Figure 1.1.

However, 78 per cent of a sample surveyed by the Department for Transport[2] said they would be willing to change their behaviour to limit climate change (see Figure 1.2). But in terms of what behaviours would most improve the environment there was a degree of wishful thinking – the top two chosen being actions either for others to do (clean engines for cars), or which individuals already do (recycling).

Actions that need people to moderate activities they cherish, like changing flying or driving habits, were downplayed. Flying is especially difficult, because there is, as yet, no low-carbon fix, and because 80 per cent of people aim to continue to fly the same amount next year, and even ten years hence – technology and tastes are leading us away from the low-carbon path.

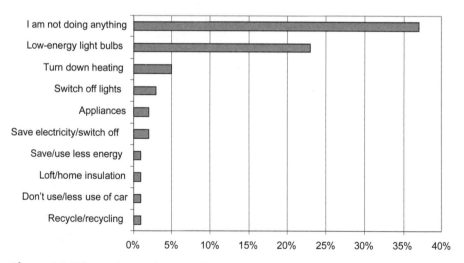

Figure 1.1 What is the number one thing you are doing to tackle climate change? (no prompts)

Note: Sample: 2130 British adults, March 2007.

Source: Ipsos MORI

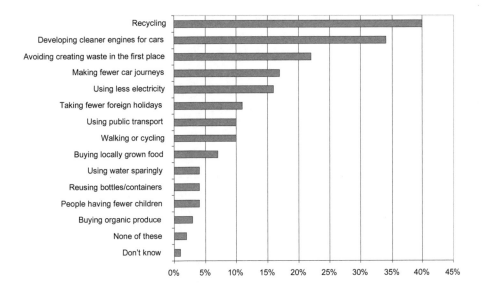

Figure 1.2 Which of the actions on this list, if any, do you think will do the most to help reduce climate change? (prompts provided)

Note: Sample: 2037 adults June 2007.

Source: Department for Transport

Psychologists recognize the dissonance between believing and doing as evidence of traumatic stress

If most people understand and believe that climate change is happening why is our response as a society so inadequate? Psychologists who have studied how people respond to traumas like bereavement say the same framework can be applied to how we view climate change.[3] Rather than engaging with the issue properly, we get 'freaked out' by the enormity of the problem and flip into the five pathological states of:

1   **denial** – refusal to believe the evidence, or more subtly, believing the threat is exaggerated;
2   **anger** – rage that climate change will spoil our lives and our futures or anger that *others* who should be responsible are not doing their jobs;
3   **bargaining** – taking inadequate actions (for example, installing and talking excessively about low-energy light bulbs) to reinforce our own self-image, but not acknowledging what we are doing is not enough;

4 **depression** – sadness, sometimes uncontrollable despondency, that we are responsible for critically damaging the world; sometimes we feel sadness at a particular feature (the glaciers) or a species or image (the drowning polar bear); and

5 **acceptance** – a measured, rational and proportionate response to the climate threat; finding out about the consequences of our actions, adjusting our behaviour to reduce the threat.

Our reactions don't usually fit into a single box. Though I like to think of myself as wavering between bargaining and acceptance, hearing that government is considering giving its OK to construct another runway at Heathrow, or to build a coal-fired power station at Kingsnorth (miles from any plausible carbon sequestration gasfield) still angers. The thought of the glaciers in the Himalayas melting within my lifetime, and the floods and droughts in Asia this will entail, leaves me desperately sad, throwing up inane, anxious questions: where will the abominable snowman hide? Will the Punjab still produce multiple harvests?

This book is written to help people settle into acceptance and find the appropriate response. Most people won't be able to get there by reading this book alone. The final chapter talks a little bit about organizations that are trying to cultivate a sense of community and shared journey for those trying to develop a carbon consciousness.

How to Read this Book

If you are reading this book, you probably don't need me to tell you that society needs to reduce its emissions of greenhouse gases. Nevertheless Chapter 2 provides a potted summary of climate science drawn mainly from the recent international science reports and some of the ethical and economic issues raised by the Stern Report.[4] The chapter goes on to calculate a sustainable level of per capita emissions that helps set a sustainable target.

Chapters 3 to 8 go through the different ways we cause greenhouse gas emissions: eating, travelling, heating our homes, operating appliances, making and throwing things away. These chapters are all organized in the same way. They start with some tips about the things we can do that will save the most emissions, the next section has statistics, trends and background data on how greenhouse gases arise, after that there are sections about what we can do to reduce emissions. Often I describe what we can do in the short term, medium term and long term. Then I go on to describe what I did myself, how much it cost and how much carbon it saved. Duncan and Angie's experiences are often included too. Each chapter rounds off with a diagram showing the carbon savings I expect to make.

Chapter 9 calculates how I did in the year overall and talks about how we can reduce our emissions through community-based activities and carbon offsetting. There is also a brief description of some of the macroeconomic effects of society reducing its consumption of energy and goods more generally.

A word on units

This book has a lot of numbers in it. I have included a list of abbreviations at the back which gives more detail, but here are some basic concepts to help make sense of what you are about to read.

The information in this book covers three greenhouse gases. Emissions of greenhouse gases are given in 'tCO$_2$e' – this means the tonnes of carbon dioxide equivalent. This is explained in more detail at the start at Chapter 2.

Energy use (electricity and gas) is measured in 'kWh'. This is the amount of energy a 100 watt electric light bulb uses in ten hours and equates to a cost of about 12p for electricity in the UK at the moment.

Notes

1   Downing, P. and Ballantyne, J. (2007) *Tipping Point or Turning Point? Social Marketing & Climate Change*, Ipsos MORI www.ipsos-mori.com/researchpublications/publications/publication.aspx?oItemId=1174 (accessed July 2009).
2   Department for Transport (2008) 'Attitudes to climate change and the impact of transport (2006 and 2007)', www.dft.gov.uk/pgr/statistics/datatablespublications/trsnstatsatt/attitudestoclimatechange2 (accessed July 2009).
3   Randall, R. (2005) 'A new climate for psychotherapy', *Psychotherapy and Politics International*, vol 3, p3.
4   HM Treasury and Cabinet Office (2006) 'Stern Review on the economics of Climate Change', www.hm-treasury.gov.uk/sternreview_index.htm and Cambridge University Press, Cambridge (accessed July 2009).

2

The Economic and Environmental Challenges

- The UK's Committee on Climate Change recommends the country should reduce its emissions of greenhouse gases compared to 1990 levels by 42 per cent by 2020 and 80 per cent by 2050.
- This means emissions per person in the UK need to fall to 7.5 tonnes of carbon dioxide by 2020. Emissions were around 13 tonnes per person in 1990 and are around 12 tonnes per person now. We need to make far faster progress.
- Individuals will have to use less fuel in the home and car (which account for about a fifth of the UK's energy use), reduce their use of electricity and non-car transport (which make up a quarter of energy use) and buy fewer goods and services.
- About two-thirds of greenhouse gas emissions from the UK economy arise from producing goods and services, especially food, complex electronics and large goods like cars. So focusing on heating, light bulbs and transport won't be enough.
- Energy use is unequal within our society. The richest 10 per cent of British households use five times more energy than the poorest 10 per cent. Addressing energy use by the well-off is where the biggest climate savings will lie.
- We cannot wait until the recession is over before we think about reducing our greenhouse gas emissions. Over the next few years we need to reduce our emissions and invest in low-carbon infrastructure as we climb out of a recession.
- We should reduce our consumption back to an affordable level and increase our investment in low-carbon technologies. If we have secure jobs or savings, now is a good time to help the economy recover by investing in energy efficiency in the home.
- We also need to come to terms with a change in our economic relationship with India and China. Even after we recover, our economic circumstances will be different – imported goods, cheap overseas holidays and cheap borrowing could be gone. So changes in our behaviour like buying locally, travelling less and keeping goods for longer will help the environment and save money.

Recession, Competition from India and China, and Climate Change

Plan A (because there is no plan B) is our five year plan to tackle some of the biggest challenges facing business and our world.
(Marks and Spencer describing its targets, which include cutting CO$_2$ emissions)

The rush of customers taking money out of Northern Rock continued for a second day on Saturday, amid concerns over its emergency Bank of England loan.
(BBC website, 15 September 2007)

The first quote is taken from the Marks and Spencer's website and describes its aspiration to reduce its greenhouse gas emissions. What is most impressive is their sense of urgency. The company has given itself five years because that's how much time there is, and as it says, *there is no plan B.*

The second quote describes the start of the credit crunch. Who can forget the scenes on television on 14 September 2007, when customers queued around the block to withdraw their savings from Northern Rock? This was when the credit crisis finally became real to the general population. There had been rumblings about the collapse in inter-bank lending in the financial press for several months. But now the tension was palpable and not just confined to the men in pinstriped suits. If banks no longer trusted one another, why should we trust them? It was this day when people were reminded of the *virtual* nature of banking. Their life savings were just data on a computerized ledger, easily appropriated by more powerful forces if Northern Rock went to the wall. If Northern Rock folded they'd be just another creditor waiting in the line for when the administrator or the bank compensation scheme paid them their dues. That could be months away – maybe even years. In the meantime, there were bills to pay and Christmas presents to buy. It made people aware of a new fear: a fear the institutions they trusted to look after their wealth could go broke, wiping out blameless customers and creditors.

But I watched the day from afar, distracted. Intellectually I understood the importance of what was happening, but I had other things on my mind. It was, after all, the day before I got married.

Though the economy is hurting, we cannot afford to take our eye off reducing our greenhouse gas emissions

I was working as an economist and policymaker in the Office of Climate Change when I decided to write this book. I wanted to take some time out and try to reduce my own emissions and write about the experience. I knew from speaking to people in North London, where I live, that others were trying to do the same. We knew climate change was happening already, the heat-waves of 2003, the drought in Australia, the retreating glaciers, the collapse of ice-shelves; every year we delay making the necessary low-carbon changes to our lives increases the risk of chaotic consequences.

This book would emerge into a world where unemployment levels in the West would be higher than for 20 years and these would persist for perhaps two years. When we recovered from our economic slumber it would be into a changed world where the centre of economic gravity moved from the West to Asia. Recovery couldn't just be more of the same. In the last recession the shedding of jobs in low-wage manufacturing and services broke the Midlands, the North and the rust-belt of the US. This one would feed higher up the economic food chain, hitting professionals and white-collar jobs too.

The credit crunch will be the economic backdrop to all our lives for some time. My own savings had been badly hurt. Angie, who I mentioned in the last chapter, has debts not savings. But poverty is no lead screen insulating her from the fallout from the credit crunch. Her income from her part-time job has slumped as customers of the alternative medicine practice where she worked stayed at home. Her biggest worry is her unsecured loan – she hasn't dared open the mail from her bank – it sits malignly on her coffee table, its bright red lettering warding her off. Duncan works in the public sector so believes his job to be secure, but he lives in rented accommodation and the prospect of buying property is off the agenda for the foreseeable future since it will take him a decade to save up the necessary deposit now that lending criteria have tightened.

Climate change was barely going to figure in most people's minds during the recession. It would hover away from the headlines, in the newspapers' inside pages, a subordinate threat.

This is even though many climate scientists say the recent Intergovernmental Panel on Climate Change (IPCC) reports have underestimated the speed at which climate change is happening. Climate systems' long time-lags mean that, unlike imprudent financial borrowing, the consequences of imprudent energy use are not felt for many decades.

Climatologists are telling us we need to move faster than we previously thought. We will look at this evidence later in this chapter. But the important message is we cannot afford to wait until the recovery before we turn our attention to the environment; we have to do it now. We need to invest in reducing our emissions at the same time as we try to mend our economy, and at the same time as the investment resources are transferring east.

The credit crunch will cause a temporary reduction in greenhouse gas emissions

My high street in Kentish Town has changed over the last year. Woolworths has gone, so too has the MFI, and one of the (admittedly over-abundant) whole-food shops. When my wife and I went out for a meal on the Friday before Christmas, we were served straight away – something nigh on unknown in any other year.

No wonder spending is down. In 2008 the number of unemployed British people rose by 250,000 to 1.9 million. The speculation is another million jobs will be lost over the course of 2009. City bonuses in 2008 were £7 billion, still a mind-boggling sum, but half their 2007 and a third of their 2006 levels. Whatever your views about the finance sector, there is no getting away from its importance to the UK economy. Figure 2.1 shows how the sector's contribution to the UK gross domestic product (GDP) in 2006 was about the same as the other three big losers so far from the credit crunch – manufacturing, retailing and construction – *combined*. A significant share of corporate taxes and exports were courtesy of the industry.

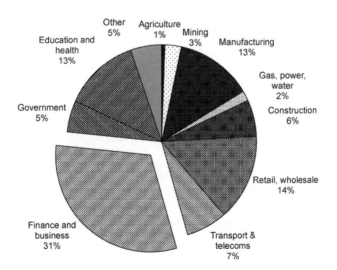

Figure 2.1 Contribution to UK GDP of different industries, 2006

Note: Total GDP was £1177 billion

Source: Office for National Statistics[1]

The severest job losses are taking place in some of the energy-intensive industries: sales of gas guzzlers are collapsing and traffic at the airports is down. For the next year or two the greenhouse gas emissions for many countries will fall because of reduced economic activity. But no economical environmentalist should take comfort in the severity and speed of the downturn. The smart way to slow a speeding car is by dabbing the brake in a controlled fashion, not by driving into a tree. When the car plants and steel mills re-open, the production lines and furnaces will still need to update their processes, otherwise they will remain locked into existing energy usage.

We need to invest in low-carbon technologies so when we recover we don't return to high carbon emissions

Will government develop policies to directly invest in low-carbon projects? I don't know. The government is running a huge deficit – spending much more than it raises in taxes. This makes it uncomfortable for government to borrow further to subsidize low-carbon investment in rail networks or renewable electricity incentives. If it did so it would have to cut back on other types of spending, or borrow further. But the latter option is affordable. At the start of 2008 the UK government's debt was 44 per cent of GDP; it will reach 50 per cent soon (if we ignore the effect of putting the liabilities of the now state-controlled banks on the government's balance sheet). But it is still lower than that of the US, and much lower than that of Japan. So borrowing to finance low-carbon investment is affordable for the country.

The other option is strengthening existing policies that stimulate private-sector investment in low-carbon technologies. But our performance in providing this leadership is woeful. I have spoken to people in the power industry who have plans on how to decarbonize their sector in their back pockets, but cannot persuade their board rooms because there is no consistent signal or economic incentive from government or the EU. They are frustrated that our declared targets for wind power and combined heat and power are not backed up by meaningful incentives or changes in regulations to make building infrastructure easier. In autumn 2008 the price of carbon dioxide in the flagship EU emissions trading market was a pitiful €25 per tonne. The policy which aims to reduce emissions by increasing the cost of polluting added a mere US$7 per barrel to the cost of burning oil. Over the year market forces drove down the price of oil by US$100 per barrel. The EU's emissions trading scheme is about as noteworthy to the investment plans of power companies as an OPEC minister's sneeze.

What does this mean for consumers and policymakers?

So what should a consumer who wants to reduce his greenhouse gas emissions and help the economy do? This question is baffling policy wonks the world over.

Alex Bowan, Sam Fankhauser, Nick Stern and Dimitri Zenghelis issued a pamphlet aimed at their former employers in the Bank of England, European Bank for Reconstruction and Development, and HM Treasury with some principles for designing a green stimulus package.[2] They argue we need to spend now – ideally in the next 18 months, but our spurt of spending should be time limited. This spending should increase economic demand, create jobs, and use factories and employees that might otherwise remain idle during a recession. Lastly we should ensure any project locks in carbon savings over time. The last point says that if government wants to stimulate mega-projects, they need to pick the right project. A nuclear power plant or a coal-fired power station with carbon capture will save 6 million tonnes of carbon dioxide every year; an extra runway at Heathrow will emit roughly the same.

Their ideas make good sense for the economical environmentalist consumer too. Those of us lucky enough to have savings or reliable jobs need to keep on spending; during a recession we can pick up good deals. In particular we should buy goods and services that employ local people, especially skilled workers in sectors badly affected by the recession – this includes, above all, construction. We should bring forward our spending plans. If family circumstances mean you need more space, then convert your loft or extend the house now. Now is also a good time to eco-refurbish your home, or repair and restore your goods. If we have to buy new, buy the lowest-carbon model.

But we also need to remain inside our budget and be especially wary of borrowing. The times of cheap credit and high returns from wealth have now passed. The majority of people are going to have to be careful about how much they spend during the next two years. This means buying fewer things and cutting back on holidays and large purchases.

India and China

Fifteen months ago I was sitting in a hotel in Kerala, India. I had just attended a friend's wedding and was feeling slightly blown-out by the experience. The ceremony had been more opulent than my own a few months earlier. India was clearly booming. The Kochi skyline seemed to be framed by the booms and jibs of huge steel cranes: the city was being constructed anew in front of my eyes – new hotels, wide roads and office blocks. Would the Portuguese founders of Fort Cochin five centuries ago recognize any of it? On the road between the airport and the hotel, billboards aimed at foreign tourists promised plastic surgery and organ transplants for a fraction of the price charged by private clinics in the West. India wasn't content to sweep up just call-centre jobs any more, but wanted the West's white-collar and professional jobs too. Why should expensively trained Indian doctors like my father come to the UK to work for the NHS when patients were prepared to come to them? Indian doctors were taking the rejection of house calls to its logical conclusion.

More recently, I was in a bar with my cousin in central London. We were catching up on news about our relatives: it had been months since we'd met – he spends time in the UK and time in India setting up a business. He'd just flown into the UK. We were talking about another cousin who works for an IT company, which was created to provide back-office IT support for a large UK company. But the Indian firm had grown into an aggressive and acquisitive giant and had broken free from its UK parent. Our cousin lives in Pune and had returned back from a trip to the US where he had been scouring around for firms to gobble up. He's looking for the US acquisition target's customers, not their employees. So there will probably be a flood of redundancies if the deal goes through. Another of our cousins, a chemical engineer based in Alberta, has been working on a project to exploit the oil sand deposits there. Extraction of oil sand is to the environment what the film *Wall Street* is to the idea of caring capitalism. It involves squirting hot water deep into the soil to extract an immensely polluting fossil fuel from the ground. The soil is strip mined, the bitumen squeezed out and the sand then discarded. Because the price of oil is falling, it looked as though my cousin will have to return to India along with other contract workers. He was unbothered, the opportunities in India are just as good, and green cards and foreign passports no longer have the same allure to middle-class Indians that they did in my parent's generation.

I am proud of my family and what my cousins are accomplishing. Back in the 1970s when we were growing up it did not seem possible we would be sitting in a bar talking about a family dispersed across three continents. 'I'm embarrassed to be related to the two of you', I say laughing, 'You, the original Slumdog Millionaire, and Ravi in Canada, whose response to climate change is "let me help you bring it on".' He replied he was glad we'd found a suitably obscure place to drink, being seen with an eco-fascist like me would kill his reputation.

I was born in a city called Nagpur. It missed out on the IT boom enjoyed by nearby Mumbai, Pune and Bangalore. But its central location in India makes it a major transport hub. Boeing has located its regional maintenance and overhaul centre there and the economy seems to be doing well. I lived there for a few years as a child and return every two or three years. The cycle rickshaws that conveyed me to school have been overtaken by flyovers and concrete. It has a population of 2.5 million, about the same as Wales. I doubt if many people reading this book will have heard of it.

The other city I grew up in was the equally obscure Newcastle-under-Lyme. It made the newspapers in January 2009 when one of its most well-known employers, Wedgwood, called in the receivers. When I was growing up in the city, 50,000 people worked in the pottery industry; at the time of the demise of Wedgwood that number had fallen to just 2000. Most of the manufacturing had already been transplanted to Indonesia. Now the only nod to the industry is in the names of the football team and the large shopping centre in Hanley. One of the other major sources of employment in the city was coal mining; the mines in Trentham and Silverdale closed ten years ago.

The two cities embody both the decline in the fortunes of companies and communities in the West and the rise of those in the East. The self-confidence of Indian business is simultaneously alarming and gratifying. The wealth of the owners of Tata, Infosys, Reliant and their like has been an inspiration to a generation of students graduating from engineering and business schools in India. To many people's minds this industrial success is overdue and a return to the world order before the Industrial Revolution took place 200 years ago. Tata – just one of several hugely successful Indian firms – gobbled up Corus and Jaguar Land Rover over the last decade, as though saying: 'You can keep the Kohinoor, but there are other jewels in the crown we'll have instead.'

India had a reputation for an ancient metaphysical and spiritual tradition. But for every Arundhati Roy or Rajendra Pachauri campaigning for water rights or leading the world's climate research agenda there are ten Indians demanding she take her place in the new world order. When I talk about my work to my cousins they listen politely. They are as aware of the issues of climate change as any educated person in the world, but the momentum of growth is dizzying and they have no desire to resist. There is a pent up anger at the West for screwing things up and then crying 'we all have to make sacrifices'. Ghandi and his penchant for hand-loomed and local systems of production are of as much interest and relevance to their day-to-day lives as Morris dancers are to ours. India is diving into energy-intensive industrialization as fast as it can. Its 1 billion people want the wealth, jobs and opportunities that its 100 million middle class already have.

I have written at length about this because this worldview is at odds with the architecture of the international carbon markets. Much of the rationale for the system of international emissions trading through markets set up in the Kyoto Protocol – the cuddly sounding Clean Development Mechanism – was centred on the idea that Western capital could be injected into poor countries to unlock low-cost, low-carbon industrialization opportunities. Revenues from the technology sales and financial services would accrue to the West.

Many of these notions have been turned on their head. China is awash with US$2 trillion of foreign exchange and a further US$200 billion of sovereign wealth; the Indian central bank's foreign exchange reserves are just US$300

billion, but its mighty private-sector industrialists are fast acquiring Western assets, and developing their own low-carbon technologies. The new Tata Nano has reinvented the motor car, stripping out cost and weight to bring the price down to Rs100,000 (around £1200). Some of the underlying rationale for emissions trading and concomitant capital flows has reversed. We in the West are selling our companies, not our products or clever financial acumen to India and China; and we are borrowing from them, not lending to them.

This disequilibrium might self-correct as we lift ourselves out of the recession. Currencies will realign and global interest rates rise. When this happens we in the West cannot expect our living standards and debt-funded consumption to return to its former level unless we rediscover how to make goods and services that can compete. It means we will be making and using more domestically produced goods. So the economical environmentalist will be looking into a future where imports and investments cost more.

Climate Change Is Already Happening

Today, I am testifying to Congress about global warming, 20 years after my June 1988 testimony, which alerted the public that global warming was underway. There are striking similarities between then and now, but one big difference. Again, a wide gap has developed between what is understood about global warming by the relevant scientific community and what is known by policymakers and the public. Now, as then, frank assessment of scientific data yields conclusions that are shocking to the body politic. Now, as then, I can assert that these conclusions have a certainty exceeding 99 per cent. The difference is that now we have used up all slack in the schedule for actions needed to defuse the global warming time bomb. The next president and Congress must define a course next year in which the United States exerts leadership commensurate with our responsibility for the present dangerous situation.

(James Hansen, director, NASA Goddard Institute of Space Studies)

A great deal of new research has been published on the science, technology and economics of climate change and the reduction of greenhouse gases. These reports try to answer three questions:

1 What is the maximum amount of greenhouse gas that can exist in the atmosphere before we get dangerous climate change?
2 What is the maximum level of global emissions consistent with this?
3 What should be a British person's share of these global emissions?

It'll come as no surprise that none of these questions has straightforward answers. The years 2006 and 2007 saw some heavy-weight reports thud onto policymakers' desks. Late in 2006 the UK government issued Nick Stern's 700-page opus *The Economics of Climate Change*.[3] After this the IPCC drip-fed us its gloomy trilogy, the snappily titled *Fourth Assessment Report* (AR4).[4] The three constituent working group reports are entitled *The Physical Science Basis* (989 pages), *Impacts, Adaptation and Vulnerability* (939 pages) and *Mitigation of Climate Change* (834 pages) – which is IPCC-speak for how should we go about reducing our emissions. They followed this up with their summary report at the end of the year. Towards the end of 2007 the International Energy Agency updated its outlook on future energy use and revised its views on the growth in world energy demand till 2030.[5] It also includes information on current trends in India and China, whose runaway economic growth will contribute greatly to the growth in energy demand.

There is no shortage of analysis or thought about what needs to be done.

What are greenhouse gases and how much have we contributed to their recent rise?

Climate change is being caused by the accumulation of a small number of 'greenhouse gases' which we are releasing into the atmosphere. They work like the glass in a greenhouse – transparent to the high-energy radiation from the sun, but relatively opaque to the lower-energy radiation that is reflected back from the Earth's surface. So they trap the sun's heat in our atmosphere. The existence of *some* greenhouse gases in the atmosphere is essential – without them the surface of the Earth would be too cold to sustain life. The trouble is that the increased concentration of greenhouse gases is causing temperatures to rise. The Kyoto Protocol has set targets for the following greenhouse gases:

- **Carbon dioxide (CO_2):** this is produced from burning fossil fuels, some industrial processes – such as cement production – and also permanently burning down forests and converting them into fields. Before the Industrial Revolution the atmospheric concentration of CO_2 was 280 parts per million (ppm). This had risen to 380ppm by 2005.
- **Methane:** this is produced from rotting vegetation *in the absence of air*. Cows create it in their stomachs when they digest grass, and it also comes from landfill sites and from crops grown underwater, like paddy rice. The concentration of methane in the atmosphere used to be 0.7ppm before the Industrial Revolution and this has more than doubled to 1.7ppm.

- **Nitrous oxide**: this is produced when fertilizers and manure break down. Increasingly, we are also getting it from cars fitted with catalytic converters. The concentration has risen from 0.27ppm to about 0.32ppm.
- **F-gases**: this heading covers a variety of different inert and long-lived man-made substances that contain fluorine. F-gases are used as refrigerants, fire retardants and in some chemical processes. These have only come into existence in the last few decades.

Aside from these gases covered by the climate change agreement are some other substances that affect the climate:

- **CFCs/HCFCs**: their use is anyway being phased out because of the damage they do to the ozone layer.
- **Water vapour**: this is, and will remain, a major climate gas but whose existence in the atmosphere is quite will-o'-the-wisp, and except for those adept at rain dancing, outside our direct control.

There are also some substances that trade – in climate discussions – under the name of aerosols. They include pollutants like oxides of sulphur (SO_X) which are responsible for respiratory diseases and making the skies in developing countries' cities foul – or to those more romantically inclined – tinged with brilliant shades of orange and red. These are effectively 'anti-greenhouse gases' shading out sunlight. There is a great book, *Catastrophe* by David Keys,[6] that suggests that several major civilizations were brought down by a bad case of global cooling when vast amounts of aerosols spewed out of a volcano in 536. At present, the concentrations of SO_X are so high that they cancel out the combined greenhouse effect of all the methane, nitrous oxide and F-gases put together. But countries in the developing world are cleaning up their vehicle exhausts and coal-fired plants, so it's likely the amount of sulphur aerosols will fall, exposing us to more global warming. Some of former President Bush's advisers have had the brilliant idea of firing these substances into the atmosphere using missiles to counter climate change. Many others think this idea is barmy.

The current stock of greenhouse gas emissions has already caused temperature rises of 0.7°C

The most recent IPCC summary document declares in uncharacteristically strident language that evidence of 'warming of the climate system as [is] unequivocal'.[7] As evidence it throws around some pretty scary facts. The last century has seen warming of 0.7°C, with the temperature currently rising at

0.13°C per decade; and 11 of the 12 warmest years since 1850 have been in the last 12 years. Sea levels have recently been rising at 3.0mm per year. The last 30 years have also seen a dramatic increase in the amount and ferocity of cyclones.

The observed rise in temperature is greatest in the far north, just as the models predict, and it has been heating up over land faster than over the sea. The widely reported break-up of the sea-ice around the Arctic has been one of the consequences, causing people to speculate that it will become possible to sail around the north of Canada to California and Asia.

How does the government select its climate targets?

The UK presently has a target to reduce its CO_2 emissions by 80 per cent by 2050. It was announced late in 2008 following advice by the Committee on Climate Change. This is one of the most ambitious targets in the world. The earlier target of a 60 per cent cut was loosely based on the state of science after the IPCC's *Third Assessment Report* (TAR) published in 2001.[8] The target was intended to stabilize concentrations of greenhouse gases at 550ppm, thereby holding the temperature rise to 2°C. Since then, there has been an environmental arms race with countries vying with each other, beefing up their long-term targets. When the heads of state of the richest eight countries met in Germany in summer 2007, they agreed global emissions should be halved by 2050 and that 'strong and early action' should be taken.

The IPCC brings together the results from the world's main climate models – including one developed by the UK Meteorological Office. Each model gives slightly different results, reflecting differences of views between the teams that created them. These models are run for an agreed range of scenarios, which specify, among other things, an agreed year-by-year change in future greenhouse gas emissions.

The models are among the most complex operating in the world. I saw one being demonstrated which could look at the evolving climate for small grids on the Earth's surface season by season for a 100 years. The IPCC's latest 2007 report explains the changes that have been made over the past six years. New data has been fed in, representing the continued accumulation of emissions of greenhouse gases since the 2001 report. The models incorporate better understanding of the underlying science. One such improvement is the inclusion of carbon cycle effects. For example, higher temperatures speed up the rate at which dead organisms decay, causing more carbon to be released into the atmosphere. Warmer (and drier) climates also make vegetation more flammable increasing the risk and emissions from forest fires. At present carbon sinks (forests and soils) absorb about half of all our releases of CO_2, so the projected disabling of ecosystem functions can have serious consequences for the climate.

The new models contain better information about the interaction between the atmosphere and the ocean. The models can now represent how climate change affects the flow of hot and cold ocean currents. These currents can have profound effects on local weather conditions. The local weather, especially in countries with long seashores like the UK, is strongly influenced by sea breezes that warm or cool coastal regions. The Gulf Stream gives the UK an abnormally warm climate for its latitude. Possible changes to the ocean currents give rise to the non-intuitive possibility that the Gulf Stream could become weaker making western Europe cooler – a process flukily anticipated in the 2004 science fiction disaster movie *The Day After Tomorrow*. Scientists regard such an eventuality as being highly unlikely.

The IPCC's new report makes grim reading

Table 2.1, reproduced from the synthesis report, summarizes the current state of thinking about greenhouse gas (GHG) stabilization levels and global average temperature rise and sea-level rise.

The models pretty much suggest that if we want to maintain long-term temperature rise to below 2–2.4°C we should have started a while ago. The CO_2 already in the atmosphere commits us to this much warming. There are already 455ppm of 'Kyoto' gases in the atmosphere; it's only the parasol effects of the aerosols that are reducing somewhat. But these gases are relatively

Table 2.1 Stabilization concentrations and resulting temperature and sea-level rise

CO_2e concentration at stabilization	Global average temperature increase	Global average sea-level rise (from thermal expansion only)
ppm	°C	m
445–490	2.0–2.4	0.4–1.4
490–535	2.4–2.8	0.5–1.7
535–590	2.8–3.2	0.6–1.9
590–710	3.2–4.0	0.6–2.4
710–855	4.0–4.9	0.8–2.9
855–1130	4.9–6.1	1.0–3.7

Notes: Atmospheric CO_2 concentrations were 379ppm in 2005. The best estimate of total CO_2e concentration in 2005 for all long-lived GHGs is about 455ppm, while the corresponding value netting off pollutants like SO_x is 375ppmCO_2e.

Source: IPCC (2007) *4-AR Synthesis Report*, Topic 5.[9]

short lived and if China and India get their acts together and clean up their car exhausts and power stations, the global cooling effect will soon be reversed. This pollution is thought to mask between 0.3°C and 0.5°C of temperature rise. We are also already committed to a sea-level rise (from thermal expansion) of 0.4–1.0m. Sea level will also rise from the melting of ice from glaciers, ice-caps and the ice-sheets of the Antarctic. At present scientists think it unlikely that the ice-caps and ice-sheets will melt this century.

If the world carries on with existing policies the concentration of GHGs is set to rise to 550ppmCO$_2$e by 2050. This commits us to a 3.0°C temperature rise and a 0.5–2.0m rise in sea level. But reality has exposed some weaknesses in the models. Two substantial ice-shelves have already collapsed: Larsen A in 1995 and Larsen B in 2002. The latter had been stable for 12,000 years and its demise took everyone by surprise. It had an area of 3250km^2 – almost as big as Essex, and a depth of 220m. Yet its disintegration only took three weeks! The climate models did not anticipate the abruptness of the loss of the ice-shelf. Instead of gradually melting away like an ice-cube in the sun, the meltwater ran into crevices in the ice, refroze and expanded, shattering the ice-shelf into pieces. At the time of writing, a video of its demise can be seen on the *New Scientist* website. If we lose the Greenland ice-sheet this would add a further 1m to sea-level rise. The loss of the entire West Antarctic ice-sheet would add a further 5m. Both of these are unlikely to occur soon, but if they did they would be true catastrophes causing the uprooting of tens of millions of people.

So far we have only been discussing the models' *average* view of the world. However, there are many factors which affect climate change that are not known with certainty. Instead of trying to come up with a single number, the scientists run the models many times over, varying the unknown factors to see what happens to temperature and sea-level rise as these unknown quantities are changed across a plausible range of values – something called Monte Carlo analysis. In any casino *on average* the croupier will make some money. However, if you look at the spread of wins and losses of individual people in the casino you'll see some people grinning and some wondering how much they'll get for their cars if they throw their keys in. The scientists have replicated this with their climate models and can work out the chance of low-probability but catastrophic climate change events.

The Stern report recommended that the world should seek to stabilize the concentration of greenhouse gas in the atmosphere between 450 and 550ppmCO$_2$e. His team of economists made use of the IPCC 2001 report for the underlying science, which, as I have said, was slightly more sanguine than the more recent report. Stern reaches his eventual conclusions by looking at the costs of reducing our emissions enough to hold them within this band and comparing them to the costs of allowing them to rise outside this range. It is a devilishly hard cost–benefit analysis to undertake – perhaps the hardest ever performed.

The Stern report argues that trying to stabilize emissions at less than 450ppm is out of question because we've left it too late and it would be too expensive. The report goes on to argue that stabilizing the concentration of greenhouse gases at above 550ppmCO$_2$e exposes future generations to unacceptable risks of dangerous climate change. At the current rate of accumulation we are expected to hit 550ppmCO$_2$e between 2030 and 2050. Climate models suggest this concentration of greenhouse gases exposes the world to a 20 per cent probability of catastrophic temperature rises above 5°C.

A rise of 5°C doesn't sound a lot compared to the differences between the seasons, or even over the course of the day but it is actually the same difference in temperature as between the depths of the ice age and now. Mankind has never known average global temperatures 5°C higher than now. The sea-level rise alone would be enough to inundate London, New York and Tokyo. Some of the many controversial issues he considers include: how do you value human lives? How do you trade off the interests of today's generation against the benefits received by future generations? Put one way the calculation seems obvious: our generation is being asked to give up holidays and restrict the use of energy to pay for the investments in new zero-carbon technologies to avoid the dislocation of millions of people; but we are asking this generation to trust imperfect science and models.

There is an ethical discussion in the Stern report about how governments should treat exposing future generations to these unlikely but catastrophic futures. Paraphrasing this fairly technical discussion the report poses the question: 'Would you get in a plane if there was a one in five chance of it crashing. No? Well why are we asking our grandchildren to climb aboard?' Its handling of risk and uncertainty has been controversial amongst economists (including those working within the UK government) since the treatment of these improbable but high-cost events is given a heavy weight in the calculations, and therefore drive its conclusion that it is economically better to act soon to avoid the risk of uncontrollable climate change, than to wait and see if new technologies develop or it becomes easier to adapt to climate change.

If we are serious in our desire to hold the rise in temperature to below 2°C we should not allow the stock of greenhouse gases to rise above 450ppmCO$_2$e at the very most – and even then we remain vulnerable to low probability catastrophic temperature change.

In April 2008 James Hansen[10], one of the world's most acclaimed climate modellers and head of the NASA Goddard Institute for Space Studies, recommended we slash the stabilization target to 350ppmCO$_2$e – i.e. demanding a reduction from the current levels of 385ppmCO$_2$e. This would require an immediate cessation of emissions and several decades for gases to be reabsorbed into trees and the sea. He and his colleagues have revised their advice after analysing the very long-term and slow interaction between climate change and the area of ice. Ice reflects sunlight back into space, cooling the Earth, so its loss ramps up climate change. Once we take account of this feedback effect he believes the long-term change in temperature is twice as high as our current models predict.

Recent evidence suggests we need to reduce our greenhouse gas emissions faster than we thought before

So how much is the world allowed to emit if we want to keep the stock of GHGs down to 450ppmCO_2e? There is no simple answer this question. If you think of the concentration of greenhouse gases like the level of water in a bath tub, our emissions into the atmosphere are like the flow of water from the tap and the natural ability of the environment to absorb GHGs is like water draining through the plug hole. If we wish to avoid the bath flooding, the flow from the tap eventually has to be the same or less than the rate the water drains. While the bath is filling, it's OK for the flow from the tap to be faster than the rate it drains, but the faster the rate of flow from the tap the shorter the length of time we have to learn how to turn the tap off.

There is no unique trajectory to achieving any particular stabilization level. Normally the assumption is that global greenhouse gas emissions keep on growing as we try to steer our Titanic of an economy off its carbon-guzzling tendencies. But once the new carbon-free technologies develop, then the emissions can fall quite sharply. Well, that's the idea.

Because greenhouse gas emissions hang around the atmosphere for so long, what is important is how cumulative emissions rise over time – the amount of water that has been added to the tub. If we plan to reduce to 'sustainable' levels in the future, but take too long about getting there, we risk overshooting in the meantime.

So where are we starting from, and where are we trying to get to? Currently greenhouse gas emissions are about 50 billion tonnes a year (50GtCO_2e) – just over half of this is CO_2 from fossil fuel use. Apart from energy-related CO_2, there are also significant contributions of CO_2 from burning forests and of methane from agriculture and mining. As mentioned earlier, this is partly masked by pollutants like SO_x.

Figure 2.2 has been reproduced from some modelling that was under-taken by Ecofys for Defra (the UK's environment ministry) in 2007.[11] It shows the amount of emissions the world can emit in order to avoid the stock of greenhouse gas concentrations rising above various different levels. The units on the y-axis on the left have to be multiplied by 3.66 to get them into GtCO_2e. The y-axis on the right shows the change in emissions relative to 1990. The

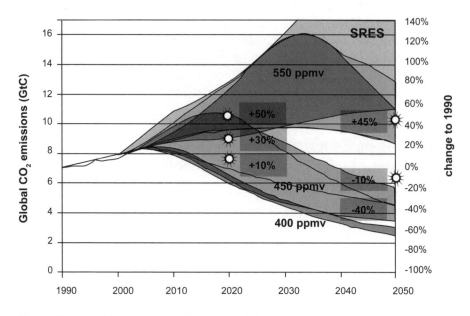

Figure 2.2 Possible trajectories for total global emissions of greenhouse gases to achieve stabilization at 400, 450 and 550ppm of greenhouse gases

Source: Defra (2007)

different lines are like different sizes of bathtub. The larger the bathtub, the longer we have to reduce our emissions and also the higher the final level of emissions. However, we also risk greater temperature and sea-level rise, and hence run a greater risk of catastrophic costs.

If we allow the 'stabilization concentration' to increase, we buy ourselves a few more years of time and higher peak emissions; but not much. The Ecofys model suggests that achieving stabilization at 450ppmCO_2e requires the world's emissions to have peaked already and fall by a quarter in around ten years, and by three-quarters by 2050. If these were distributed equally around the world, emissions would peak at *6.7tCO_2e per person now and fall to around 2.4tCO_2e by 2050* (assuming the world's population grows to 9.2 billion). It's also saying we mustn't allow emissions to rise above 40GtCO_2e, but they're already at 50GtCO_2e – oops!

But far from falling, the International Energy Agency[12] reference scenario forecasts energy-related CO_2 emissions will grow from 27 to 42MtCO_2 between 2005 and 2030 (if you include non-CO_2 greenhouse gases and CO_2 from clearing forests, the numbers would almost double). Present trends aren't even in the right direction. What we are saying here is that the world needs to get its act together and make meaningful changes as fast as possible so they are in place over the next decade.

The UK government set up the Committee on Climate Change[13] to give advice on the maximum emissions targets ('budgets') the UK should apply for the next 5 to 15 years. It reached similar conclusions to Ecofys, saying global emissions should peak in 2016 and fall by 3 per cent per year thereafter. If distributed equally around the world this implies emissions per person *should be between 2.1 and 2.6tCO$_2$e in 2050.*

The Committee recently published a carbon budget for the UK, based on a thorough scientific and technical assessment of the science of climate change and the technologies available to reduce emissions. At the time of writing, the budget is being considered by government. I have given its 'intended' budget on a per person per year basis in Table 2.2. They recommend emissions dropping to 7.5tCO$_2$e per person by the period 2018–2022.

Table 2.2 Greenhouse gas budgets for the UK

Budget Years		2008–2012	2013–2017	2018–2022
Total Budget	Mt	3018	2679	2245
Annual budget	Mt	604	536	449
Emissions/person	tCO$_2$e/person	10	9	7.5

Source: Committee on Climate Change (2008)

Developed countries need to reduce their emissions so that less developed countries can improve their well-being

Figure 2.3 shows the variation in fuel-based emissions per person across the world. If you included emissions from forestry clearance and methane, the figures would look much higher for many of the poorer nations in particular.

Before we all get depressed about the impossibility of the task ahead, it is worth reminding ourselves what our historical emissions looked like. Figure 2.4 shows the CO$_2$ emissions from burning of fossil fuels over the past 250 years. Until 1800 we were complete neophytes relying on renewable sources of energy like wind (sailing ships and windmills), water (water mills) and biomass (wood and whale blubber). We then got into our stride fairly quickly, and by 1950 we really set off! The graph shows that we were last emitting around 10MtCO$_2$e in 1970, so we have to go back to global energy use from the time of the swinging 1960s rather than the Victorian or Stone Age. There is a fascinating literature showing that, at least in the West, there has been no overall rise in happiness for the past 30 years so greater consumption and energy use hasn't translated into well-being. We return to this theme in the final chapter.

Figure 2.3 Regional per capita emissions of carbon dioxide from fuel use, 2006 (tCO$_2$ per person)

Source: US Energy Information Administration (2008)[14]

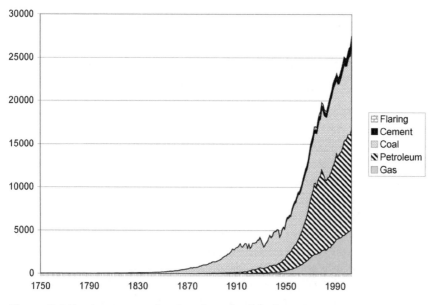

Figure 2.4 Total emissions of carbon from fossil fuel combustion, 1750 to 2001 (MtCO$_2$)

Source: US government's Carbon Dioxide Information Analysis Centre

Reducing Emissions

It takes years for economic systems to change so we have to act now

We are causing the concentration of greenhouse gases in the atmosphere to rise at about 2.5ppm per year. Why not wait another few years and then really knuckle down? Even better, why not undertake some gratuitous over-consumption now, before *they* really clamp down?

This strategy of cramming all our effort at the last minute might work when revising for exams, but there are at least two good reasons for believing it won't work for reducing greenhouse gas emissions. First, because it is the stock rather than the flow of greenhouse gases that is the problem; it makes sense to cut out any easily avoided carbon dioxide now when it's cheap. Later, when it becomes trickier to reduce emissions, we will rue those early low-cost options we should have taken care of years back.

Without wanting to sound like a pension salesman, there is a good analogy with the pensions industry. If we get into the habit of making annual payments every year early in our lives, then this means we only have to deny ourselves the occasional meal or buy a slightly less grand car in order to finance our pension. If we leave it to the last ten years of our careers we suddenly find we need to take huge cuts in our standard of living to make the pension pot big enough to live off. (That did sound like a pension salesman.)

Second, it takes the economic system time to change – sometimes decades. When you buy a car, you are pretty much stuck with it for its ten-year lifespan. A petrol-engine car with a 1.3 litre engine will keep on emitting around 150g of CO_2 per kilometre driven for its ten-year lifespan, no matter what super-duper hydrogen fuel cell gizmo is fitted to newer cars. Such longevity is worst in our transport infrastructure and developments. The routing of many of our roads has persisted from Roman times, seeing off the dark ages, the plague and the rise and fall of the British Empire. The layout of neighbourhoods and suburbs might persist for hundreds of years. Anyone who has travelled in Los Angeles will have noticed how difficult it can be to get around without a car. There is no quick fix that will suddenly make the city a haven for cyclists or pedestrians overnight. Any mass transit or low-carbon transport system is going to have to deal with LA's low population density, and long-distance travel patterns. Our appetite for using fossil fuels can be compared to an ocean liner heading in the wrong direction. For the next few miles the direction of travel will be dominated by the vessel's momentum; it can be swayed from this course but it might take decades to do this. It is for this reason that former Prime Minister Blair[15] said 'But without radical international measures to reduce carbon emissions within the next 10 to 15 years, there is compelling evidence to suggest we might lose the chance to control temperature rises.'

Emissions should be reduced in the cheapest way possible

Economical environmentalists have an aversion to spending money to no good effect – it makes them come out in a rash. We start from the premise that natural resources and people's time are scarce and should be used where they deliver the most benefit. We are also suspicious folk, prone to rather jaundiced views about some of the statements made by both environmentalists and businesses. To our way of thinking, there's nothing quite as effective as inserting the word 'green' or 'organic' on a product to legitimize hiking up its price. On the other side, there are some well-intentioned actions intended to save the planet which are, at best, useless and, at worst, harmful. Is an energy-from-waste plant really so bad, given the difficulty we have finding markets for recycled paper, textiles and plastics?

Economical environmentalists are also interested in the real underlying costs of the energy-saving measures being taken. This means stripping away the government subsidies which modify the prices people privately experience. For instance there are some pretty hefty subsidies to encourage the installation of photovoltaic (PV) panels. Part of the motivation for these grants is that some of the high costs arise because the technology is still immature and the production and installation costs will fall as the market expands and we exploit learning-from-doing savings. There are certainly good reasons to believe this will happen; they have come down an order of magnitude between 1985 and 1995. This fall in price as a technology matures is well documented and shown graphically in Chapter 6 for a variety of electricity technologies.

But some of the costs of setting up a PV panel, for instance the installation cost, are likely to remain relatively high for the foreseeable future. We need to take care not to let the pattern of grants tempt us into making poor financial decisions.

This divergence between the price faced by customers and the true resource cost can also go the other way. Currently prices being paid for low-carbon energy and services might be too low because networks and product marketing have been developed and optimized for fossil fuel-based energy and goods. For instance if you generate electricity at home your local electricity supplier offers you peanuts for any electricity you don't need (and might even charge you for a two-way meter). You might as well be giving the electricity away for free. This is not because they are thieves, or because they are hostile to people generating their own power. It is because the electricity you are trying to sell is of low value to them. At the moment they have no idea how much will be produced, or where it will be produced and therefore cannot avoid any of the costs associated with supplying the power. I once had to organize a conference in Wales where the client insisted that we provide translation facilities in case anyone in the audience wished to address the floor in Welsh. We paid for two translators to attend and they never opened their mouths once – apart from expressing their gratitude for their healthy pay cheques. The cost of the translators was avoidable, but only if we had done more planning and established before the conference that none of the invited delegates wanted to speak Welsh, so we could have cancelled the hire. Similarly, unplanned micro-generation from solar panels is of little value to the local grid if they have not anticipated how much power it will deliver and planned their purchases from large power stations accordingly. However, there is nothing to stop power companies, in the future, using day-ahead weather forecasts to anticipate solar output from their customers' micro-generation and change their orders.

Current Emissions in the UK

Emissions of greenhouse gases per person in 2004 in the UK were $12.2tCO_2e$ per person. These figures were drawn from the Office for National Statistics (ONS) environmental accounts.[16] These numbers include emissions from international aviation and shipping, which are normally excluded from national emissions figures because there is no agreement on which country's books emissions should appear on. Should it be the country where the fuel is bought or sold, or shared between the two nations? This might sound a fairly prosaic argument, but it is important to a number of states that make a good living as international transport hubs, like some of the Middle Eastern oil-exporting countries, and sadly the UK – hence the government's enthusiasm for expanding Heathrow. In 2004, UK emissions from aviation and shipping amounted to about $65MtCO_2e$ – about 9 per cent of greenhouse gas emissions.

If we follow the advice given by the Committee on Climate Change, average emissions have to fall to $7.5tCO_2$ per person by 2020 – a 40 per cent cut.

UK GHG emissions are concentrated in power generation, manufacturing, transport and households

So where in the economy do these emissions take place? Figure 2.5 shows how much greenhouse gases are emitted by different UK industries.

People, through the use of cars and gas central heating, are only directly responsible for a fifth of emissions. Major sectors of the economy, like finance, retail and education, which employ vast numbers of people, are together only responsible for 4 per cent of greenhouse gas emissions directly, barely half that of agriculture or waste. Not too surprisingly, sectors like electricity and

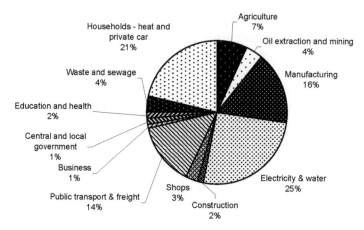

Agriculture
7%

Households - heat and
private car
21%

Oil extraction and mining
4%

Waste and sewage
4%

Manufacturing
16%

Education and health
2%

Central and local
government
1%

Business
1%

Public transport & freight
14%

Shops
3%

Construction
2%

Electricity & water
25%

Figure 2.5 UK greenhouse gas emissions by economic sector, 2005 (percentage of total GHG emissions of 733MtCO$_2$e)

Source: Office for National Statistics (2007)[17]

water are highly fossil fuel intensive and emit a quarter of UK emissions. The UK's enfeebled manufacturing sector is still responsible for a sixth of emissions – largely through fossil fuel-gobbling sectors like oil refining, steel production and cement production.

Emissions from goods and services cause more than half our emissions

If we are trying to reduce our emissions we need to take account of all the GHGs hidden away in making all the goods we buy.

Figure 2.6 shows conceptually how you might go about linking emissions from the different sectors to individuals in the UK.

Quite a lot can be readily linked to easily recorded purchases – in particular anyone can measure their use of gas for heating (1.5 tCO$_2$e per person) or petrol/diesel in their private cars (1.0tCO$_2$e per person). Together these account for a fifth of UK emissions. Emissions from public transport, planes and electricity are also easy to allocate back to individual decisions – together these make up another 25 per cent of emissions (3.1tCO$_2$e/person). A flight to Australia is clearly emits more than a train journey to Brighton, and the emissions of both journeys are quite easy to calculate.

But finding the GHG emissions from most goods and services is a bit like finding the opposite ends of a string of spaghetti while it's boiling in a pot. We can't duck the questions since half of the UK production of greenhouse gases is from the rest of the economy – around 6.4tCO$_2$e/person. Just consider the purchase of a hamburger from a fast food restaurant: we would need to include

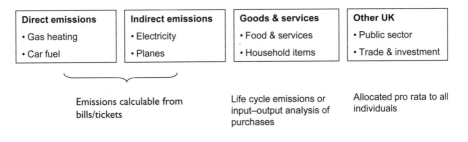

Figure 2.6 How our purchases give rise to emissions

emissions from agriculture (to produce the beef patty), fertilizer sectors (to nourish the cereal crop that makes the bun), the food manufacturing industry, the freight industry and finally the retail sector. And to make it more complicated these emissions might change over the course of the year, for instance if the restaurant owner finds a cheaper bun supplier located in another country, or decides to ditch the gherkins from his hamburger altogether.

How do we go about unravelling the spaghetti of business interactions that go into the production of the simplest goods? Inevitably we are going to have to look carefully at our purchases. But how to go about navigating the web of connections – those economic filaments: hauliers, loans, spending on plant and machinery – that distribute our spending to all the different businesses that play a role in getting the product to our door?

These non-obvious indirect emissions of greenhouse gases can be approximated using an analytical technique called input–output analysis. This uses information about how much one industry spends on the outputs from other industries and allocates the emissions to the purchasing industry. By using some cunning mathematics devised and operationalized by the Nobel prize winning economist Wassily Leontief in the 1940s (who actually used this approach to study environmental and resource depletion needs back in the 1960s) it is possible to associate the indirect energy use and greenhouse gas emissions back to the goods bought by households. The ONS publishes these data for 91 different products and services. Amazingly, Leontief calculated the US's input–output tables for 500 industries back in the 1940s in one of the first uses of computers for mathematical modelling – quite a feat given the quality of economic statistics and computational hardware – using a computer called the Harvard Mark II which was about as sophisticated as a slide rule.

The information in Figure 2.7 is taken from a 2004 paper by the environmental accounts branch of the Office for National Statistics. Statisticians at the ONS looked at the detailed purchasing behaviour of people in different regions and in different household types in the UK and using the input–output tables and some clever maths calculated the embodied emissions arising from all inter-industry purchases, according to the value of goods one industry sector buys from another industry sector.

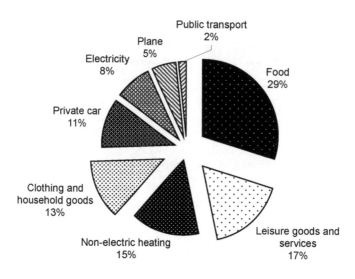

Figure 2.7 Average direct and indirect UK emissions, 2001 (excluding emissions from government, trade and investment)

Source: Francis (2004)[18]

The pie chart in Figure 2.7 shows 60 per cent of our emissions are 'indirect', arising from the production of food, leisure goods, and clothes and household goods. So, for instance, the pie chart shows that food is responsible for a whopping 29 per cent of emissions (outside of government, exports and investment) – more than transport and electricity put together. This is because food production entails emissions from the food chain – growing, manufacturing, distributing and retailing – as well as from the purchase of carbon-intensive goods and services like fertilizer and international aviation, and also because food is bulky and perishable and it therefore takes considerable energy to distribute.

One of the surprising results was that even in 2001 the average Londoner emitted slightly more from his flights (2.1tCO_2e per household) than he did from his car (2.0tCO_2e per household) – emissions from aviation grew by a fifth between 2001 and 2006. This is what having the world's best-connected airports (and pretty good public transport) and the country's worst congestion does for you. I can attest to this: I have reached Turkey in the same time it sometimes takes me to drive to Birmingham from my North London home.

Emissions also arise on our behalf from the public sector (schools, hospitals and government) and through the production of goods for export. These cannot easily be allocated to individuals. The fairest way of attributing them is to simply split them equally across all the people in the UK. But they were only 3 per cent of emissions, so they can be ignored for the purposes of setting the target.

Box 2.1 *Life-cycle analysis*

Life-cycle analysis is a technique for calculating the total environmental effects of goods and services, assessing how much energy goes into the production, use and disposal of the food. In the case of agricultural produce this might include the environmental impacts not just of growing foodstuffs but also any emissions from businesses making feedstuffs, fertilizers and agrochemicals, which are environmentally important parts of the modern 'food chain'. In theory we might also want to think about the emissions arising from the production of capital items used in food production, like the warehouses, shops, tractors and trucks that are used by the food industry. Usually the analyst has to make a pragmatic decision about drawing the system boundary in such a way as to capture the most important impacts only, especially where these are likely to differ significantly between the goods and services being compared.

How much do we emit?

In 2007 we emitting around $10tCO_2$ per household from the use of home energy, flying and petrol/diesel. But it's worth digging under these numbers to see how these were spread across different people in society.

How much we earn has a huge bearing on the amount of energy we use. The poorest 10 per cent of households, earning an average of £9000, emit just $4tCO_2$. The richest 10 per cent of households emit more than this on their flights alone, and five times as much as this altogether. This is both shocking from a fairness point of view and restricts the type of policy we can use to reduce emissions. If we have one price for carbon dioxide across all uses of carbon dioxide, politicians will feel inhibited from increasing the price too much because of hurting the poor. Policies that increase prices to say £100/tCO_2 will be resisted because of the serious effects on fuel poverty, but this might be the level necessary to inhibit the rich from flying.

This is particularly pertinent to adding a new runway at Heathrow. The government argues they're tackling aviation through putting its emissions in the carbon market. But could a price that discouraged people from flying to a skiing holiday also allow everyone to keep their home warm? No one I know is talking about the price of carbon dioxide in the market rising to more than €100/tCO_2 because this would hurt poor households and the competitiveness of business. The poorest households can eat cake in the café, while the richer members of society will carry on eating gateaux in their gîtes.

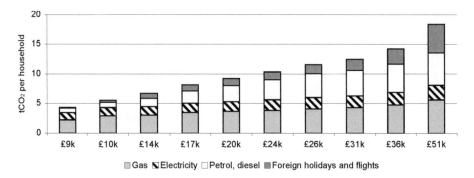

Figure 2.8 Approximate emissions of carbon dioxide according to income of household, 2007

Source: Author's calculations based on ONS data.[19]

My own carbon emissions

I want to reduce my emissions, but am conscious that apart from working as an environmental and energy economist I have nothing else to commend me to the job of downsizing my emissions. I cycle to work, but I like my meat. I drive my fuel-efficient car sparingly, except for a round trip to Birmingham every fortnight. I fly a few times a year. If this is all getting to sound a little like Alcoholics Anonymous, I have to also confess a worrying ambiguity in my ambitions for this project, and my capability to deliver any changes.

But am I really going to be able to pull this off (see Figure 2.8)? I am possibly the least practical person I know. If the capacity to make things with your own two hands was ever the subject of natural selection the Vaze genes would never have made it out of the cave … perhaps not even the primordial soup. If there's anything that needs to be done involving changing the fabric of the house, installing devices or growing things, then I'm going to have to pay someone to do it for me. More unsettling is the realization I don't really want to change my life very much either. I like skiing and I've enjoyed holidays in far-flung places. I've come to the slightly disturbing realization that, though I want to reduce my emissions, I don't want to change the way I live.

A slightly broader question that many grapple with, perhaps subconsciously, is: *why should I cut back?* Why should I be the altruist, while others carry on emitting to their heart's content? Jeremy Clarkson seems to have the best fun, blithely unconcerned while the Ferrari he test-drives belches climate chaos – does he not feel the smallest morsel of guilt or doubt? Compared to such hardcore polluters, my own minor climate indiscretions seem small-scale. Why not carry on a little longer until someone else – the government, the London mayor or the European Union – forces the change?

Table 2.3 First-cut assessment of my CO_2 emissions

	Measurement unit	CO_2 per unit	Quantity	Personal tCO_2
Car use	km	143	16,000	1.1
Electricity	MWh	455	1.496	0.3
Gas	MWh	0.200	4.64	0.5
Plane journeys[b]	L fuel per passenger-km[a]	0.045	10,720	2.4
Total				4.4

Notes: [a] Assumes Jet A fuel has a 77 per cent specific gravity, and is 84 per cent carbon. [b] Emissions for plane journey are for my personal flights and exclude my wife's and children's.

Sources: Car use: my car's operational manual. Electricity and Gas: BERR's Digest of UK Energy Statistics.[20] Plane journeys: Wikipedia data relating to fuel consumption for a 75 per cent loaded Boeing 737-500 on a long-haul flight; this slightly understates emissions as the short-haul flights would have had poorer fuel efficiency.

Now is the time of reckoning, working out my own numbers. I will do a back-of-the-envelope calculation in this chapter based on my bills (see Table 2.3). In later chapters I will return to these figures and work out how they can be economically reduced.

Altogether I have clocked up almost four and a half tonnes of direct, public transport and electricity emissions. All the hours and hours I spent driving back and forth to Birmingham every fortnight emits less than the 20 or so hours I spent in the plane in the year. But this is not the whole story. Energy goes into making and transporting all my other purchases: food, clothes, CDs, books and all the services I buy. And the food production, record and book publishing industries all make purchases too. According to the ONS, the average indirect emissions from these other goods and services are around 6.4 tonnes per person. This chapter has so far set out the challenge. I, through my direct actions and purchases, emit something like $11tCO_2e$ – pretty close to the UK average. My goal is to reduce them by a nice, round 40 per cent. The numbers at this stage are fairly back-of-the-envelope. Over the course of the following chapters I will look at the science and economics behind these purchases to work out how to reduce them.

Notes

1 Office for National Statistics (2008). Supply and use balances from *United Kingdom National Accounts The Blue Book*. Figure quotes gross value added at basic prices.

2 Bowen, A., Fankhauser, S., Stern, N. and Zenghelis, D. (2009) *An Outline of the Case for a 'Green' Stimulus*, Grantham Research Institute on Climate Change and the Environment, www.lse.ac.uk/collections/granthamInstitute/publications/An%20outline%20of%20the%20case%20for%20a%20'green'%20stimulus.pdf (accessed June 2009).

3 HM Treasury and Cabinet Office (2006) 'Stern Review on the economics of Climate Change', www.hm-treasury.gov.uk/sternreview_index.htm and Cambridge University Press, Cambridge.

4 IPCC (2007) *Climate Change 2007: Synthesis Report. Contribution of Working Groups I, II and III to the Fourth Assessment Report of the Intergovernmental Panel on Climate Change*, Core Writing Team, R. K Pachauri and A. Reisinger (eds), IPCC, Geneva, Switzerland, available at www.ipcc.ch/publications_and_data/publications_ipcc_fourth_assessment_report_synthesis_report.htm.

5 International Energy Agency (2007) 'World Energy Outlook 2007' OECD/IEA, Paris, www.iea.org/textbase/nppdf/free/2007/weo_2007.pdf (accessed July 2009).

6 Keys, D. (1999) *Catastrophe. An Investigation into the Origins of the Modern World*, Ballantine, New York.

7 IPCC (2007) *Climate Change 2007: Synthesis Report. Contribution of Working Groups I, II and III to the Fourth Assessment Report of the Intergovernmental Panel on Climate Change*, Core Writing Team, R. K Pachauri and A. Reisinger (eds), IPCC, Geneva, Switzerland, available at www.ipcc.ch/publications_and_data/publications_ipcc_fourth_assessment_report_synthesis_report.htm.

8 IPCC (2001) *Climate Change 2001: Synthesis Report. A Contribution of Working Groups I, II, and III to the Third Assessment Report of the Intergovernmental Panel on Climate Change*, R. T. Watson and the Core Writing Team (eds), Cambridge University Press, Cambridge, available at www.ipcc.ch/ipccreports/tar/vol4/index.php?idp=0.

9 IPCC (2007) *Climate Change 2007: Synthesis Report. Contribution of Working Groups I, II and III to the Fourth Assessment Report of the Intergovernmental Panel on Climate Change*, Core Writing Team, R. K Pachauri and A. Reisinger (eds), IPCC, Geneva, Switzerland, available at www.ipcc.ch/publications_and_data/publications_ipcc_fourth_assessment_report_synthesis_report.htm, Topic 5.

10 Hansen, J., Sato, M., Kharecha, P., Beerling, D., Berner, R., Masson-Delmotte, V., Pagani, M., Raymo, M., Royer, D. and Zachos, J. (2008) 'Target atmospheric CO_2: Where should humanity aim?', *Open Atmosphere Scientific Journal*, vol 2, pp217–231, reproduced at http://arxiv.org/ftp/arxiv/papers/0804/0804.1126.pdf (accessed June 2009).

11 Ecofys (2007) *Factors Underpinning Future Action 2007 Update*, for the Department of Environment, Food and Rural Affairs.

12 International Energy Agency (2007) *World Energy Outlook 2007*, International Energy Agency, Paris.

13 Committee on Climate Change (2008) *Building a Low Carbon Economy*, The Stationery Office, London, p21.

14 US Energy Information Administration (2008) *World Per Capita Carbon Dioxide Emissions from the Consumption and Flaring of Fossil Fuels, 1980–2006*, www.eia.doe.gov/iea/carbon.html (accessed June 2009).

15   Prime Minister's comments at the launch of the Stern Review, 30 October 2006. www. number10.gov.uk/Page10300 (accessed July 2009).

16   The 93-sector industrial disaggregation of UK emissions is found on the ONS website at   www.statistics.gov.uk/CCI/nugget.asp?ID=155&Pos=1&ColRank=2&Rank=448 (accessed June 2009). The results are also published in a more aggregated form in the 'Blue Book' on National Accounts.

17   Office for National Statistics (2007) *Environmental Accounts Autumn 2007*, www. statistics.gov.uk/downloads/theme_environment/EADec2007.pdf   (accessed   June 2009).

18   Francis, P. (2004) *The Impact of UK Households on the Environment Through Direct and Indirect Generation of Greenhouse Gases*, Office for National Statistics, www. statistics.gov.uk/downloads/theme_environment/Impact_of_households_final_report. pdf (accessed June 2009).

19   Office for National Statistics (2008) *Family Spending*, 2007 edition, Palgrave Macmillan, London, Table A8, 'Expenditure and food survey'.

20   BERR (2008) *Digest of UK Energy Statistics 2008,* published on BERR website www.berr. gov.uk/energy/statistics/publications/dukes/page45537.html (accessed on July 2009).

From Field to Fork:
Reducing the
Environmental
Impacts of Eating

This chapter covers greenhouse gas emissions from growing, transporting, preparing and storing the food we eat. These activities account for about a fifth of the UK's greenhouse gas emissions. The good news is that there is plenty of scope for their reduction. I halved my own by making just seven changes:

1   Cutting out beef, lamb and reducing dairy products. Cattle and sheep emit massive amounts of methane; sustainably caught fish and soya can substitute for beef and milk products.

2   Going organic. This avoids emissions from producing nitrogen fertilizer. Organic farming also increases the amount of carbon stored in the soil.

3   Stopping eating food grown in greenhouses or food that's been air-freighted to the UK. Some supermarkets have started labelling air-freighted products so they should be easier to spot.

4   Replacing chilled soups and vegetables with their canned alternatives. Storing and transporting chilled food takes large amounts of energy and also releases climate-unfriendly refrigerants. Canned foods retain the nutrients and their packaging is easy to recycle. Unopened cans store easily – so less is wasted.

5   Buying the most fuel-efficient fridge on the market and keeping it defrosted.

6   Taking a doggy bag to restaurants and cutting down on the amount of food I throw away at home. This provides triple benefits – less food needs to be grown, transported and prepared, there are less methane emissions from the landfill site and it saves money

7   Using the microwave instead of the cooker to reheat food or to heat small amounts of water.

The act of putting into your mouth what the earth has grown is perhaps your most direct interaction with the earth. (Frances Moore Lappe)

Introduction

Keeping my emissions of greenhouse gases from eating to sustainable levels ought to be one of my easier challenges. Food contradicts Gordon Gekko's most famous dictum. In the case of food greed is *not* good; greed thickens the arteries and handicaps one's prospects with the opposite sex. As we have become richer we can, and do, over-consume other products with impunity, even with aplomb; we fly further afield, buy bigger homes and flashier cars. But our capacity to eat is limited by our metabolism.

At the purely biological level the average person, world over and for many generations, has the *same range of food* intake – between 2000 and 3000 kilocalories of energy and 50g of protein. If we eat much more than this we put on weight, eat much less and we starve. Even the basic foodstuffs have not changed over the millennia. Mankind's diet consists in large part of the same mix of domesticated plants (wheat, barley, potato, rice, soya) and animals (chicken, pigs, cows, sheep and lately salmon) that we domesticated 10,000 years ago.

Apart from deriving nutrition from food we have other objectives from food. We care about its taste. We might believe that farmers and fishermen should be paid a fair price for their work, that animal welfare be protected and that we reduce the amount of freight vehicles clogging up the roads. Growing and processing food can also be a major tool for international development – it's one of the few sectors where African economies could outperform our own if we gave them fair access to our markets. So this chapter has to touch upon these other issues too, if the suggestions are going to make sense or have any general applicability to others.

Overview of emissions from eating

We are digging our graves with our teeth. (Thomas Moffett)

Figure 3.1 shows the greenhouse gas emissions from eating that arose at the different stages of the food chain in 2004 – the raw data, come from the ONS environmental accounts. According to these data, eating gives rise to 135MtCO$_2$e of GHG emissions – making up around 18 per cent of total UK emissions. This is a little higher than the 106MtCO$_2$e figures calculated by the Food Climate Research Network (FCRN) which are quoted in a report

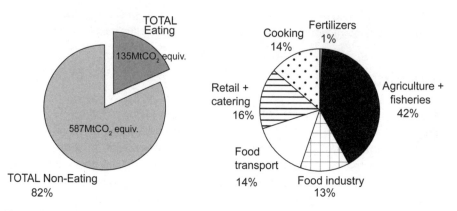

Figure 3.1 Greenhouse gas emissions from 'eating'

Source: Derived from the Office for National Statistics environmental accounts.[1]

produced by AEA Technology for the UK ministry of agriculture (Defra).[2] My figures include emissions from fertilizer production (about 5MtCO$_2$e in 2005). Even so, they are likely to slightly underestimate true emissions because they only look at the food that is grown and processed in the UK. The UK is a net importer of foods so we are missing out on the emissions produced in other countries on behalf of our consumption.

The figure of 135MtCO$_2$e for the UK is the equivalent to 2.25tCO$_2$e per person, about a third of my goal. If I am to become sustainable I need to make some inroads into tackling emissions from eating.

Different stages of the food chain

Let's see how GHG emissions come about in the different stages of getting food from the farm to the fork. Figure 3.2 shows the different stages in the production and distribution process that give rise to GHGs.

Modern agriculture consumes about a million tonnes of nitrogen fertilizers a year. Fertilizer production is energy intensive (emitting the equivalent of around 2MtCO$_2$e) and more importantly also emits large quantities of nitrous oxide (equivalent to 3MtCO$_2$e). So there might be scope for reducing emissions by switching to crops that use little or no fertilizer. We also use phosphate and potassium fertilizers but their production is much less GHG intensive than that of nitrate.

Farming and fishing emit around 54MtCO$_2$e. Nitrous oxide accounts for just over half and methane 37 per cent.[3] These gases bubble off in relatively small quantities but have much more global warming effect than CO$_2$.

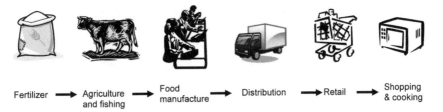

Fertilizer ➝ Agriculture and fishing ➝ Food manufacture ➝ Distribution ➝ Retail ➝ Shopping & cooking

Figure 3.2 Source of greenhouse gas emissions from producing, transporting and preparing food

Emissions from food manufacturing are tricky to quantify because fewer statistics are collected by government. The ONS data suggest emissions are $17.5MtCO_2e$. The AEA study reports that about 75 per cent of these emissions arise from heat-based operations like heating, cooking, distilling and drying – so there might be some scope to look at the degree of processing and energy intensity of production as a means of slimming the carbon footprint. Distribution emissions of $19MtCO_2e$ are almost entirely of CO_2 arising from diesel for road haulage, and aviation fuels used for air-freighted goods. Retailing and catering emissions of $21MtCO_2e$ mainly arise from purchases of electricity for lighting and refrigeration. Store fridges inadvertently emit significant HFC-based refrigerants. We directly produce around $19MtCO_2e$ of emissions from travelling to the shops, cooking and from the electricity used by fridges.

Given the huge scale of the farm to fork emissions from eating I am going to have to carefully dig into the data and answer the following questions:

- Do we really need to buy so much food?
- How much GHG does the cultivation of different commodities emit?
- Does selecting different types of production (free-range, organic, glasshouse and conventional farming) make much difference?
- Is it possible to select food that embodies little processing energy?
- How do I reduce the amount of CO_2 released through the transport of my food?
- Where is the best place to eat – cooking food at home from the raw ingredients, or microwaving a TV dinner; or out of the house in canteens or restaurants.

This should be fun. But before we start it might be worth describing how much food we presently eat.

Do We Really Need to Buy So Much Food?

I never diet. I smoke. I drink now and then. I never work out.

(Naomi Campbell)

Fortunately supermodels are not the only source of insightful tips on diet and exercise. We also have Miss Piggy's sage and pragmatic input: 'Never eat more than you can lift.' There is probably no better metaphor for our unsustainable lives – our environmental obesity – than the amount we overeat. The dominant theme in this section is: as a country we are pigging out and there are opportunities to trim some of our emissions by buying less. Surprising though it might seem, average food intake has actually fallen by 20 per cent between 1974 and 2004.[4] Also, data suggests we have increased the amount of formal exercise we take – by around 0.6 hrs per week – between 1998 and 2006.

So things are looking up? Well actually no – as a country we are still putting on weight. This is because a generation ago people didn't have all the labour-saving gadgets we have today; workers spent more of the day *working* rather than pushing a mouse around a plastic mat and fewer people lived in centrally heated homes. On average we are eating some 10–15 per cent more food than is necessary. People are notoriously unreliable in their responses to food (and alcohol) surveys, so even though government's statistical surveys suggest we are eating less than we need, alternate sources of data suggest these surveys tend to underestimate true consumption by up to 25 per cent.[5] Figure 3.3 shows the consequences. The numbers of morbidly obese make particularly depressing reading. In 1993 less than 1 per cent of people were dangerously (morbidly) overweight. By 2006 the numbers of super-sized people had doubled.

The reason why we need to consume less energy is that we are burning off less keeping warm. Many people now barely know what it is to be cold – the average temperature in people's homes has risen by 6°C between 1970 and 2004 to 18°C as central heating has become almost universal and insulation in homes and offices has improved.[6]

Other EU countries are not as bad as us. According to an EU survey, it's now 'official': the British *are* the most gluttonous people in Europe. Even the not-noticeably-svelte Belgians and Germans weigh in on the scales at less than us. A whopping 60 per cent of us are overweight or obese, compared to just 37 per cent of French (see figure 3.4). Most of us could eat fewer calories, save the planet and our girths in one fell swoop.

To make matters worse, we buy much more food than we eat. A large part of our purchases never make it out of the cellophane. A survey by the Waste & Resources Action Programme (WRAP) showed that on average we each

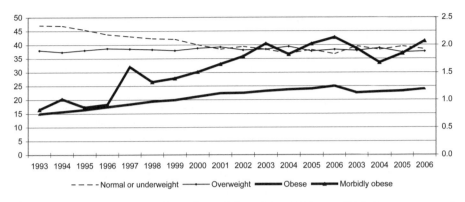

Figure 3.3 Body mass index of English adults 1993 to 2006 (percentage of population)

Note: Percentage of population Normal or underweight, Overweight and Obese should be read on the left-hand axis; Morbidly obese on the right-hand axis.

Source: The National Health Service Information Centre (2006)[7]

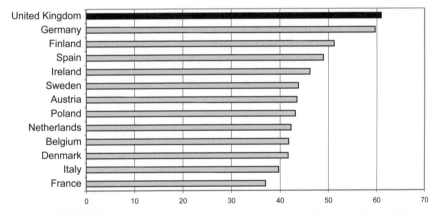
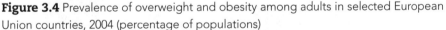

Figure 3.4 Prevalence of overweight and obesity among adults in selected European Union countries, 2004 (percentage of populations)

Source: Elmadfa, I. & Weichselbaum, E. (2004)[8]

throw away a third of the food we buy.[9] A total of 6.7 million tonnes of food is avoidably wasted each year, worth £420 per household – 4.1 million tonnes of this still in the packet whole and untouched, some of it still in date. The two-for-one offer is not such a smart buy when one of the two so often ends up in a landfill site.

With trepidation I decided to see how my own food intake measured up. I was getting married in September. It was a source of minor anxiety that I didn't disgrace myself on the wedding photos too much; especially by contrast with my hourglass-proportioned fiancée.

I kept a detailed diary of my food consumption for a week. This entailed weighing everything I cooked or imbibed at home. I balked at the idea of taking my scales to the office, but by the end of the week I had developed an eye for gauging the weight of food from the size of the stack. Most days I ate in Defra's rather good canteen. Not too long ago the department used to have a scandalously atrocious canteen, which only managed to avoid the ignominy of poisoning its clientele by serving food so bad that it drove most of its victims away.[10] Things have changed now and the canteen is popular with staff, and has a good range of reasonably priced food with Fairtrade and vegetarian options. However, the tradition of awful food lives on in the catering provided for meetings. This consists of mystifying platters of sandwiches which invariably dumbfound invited guests and provide a useful and vaguely apologetic icebreaker for the first minute of any meeting. While keeping my food diary I realized I eat a distressingly large number of biscuits at work. It was a little difficult to work out their ingredients – as far as I can make out they have no analogues in the market economy – they are an outcome of the public sector procurement process, which is akin to modern day foodstuffs the same way the archaeopteryx is related to birds.

To my surprise I found I ate more than the average British person. According to the large number of diet calculators on the internet,[11] I need to eat around 2800 kcal per day to keep me going – a little more than the average person

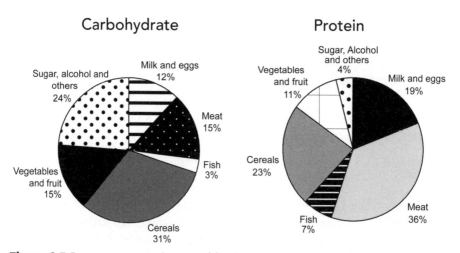

Figure 3.5 Percentage contribution of food types to average daily total energy and protein intake

Source: The National Diet & Nutrition Survey: adults aged 19 to 64 years; sample undertaken July 2000 to June 2001[12] ONS on behalf of Food Standards Agency and Department of Health.

because of all my cycling. Coincidentally, this is almost exactly how much I do eat, despite my children's and wife's incredulous views to the contrary. For the next few days after this discovery I strutted around as proud as punch (wedding photograph ... bring it on) before realizing that unlike most of the rest of the UK there was little scope for me to cut back my emissions simply from dieting. However, there was still a small sliver of hope, my protein consumption is higher than necessary – 80g compared to a recommended minimum intake of 50g. There is therefore some scope to rebalance my diet by substituting climate-friendly plant products for climate-unfriendly animal products.

Figure 3.5 shows how the different foodstuffs contribute to protein and carbohydrate intake for the average person.

I am taken aback by the high proportion of my calories (20 per cent) and protein (30 per cent) derived from dairy and eggs – quite a lot more than the average person. Cattle are a major source of methane, and the damage to the environment is just as real whether you consume your cow as a steak or as stilton. Thinking about it again this does make sense; I drink about 2.5L of milk a week, mostly in the form of cappuccinos, and get the same amount of protein and carbohydrate again from cheese. I always assumed I ate much less of animal products. My (now) wife is vegetarian and this rather stifles the number of times I can eat meat – I get assailed with killer lines like 'You can't possibly use that frying pan to make a lentil bake, I saw you cook *sausages* in it last month.'

About 15 per cent of my carbohydrate intake comes from sugar. This is probably an underestimate since I have not recorded all the sugars that slip into the diet through ostensibly savoury food like baked beans that actually have added sugar.

How Much GHG Emissions Come from Growing the Different Foodstuffs?

I do not like broccoli. And I haven't liked it since I was a little kid and my mother made me eat it. I am President of the United States, and I'm not going to eat any more broccoli. (George Bush, 41st President of the US)

And sadly you don't have to be a former leader of the free world to assert your dietary preferences so forcibly. When I tell my kids there are going to be some changes to our diets as we are on a mission to save the planet my daughter is suitably supportive. 'Sure Dad', she enthuses. 'We are doing a project on climate change at school.' My son echoes her words, but not with quite the same vigour. Our first meal is a useful wake-up call: 'Yuk', he shudders as he draws a fleck of spinach out of his mouth to join the rest of the green mush that sits aside his plate. All the pizza's spinach, mushrooms, pepper and onion are arranged in neat stacks around the plate, the tuna, olives and cheese are all gone. His Star Wars-style strategic defences against vegetable intrusions would make the second former President Bush drool. Without the benefit of tens of billions of dollars' worth of microwave detection technology, my son can locate and negate any dietary incursions that don't meet his approval. Quick – someone sign him up for the Department of Defence.

Do I really need to re-educate my kids on their diet? How much do the agricultural commodities actually matter? Sadly, yes. As shown in Figure 3.1, over 40 per cent of the total emissions from eating come from growing food. And there are huge opportunities to reduce these emissions by choosing the underlying agricultural products more carefully. I grasp the leftovers from the pizza purposefully in my fingers realizing that it is my duty to instil in him a sense of rationality and decency. I say: 'Steady on old boy. These vegetables are good for you, and we all have to make little sacrifices in order to mitigate the threat of global warming.' Or words to that effect. He nibbles the edge of the pile of vegetables and then shoots off. 'I'm full. You eat it.'

Figure 3.6 gives the relative 'life-cycle' emissions of greenhouse gases per tonne of produce. The liquid milk has been converted into its dry matter equivalent (as though it were being bought as cheese rather than in its liquid form) to make it easier to compare with the other produce. As George Orwell famously quips in *Animal Farm*, 'All animals are born equal – but some are just more equal than others.' Pigs are the Snowball of the climate-friendly farm, quietly delivering the bacon without wrecking the environment; while cattle are the Napoleon figures, their placidity belying their berserk methane and nitrous oxide emissions.

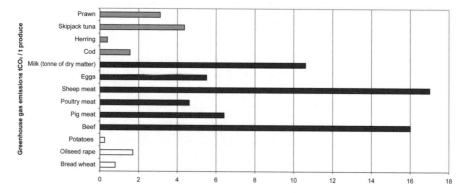

Figure 3.6 Greenhouse gas emissions per tonne of agriculture and fishery produce
Source: See text.

The emissions from vegetable-based commodities are on average 0.9tCO$_2$e per tonne of produce. Animal-based products are a little over ten times more at 10tCO$_2$e per tonne. Captured fish emits between 0.35 and 4tCO$_2$ per tonne caught – significantly lower than any other animal-based food. So it looks as though substituting fish for meat and dairy products might yield some big greenhouse gas savings – especially if I switch to oily fish like mackerel or herring. We have to be careful when making these comparisons by weight since the different commodities differ greatly in the amount of calories and protein per unit mass they provide.

Most of the numbers in Figure 3.6 are from a study by Silsoe College for Defra.[13] The Silsoe study didn't look at fishing so I had to use other sources of information. If you are hoping that fish products might be a means of sneaking animal proteins into your diet, let me give you some hope. Eating fish gets a bad press. Listening to some environmentalists you would think that all fish are about to go extinct. This is of course a ridiculous generalization. The seas make up about 70 per cent of the world's surface and only 750 species of fish are caught for food. The fact that many species are being overfished no more means we should boycott all fish, than the plight of tigers and rhinos means we should boycott venison.

We land about 650 kilotonnes (kt) of fish in the UK;[14] aquaculture accounts for a further 150kt.[15] Sea fishing is energy intensive, giving rise to substantial CO$_2$ emissions, but unlike agriculture there are few emissions of methane and nitrous oxide. Emissions from caught fish vary depending on the species being targeted: relatively bountiful species (herring, mackerel and whiting) which swim close to the surface of the water require less energy to catch than the bottom-dwelling species that are caught by trawlers. Trawlers drag heavy and destructive fishing gear over the bottom of the seabed, scraping the rock to catch cod, haddock and some shellfish species. Peter Tyedmers, a Canadian academic, looked at the energy use, including the energy embodied in the boats and gear, in 54 different fisheries around the world.[16] The CO$_2$ emitted from targeting different species varies significantly. Bottom-dwelling species like cod release 1.6tCO$_2$ emissions per tonne of fish landed. Small, abundant surface-swimming species like herring take an average of just 0.39tCO$_2$ per tonne of fish landed. North Atlantic prawn takes 3.1tCO$_2$ per tonne. Catching less-bountiful surface-swimming species like skipjack tuna is more energy intensive, emitting 4.4tCO$_2$ per tonne landed. I am not interested in eating tiger prawns or anything grown in mangroves. By and large, the more expensive the fish the scarcer it is and hence more carbon intensive to catch – so you are better off eating cheap species.

One has to be careful when comparing across different life-cycle studies, as researchers differ in what items are included. The Tyedmers study for fish only looks at CO$_2$ (emissions of other GHGs are likely to be small). The

Silsoe research on agriculture undertook a much more complete analysis and included greenhouse gas emissions from producing inputs like fertilizers – even those from making the agricultural machinery. Even so, it looks likely that fish is a highly climate-friendly source of protein, especially in comparison to meat.

The heating of horticultural crops in greenhouses can make some fruit and vegetables as carbon intensive as livestock

I have excluded horticultural crops from the discussion so far as they are very much a special case. UK horticulture is a highly intensive form of industrial production whose only affinity with agriculture is that the word ends in '-culture'. It is so energy intensive, cheerfully spending £29,000 in fuel *per hectare per year* (which is more than twice the value of the land), that when the Climate Change Levy was introduced in 1998 the sector requested a special dispensation from paying the tax (not a particularly exceptional request from industry lobbyists) and got it (a mind-boggling exception which baffled all the other trade associations who were also busy lobbying the Treasury with equally compelling arguments from their own down-at-heel memberships) – the only sector to do so.

The Silsoe study analysed emissions from tomatoes grown in heated greenhouses. A heated glasshouse produces about 370 tonnes of produce per hectare (t/ha); in comparison, a field of wheat only produces 6t/ha. Prices for horticulture are high too: a tomato grower receives £620/tonne (tomatoes can easily retail for £2000/tonne), compared to a mere £75/tonne received by grain farmers. Growers have every incentive to work their greenhouses to death. Not surprisingly, GHG emissions from tomatoes grown in heated greenhouses are huge – at just under $10tCO_2e$ per tonne of produce – way above other plants and vying with beef and mutton for the title of the most climate-deadly UK food. It is actually possible to grow tomatoes in the UK without heating at all, but the growing season runs from July to October, rather than March to November and the yields per hectare are much lower – a mere £53,000/ha, still a sum any cereal farmer would commit heinous crimes for.

UK horticulture is cleaning up its act somewhat. Planet Thanet has recently opened the biggest horticultural farm in the UK. With an area of 51 hectares, equivalent to 80 football pitches, it'll grow 15 per cent of UK production of horticultural crops. It uses gas-fired combined heat and power (CHP) to make electricity, which it sells to the grid, and heat, which is used in the greenhouses. Some of the CO_2 is also used to enrich the atmosphere in the greenhouses. CHP is normally considered to be 30 per cent more efficient than producing the heat and power separately. An improvement, but still not as good as importing the crop by road from Spain.

Box 3.1 *Greenhouse gas emissions from tomatoes grown in Spain and the UK*

Tomatoes grow best at a temperature of 19–21°C – which we only experience in the UK for a few months in summer. So there is a lot to be said for importing horticultural crops grown in countries with warmer climates. Around 100,000 tonnes of tomatoes are grown in the UK each year, and 320,000 are imported mainly from Spain and the Canary Islands, and the same amount again from The Netherlands.

Table 3.1 shows the total CO_2 emissions from growing and transporting tomatoes from the UK and Spain. Imported tomatoes give rise to just a quarter of the emissions of tomatoes grown domestically. It was assumed that the Spanish tomatoes were driven 1079 km by road and travelled 182 km by sea. The data below omits the emissions from fertilizer production and application, and from the production of the glass houses (used in the UK) and poly-tunnels (used in Spain). Nor does it consider the large amounts of water consumed by tomato growth which is an important sustainability consideration in Spain.

Table 3.1 Emissions of carbon dioxide from tomatoes grown in Spain and the UK (kg per tonne of crop)

	Spanish	British
Gas	0	1858
Electricity	519*	536
Transport to UK	111	
Total	630	2394

Note: * Emissions from Spanish electricity may be overestimated as more carbon-intensive UK data was used. Electricity for lighting in Spain might be overstated due to greater 'free' sunlight.

Source: AEA (2005)[17]

The other way we can eat out-of-season tomatoes is by using waste heat discarded by industry or power production. The UK imports around the same quantity of tomatoes from The Netherlands as it does from Spain. Dutch greenhouses use heat from power stations to provide warmth and elevated levels of CO_2 (which acts as a fertilizer) for their crop. However, some commentators say that even with these climate-friendly production practices Dutch horticulture is still responsible for 2.4–3.4 per cent of the country's GHG emissions. Few of the UK's greenhouses use waste heat – the main exception is the Cornerways tomato nursery run by British Sugar and heated from its Wissington sugar factory. There remains huge potential for making more use of this cheap waste resource. Potential sources of heat include power stations (the hot exhaust gases are passed through heat exchangers to prevent pollutants from coming into contact with the crop) or energy-intensive food production like distilleries or sugar refining. So try buying local seasonal produce, or produce grown using waste heat.

Organic and free-range foods: Do they reduce greenhouse emissions?

Organic farming eschews the use of chemical fertilizers and pesticides, and uses traditional methods to supply nutrients and protect crops. Nitrogen (as ammonium or nitrate) is by far the most GHG-intensive agrochemical used in conventional agriculture. If organic farming avoids nitrogen fertilizers surely it must be much better for the environment?

Unfortunately the answer is not quite so clear-cut. Organic farming is less productive than conventional farming. Yields per hectare are between a quarter and a half less than conventional farming, so more tractor fuel is needed to produce the same quantity of crop. Organic farming still needs the introduction of nitrogen into the soil; the organic alternatives to artificial fertilizer are themselves a source of nitrous oxide. In the organic system, nitrogen is added either by planting a 'break' crop like peas or beans every few years – the roots of these legume species shelter bacteria that fix nitrogen from the atmosphere into the soil – or by applying manure to the crop. The emissions of nitrous oxide from the farm manure have to be split between the crop and the animal products. The real issue is whether using the manure in organic farms emits more nitrous oxide than the disposal methods used by conventional farms. So the question of whether an organic crop is better for climate change needs to be measured empirically.

Sadly there is hardly any UK research on the subject. The only paper I could find was a 'modelling'-based study from Silsoe College for Defra.[18] It suggests the GHG savings for crops are a fairly modest 2 per cent for organic wheat and 5 per cent for oilseed rape. Their analysis assumed the organic farms had no manure, and also made fairly onerous requirements for the land to rest between crops, which pushes down the productivity of the land and raises the emissions per tonne of product. The research also looked at organic systems of animal production. The results were mixed: energy-related emissions were 15–40 per cent lower than conventional farming, but organic egg and poultry meat released 15 and 30 per cent more, respectively, than their conventional counterparts. Gundula Azeez and Peter Melchett from the Soil Association criticized the work, saying the organic systems being modelled bore no relation to real life; organic farms combine livestock and crops so wastes from the first can be used as inputs into the second.[19] This is ignored in the Silsoe research.

Research carried out in other countries is more positive about organics. In 2007, a Swiss research institute for organic farming issued a report with the UN's International Trade Centre, reviewing the literature on emissions from organic and conventional farms in Germany and The Netherlands.[20] The results were highly variable. The German data showed that emissions from organic farming were lower, while the Dutch results found them about the same. A diagram from the study is reproduced in Figure 3.7. The results exclude savings from avoiding emissions of nitrous oxide from the production of fertilizer, and also the increase in the amount of carbon locked up in the soil from organic farming.

The soil association believe that emissions per kg are between 15 and 40 per cent lower from organic.[21] For the purposes of calculating my footprint I have taken the Soil Association's results at face value and will assume the switch to organic will reduce the emissions from the growth of the food I eat by 25 per cent. The reality is probably much subtler, for instance that the use of some pesticides might actually boost yields without increasing emissions. So it's not organic per se that saves greenhouse gas emissions, but the use of strategies to minimize the addition of artificial nitrogen. Similarly, greater use of a manure on conventional systems might also generate carbon benefits without meeting organic standards.

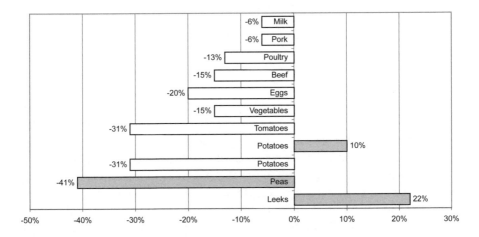

Figure 3.7 Emissions from organic farming systems relative to conventional systems for Dutch and German farms (percentage change in GHG emissions)

Note: White bars are results from Germany, grey bars from The Netherlands.

Source: UNCTAD/FiBL (Research Institute of Organic Agriculture)

Free-range poultry, for both eggs and meat, gives rise to higher emissions than the battery variety – since one of the few things being scrunched up, 15 animals to the square inch, has going for it is that it keeps you warm. The Silsoe study estimates the increase in GHG emissions from free-range as being about 20 per cent for meat and 10 per cent for eggs. The GHG emissions for free-range pigs were the same as those for indoor pigs. We are well aware of the animal welfare issues arising from intensively raised pigs and poultry. Despite the climate emissions penalty I'm going to carry on eating free-range produce.

What I Did and Didn't Do

I have recast my diet into its underlying agricultural commodities and calculated the greenhouse gas emissions from the production of the commodities (see Table 3.2). I have been fairly rough and ready, for instance converting biscuits into 50 per cent wheat, 25 per cent vegetable oil and 25 per cent sugar, or assuming that pork sausages are 100 per cent pig-meat. There are several good books detailing the adulteration undergone by our food – some of it for relatively benign reasons, for instance to extend its shelf life, but much of it replacing high-cost ingredients with cheaper substitutes. The table below shows my food intake according to the main agricultural commodities. I have combined the fruit and vegetable products by weight, splitting them according to whether they have been sourced in the UK, in mainland Europe and outside Europe. This is to work out the energy used to transport them to my home.

So which of these agricultural commodities are to blame for all the greenhouse gases? Figure 3.8 shows the GHG emissions from growing the plants and raising the animal products I consumed in my test week. Dairy products, or more specifically my latté and cheese consumption, were the most important source of emissions. I am not a big beef eater but my single 180g burger emitted five times more GHG than the combined emissions of my three fish meals! I also ate a fair amount of tomatoes and mushrooms grown in greenhouses, which pushed up the emissions from my fruit and vegetables.

Overall milk and cheese made up about a third of my emissions, greenhouse crops and beef were about a sixth each. Despite being half of my emissions, beef and dairy products only make up quarter of my calorie intake and a third of my protein. The cultivation of the other farmed meats is not quite as GHG intensive but they're not that far off. At the other extreme cereals and potato only made up about 5 per cent of my GHG emissions, yet accounted for about a third of my energy and protein intake. I was surprised at the high proportion of protein derived from plants. You don't need to eat meat or animal products to get proteins. My other big issue was the amount of food

Table 3.2 My weekly food and drink consumption by agricultural commodity (excluding still and fizzy water)

	Quantity (g)	energy (kcal)	protein (g)
Milk and milk products	2984	3519	161
Eggs	240	360	30
Beef	180	275	15
Pork	400	870	38
Chicken	180	195	20
Herring and mackerel	125	310	26
Cod and haddock	140	140	32
Prawns	110	70	17
Sugar	642	2868	28
Potatoes	559	1453	32
Wheat	1598	4898	133
Oilseeds	509	2592	24
Fruit and Vegetables (UK)	619	320	16
Fruit and Vegetables (mainland Europe)	1690	654	22
Fruit and Vegetables (outside Europe)	1780	1503	43
Weekly intake	11,754	20,027	635
Daily intake	1679	2861	91

Notes: Quantity in wet weight before cooking, includes beverages except water. Assumptions: sausages = 100% pork; chocolate = 25% sugar, 25% milk, 25% cocoa butter, 25% vegetable oils; biscuits = 50% wheat, 25% sugar, 25% oilseeds; spring rolls = 50% wheat, 25% fruit and vegetables (UK), 25% oilseeds.

that I threw away, most of it was outrageously climate-costly lettuce and herbs which always end up in the bin by the end of the week, as did about half the food I ordered in restaurants (I tend to favour curry houses, cafés and occasional flurries in gastro-pubs).

I decided to make four adjustments to my diet: I substituted beef with fish, replaced milk with its soya equivalent, gave up fruit and vegetables grown in greenhouses and lastly stopped throwing away food from restaurants and started asking for a doggy bag. I considered giving up dairy cheese too; there are certainly soya cheeses available on the market, which I tried. The less said about the experience the better.

Reducing milk, beef and lamb consumption can make a significant reduction in our emissions from food

Were these changes easy? Let me come clean – basically I like meat, I do occasionally lapse into a few weeks of vegetarianism, usually in that puritanical period in the first two weeks of January when the New Year's resolutions are still fresh in my mind. I didn't want to make the mistake of going fully vegetarian because I knew I would not be able to sustain it. Is reducing our reliance on beef and dairy really necessary? Grazing land is very much part of the fabric of the UK countryside. Some people make the argument that eating beef and lamb utilizes areas of the country too wet or too hilly to grow cereals, land that would otherwise revert to some ugly, barren T. S. Eliot-esque Waste Land – 'I will show you fear in a handful of dust.'

There are two arguments against this reasoning: first, cattle production uses large amounts of cereals that we could eat and, second, cattle are prodigious emitters of methane and nitrous oxide. The UK climate means that livestock have to be fed cereals and concentrates in winter when it is too cold for the grass to grow. Livestock eat more than half the 20 million tonnes of cereal we produce. Cows are also awesomely inept at making beef and milk out of plant matter. A UK beef cow slaughtered at 24 months yields around 300kg of meat. During her lifetime a cow will eat 3500kg of grass (dry matter), 15kg of milk substitute (sadly for the calf; her mother's milk is too valuable to be wasted on her children) and 1100kg of cereals. Put another way you have to put around 15 units of food into a cow to get one edible unit of meat out. Energetically, we would be much better off editing the cow out of the picture and eating the soya and cereal concentrates ourselves and doing something useful to the grassland like planting windmills. Not everyone will like this message, but a climate puritan would stop eating beef and lamb altogether and grow trees instead. For the next few decades the soil and timber store some carbon and hopefully produce some timber afterwards. It is theoretically possible to stock fewer cattle and conserve grass as hay and silage for the winter months – but yields are much lower and you still need protein supplements.

And cows are to the environment what landmines are to a stroll in the Vietnam countryside; in her life a cow will produce 70kg of methane (equivalent to 1600kg of carbon dioxide) and 3600kg of manure, itself a potent source of the GHG nitrous oxide. When I said this to myself enough times, I finally convinced myself to give up beef and milk. Though see Box 3.2 about how it's quite possible to take another view.

> ### Box 3.2 *Minimizing the emissions from raising beef and dairy*
>
> My friends Tony and Ann run a livestock farm in the Home Counties. They feel beef and dairy will continue to play an important part in our diets for the foreseeable future. As well as this, raising beef is a way of life: Ann's family had raised beef (and in earlier times dairy too) for many generations. They well understood that their cattle emitted methane and nitrous oxide. To them the issue was how to tame the cow's environmental impacts. This meant understanding how many cattle could be safely raised, and modifying the cow's diets to reduce the methane emissions. The cow's wastes, properly managed through anaerobic digestion, instead of being a source of nitrous oxide could be converted to fertilizers and energy.
>
> The weather on the farm was mild so the cattle were largely fed from grass and silage. They tried to minimize the use of concentrates, though last year it had rained all summer which meant they weren't able to conserve much of the grass for winter. Tony sold a proportion of his beef within the community – informally trading with local horticulture and vegetable producers. After he had the cattle slaughtered he sold sides of beef to locals; they stored the meat in the freezer. His meat had a good reputation locally and by cutting out the middleman both he and his customers got a fair price and it minimized the distances the meat travelled.

Fish are a good alternative source of protein, but you need to be careful to select a sustainable fishery; soya is another excellent source of protein but its cultivation can threaten tropical forests.

Readers might struggle with some of the above. By eating fish aren't you contributing to humanity's Tet offensive to obliterate global fish stocks? Not if you are selective in which fish species you choose to eat. Many fisheries, even some close to home, are faring quite well. According to ICES – the international agency whose job it is to advise on the state of the international fish stocks in the Atlantic – the following stocks were in a healthy state in 2006: sardines, haddock (except for haddock caught in the West of Scotland) and Norwegian herring. Plaice was at risk, and so too was hake. Sole and cod remain in trouble, even the normally sustainable cod from Iceland and Faeroes is under threat, and to my surprise mackerel is now being unsustainably harvested. If you want to take a look at up-to-date advice provided by the fisheries scientists you can take a look at their website: www.ices.dk/advice/icesadvice.asp.

A couple of words on the terminology you will need to know if you ever dip into these reports: information on the health of the fish stock is organized according to species and region of water. The EU seas are divided into a number of different divisions that broadly reflect the geographic boundaries that the more homely fish species tend to stick to. The term 'recruitment' is the number of fish that survive to reproductive age (fish are more fecund than Genghis Khan, but the vast majority of the young never make it to puberty), SSB (spawning stock biomass) is the weight of sexually mature fish, and the TAC (total allowable catch) is scientific advice on the weight of fish that can be safely caught. ICES synthesize the data collected by the marine scientists from its member states and provide their advice based on the number and age distribution of fish within the region. Fish populations can be extremely volatile – the health of a stock can change substantially from one year to the next through births, predation, climate and, of course, fishing effort.

How about replacing milk with soya milk? Doesn't soy production cause deforestation in the Amazon? The majority of soya consumed in the UK is indeed imported from Brazil. One study undertaken for Defra put the proportion as high as 59 per cent and even more if we add in the soy that comes into the UK via staging countries like The Netherlands.[22] Soya is mainly produced in the south of Brazil near Rio and São Paulo, though soya farms are expanding northwards on land that was recently forested. However, dairy cattle are themselves big consumers of soya concentrate; in a way, cow's milk is just an inefficient means of drinking soya beans. At least if you consume the soya milk directly it is easier to geographically source it to use existing, preferably European, arable land. The brand I'm buying exclusively uses soya grown in the south of France. It has proved more challenging trying to get canteens, cafés and restaurants to supply me with soya milk. My former employer Defra's canteen was fine (where I consumed most of my soya milk), so too are about half of the places I frequent around North London.

In terms of acceptability – I have got used to the milk and quite enjoy it. Not all our visitors do, certainly the builders who carried out our loft conversion would have no truck with it. It does tend to split when it's added to boiling hot water – but cunningly I no longer make my tea or coffee with boiling water, but more of this later in this chapter. The soya yoghurt tastes OK, just not like yoghurt.

Better labelling of air-freighted foods and box schemes make it easier to avoid fruit and vegetables grown in heated greenhouses or air-freighted to the UK

Reduction of emissions from my vegetables was achieved by buying my fruit and vegetables from Abel and Cole's excellent box scheme (see Box 3.3). The company eschews air-freight and the use of heated greenhouses, which dramatically reduces the emissions from cultivation (and transport). I expected their produce to be significantly more expensive than buying from the supermarket or even the local organic shop. I did a quick price test. This week's box contained 5.5 kg of seasonal fruit and vegetables and cost £14.80. I was surprised to find that the same food from Tesco's online site was £10.30 for the non-organic food or £12.00 for the organic equivalent plus a £5 delivery charge. It is possible to shop more cheaply in Tesco by picking the Value range where it exists or the two-for-one offers, but I rarely buy either of these – the former because I am too snobbish and the latter because I always end up binning the second pack. I was surprised to find Abel and Cole's box cheaper than I expected. Box services like Abel and Cole are not cheap if you pick your own selection of produce rather than their in-season selection, also their meat and deli is cripplingly expensive.

Angie and Duncan were both aware of food miles. Angie tended to buy seasonal produce by default, since it was usually good value. The annex at the end of this chapter lists seasonal vegetables and meats for the different months. In winter it might be worth relying on tinned vegetables to get some variety.

Duncan only eats meat at weekends and even then just chicken and fish. He has a preference for organic food. The price is off-putting, but he's happy to spend a bit more on food items he likes. When he eats organic it tends to be organic vegetables and cereals rather than organic meat, since he believes there are likely to be more pesticide residues on leafy greens than in chicken or milk. 'I knew about the amount of energy that goes into air-freighted food, but didn't know how bad greenhouses are.' His main constraint is time – lunches especially are always in a rush. He occasionally eats ready-made sandwiches for lunch, falafel or cheese, or ready-made fresh soups which he finds nutritious and tasty.

The last change I have made to my diet is reducing the amount of food wasted. I eat out at least two or three times a week. I have never managed to finish even a one course meal in a restaurant even though I have almost died trying, ditto with pub grub, where managers seems to obtain a perverse sense of fulfilment in confronting me with overwhelming quantities of food. Now I have started to ask restaurants to box any uneaten food, which I usually have for breakfast the next morning. I haven't summoned the courage to do this in pubs or at business meals yet. It saves money and so far there have been no complaints from the staff.

Figure 3.8 shows the impacts of these relatively minor changes to my diet. For good measure I also compared these with the emissions from the average British person.

My emissions from eating dropped by about 55 per cent as a result of ditching the milk, beef and heated-greenhouse-grown vegetables. Not bad going.

Box 3.3 *Organic box scheme*

My sister-in-law suggested I should try out her home delivery box service. I smiled wanly and thought to myself, 'What an excellent idea if you're bored with having any time for a social life, friends over for dinner or any sense of enjoyment from eating at home.' My own view about organic box schemes had become a little sclerotic after using a scheme a decade earlier. Then the fruit and vegetables had looked about as appealing as a tumour, and eschewing packaging the company had instead wrapped every turnip, potato and carrot in half a kilo of mud and foliage. I swear I expended more energy scrapping manure and soil off the produce than my digestive system could possibly have recovered from the food.

Nonetheless, I joined the Abel and Cole scheme. Like several other box schemes the company has greatly extended its range of products and presently offers around 500 items, including different fruit and vegetable box configurations, dairy products, meats, breads, pantry items, drinks, cookery books, deli items and cleaning products. All the products are organic and the packaging is largely returnable. Food is sourced as locally as practical, but in order to give the boxes variety (especially in spring) they do include sea-freighted goods from the southern hemisphere. The company choose the time and day of delivery to reduce the amount of trips from the depot to people's homes. The driver tells me he does 80 drop-offs in my neighbourhood in North London. The price of the basic fruit and vegetable boxes and dairy products are comparable to organic produce from supermarkets, though meats are significantly more expensive than the supermarkets' organic ranges, reflecting the very high welfare standards used by the farms.

When my first organic box arrived I was confronted with a kilo of cabbage, half a kilo of pak choi and the challenge of converting it into a banquet for ten. 'Help – what do you do with cabbage?' I spluttered. 'It used to big in the gulags', my wife pointed out *a propos* to absolutely nothing. A few hours later a copious volume of cabbage soup was simmering away in our pressure cooker (the only vessel big enough to cook it in one go), its fibrous structure effortlessly resisting the thermal onslaught we dished out. The once crisp pak choi had been reduced to its constituent molecules and had melded into the tofu. One of our guests had spent nine years in Hong Kong and knew the difference between pak choi and the glue we proposed to serve her. But the food actually tasted quite good, as did the starter and fruit salad. Since that first week I look forward to trying out different foods and I am eating a much more healthy and varied diet than ever before.

It's become much easier to dramatically reduce your emissions from food by signing up to a home delivery box scheme. Numerous home delivery box schemes have sprung up. At the time of writing, the website www.boxscheme.org lists 134 home delivery services in the UK. Much of the grunt-work of reading the labels and researching the websites to eliminate air-freighted, artificially heated, inhumanely reared and non-organic produce is outsourced to the managers of the schemes.

Well-run box schemes can dramatically reduce the transport emissions by entirely eliminating air freight and the drive to the supermarket; they might also reduce road haulage emissions by sourcing much more from small local farms. I did some bone-crunching calculations which suggest the ingredients of the box journey less than half the distance driven by the typical UK food. However, some of the canned foods are sourced from ethical businesses which are often quite far away – the canned fish I bought was caught in Spain and processed in Germany.

Recipe for lassi

If you are ever stuck with a load of leftover natural yoghurt, add half a tub to a glass of cold water, half a teaspoonful of cumin, a pinch of salt and a couple of ice cubes and whisk to make a delicious salt lassi. Works great with soya yoghurt too.

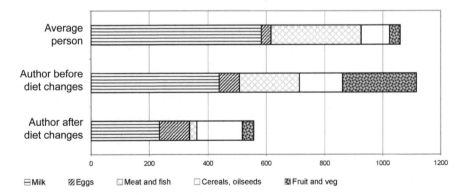

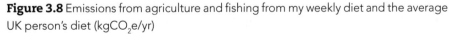

Figure 3.8 Emissions from agriculture and fishing from my weekly diet and the average UK person's diet (kgCO$_2$e/yr)

Sources: Author's diet from author's calculations; Average person from ONS (2006).[23]

Box 3.4 *Beans vs beef: Battle of the greenhouse gas emitters*

Vegetarians find beans, especially soya, an excellent source of proteins. However, as immortalized in the campfire scene in *Blazing Saddles*, the consumption of beans does have its own unfortunate side effects. Eating beans causes flatulence because our bodies cannot digest some of the sugars. The sugars pass into the colon where they are fermented by bacteria which produce hydrogen, carbon dioxide and some methane.[24]

A daring researcher established that when volunteers were fed 10g per day of the offending sugar his volunteers doubled their wind production to 0.7 litres per day.[25] Half of this was hydrogen, a tenth carbon dioxide and a tenth methane. The addition of 10g per day of the sugar increased methane emissions by 0.025g per day.

However, these indigestible sugars only make up about 5 per cent of the mass of dry soya,[26] so the additional methane emissions from eating 1kg of soya beans is a modest 0.125g methane.

By contrast, a 500kg cow produces 70kg methane over its lifetime, equivalent to around a 0.25kg of methane for every kg of meat. No wonder cows aren't invited to cowboy fireside sing-songs!

Is it possible to select foodstuffs that embody little processing energy?

The processing of food accounts for about 13 per cent of the field-to-fork emissions. It is difficult to obtain public information about how energy is used within the food industry. The data are largely commercially sensitive and therefore not publicly accessible. There is, however, a lot of green bumf on the corporate websites. Much of this is misleading. In a project I was involved in, one of my team-mates had to visit a combined heat and power plant of a major food producer. The extravagant claims on their website were not borne out on the ground; the site used 30-year-old technology and had spurned several offers to modernize their processes and use more energy-efficient plant.

Nonetheless, it is possible to use a few generic sources of information to steer food purchasing away from energy-intensive foods. A study for Defra by AEAT[27] shows that the most energy-hungry parts of food production are the heating of water (49 per cent of energy use), direct heat (19 per cent, used to fry or roast food), motors (16 per cent, to cut, shred and mix food, and to power conveyor belts), electrical heating (for electric ovens), refrigeration (6 per cent) and compressed air (2 per cent). Too much information! Maybe, but the point I am trying to make is that most of the energy used by the food industry is to cook food, or heat water to boil the raw ingredients. Relatively little is wasted on refrigeration, since in these days of just-in-time production ingredients do not tend to hang around for long at the factory. Cutting and moving the food around the plant (conveyor belts) uses little energy too. To reduce the emissions from food manufacture we need to think about which foods take the least heat to cook. In a way, preparing food on an industrial scale is not all that different to cooking food in the home. You only put enough heat into a food to cook the ingredients, too much heat and it will become mush, too little and it will be raw. Foods that take a long time to cook at home like mutton or chick peas will also take a lot of energy to cook in the factory.

Foods vary considerably in the energy needed to prepare them. Operations like distilling or drying are highly heat intensive. The doctor's favourite hate figures, salt and sugar, are both produced from the energy-hungry driving-off of water, so should be equally despised by the climate conscious. The water is literally boiled off from the brine or sugar syrup in a partial vacuum. Try it at home and see how much energy it takes. The UK consumes a staggering 100kg of salt per person per year (not just in food, also used for de-icing roads), and over 30kg of sugar. The production of most dry foods requires much more energy than the production of equivalent foods with higher water content: honey and soy sauce could occupy the same dietary niche as sugar and salt but with less input of heat. It is possible to heat and dry foods using much less energy – in India chillies and salt are dried in the sun; UK farms still use sunlight to make hay, or so the saying goes. A Swedish researcher (Carlsson-Kanyama) has collected information on the energy in various cooking operations. I have converted her data into emissions assuming that natural gas was used as the energy source (see Table 3.3). Care should be taken with this table as it is drawn from a range of different academic studies.

The food industry is well aware of consumers' interest in sustainability issues and there is a lot of good work being done. Both the UK's major sugar firms are cutting their emissions. British Sugar (which makes sugar from domestic sugar beet) has invested in combined heat and power and uses the low-grade heat from one of its plants to provide heat for growing tomatoes.

The food industry has submitted information on their energy consumption to Defra in fulfilment of their Climate Change Agreements. Figure 3.9 is drawn from this fascinatingly informative series of 'voluntary' agreements that were negotiated between Defra and industry trade associations back in 2001.[28] Businesses agreed to improve their energy efficiency in exchange for a reduction in the amount of energy tax (climate change levy) they paid on the fuel and electricity purchases. The information below is the target reduction in emissions which the firms had agreed to exchange for the reduction in taxes. I have made the assumption that the firms' energy use is an equal mix of gas and electricity. My daily Mars bar is not looking like a tenable feature of

Table 3.3 Range of CO_2 emissions from carrying out various food processing tasks

	Emissions (kgCO$_2$/kg product)	
	Low	High
Pasta fabrication	0.06	0.17
Milling flour	0.02	0.18
Canning vegetables	0.14	0.26
Pickling	0.19	0.30
Juice from fresh oranges		0.32
Freezing		0.52
Chocolate production		0.59
Chip fabrication	0.76	1.03
Drying	0.36	1.07
Canning meat	0.36	1.72
Freeze-drying onions	1.66	2.95
Instant coffee		3.44

Source: A. Carlsson-Kanyama[29]

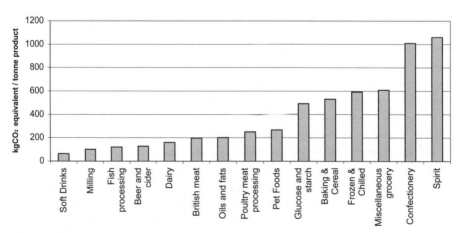

Figure 3.9 Target emissions of greenhouse gases from the food manufacturing industry, 2004

Source: Calculations from climate change agreements, Defra (2001)

my diet (about 1kg of CO_2 for every 1kg of chocolate), but fish is still looking good.

Spirits and beer are at opposite ends of the energy-efficiency spectrum as a result of the large amounts of heat needed in the distillation process, and also because the act of distillation reduces the mass of the product.

So the rather obvious take-home message is to try and consume foods that take the least amount of cooking – salads are in – and avoid foods with large quantities of artificially dried ingredients. Simple mechanical actions like milling, mixing and chopping of foods are fairly benign. In terms of preserving foods, the operation of canning is better than freezing and as an added bonus requires no ongoing refrigeration energy use either. Drying takes more energy still.

How do I reduce the amount of CO_2 released through the transport of my food?

Shipping is a terrible thing to do to vegetables. They probably get jet-lagged, just like people. (Elizabeth Berry)

Emissions from food transport account for about 14 per cent of the field-to-fork total, lower than one might assume given the amount we read about food miles. Perhaps the reason why food ingredients' peripatetic existence so attracts environmentalists' ire is it doesn't seem fair that our food gets to fly so much more than we do. And so much of this mileage seems unnecessary. There is a scene from the 1970s comedy *The Good Life* where Tom Good tries to sell the surplus produce he's grown in his garden, to one after another local shop. Finally he manages to find a store willing to buy the produce, but the catch is they want him to deliver the same quantity every week. I worked on a project on the fishing industry and found that the centralized buying actions of supermarkets insisting on mega-large contracts pretty much precluded many UK fishermen from selling to UK supermarkets. The buyers were only interested in talking to large consolidated sellers that would assure them of delivery of consistent and high-quality fish all year round. The UK's decentralized fishing industry has found it hard to fulfil such demands and sold much of its produce to other countries. So we have the spectre of trucks full of fish passing each other in Calais.

Defra commissioned a fascinating report on food miles.[30] Figure 3.10 summarizes the findings. Heavy goods vehicles are the largest source of greenhouse gas emissions, about 40 per cent of their emissions taking place outside the UK. The last three miles of the average food journey – in the family car – accounts for a staggering 13 per cent of all the emissions. This isn't too surprising if we consider the physical reality of the average shopping trip – driving 1 tonne of car and wailing family through congested suburbs to convey 11kg of food back home. Aviation and sea transport both emit around 10 per cent of greenhouse gas emissions, though with starkly different emissions intensities.

More important than food's frequent-flyer scale air miles is its road mileage; over half of the emissions of food transport arise from domestic and international road haulage. In 2006 heavy goods vehicles carried 42 billion tonne-km of food around Great Britain,[31] and food made up 27 per cent of the load borne by HGVs. (These numbers exclude the movements of non-food goods used by the industry, like pesticides, fertilizer and fuel.) Altogether 358 million tonnes of food and drink were carried an average of 117km, just within the UK. The figure of 358 million tonnes is a staggering amount – way more than we eat and drink. I calculated the total amount of food and drink we ingest as 66 million tonnes per year (calculated from the mass of UK agricultural production + net imports + volume of beer produced + volume of soft drink sold – the mass of animal feed).[32] Forget about international movements – based on the numbers above, the food travels on average 632km *in the UK alone*.

How can this be? We only consume about 1.1 tonne of food and drink a year, but the UK freight industry carries six tonnes of food on each of our behalves every year. The difference arises because food gets on and off trucks on average five times between the field and the supermarket. This is the result of the rather bizarre cost-minimization tactics pursued by food retailers and wholesalers. Food distribution takes place through a small number of vast distribution points. Their size permits stores to gather and dispatch the 40,000 or so products sold by the largest superstores. This suits the supermarkets well. It permits the stores to carry a huge range of products, it reduces their own storage costs but it makes others continually deliver small amounts of commonplace, little-processed food absurdly long distances.

George Monbiot describes in his book *Heat* the peregrinations of some produce grown in the Vale of Evesham and sold in a supermarket just a few kilometres away.[33] Their vegetable's epic journey to just-round-the-corner entailed a journey to Herefordshire, then a pack-house in Dyfed, Wales, then a distribution centre in Manchester, and back again to Evesham amassing 670km of travel with no real added value along the way, spookily similar to the figure I calculate above.

Figure 3.10 shows the proportions of CO_2 emissions and distance-weight attributable to each leg of foods' journey from field to fork. Though *shipping* dominates distance-weight figures, reflecting the huge mass of grains, fruit and vegetables moved long distances around the world, it only makes a modest contribution to CO_2 emissions, such is the carbon efficiency of shipping.

The efficiency with which we convey food varies significantly according to the form of transport used. The poorest performer is the humble family car

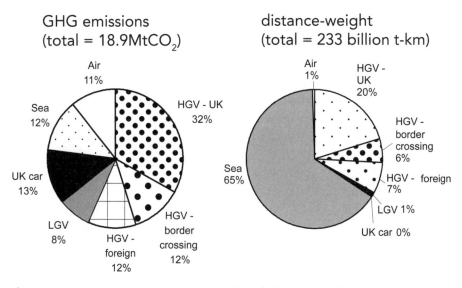

Figure 3.10 Greenhouse gas emissions and total distance-weight, 2002

Notes: LGV = light goods vehicle; HGV = heavy goods vehicle.
Source: AEA Technology (2005)[34]

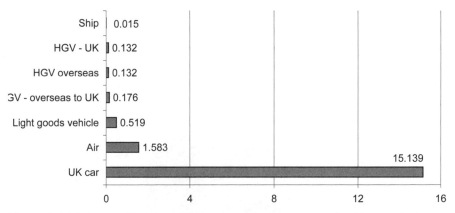

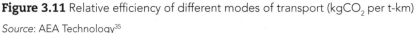

Figure 3.11 Relative efficiency of different modes of transport (kgCO₂ per t-km)
Source: AEA Technology[35]

used to convey the food the last few miles from the supermarket to the house. This emits on average 15kg of carbon dioxide for every tonne-km carried. The ship that brings the case of Chilean Merlot emits a mere thousandth of this – just 15 *grams* of carbon dioxide per tonne-km, this is ten times less than the heavy goods vehicle (HGV) and a hundred times less than the plane! It's not even visible in Figure 3.11 when they are all plotted on the same scale.

The trouble with air freight is not just its inefficiency, it's the fact
it makes possible the inefficient transport of foods over very long
distances

Air-freighted food gets some bad publicity: it deserves it. While only 1.5 per
cent of fruit and vegetables eaten in the UK are air-freighted, they account
for 40 per cent of transport emissions from fruit and vegetables. Air freight
is mainly used for high-value, perishable goods like fish and fresh fruit and
vegetables. Less perishable exotic fruit like Kiwi and bananas are ship-borne
and ripen in the vessel.

The transport of Kenyan green beans emits 20–26 times more CO_2 than
seasonal UK beans.[36] Because the emissions of CO_2 are at high altitude they
give rise to far more global warming than low level emissions. The latest IPCC
data suggests emissions might be between two to four times worse than CO_2
emitted at ground level[37] – more about this in the next chapter. Canning vegetables takes very little energy (around $0.2kgCO_2e$ per kg vegetable compared
to $11kgCO_2e$ for flying them from Kenya), so is a good way of eating seasonal
vegetables out of season.

In 2004, 183kt of food and flowers were flown into the UK.[38] Figure 3.12
shows the proportion by weight coming from the different regions of the
world. There is also a list of the 15 largest exporters by mass too. Air freight is
often associated with Kenya and other sub-Saharan countries. Other countries
air-freight food to us too, the US is our second largest air-freighted supplier
and even Iceland gets into the top 15 by dint of its fish sales.

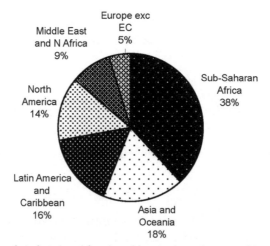

Figure 3.12 Source of air-freighted food and horticulture imported into the UK (kt/yr
of different produce , and % of kt mass from different countries)

Source: HM Customs and Excise [39]

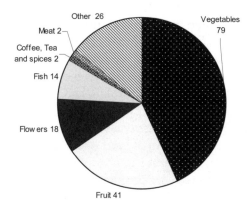

Figure 3.13 Mass of various food and horticulture commodities air-freighted into the UK, 2004 (kt)

Source: HM Customs and Excise[40]

But Kenya is the largest source by a long way, accounting for about 18 per cent of our air-freighted imports by weight (about a fifth of this is flowers). Figure 3.13 shows the types and importance of perishable foods and flowers that are imported. Fruit and vegetables are the most significant in terms of weight.

I eat around 10kg per year of Alfonso mangoes, baby corn and other exotic vegetables. Their air transport accounts for 10 per cent of my emissions from food transport and these release around 100kgCO_2 per year, but provide only 2 per cent of my food intake!

We could easily manage without the food air-freighted into the UK. However, weighing against this on the moral scales is the economic opportunity it provides sub-Saharan Africa. My wife was born and raised in Kenya and my father-in-law still lives there. I am conscious that horticulture provides valuable jobs. One NGO that is often quoted in the press says that the sector directly employs 120,000 people in sub-Saharan Africa and ten times more indirectly.[41] In 2007 the Kenyan horticulture sector exported KSh67 billion (about £0.5 billion) worth of produce. Of this, £100 million was for sales of fresh produce to UK supermarkets.[42] However, there is a significant gulf between the money paid by the UK consumer and the money reaching ordinary Kenyans. Of the £10 to £20 per kilogram paid for produce, between £1.50 and £2 per kilogram are paid in air-freight costs;[43] retailers will typically receive about 50 per cent of the price. A myriad of other businesses will receive their cut: insurers, marketing staff, foreign exchange traders, road hauliers and customs (Kenya is too rich to qualify for zero-rate tariffs offered the poorest countries). Less than a third of my spending will go to into the Kenyan economy and only a fraction of this to the poorest farmers.[44]

There's a darker side to the Kenyan horticulture industry too.[45] Much of the industry is concentrated around the shores of the beautiful Lake Naivasha, 60 miles north of Nairobi. The lake is now under pressure from over-abstraction of water and from pesticide and fertilizer residues. The low wages paid to the farm labourers (around £50 per month) have been the subject of disputes and walkouts. In the business of trading off environment against development, we need to think about the effectiveness of air-freighting horticulture produce as a means of transmitting financial resources to developing economies. On balance and to my mind, air-freighting of food is fundamentally an unsustainable business and it would be a mistake to encourage continued investment. To offset this, I will try and increase my consumption of sea-borne goods from the same countries.

Table 3.4 is reproduced from a document by the Soil Association in which they argue against air-freighted produce being included within the definition of 'organic food' because of the associated emissions. If you decide you want to avoid air-freighted goods, here are the products to look out for.

Table 3.4 Is the produce you buy likely to be air-freighted?

Air-freighted product	Country of origin
Green beans	Egypt, Zambia, The Gambia, Kenya
Baby sweetcorn	Thailand, Zambia
Asparagus	South Africa, Thailand
Podded peas	Egypt, Zambia, The Gambia, India
Limes	Dominican Republic, Mexico
Avocados	Mexico
Spring onions	Egypt, Thailand
Pineapple	Ghana
Sweet potatoes (early season only)	US
Grapes (early season only)	Egypt, Mexico, South Africa

Source: Soil Association (2007)[46]

It isn't by any means just supermarkets that fly in food. Some of the local delis are even worse. Our nearest insists on importing fresh pasta from Italy, since anything less would not be authentic. I challenged him on this and he came out with the usual refrain – that the plane was going to fly and his custom made no difference to the number of journeys. This is of course a fallacious argument. Air freight is quite likely carried in the belly of scheduled flights.

Unlike passenger flights which pay air passenger duty, air freight pays no taxes. The overall profitability of the route is determined by the revenues from air freight and passenger receipts. Because of the slim margins, revenue from air freight can make a sizeable impact on profitability. His client numbers seem to be dwindling and it's unlikely his business will survive the credit crunch. But I do wonder why we carry on believing that we should pay a premium for importing something by air that can be so easily be manufactured in the UK.

Replacing the consumption of soft drinks with tap water is a great way of reducing emissions from transport

> *It borders on morally being unacceptable to spend hundreds of millions of pounds on bottled water when we have pure drinking water, when at the same time one of the crises that is facing the world is the supply of water.*
> (Phil Woolas, UK Minister for the Environment, Defra)

Retailing at £1 but requiring a fraction of a penny to produce, bottled water is a dream come true for the manufacturer. The marketing people have somehow managed to daub it with the reputation of being a health drink which, I suppose, in comparison to lemonade and cola, it probably is.

One way of reducing emissions from transport is by replacing bottled water and other soft drinks with tap water. The UK consumes a whopping 14 billion litres of soft drinks per year (bn L/yr), and within this the consumption of bottled water had grown to 2.2 bn L/yr by 2006. If these travel the average haul of 119km to the supermarket and are conveyed home by car, then this represents transport emissions of some $1.5MtCO_2$, or $25kgCO_2$ per person – mainly from the trip home. The figure will be even higher if the water is imported – you can even buy bottled water from Fiji. I would love to boycott the stuff but I never drink it anyway. As well as the transport emissions, a further $1.9MtCO_2$ of emissions are associated with the production of soft drinks.

But there seems to be a shift in tastes and people were ordering tap water more, even before the credit crunch. Maybe the marketing disaster that was Coke's failed launch of the Dasani brand put paid to any claim of healthiness. The water, which was extracted from the pristine and untouched wilderness that is Sidcup, had become contaminated with bromate through the 'purification' process, and countless bottles had to be recalled.

Restaurants, especially the upmarket ones, are the worst culprits at foisting these pointless drinks upon us. In my local pizzeria I quizzed the retailer about why he insisted on selling Italian bottled water which had been transported over 1000 miles by road. It was just a matter of national pride. The UK's environment ministry, Defra, has banned bottled water from meetings and invested taxpayer's money ... wait for it ... in plastic jugs, just like in the old days. (The same cannot be said for the House of Commons which is said to spend £60,000 a year on bottled water.)

Food retail and catering

The selling of food to the final consumer accounts for 16 per cent of GHG emissions; roughly half from the retail sector and half from the catering sector.

Tesco has produced an interesting breakdown of GHG emissions from its UK operations.[47] About half came from the purchase of grid electricity (chiefly for refrigeration and lighting), about a quarter from the release of the refrigerant HFC from its fridges and freezers and much of the rest came from transport and wholesale operations. If Tesco is anything like the rest of the retail sector (it makes up 20 per cent of the sector so to an extent it *is* the retail sector), this suggests that the use of chilled cabinets in supermarkets and corner shops are responsible for almost 5 per cent of food's GHG emissions. I checked this figure against some other sources. Tara Garnett from the Food Climate Research Network claims that food refrigeration (during production, transport, retail and home storage) contributes 3–3.5 per cent of UK's *total* GHG emissions.[48] Swedish academics, Annika Carlsson-Kanyama and Mireille Faist, estimate that the open cabinet requires 50 times more energy to keep cool than a refrigerated room, around the same amount of energy as transport from the farm to the food processor.[49]

The supermarkets are all responding to consumer (and workforce) pressures and trying to reduce the amount of GHG emitted per square foot of space. Sainsbury's and Tesco have both set themselves ambitious targets to reduce their store emissions by enhancing energy efficiency (especially in new stores) and by replacing HFC-based refrigerants with non-GHG ones. The Co-op is sourcing its power from renewable electricity, though there is an issue about how much carbon this strategy actually saves since in the UK the bottleneck restricting the penetration of renewable power is supply (planning permission and grid connection) rather than demand.

However, these aspirations are still a long way from the reality of what occurs in store. Too much electricity is wasted by stores over-illuminating their products and maintaining huge open cabinets of chilled foods. My local Sainsbury's and Tesco convenience stores are about 250 square metres in size. Their outer walls have a 25 metre garland of chilled cabinets – containing high-value, high-margin perishable items: pre-cut salads, meats, bottled water (which, having managed to withstand storage for hundreds of years beneath the Scottish Highlands at ambient temperatures, needs to be chilled for the last few hours of its life) and the ubiquitous ready meals. Additionally, the stores each had around 120 spot or strip lights and a handful of air-conditioning vents. The shops were a bit of an environmental nightmare, making no effort to use natural sunlight or basic insulation. The selection of products is aimed at maximizing the profits with scant care for the energy needed to store or package the foods. Out of curiosity I tested the electricity demand of the chilled cabinets in my local Costcutter store. One sorry-looking appliance drew 250W and was on 24/7 all year round. Its emissions are about 900kgCO_2 per year. A slightly smaller cabinet with basic insulation (a see-through plastic door) still drew 127W. The average home fridge uses barely 30W.

We have become so used to buying perishables like ready foods, dairy products and pre-cut vegetables that we have almost forgotten about life without them. In a fascinating account of life before fridges recounted in her Food Climate Research Network (FCRN) synthesis paper,[50] Tara Garnatt refers to the demise of the old fashioned larder – which pretty much exited from the design of homes after 1960 after the fridge became an instant must-have product. What could be more wholesome than food transferred from the chilled cabinet, to the car, to the fridge so it could retain its fresh and nutritious goodness?

Before chilled foods our ready meals came from the can. Canning was developed soon after the Napoleonic Wars. It was briefly fashionable in the mid-nineteenth century, but – aside from Andy Warhol's iconic paintings of Campbell's soup – has captured the zeitgeist about as successfully as corsets or surgical bandages. The process of canning sterilizes food by sealing it in metal and then cooking it at temperatures above 116°C to kill off all the microbes. Supermarkets do not display canned foods prominently because they keep for a long time and are cheaply distributed so can be stocked by rival independent stores, which is pretty much the opposite of the qualities they're looking for from a profit maximization viewpoint. Canned foods have the reputation for being less healthy than fresh produce – this is what I believed too. I tried to find evidence to support this but the only independent research I could find was from the British Nutrition Foundation which says the complete opposite:[51]

Canned food, contrary to popular belief, can form part of a healthy balanced diet. It's often assumed that canned foods are a poor source of vitamins and minerals. Canned foods in many cases provide similar amounts of vitamins and minerals to fresh equivalents, and are often a good source of protein and fibre too.

They go on to say that canned foods are often produced soon after harvest so retain their nutrients. Counter-intuitively canned foods might even be *more healthy* than the manky old 'fresh' carrot that's been at the back of fridge for the last two weeks. The other option to canning is vacuum-packing. Our local health food shop stocks some delicious vacuum-packed ravioli which retails at a similar price to the chilled food but does not need to be stored at a low temperature.

Box 3.5 *Impact of supermarket practices on greenhouse gas emissions*

Supermarkets are setting themselves stringent GHG reductions targets and are acting fast to meet them. For instance, Tesco's store at Diss incorporates a number of energy-saving features including clear Perspex windows to make better use of natural light, wind turbines to meet some of its electricity needs, movement-detecting lighting and better management of cooling. Famously, Tesco has also announced the creation of a £100 million fund to spend on installing renewables and combined heat and power in its stores.

However, supermarkets' practices can contribute to the increase in food miles and energy consumption in other parts of the food supply chain. In particular, supermarkets have reduced the number of locations ('regional distribution centres', RDCs) to which manufacturers can deliver food, so increasing the distances that manufacturers have to transport their goods. The supermarkets are also transferring the cost of maintaining inventories onto manufacturers.

The first can result in the well-known logistical anomalies, such as the one described in the Food Miles report that features the epic migration of a sandwich made in Derbyshire which journeys 160 miles around the country before making its way back to a Derbyshire shop a few hundred metres from the factory.[52] Supermarkets have in the past provided no local discretion to store managers to source from nearby farms or producers, apart from a few early morning items like bread, milk and eggs. Instead food producers have to funnel all their deliveries through the supermarkets' 70 or so regional distribution centres – each serving vast hinterlands. For instance, Sainsbury's current strategy seeks to replace its present 21 depots with 9 'fulfilment factories' and 4 other depots[34] spread near to the motorway network – there is no RDC in Wales, so all food sold in Welsh Sainsbury's would have to be trucked from England.[53]

Supermarkets' efforts to cut their own inventory costs give rise to more frequent and less efficient logistics for their suppliers. The movement of frozen foods is a particularly energy-hungry part of the food distribution system. Researchers at Herriot-Watt University write about the 'quick response' demanded by supermarkets from the suppliers of frozen food.[54] Around 65–70 per cent more energy is required to distribute frozen food than ambient food. Since 1995, supermarkets' lead times have dropped from 6 days to 3.7 days, the frequency of delivery has risen from 2.1 to 3 per week and the average consignment size has declined from 11.7 to 9.8 pallets per truck.

I have decided to stop buying chilled foods from supermarkets because of their wasteful energy-use practices, and the role they play in creating unnecessary food miles. It's a tough call because it's also true they are doing quite a lot to reduce their emissions and to improve the information they provide customers. Box 3.5 talks in more detail about the pros and cons of supermarkets.

Swapping the modem for the motor can make a significant saving

Emissions from driving the food the last leg of its journey home from the supermarket account for about 13 per cent of emissions on average. While on average each car is driven 580km a year to and from food shops; ours barely scrapes in 10km a year. I can declare rather smugly that I usually walk or cycle to my nearby shop. Having groceries delivered to the home can therefore make a big difference.

A range of studies reviewed by Cairns and colleagues suggest that internet shopping for groceries can reduce traffic demand by those doing the shopping by more than 70 per cent since the delivery companies can consolidate the orders of several nearby homes into a single journey.[55] Emissions savings are less pronounced because they use large vehicles. However, the amount of emissions savings depends on how fussy you are about the specific time of delivery. Ocado and Tesco both deliver within a two hour slot but this convenience has a carbon price, reducing their ability to minimize the travel by their vans. The motor manufacturers' association even claims that emissions from road transport will rise as supermarkets' reduced flexibility to schedule means that the vans return back to the depot after just two drop-offs. Mitigating against this, the supermarkets typically impose a delivery charge which has had the effect of making people place larger and less frequent orders – Tesco home shoppers spend an average of 120 per cent more than in-store customers, their average shop being £91 compared to the average of £41 for in-store customers.

The best home delivery system that I have encountered is the Abel and Cole system where customers are given no option but to take delivery at the time and day specified by A&C. Sounds harsh but it works for me. My driver tells me his 80-home round journey is about 70km long, including the journey to and from the depot in Wimbledon. This represents an 80 per cent reduction in the amount of mileage to convey the goods home. However, weighing against this is that few people completely abandon their shopping trip, and the Abel and Cole transit van's fuel economy (24mpg urban average) is about two-thirds the average for the typical car. So my guesstimate is that the home delivery service probably reduces emissions from the journey home by about 60 per cent. The company is also presently trialling biodiesel from locally grown oilseed rape which will make further reductions.

Box 3.6 *Low-carbon food on a budget*

Angie was a little shy about showing me her kitchen. 'The room is a complete mess', she explained. 'But I've got a old fridge in there – it's a seven-year-old Bosch, still works a treat, mind. I wish it was frost-free as I never get around to emptying it. My son got me the microwave before he passed away.' I suggest she defrost the fridge and move it away from the window as it was in the sunlight. She should also keep an on eye on Freecycle (described in chapter 7) for a newer fridge.

Keeping the food bill down was her first priority. We found that eating low carbon could be quite cheap. She liked meat, and ate sausages and bacon two or three times a week. She didn't much care about organic food, finding it pricey, but did eat organic eggs – as much for welfare reasons and health as anything else. She ate cheese most days. I showed her a picture of Quorn and she looked at me suspiciously. 'You're not a Quorn salesman are you? You do go on about it.' She agreed to try the Quorn cottage pie once to see how it tasted.

I certainly learnt a thing or two from her about planning. She was extremely economical with her time, purchasing her food in Iceland two or three times a week near the clinic where she worked. Three small bags of shopping was the limit to what she could carry on the bus. She cooked everything in bulk: the frying pan would accommodate an entire packet of sausages; her big saucepan could make several servings of stew in one go. She'd pack the uneaten food into single-portion freezer bags once it had cooled. I took copious notes.

She took me to inspect her freezer. A 20th century Mrs Beeton for sure – I was impressed how much food she fitted in her freezer. My own contained a lonely tray of ice cubes, a tub of half-eaten Häagen-Dazs and a frozen bottle of bubbly, which someone had put in the freezer to chill one party, and probably needs to be extricated by a bomb-disposal squad.

'I don't suppose you buy organic food from Abel and Cole either', I said. She shook her head, distressed I was mocking her. 'I couldn't afford that.' But she did buy local and asked if I knew what fruit and vegetables were in season in the different months so she could keep an eye out at the shops. (The list is reproduced as an annex to this chapter.)

I have refrained from making any comment about farmers' markets. Some people swear by them – I don't. My own experience with them has been a bit hit and miss. My last visit consisted of a five-mile drive, to see stall after stall selling homemade Devon boar sausages and the like. I have come back with nothing more than a sprig of parsley and a jar of some fruit conserve (I think that means jam). My visits have been fun, but I suspect not achieved much on the climate front since the farmers have driven their environmentally disastrous ancient white vans halfway across the country to sell a few kilos of produce. The only reason this makes financial sense is because of the subjugation they suffer at the hands of the supermarket buyers. They aren't doing this for the environment; it's to escape their bondage.

So what's the take-home message of this? Food miles, the distance actually travelled by the food, is less important than the mode of transport used to convey the food. The worst thing to do is drive long distances in your car on a weekly basis for the food shopping. It makes much more sense to shop locally for the fresh food and shop infrequently from the supermarket, and to then buy in bulk. If you are addicted to the choice you get from supermarkets, the trick is to get them to deliver.

Is it best to eat at home, cooking from raw ingredients or microwaving a TV dinner, or out in a canteen or restaurant?

We live in an age when pizza gets to your home before the police.

(Jeff Adler)

Recipe: A series of step-by-step instructions for preparing ingredients you forgot to buy, in utensils you don't own, to make a dish the dog wouldn't eat.

(author unknown)

I like cooking, but I have a sneaking suspicion that cooking from raw ingredients takes an inordinate amount of energy and is more of a leisure activity than a cost-effective means of keeping my CO_2 emissions at bay. The trouble with cooking at home is that most people cook in small batches, so most of the energy goes into heating up the kitchen, oven, or pots and pans and relatively little into exciting the food molecules.

Environmentally speaking, the questions I am interested in tackling are 'How should I cook to reduce my emissions?' and 'Is it better to cook food at home, to heat ready-made food in the microwave or to eat out?' My current split probably leans towards the second and third options.

It's proved impossible to give a definitive answer to this question since it depends on whether you are cooking for just yourself or a family (the more in one go the better), how well you and the restaurant minimizes the wastage of food, and the underlying ingredients being used. It clearly takes more energy to cook a solitary fish-finger in the oven than to rustle up a salad. Even the seemingly uncontentious statement 'super-sized pub grub is a bad thing' is difficult to be 100 per cent confident about. Confronted with an unsettlingly large goulash in a Hereford village pub (cooked by a *Polish* chef – the globalization of our food chain and hospitality sector never fails to impress), I made a determined and ultimately successful bid to finish off the impossibly large meal. I asked whether much food gets thrown away. The waitress pointed to the contented-looking kitchen dog: 'He eats all the leftover meat. Waste vegetables go to a nearby farm. Nobody ever touches the garnish but they complain if we leave it off.' *I even ate the garnish!* I thought with a touch a pride, as we waited for air rescue to winch me to my car.

It's difficult to find up-to-date information on the precise use of energy for cooking within households. The data in Table 3.5 are drawn from a study that Brenda Boardman and colleagues in Oxford undertook based on 1998 data about the use of kitchen appliances. The most up-to-date government statistics show that household use of energy for cooking has risen by 6 per cent since 1998, while that for cooling had fallen by the same amount, reflecting the tightening of standards for fridges. On average the cooking and storing of food emits about 0.27tCO$_2$e per person, about half in fridges and half from cooking.

Table 3.5 shows the emissions and costs of running kitchen appliances over a year for the average family. Fridges and freezers are by far the largest

Table 3.5 Ownership and energy consumption of kitchen appliances, 1998 (per household)

	Ownership per household	kWh per appliance per year	kWh per household per year	Emissions (kg/yr)	Cost of energy (£/yr)
Hob – electric	0.46	270	124	65	13
Oven – electric	0.57	245	140	73	15
Hob – gas	0.49	270	132	27	5
Oven – gas	0.38	245	93	19	4
Kettle	0.95	170	162	85	17
Microwave	0.77	85	65	34	7
Refrigerator	0.43	300	129	67	14
Fridge-freezer	0.6	650	390	204	41
Upright freezer	0.24	500	120	63	13
Chest freezer	0.18	460	83	43	9
Total			1438	681	136

Notes: Emissions from electricity are assumed to be 0.52kgCO$_2$e/kWh and from gas 0.206kgCO$_2$/kWh; cost of electricity 10.5p/kWh; gas 4p/kWh (2008 prices).

Source: Boardman et al (2005)[56] Table 6.1, and my guesstimate of the penetration of gas hobs and gas ovens.

source of emissions in the kitchen, accounting for over half of emissions and costing £76 a year to run at today's electricity prices. My own fridge-freezer's measured electricity consumption (on a fairly brisk spring day) was the equivalent of 290kWh per year (152kgCO$_2$ per year, £30 per year) – which outperforms the figure in the table by 55 per cent. Our own household (of exactly 2.5 people) uses an A-rated frost-free Bosch which is now about three years old and which we selected for its energy efficiency.

The energy-efficiency standards of fridges have risen dramatically since the data underpinning the table were collected; so much so, that anything lower than A band fridges are passé and the best ones are A+ and even A++. I had a look at fridges on a number of websites. I could find nothing on the market worse than a B. That said, even within the A-class there is a 45 per cent difference in energy efficiency between the best and the worst. It seems as though manufacturers have largely withdrawn the least efficient models from the market, but haven't yet made use of the new higher bands. There are exceptions: Miele make a number of A++ models. Tests by the Oeko institute in Germany suggest that A++ fridges are about €20 more expensive but save about €17 per year in electricity bills.

Table 3.6 shows the relative efficiency a fridge needs to attain to be marketed in a particular band. The top band A++ can use as little as half the energy of others on the market, and a quarter of the energy of pre-1990 models. Always buy as small a fridge or freezer as meets your family's needs. It's worth remembering that the Energy Efficiency Index rating compensates

Table 3.6 Energy efficiency of fridges and freezers

Energy-efficiency class	Energy-efficiency index: I
A++	I ≤ 30
A+	30 ≤ I < 42
A	42 ≤ I < 55
B	55 ≤ I < 75
C	75 ≤ I < 90
D	90 ≤ I < 100
E	100 ≤ I < 110
F	110 ≤ I < 125
G	125 ≤ I

Source: The Energy Information (Household Refrigerators and Freezers) Regulations 2004, Statutory Instrument 2004 No: 1468. The value of 100 (which is the division between D & E bands) was the average performance in 1993.

the model for size, frost-free capability, relative size of freezer compartment and features like ice makers. While it is quite possible to buy the fridge equivalent of a hummer – one of those walk-in, Tardis-style domestic fridges – that still shrouds itself in an A rating cloak, you'd be kidding yourself this was going to save the planet.

Once you've taken the decision to the buy the fridge there are a few things to do to reduce the emissions further: keep the temperature at 6°C for a fridge and −18°C for a freezer; locate the appliance in a cold room, or least away from the cooker; keep it about three-quarters full and defrost it from time to time. Fridges work by expelling the heat from the inside through the radiator at the back. Anything that makes it hard to expel the heat – like a hot external environment, or dust – will make the motor have to work harder. There are also a couple of gadgets on the market to improve the efficiency – the SavaPlug – which moderates the power fed to the fridge a second or two after the door is closed. This is to avoid the fridge drawing more power than it needs once the motor has got going. Unfortunately the device is not compatible with my fridge.

Here are the fairly paltry changes I have made in refrigeration: I moved the fridge away from the wall, removed all the cardboard and papers that had accumulated behind the fridge and dusted the radiator, made a solemn promise to myself to defrost items in the fridge, to allow the food to cool before putting into the fridge and to try to open and close the door more slowly to avoid unnecessary release of the chilled air. None of this is rocket science. I'm also going to investigate whether I can update my already A-rated fridge in an environmentally benign way (more on that in the waste chapter). I'll have to wait until it needs replacing to make any significant savings.

Perhaps there is some scope for reducing my emissions from cooking. The next bit is going to get deeply anally retentive so please skip it if you don't like this sort of thing. When I say cooking, let me be more precise about what I mean. My wife and I probably cook more frequently than most people like us, but we don't cook like our parents used to; what we do is make coffee and tea, reheat food bought from shops, prepare salads and sandwiches and perhaps four meals a week cooked from raw ingredients – mainly as a result of the box scheme.

Since there are 2.5 of us living in our household our entire emissions from cooking are only $81kgCO_2$ per year. In terms of energy savings, it is worth reminding ourselves about the basic physics underpinning cooking. When you cook, you are trying to heat the food up and heat up as little of everything else as possible. Different materials take different amounts of heat to warm up. Water is particularly bad, needing ten times the energy to warm as iron and about five times as much as aluminium.

Table 3.7 My household's energy use, emissions and fuel costs from cooking

	Units	Usage (per week)	Energy use (kWh/unit)	Energy use (kWh/yr)	Emissions (kgCO$_2$/yr)	Cost (£/yr)
Kettle	cups	28	0.06	87	45	9.17
Microwave	minutes	70	0.020	73	38	7.64
Coffee maker	cups	7	0.06	22	11	2.29
Toaster	rounds	6	0.04	12	6	1.31
Oven/grill	minutes	30	0.042	65	34	6.83
Gas hob	minutes	210	0.03	364	75	14.56
Everything else*	minutes	5	0.001	0.21	0.1	0.02
Total				624	210	42

Note: * Everything else means a food processor, electric hand-held whisk and expresso maker.

A Defra study on life-cycle emissions from food puts the relative energy requirements for different styles of cooking at: microwaving 0.8MJ/kg, roasting 9MJ/kg, boiling 3.5MJ/kg and frying 7.5MJ/kg.[57] This is borne out by a different study of the energy balance for eating chicken either as a ready meal or cooking it from scratch in the oven;[58] this showed that emissions from cooking the chicken at home were about 40 per cent higher than simply microwaving a ready meal. Because this study was primarily about food miles they equated this energy penalty from home cooking to an extra 9000 miles of travel for the ingredients.

Apart from warming up your chicken tikka masala, microwave cookers can also be useful for making individual cups of hot water. By way of comparison my 1.4 kW microwave takes 90 seconds and consumes around 0.03kWh of energy to heat a cup of hot water sufficient to make a cup of coffee; if you accurately measure 1.5 cups of water into an electric kettle you could make a cup of tea with the same amount of energy, but a quarter-filled electric kettle – which is what I usually do – takes three minutes and twice as much energy (a full kettle took nine minutes to boil). Using the gas ring is intrinsically more carbon efficient than the electric kettle, but since my gas kettle weighs just over 1kg this proves an inefficient means of heating just one or two cups of water. The gas ring heats water from the outside in so you have to get the metal really hot before the water will boil. I decided from now on to use the microwave to make myself and my wife hot drinks, and use the gas hob when we were heating up a large amount of hot water. I reckon this will save me about 20kgCO$_2$e per year.

> **Box 3.7 *Low-carbon eggs***
>
> 'I'd stay outside if I was you – you might find what I'm doing disturbing.' The kitchen door sprung open immediately.
>
> 'Please don't tell me you tried to boil an egg in the microwave. For someone who thinks they're intelligent, you do some really stupid things', said my wife as she observed me scraping bits of boiled egg from the inside of the microwave. 'Everyone knows you can't boil an egg in that thing. They blow up.'
>
> I kept quiet; somehow saying that I wasn't boiling the eggs, simply reheating them didn't seem a strong enough retort.
>
> The issue of the most energy-efficient way of eating eggs had vexed me for a week now. I had boiled and shelled four eggs a couple of days ago and was trying to find the best way of heating them up again. It didn't look good. Four eggs (240g) in 1000g of water and pan – and then there was the matter of reheating them. Making an omelette had a more favourable ratio of mass of food to mass of utensil, but two-day-old omelette tastes rubbish. The best solution seemed to be to make microwaved scrambled egg: whisk the egg, add milk (soya of course), heat in the microwave for 45 seconds give another stir and then another 45 seconds in the microwave. Total GHG emissions from cooking was $0.02kgCO_2e$ – about a fifth of the energy used to boil a single egg.

Microwave cookers are also very efficient at warming small quantities of food. Many things can be heated up in seconds which would take minutes under the grill or in the boiling pan. For instance a baked potato cooks in just ten minutes in a microwave, a portion of carrots or peas sufficient for two people take between three and six minutes in a microwaveable plastic container.

How about eating out?

I nosed around the kitchens of a couple of cafés and restaurants to see whether their mass production of food was more efficient than mine. One would expect someone cooking loads of food to be much more efficient since there is less metal/oil/water being heated per unit of food. Our slightly posh Italian restaurant cooked individual portions from scratch and didn't appear to offer any savings over home cooking that I could discern. The Indian takeaway on the other hand did seem pretty efficient. The chef parboiled a huge vat of rice, which he finished off when an order came in; the tandoor oven was well insulated, used gas and was in almost constant use to make the breads and chicken on a skewer.

Bringing It All Together

This section discusses how the changes I made to my diet contributed to my goal of reducing my emissions. At www.economicalenvironmentalist.co.uk there are some downloadable sheets and an online calculator to allow you to do the same for your diet.

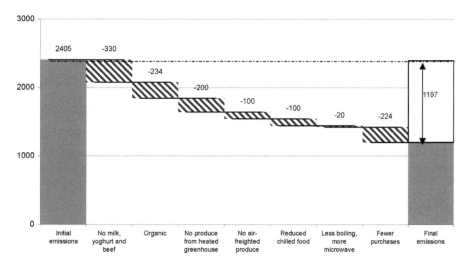

Figure 3.14 Summary of the GHG impacts of the changes in my diet ($kgCO_2e$ per year)

Source: My calculations (see text).

Cutting out beef and lamb and reducing dairy products

This reduced my emissions by 330kg per year, mainly through replacing the milk with soya milk and soya yoghurt. I carried on eating dairy cheese which is much more GHG intensive per unit mass than milk, hence the remaining dairy GHG emissions (see Table 3.8).

Going organic

As described earlier, the quality of information on the relative GHG emissions from organic and conventional agriculture is weak. I have assumed going organic avoids all the emissions from the fertilizer industry ($94kgCO_2e$ per year) and a quarter of those from agriculture (a further $140kgCO_2e$ per year).

Table 3.8 My weekly meat, fish and dairy consumption and annual greenhouse gas emissions

	Food intake		Annual GHG emissions	
	(g/week)		(kgCO$_2$e)	
	Before	After	Before	After
Milk and milk products	2984	425	439	234
Beef	180	0	150	0
Pelagic fish	125	310	1	1
Demersal fish	140	140	10	24
Shell fish	110	70	17	0
Soya milk	0	2500	0	21
Total	3539	3445	616	280

Stopping eating food grown in greenhouses or food that's been air-freighted

I probably ate more greenhouse and air-freighted food than most so the savings from this were quite sizeable. Abandoning these saved me 200kgCO$_2$e from produce grown in heated greenhouses and 100kgCO$_2$e from stopping use of air-freighted food.

Replacing chilled soups and vegetables with their canned alternatives

I have assumed that the transport and display of chilled foods by retailers accounts for 5 per cent of the total life-cycle emissions from eating. I wasn't able to eliminate these entirely because of my continued consumption of cheese; nonetheless, I counted savings from retail of just 100kgCO$_2$e. Nor was I able to make any inroads into reducing use of fridges in catering.

Using the microwave instead of the cooker to reheat food or to boil small amounts of water.

Slim pickings here. All I can really claim is 20kgCO$_2$e from heating my water in the microwave instead of the kettle. I also saved a bit by reheating food in the microwave.

Buying the most fuel-efficient fridge on the market and keeping it defrosted

I already had a highly energy-efficient fridge so it makes no sense for me to change it. I made a few promises to keep it stocked correctly but I can't claim it'll save me any energy. The average fridge-freezer in 1998 caused the release of about 300kgCO$_2$e from its power consumption. There's scope to halve these emissions or better by going for the most energy-efficient fridge.

Taking a doggy bag to restaurants and cutting down on the amount of food I throw away at home

My food consumption dropped by over 15 per cent: about half of this was because I ate less, about half because I reheated old food, including an Indian restaurant meal. This showed up in as a reduction in the food I bought and cooked. There was probably some reduction in the amount I cooked but I didn't monitor this.

As well as these fairly generic suggestions I was able to make a dent in my emissions through my box service. These now account for about a third of the food I consume by weight (mainly because of the soya milk). The domestic food miles from road freight for these purchases appear to be about half of those for standard groceries as there are only three domestic transfers instead of five and the distance is a little shorter. I estimate annual savings might be around 20kgCO$_2$e. It is hard to judge whether there is any reduction in road or sea freight outside the UK.

Table 3.9 shows how the emissions reductions are spread across the different parts of the food chain.

Table 3.9 Emissions from eating, before and after dietary changes (kgCO$_2$e/yr)

	Before	After
Fertilizers	94	0
Agriculture + fisheries	1265	417
Food industry	290	260
Food transport	316	196
Retail + catering	356	260
Cooking and domestic fridge	84	64
Total	2405	1197

Table 3.10 gives the average weekly food consumption for different household types so you can compare your own consumption against others. My own data (Table 3.2) before I changed my diet was not too different from the average 'single' person except that I ate more fish and less meat than the average person and very few soft drinks.

Table 3.10 Purchased quantities of food and drink for average UK households (grams or millilitres per week per person)

Eating in	Unit	Single person	Couple with two children	65–75 year old
Milk and milk products excluding cheese	mL	2416	1839	1563
Cheese	g	137	104	95
Carcass meat*	g	241	170	164
Non-carcass meat and meat products	g	935	673	670
Fish	g	240	126	128
Eggs	g	124	68	69
Fats	g	231	127	123
Sugar and preserves	g	184	84	79
Fresh and processed vegetables	g	2220	1553	1428
Fresh and processed fruit	g	1665	1218	955
Bread	g	861	582	543
Flour	g	51	38	55
Cakes, buns and pastries	g	219	135	87
Biscuits and crispbreads	g	206	156	101
Other cereals and cereal products	g	544	511	548
Beverages	g	89	38	25
Other food and drink	g	847	731	693
Soft drinks	mL	1682	1850	1931
Confectionery	g	140	123	83
Alcoholic drinks	mL	804	675	751
Total food	g	12,892	10,003	9257
Total drink	mL	2486	2525	2682

Eating out	Unit	Single person	Couple with two children	65–75 year old
Indian, Chinese or Thai food	g	38	26	40
Meat and meat products	g	80	71	95
Fish and fish products	g	19	10	12
Cheese and egg dishes or pizza	g	21	24	23
Fresh and processed potatoes	g	76	67	71
Vegetables	g	42	23	26
Salads	g	24	13	17
Rice, pasta or noodles	g	18	17	18
Soups	g	10	7	10
Breakfast cereals	g	0	0	0
Fresh and processed fruit	g	10	27	15
Yoghurt and fromage frais	g	3	3	4
Bread	g	7	8	7
Sandwiches	g	74	74	96
Other food products	g	99	131	213
Beverages	mL	161	93	80
Soft drinks including milk	mL	234	373	457
Alcoholic drinks	mL	793	298	720
Confectionery	g	7	19	14
Ice cream, desserts and cakes	g	28	28	21
Biscuits and chocolate	g	3	4	3
Crisps, nuts and snacks	g	6	10	11
Total food	g	566	562	698
Total drink	mL	1188	764	1257

Note: * Roughly half of the carcass meat eaten is beef, lamb or mutton.

Source: ONS Expenditure and Food Survey (2008)[59]

Notes

1   Office for National Statistics (2006) Environmental accounts detailed 91 industry disaggregations of emissions for 2004. These can be accessed as Excel spreadsheets at www.statistics.gov.uk/statbase/explorer.asp?CTG=3&SL=&D=4261&DCT=0&DT=32# 4261 (accessed on July 2009). More recent data is available at lower levels of industrial/ fuel disaggregation.

2   AEA Technology (2007) *Scoping Studies to Identify Opportunities for Improving Resource Use Efficiency and for Reducing Waste through the Food Production Chain*, Report to Defra.

3   Office for National Statistics Environmental Accounts.

4   Defra (2006) *Food Statistics in Your Pocket*, Chart 7.6.

5   In the feasibility study for the National Diet and Nutrition Study, estimates of energy intake using the seven-day weighed dietary record methodology were compared with measurements of energy expenditure using the doubly labelled water (DLW) methodology.

6   BERR (2008) *Heat Call for Evidence*, www.berr.gov.uk/files/file43609.pdf, Figure 1.2.

7   The National Health Service Information Centre (2006) *Health Survey for England 2006 – Updating of Trend Tables to include 2006 Data*.

8   Elmadfa, I. and Weichselbaum, E. (eds) (2005) 'European Nutrition and Health Report 2004 Forum Nutr', Kargar, Basel, vol 58, pp47-61.

9   WRAP (Waste & Resources Action Programme) (2008) *The Food We Waste*, http://wrap. s3.amazonaws.com/the-food-we-waste-executive-summary.pdf (accessed June 2009).

10 Defra is the Department for Environment, *Food* and Rural Affairs. I am sure the press would have been delighted at the idea of an outbreak of salmonella or botulism emanating from our canteen.

11 www.caloriesperhour.com/index_burn.php features a US-based calorie calculator that gives metabolic rates for loads of different activities including cycling, running, walking and in-line skating (it was produced in the West Coast US after all).

12 Hoare, J. and Henderson, L., ONS (2002) *The National Diet & Nutrition Survey Summary report: adults aged 19 to 64 years; sample undertaken July 2000 to June 2001*. A survey carried out in GB by ONS on behalf of FSA and Department of Health, www.food.gov. uk/multimedia/pdfs/ndns5full.pdf (accessed July 2009).

13 Williams, A.G., Audsley, E. and Sandars, D.L. (2006) *Determining the Environmental Burdens and Resource Use in the Production of Agricultural and Horticultural Commodities*. Main Report. Defra Research Project IS0205. Cranfield University, Bedford and Defra. Available on www.silsoe.cranfield.ac.uk, and www.defra.gov.uk.

14 Marine and Fisheries Agency (2007) *UK Sea Fisheries Statistics*, Table, www.mfa.gov.uk/ statistics/documents/UKSeaFishStats-Summary-07.pdf (accessed July 2009).

15 Prime Minister's Strategy Unit (2004) *Net Benefits: A Sustainable and Profitable Future for the UK Fishing Industry*, Cabinet Office, p28.

16 Tyedmers, P. (2004) 'Fisheries and energy use', Table 2 in *Encyclopaedia of Energy*, vol 2, overall editor Cleveland Cutler, Elsevier, Vol 2, Table 2, Amsterdam pp 683–693. Online version available at: http://knovel.com/web/portal/browse/ display?_EXT_KNOVEL_DISPLAY_bookid=1714&VerticalID=0. Conversion to CO_2: author's calculation using emissions factor of 857kgC/tonne fuel and specific density of 900g/L.

17 AEA (2005) *The Validity of Food Miles as an Indicator of Sustainable Development:*

Final Report, ED50254 Issue 7. Report for Defra available at https://statistics.defra.gov.uk/esg/reports/foodmiles/default.asp (accessed on July 2009).

18 See 13 above.

19 Gundula Azeez and Peter Melchett from the Soil Association criticize the work for assessing performance of organic farms without taking account of the nitrogen flows between livestock and cereal in mixed farms and for ignoring soil carbon effects: pers com.

20 International Trade Centre (of the UN) and FiBL (Research Institute of Organic Agriculture) (2007) *Organic Farming and Climate Change,* UNCTAD/WTO, www.fibl-shop.org/shop/pdf/mb-1500-climate-change.pdf (accessed July 2009).

21 Gundula Azeez, formerly climate adviser at the Soil Association, pers com.

22 Wilson, S. (2006) *Case Study: Soy Production and Export from Brazil,* report to Defra.

23 ONS (2006) *UK Purchases and Expenditure on Food and Drink and Derived Energy and Nutrient Intakes in 2004–05,* ONS.

24 Altman, F. (1986) 'Downwind update: A discourse on matters gaseous', *Western Journal of Medicine,* vol 145, no 4, pp502–505, www.pubmedcentral.nih.gov/pagerender.fcgi?artid=1306982&pageindex=2#page (accessed June 2009).

25 http://tafkac.org/medical/death_by_flatulence.html (accessed June 2009).

26 Based on stachyose and raffinose contents. Suarez, F.L., Springfield, J., Furne, J.K., Lohrmann, T.T., Kerr, P.S. and Levitt, M.D. (1999) 'Gas production in humans ingesting a soybean flour derived from beans naturally low in oligosaccharides', *American Journal of Clinical Nutrition,* vol 69, pp135–139, www.ajcn.org/cgi/reprint/69/1/135.pdf#search=%22raffinose%20concentration%20beans%22 (accessed June 2009).

27 AEA Technology (2007) *Scoping Studies to Identify Opportunities for Improving Resource Use Efficiency and for Reducing Waste through the Food Production Chain,* Report to Defra.

28 These do not make scintillating reading but they can be found at www.defra.gov.uk/Environment/ccl/agreements.htm. The food and drink agreement has a number of sub-agreements within it.

29 Carlsson-Kanyama, A. and Faist, M. (2000) *Energy Use in the Food Sector. A data survey.* AFR report 291, February 2000 – *Appendices.*

30 AEA Technology (2005) see 17 above .

31 Department for Transport (2005) *Road Freight Statistics 2005,* Table 1.14. Category covers agricultural products, beverages and other foodstuffs.

32 My calculation is based on the supply of agricultural commodities taken from Defra, *Agriculture in the UK,* 2007 edition. Added to this is the entire output of beer and soft drinks from trade bulletins. There is likely to be a small amount of double counting.

33 Monbiot, G. (2006) *Heat: How to stop the planet burning,* Allen Lane, London.

34 AEA Technology (2005) see 17 above.

35 AEA Technology (2005) see 17 above.

36 Marriott, C. (2005) 'Plough to Plate by Plane: An Investigation into Trends and Drivers in the Airfreight Importation of Fresh Fruit and Vegetables into the United Kingdom from 1996 to 2004', MSc dissertation, University of Surrey.

37 Grassl, H. (2007) *Climate Forcing of Aviation Emissions in High Altitudes and Comparison of Metrics: An Update according to the Fourth Assessment Report, IPCC 2007,* Max Planck Institute for Meteorology, Hamburg.

38 Database kindly supplied by Paul Watkiss, author of the 2005 AEA report on Food Miles. Data originally purchased from HMRC.

39 HM Customs and Excise (now HM Revenue and Customs) extracted in 2003 and relating to trade flows in 2002–2003. Author grateful to Paul Watkiss, then at AEA Technology, for access to raw data.

40 See above.

41 MacGregor, J. and Vorley, B. (2006) 'Fair Miles'? The Concept of 'Food Miles' through a Sustainable Development Lens, International Institute for Environment and Development, www.iied.org/pubs/display.php?o=11064IIED&n=12&l=25&s=SDO (accessed June 2009).

42 Kenyan High Commission, Grown Under the Sun, http://grownunderthesun.com/facts.html (accessed June 2009).

43 Kenyan Agricultural attaché, London, pers com.

44 Peter Robbins, author of Stolen Fruit: The Tropical Commodities Disaster, pers com.

45 Food and Water Watch (2008) Lake Naivasha Withering Under the Assault of International Flower Vendors, January (extracted July 2009) www.canadians.org/water/documents/NaivashaReport08.pdf.

46 Soil Association (2007) Should the Soil Association Tackle the Environmental Impact of Air Freight in its Organic Standards?, www.soilassociation.org/LinkClick.aspx?fileticket=%2Bsuqx5aaMko%3D&tabid=234 (accessed June 2009).

47 Tesco (May 2007) Measuring Our Carbon Footprint, reviewed by environment auditors Environment Resources Management Ltd, www.tesco.com/climatechange/carbonfootprint.asp (accessed June 2009).

48 Garnett, T. (2008) Cooking up a storm: Food, greenhouse gas emissions and our changing climate, Food Climate Research Network, Centre for Environmental Strategy, University of Surrey, www.fcrn.org.uk/frcnPubs/index.php?id=6 (accessed July 2009).

49 Carlsson-Kanyama, A. and Faist, M. (2000) Energy Use in the Food Sector. A data survey. AFR report 291, February 2000 – Appendices.

50 Garnett, T. (2008), see 48 above.

51 British Nutrition Foundation (2008) www.nutrition.org.uk/home.asp?siteId=43&sectionId=435&subSectionId=323&parentSection=299&which=1 (accessed July 2009).

52 AEA Technology (2005) see 17 above.

53 Sainsbury's (2002) Sainsbury's Automated Depots ... A Suppliers Guide, www.sainsburys.co.uk/sid/Documents/UpstreamGuide-Final.pdf (accessed June 2009).

54 McKinnon, A. and Campbell, J. (1998) Quick Response in the Frozen Food Supply Chain: The Manufacturer's Perspective, Edinburgh Logistics Research Centre, Herriot-Watt University.

55 Cairns, S., Sloman, L., Newson, C., Anable, J., Kirkbride, A. and Goodwin, P. (2004) Smarter Choices: Changing the Way We Travel, University College London, Transport for Quality of Life Final Report to the Department for Transport, The Robert Gordon University and Eco-Logica, London.

56 Boardman, B., Darby, S., Killip, G., Hinnells, M., Jardine, C.N., Palmer, J. and Sinden, G. (2005) 40% House, Environment Change Institute, Oxford University.

57 Defra (2006) Environmental Impacts of Food Production and Consumption, research report completed by Manchester Business School.

58 AEA Technology (2005) see 17 above, p74.

59 ONS (2008) Family Spending – A report on the 2007 Expenditure and Food Survey, www.ons.gov.uk/about/who-we-are/our-services/unpublished-data/social-survey-data/efs.

Annex: Seasonal Fruit and Vegetables

Month	Fruit and vegetables	Fish and meat
January	cabbage, cauliflower, celeriac, forced rhubarb, leeks, parsnips, turnip, shallots, squash	goose, lobster, scallops
February	cabbage, cauliflower, celeriac, chard, chicory, forced rhubarb, kohlrabi, leeks, parsnips, spinach, swede, turnip	mussels, halibut, guinea fowl, lobster
March	beetroot, cabbage, cauliflower, leeks, mint, mooli, parsley, broccoli, radishes, rhubarb, sorrel	sardines (fresh ones!), lobster
April	broccoli, cabbage, cauliflower, morel mushrooms, wild garlic, radishes, rhubarb, carrots, kale, watercress, spinach	spring lamb, cockles
May	broccoli, cabbage, cauliflower, gooseberries, parsley, mint, broad beans, rhubarb, new carrots, samphire, asparagus	sea bass, lemon sole, sardines, duck, trout
June	carrots, cherries, elderflowers, lettuce, strawberries, peppers, asparagus, redcurrants, peas, rhubarb, gooseberries, tayberries, tomatoes, courgettes, broad beans	Welsh lamb, crab, salmon, grey mullet
July	carrots, gooseberries, strawberries, spinach, tomatoes, watercress, loganberries, sage, cauliflower, aubergines, fennel, asparagus, cabbage, celery, cherries, lettuce, mange-tout, nectarines, new potatoes, oyster mushrooms, peas, peaches, radish, raspberries, rhubarb, tomatoes, French beans	trout, pilchards, clams, pike, pigeon
August	carrots, gooseberries, lettuce, loganberries, raspberries, strawberries, cauliflower, aubergines, nectarines, peaches, peppers, courgettes, rhubarb, sweetcorn, greengages, basil, peas, pears, apples, French beans, tomatoes	crayfish, hare, skate, john dory (that's a fish)
September	apples, aubergines, blackberries, cabbage, carrots, cauliflower, cucumber, damsons, elderberries, figs, French beans, grapes, kale, lettuce, melons, mushrooms, nectarines, onions, peppers, parsnips, peas, peaches, pears, potatoes, pumpkin, raspberries, rhubarb, spinach, sweetcorn, tomatoes	duck, venison, oysters, sea bass, grouse, mussels, partridge, wood pigeon, brown trout

Month	Fruit and vegetables	Fish and meat
October	apples, aubergines, beetroot, cabbage, carrots, cauliflower, courgettes, grapes, lettuce, marrow, mushrooms, parsnips, potatoes, squash, tomatoes, watercress	guinea fowl, partridge, mussels, grouse, oysters
November	cabbage, pumpkin, swede, cauliflower, potatoes, parsnips, pears, leeks, quinces, chestnuts, cranberries, beetroot	grouse, goose
December	celery, cabbage, red cabbage, cauliflower, celeriac, pumpkin, beetroot, turnips, parsnips, sprouts, pears, swede	wild duck, goose, sea bass, turkey

Source: www.sustainable.org

4

Getting from A to B: Reducing Emissions from Travel

Now

- Keep your driving speed to below 70 miles per hour (mph); peak fuel efficiency is at 55mph for most cars, driving at 80mph hurts fuel efficiency between 20 and 70 per cent.

Soon

- Look at your regular car trips and see how you can increase the number of people you carry. If you drive long distances look into car sharing. This can halve your emissions and save money. Many workplaces operate travel-to-work schemes, alternatively organize one yourself.
- Next time you buy a car think carefully about whether you really need it. Not owning a car can save you thousands in avoided depreciation, insurance and maintenance costs. Public transport and bikes can be just as fast in cities. Many cities have car clubs on a nearby street. Car hire, food delivery and taxis can fill some of the other gaps.
- If you need a car, buy a small fuel-efficient car for your regular journey. Smaller cars are much cheaper to run, and depreciate less.
- Holiday close to home. If you need to fly to another continent, make the most of it, organize a long leave so you can really see the country.

Longer term

- Think carefully about how you can reduce the length or frequency of your regular journeys. Work from home part of the week, using email/IT. If your daily commute is your biggest source of emissions (it is for many of us) consider moving closer to where you work, or changing job. It can improve the quality of your family life, as well as reducing emissions.

Our Travel Patterns

This chapter is about how we can reduce our greenhouse gas emissions from travelling. According to the ONS environmental accounts private transport by car accounted for about 69MtCO$_2$, public transport a further 9.5MtCO$_2$ and emissions from flying 39MtCO$_2$, in 2004.[1] The Department for Transport forecasts that aviation is expected to more than double by 2030.[2] Together these presently comprise a little over 16 per cent of UK emissions.

Trying to decarbonize my routine travel is the bit I am dreading because I start from a high base, but one I doubt I can do much about. For most of the week I feel über-Green, weaving my way through the traffic on my Brompton expending a few calories of tofu-fuelled energy getting about. But then once every fortnight I have a carbon blowout, scorching up to Birmingham in my oversized car to pick up my kids. I have always given trains the cold shoulder – presuming they are too expensive and too time consuming when you take account of the end-to-end travel. But the flights are what will do me in. It sounds a bit weaselly, but my family, like many among the Indian diaspora, is deposited over three continents – so family get-togethers often take place in another continent inaccessible except by plane.

We are travelling more as we get richer and have more free time

Emissions from personal transport have been growing fast because we are travelling around more. In 1952 on average we travelled just 10km per day; today the average person travels 50km per day. Figure 4.1 shows that most of the growth has been through the use of the car and more recently the plane. In 2006, cars and planes accounted for 62 per cent and 26 per cent of our travel, respectively. Buses were more important than cars as recently as the mid-1950s. Figure 4.2 shows the decline in the use of bicycles and the steady use of motorcycles. It's worth mentioning that even in the misty-eyed heyday of bicycles half a century ago they only accounted for 10 per cent of travel.

Cars are very much part of the fabric of our society. Three-quarters of households own cars; there are 60 cars for every 100 adults in Britain. But cars are not ubiquitous: a quarter of households don't have access to private cars, 35 per cent in conurbations like London. For these households the quality of public transport and the hassle and cost of car ownership tips the balance against owning private cars. Though the press suggests 2008 as being apocalypse for the car industry, we still purchased 2.1 million new cars; this was more than in any year before 1985, and more than the years between the early and mid-1990s. Our love affair with the car has not ended; we're just spending a bit of time apart.

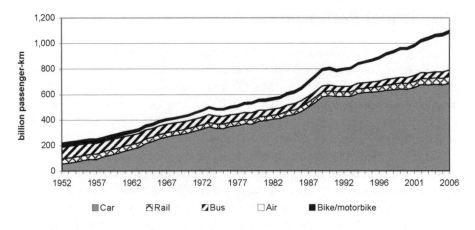

Figure 4.1 Passenger transport by mode 1952–2006 (billion passenger-km)

Source: Transport Statistics GB, 2007 and 2008 editions,[3] Figure 1.1; Air: created from Tables 2.1 and 2.4 to include international as well as domestic flights.

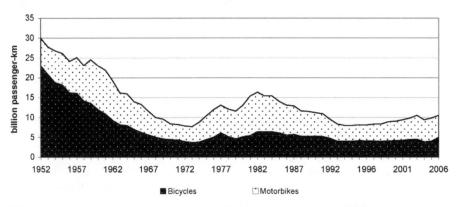

Figure 4.2 Passenger transport by bicycle and motorcycle 1952–2006 (billion passenger-km)

Source: Transport Statistics GB, 2007 and 2008 editions, Figure 1.1

Why do people travel?

About a third of travel is for commuting. Much of the rest is ad hoc trips to friends, shops and for fun. Cars are the dominant form of transport for all UK travel

Before looking at how we might reduce our routine transport emissions, it is worth thinking about why we travel and why it's grown so much. Trips arise for a purpose: to get people to work, education or for days out.

Thinking about trips in terms of their purpose can be useful since there are similarities in terms of their distance, timing, frequency and regularity. For instance, taking your five year old to school is likely to be a similar journey to that of other parents in your street. The length of the trip is usually pretty short since state schools turn down pupils that live far away. The rigid start and finish times mean the journey takes place in the rush hour; indeed conveying six million children to and from school pretty much defines the rush hour. Trips to visit friends often take place at weekends or evenings, on half-remembered roads. A commute to work can be a short walk or a daily round trip of 100 miles, repeated over and over again sometimes for decades. Most regular trips are not a source of fun or enjoyment of themselves. They are a means to an end. People's ambition for a journey is that it should be punctual, of predictable duration, quick, safe, convenient and clean. Climate change considerations probably come some way after all these.

Figures 4.3–4.6, taken from the National Travel Survey, show the distance travelled by purpose and the mode of travel. The average person travels 7000 miles a year domestically, roughly 20 miles a day. Business travel, at around 10 per cent of travel, has been stripped from the data. The annual travel of 6500 miles of non-business travel has remained more or less constant between 1998 and 2006 – suggesting that the thirst for travel might be reaching a plateau.

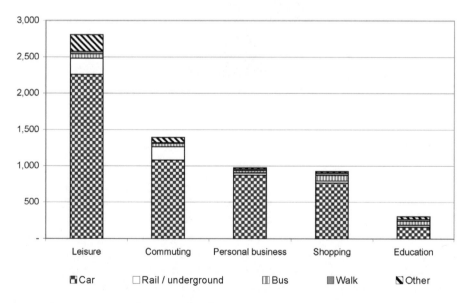

Figure 4.3 Average distance travelled per person per year within UK, 2006 (miles per year)

Source: Department for Transport (2006) National Travel Survey, Table 7.2

Commuting and education trips are regular trips, which occur week in, week out. People are interested in doing them as quickly and cheaply as they can. Because we undertake these trips regularly there is time to experiment with different options to find which form of travel works best for you, and perhaps even cooperate with others making similar journeys to reduce the reliance on cars. But over a half of household travel, and most of the growth over the last ten years, has been for leisure and personal purposes. These do not occur as frequently as commuting and school drop-offs. There is less time and inclination to experiment; and unless there is a blindingly obvious public transport option, most people either drive, walk or cycle.

The pie chart in Figure 4.4 breaks down the leisure and personal business travel into its components.

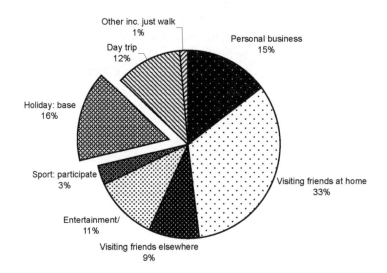

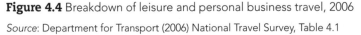

Figure 4.4 Breakdown of leisure and personal business travel, 2006

Source: Department for Transport (2006) National Travel Survey, Table 4.1

About a third of trips are for visiting friends at their homes. With these trips both the start and destination can be away from city centres, the traditional hubs for public transport, making them hard to undertake with scheduled public transport. They also often occur outside of office hours when public transport has reduced frequency. But about half the trips are to sites of enter-tainment, escort trips (e.g. hospitals), personal business trips (banks, post offices, etc.) and sporting facilities which are often reasonably well connected to public transport.

There has been growth in holiday travel. The *holiday base* trip is the annual peregrination where carloads of us wend our way down to Cornwall or up to the Lake District. These occur once a year in July and August but account for about 500 miles of travel per person per year. We have also become keener on day trips and weekend breaks. These have been made possible by broader ownership of cars – allowing fast and spontaneous door-to-door travel to locations that are hard to get to anyhow else. These sorts of journeys can be hard to cater for by public transport since they are often at unsocial times and using routes people are unused to. Cars forgive us for the last minute delays if the baby needs changing or abrupt cancellations when it starts raining. Cheap pre-bought public transport options are more grudging of such winsomeness.

The average length of trips has been increasing but we haven't been prepared to travel for longer periods of time

Below are some statistics that you don't often see juxtaposed together. They show how, over the past 30 years, the distance travelled by the average person rose until the late 1990s. Since then the travel distances have plateaued out. We are making more trips per year, and slightly longer trips. But the average time spent on a trip has been pretty constant for 30 years. British people seem to be hard-wired to tolerate up to 30 minutes travel a day each way, and then they get fed up. Most of this growth in length of trip has occurred through a switch to driving and taking the train and away from slower forms of transport like cycling and buses. Car ownership has risen by 50 per cent over the last 20 years. So the general picture is that we drive more and take longer trips through more congested roads.

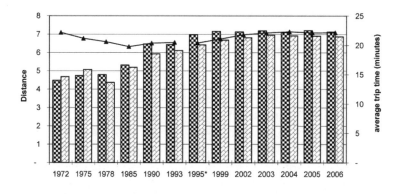

Figure 4.5 Distances travelled and average length and duration of trip per person

Note: Data from 1995 onwards has been weighted, causing a one-off uplift in trip numbers, distance travelled and time taken between 1993 and 1996.

Source: Department for Transport (2006) National Travel Survey

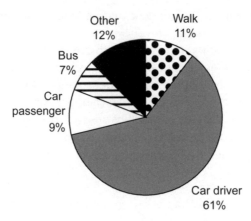

Figure 4.6 Mode of travel for commuting trips

Source: Department for Transport (2006) National Travel Survey

Commuting

Commuting is the most commonly cited reason to travel after leisure. Figure 4.6 shows that almost two-thirds of commuting is by car. This accounts for 30 per cent of all domestic travel. In more than four out of five journeys the driver travels alone. If we reduce the amount of vehicle mileage for commuting we could make a big dent in emissions, and also reduce congestion. Commuting is the longest journey people regularly make (averaging 8.7 miles) outside of business travel (averaging 19.4 miles). Walking and cycling are feasible for short distance commutes but for many driving and public transport or a combination of these are the only feasible option.

Reducing emissions from transport means cutting emissions from driving

Despite the fervent hopes of some environmentalists, cars are not about to go away. They will remain the main vehicle for transport for many years for most people. It is therefore much more important to improve the carbon performance of cars than to restrict car travel. Recent public attitude data[4] suggests that while 82 per cent of people agree with government doing more to persuade people to buy more fuel-efficient cars, only 42 per cent of people agree with any curbs on 'people using their cars as much as they want even if it damages the environment'. Further, 69 per cent of people say they would be prepared to pay a little more for a less environmentally damaging car. There is little basis to believe people are prepared to drive less; 70 per cent say their use of the car has stayed the same or gone up over the past 12 months.

It's easy to get swamped by all the advice and tips on how to cut back on transport: walk to the corner shop instead of driving, don't fly, exchange your gas guzzler for a Prius. All of these will help but the costs and benefits vary wildly.

The next section tries to make sense of the options available to the average person. Of course there's no such thing as the average person; some of us live in the country, others in cities; some have hectic lives combining work with child care, others have time on their hands; some people hate driving, others could not conceive of life without their cars.

The options are organized as follows:

Immediate changes you can make

- Changing driving habits: the fuel efficiency of cars varies depending on the speed and style of driving – particularly the amount of accelerating/braking you perform as you wriggle through traffic.
- Sharing the journey: increasing the amount of passengers carried makes little difference to the emissions from the vehicle but improves the emissions per passenger-kilometre.
- Not travelling: the internet and improvements in information technology more generally mean you can work, shop, talk or videoconference from your own home. Offices are more tolerant about working from home one or two days a week. Travelling less is therefore a real option.

Changes you can make within five years

- Selecting a more fuel-efficient vehicles: there remains huge scope for improving our car's energy efficiency by simply selecting the smallest, most carbon-efficient car. As consumers we can take advantage of the efficiencies from lower weight, better aerodynamics and engine design.
- Replacing a car journey with lower-carbon public transport or bicycle: we can even be quite inventive, mixing and matching different modes. A fold-up bike can complement a train making the end-to-end trips more straightforward. Or a ferry/car combination can reduce the need for flying into Europe and save money.

Long-term changes

- Moving house or changing job to reduce transport: most people choose where they live and work for a whole raft of reasons. Commuting can get intolerable after a while. Moving closer to our place of work can reduce emissions and improve the quality of life.

Actions Individuals Can Take Immediately to Reduce their Transport Emissions

Changing driving practices saves money and reduces emissions

Cars use energy to speed up and remain in motion. Energy is used by cars:

- to accelerate;
- to overcome air resistance so as to stay moving once they've got going;
- to overcome all the buckling and reforming of the tyres as the car moves over the road (rolling resistance); and
- to power heating/air conditioning and other gizmos.

The amount of energy needed to accelerate is proportionate to the vehicle's weight. The relationship between fuel use and air resistance depends on the amount of air the car has to push out of its way to get through the atmosphere. The car's air resistance is increased by anything that impedes air flowing smoothly over the car and off the boot. The car's shape makes a great difference – the more streamlined the less turbulence. The physics mean that if you double your speed you quadruple the air resistance, if you triple your speed you increase air resistance ninefold – for the mathematically inclined there is a quadratic relationship between speed and energy needed per unit of distance travelled. Air resistance only starts to be an issue when the speed reaches 30mph. Combustion engines work best when they are performing at less than 2000 revs per minute for diesel and 2500 revs per minute for petrol. The best speed to drive is therefore around 44–50mph in your car's highest gear. At this speed air resistance isn't yet a major issue and the engine is working efficiently. It's a little different for electric or hybrid vehicles; their motors are efficient at all speeds.

So much for the theory. What does the evidence say? While every vehicle handbook tells you driving above 60mph hurts your fuel efficiency they clam up on telling you by how much. Luckily for us, a German auto magazine *Autobild* organized a Top Gear-style test on a 12.5km circuit, putting a variety of (largely Teutonic) vehicles through the test.[5] Figure 4.7 shows how fuel efficiency drops with speed. Ouch – speed hurts! Increasing it from around 50 to 70mph adds between 20 per cent to 70 per cent to fuel use depending on the car.

Adding a rooftop bike rack to the BMW added 11 per cent to fuel consumption at 60 mph, rolling the top down on the Mercedes convertible added 5.8 per cent to fuel consumption.

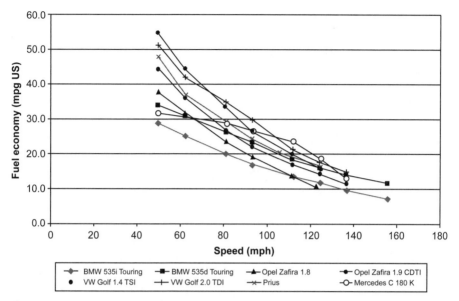

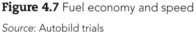

Figure 4.7 Fuel economy and speed

Source: Autobild trials

Altogether about 5–15 per cent of the fuel use by a car is to overcome un-necessary rolling resistance. If the tyre pressure is low the tyre has to flatten and recover its shape (causing it to heat up) more than is necessary to ensure a smooth ride – a 25 per cent loss of pressure is said to increase fuel consumption by about 2 per cent. About two-thirds of drivers drive with under-pressure tyres. More importantly, under-pressure tyres wear out more quickly and are less safe because they give poorer control. It's not possible or desirable to remove all rolling resistance from cars as we need tyres to smooth out all the bumps and imperfections in the road surface. Researchers say installing low rolling-resistance tyres can improve fuel economy by between 1.5 and 4.5 per cent.

We can also simply drive better. This means we should:[6]

- anticipate the need to change speed to avoid stabbing at either the accelerator or the brake;
- remove bike racks, roof boxes and roof racks, which hurt the aerodynamics;
- remove as much unnecessary weight as possible;
- try not to get lost, and avoid driving when the roads are congested; and
- keep the tyres properly inflated.

The Energy Saving Trust claim these measures will improve fuel perform-ance and save £190 per year. The Driving Standards Agency put some drivers through a two-hour boot-camp (or maybe tyre-camp) to teach eco-driving. This reduced their fuel use by 8.5 per cent – saving money and emissions.

Cars also use fuel to run the air conditioning: this can cause a deteriora-tion of between 10 and 20 per cent in fuel efficiency. If you're driving in towns you're better off keeping the windows rolled down. Once your speed goes above 45mph the drag from open windows starts to become an issue and by 55mph open windows reduce fuel consumption by 20 per cent. Putting the fan on has no effect on drag or fuel efficiency, so it is a better means of keeping cool once the air temperature in the car has been brought down to a tolerable level.

Speed bumps also hurt energy efficiency. Stabbing on the brake and punching the accelerator is exactly what we're supposed to *not do* to save fuel, but is pretty much exactly what we *do* do when we encounter speed bumps. Not only do those killer bumps take out our car's underside, they also kill fuel efficiency. One study by the Transport Research Laboratory[7] found the average emissions of CO, HC, NO_X and CO_2 from cars increased by up to 60 per cent following the introduction of traffic calming measures. In theory there are offsetting benefits from speed bumps in terms of safer streets for children, though there is an interesting debate in the US whether these benefits to health are outweighed by the negative health effects from delays to emer-gency vehicles, especially ambulances, which have to navigate the obstacles at a crawl to carry their passengers in comfort. An interesting alternative to speed bumps are area speed cameras which monitor the time taken to travel through a neighbourhood, work out the average speed and send out their penalty fines accordingly. Somehow I doubt these would be popular with the car lobby groups, either, though they're fine on air quality and climate emis-sion grounds. The government is trialling these in some areas on an experi-mental basis.

Cramming more people into the vehicle

Increasing the number of people borne by a car usually makes great environ-mental sense. A commuter sharing the journey with another can immediately halve emissions.

There are a number of travel-dating websites to help match driver to passenger. A list of some of the websites can be found under 'related sites' on the government's website www.transportdirect.info. Most of them are free but one asks for an initial subscription fee (the company asks you to believe that your providing them with your credit card details enhances safety!). One or two require an employer or school to be registered before they will accept

Box 4.1 *Car-share websites*

One of the UK's more successful car-share services is Liftshare, www.lift-share.org, which at present accounts for about 85 per cent of the market. Ali Clabburn set up Liftshare in 1997 while he was still a student at Bristol. The organization's big break came in 1999 when the Glastonbury festival approached it to build a branded website to help get people to the musical mudbath.

The company has won a clutch of awards for technical entrepreneurship and innovation. In June 2008 there were 240,000 registered users, with 6000 new members joining a month. Carbon dioxide savings are estimated at $16MtCO_2$ per year. Liftshare also operates 1800 branded car-share systems on behalf of businesses, schools and events. Such organizational websites account for the majority of registered users. Often companies will provide additional incentives to staff to participate. For instance, Alliance and Leicester, and Sky, provide priority car parking zones for permit holders. The site needs a Liftshare administrator working within the company; the website itself is fully automated and the local administrator might spend a day a month administering or publicizing the facility.

The company has extended this concept of trip matching to bicycle and walking journeys through BikeBudi and WalkingBudi for those worried about the safety of travelling alone, and TaxiBudi to share the cost of a taxi journey.

As with other car-share websites only a proportion – about 35 per cent for Liftshare – of journeys registered with the website successfully result in a match. The branded websites achieve a higher rate of matches (43 per cent was reported in 2004). Generally there are more people looking for lifts than there are drivers.

trip details; some also target one-off events like Glastonbury which create a huge number of extra journeys and are poorly served by public transport. Box 4.1 tells you about the most successful car-share website – Liftshare.

Workplace travel plans can reduce car usage by 15 per cent

The most frequent use of car-sharing is for the journey to work, often enabled through a company's workplace travel plan. The travel plans are most common in companies sited outside town centres. Sometimes local authorities insist companies produce travel plans as a condition for granting planning permission to the development. The plans vary in their content but most encourage employees to use public transport or to walk or cycle to work.[8]

According to the transport expert Lynn Sloman, successful travel plans rely on one or two employees (especially senior ones) cajoling their organization to implement carrots and sticks to encourage their staff to reduce their use of cars.[9] Incentives include charging car-sharers less to park their cars, providing them dedicated parking spots close to the office or just good marketing within the company. Successful schemes also include measures like the establishment of shuttle buses to nearby stations or town centres, and subsidizing or rerouting public transport options. The provision of better cycling or walking facilities (showers, cycle sheds, on-site cycle lanes) can sometimes make a difference but are often limited by factors outside the site's direct influence – for instance having unbroken pedestrian and cycle lanes to the major residential areas.

Box 4.2 *Car sharing is a great way of reducing emissions from commuting (and school runs) but requires driver and passenger to coordinate their travel times*

Jane used to drive a colleague to work for three years; the journey was a 50-mile round trip. She was motivated by her desire to reduce CO_2 emissions. She found her passenger through the company's car-share scheme. The costs of the petrol were split equally and the passenger also contributed £5 per week to cover the depreciation of the car.

The main compromise she had to make was the commitment to log off/walk out of meetings at the scheduled departure time. She also had to communicate any leave or meetings away from the office to give her passenger time to pre-book cheap rail tickets. Luckily these breaks in travel occurred only one day in ten.

There were tensions – Jane worked in the marketing department and often needed to work late especially in the run-up to the launch of new product. Sometimes on the journey back, especially after a long day, she wanted to unwind and begrudged the pressure to make small talk.

There was an imbalance in the relationship. Jane gave a lift largely for altruistic reasons, though the money was nice. For the passenger the lift provided a substantial benefit – cheap, convenient, door-to-door transport. She couldn't drive herself so the only option available to her was to make the difficult public transport trip. Overall, the car-share displaced the passenger's use of public transport; but she did avoid a complicated and time-consuming journey on train, bus and foot.

This result is fairly typical of results from the car-sharing literature: this finds that the passengers usually defect from buses or trains rather than their own cars.[10] Once people have forked out for their car they will not usually choose to be another person's passenger.

Car-sharing can be a successful component in the travel plan. Car-sharing's main advantages are that it offers door-to-door travel, saves money if costs of the journey are split between the driver and passengers, and can also relieve the monotony of the commute, though the flip side of this is that many people prefer their own company.

In an evaluation of 20 organizational travel plans, researchers calculated that on average they resulted in an 18 per cent reduction in car journeys – and the best achieved a 52 per cent cut (though this could be largely explained by moving the headquarters from a business park to a central location close to a railway station).[11] According to the Department for Transport, just 1 per cent of people participate in formal car-sharing schemes run by employers.[12] The main reason people choose to do so appeared to be convenience (cited by 63 per cent), because they couldn't drive (25 per cent) and because of lack of suitable public transport (23 per cent). Only 15 per cent cited environmental reasons or reducing congestion as a rationale.

In some countries governments reserve motorway lanes for high occupancy vehicles. This is regarded as an effective means of encouraging car-sharing. Work has started on creating the first one in the UK: a 1.7 mile stretch on the M62, at a cost of £3.95 million – expensive but much cheaper than building another lane on the motorway. Plans for a second one, between junctions 7 and 10 of the M1, have just been scrapped for being too dangerous – odd considering that other countries have managed it.

Not travelling

The internet, email and better communications are making it much easier to shop, work and maintain a social life without travelling.

Part of the reason for the collapse of many of the high street retailers in the 2008 recession has been the burgeoning growth in internet shopping. Why travel into the town to Zavvi's when you can buy a much larger selection of CDs, DVDs and books off the internet? Internet spending is forecast to be 11 per cent of total retail spending by 2015, and 50 per cent for music and video. I have already discussed the advantages of swapping the motor for the modem in the food chapter.

Teleworking can also make a big dent in emissions, especially if we refrain from making fewer but much longer trips instead

A recent article by the Office for National Statistics suggests that the proportion of home-based workers has now grown to about 3.1 million.[13] These either mainly work from home, or are based at home and rely on telecommunications to keep in touch with the office. Academic researchers have found reductions in commuting of between 48 and 77 per cent by teleworkers, even allowing for some extra nipping-to-the-shop type car trips in the middle of the day.[14] These findings are based on interviews with staff. Many people choose to work from home for part of the week. Often employers are keen too, since it economizes on office space.

But some of the savings in transport from working from home are undermined by changes in business practice. Project-based work sometimes uses home-based workers drawn from disparate offices scattered around the country, or indeed the world. So when team meetings do take place, journey times might be hundreds of miles long. In a project I worked on, the team consisted of staff living in Warrington, Yorkshire, Bristol, Reading and London. Travel to our weekly team meeting in the Docklands area of London took some team members four hours *each way*, rather defeating the rationale for home-working. One team member was located in Spain so his weekly commute was 2000 miles. The worst culprits are the large management consultancies, and I know a few people who have become burnt out after a few months commuting across the Atlantic on a weekly basis – reeling like boxers punch-drunk from constant jet-lag.

But despite these trends of people moving away from the place they work, or national and international employers creating geographically disparate teams, technology gives us the capacity to massively reduce the need to travel.

Videoconferencing technology is improving and becoming more affordable all the time. Members of my family, spanning three generations, gather round their PCs in India, the US and the UK every few weeks and chew the fat on Skype. Skype (www.skype.com) is free, it has over 300 million account holders, who use it on average for 50 minutes a year each. But it still feels clunky – like TV technology from the 1950s – with people zooming in and out of the field of view and the sound or picture cutting out. In spite of that, together with email, internet photo albums and the cheaper international phone calls, it is knitting our family more closely than we would have thought possible when we first emigrated in the 1970s and 1980s. To my mind it's still unclear whether this is satisfying our desire to physically meet or just whetting our appetites for 'a proper encounter'.

But it's in the business world that the real advances are being made. The internet hardware provider Cisco Systems has set itself ambitious targets to reduce the amount of flying by its staff. In 2007 it invested US$22 million in videoconferencing technologies and claimed a substantial reduction in flying. Their TelePresence units provide videoconferencing suites which give participants in up to seven offices the impression they are sitting are in the same room. It seeks to roll out home broadband with videoconferencing in selected cities.

Changes to Be Made over the Next Five Years

Choosing a more fuel-efficient vehicle

And for personal transportation? That means banning 'gas guzzlers' and steadily increasing the total efficiency of any vehicle sold. You can buy the roomiest, vroomiest car, as long as it meets the efficiency standard.

(Mark Moody-Stuart, former CEO, Shell)

When Shell's former boss calls for the banning of gas guzzlers you realize how little faith we can have in market measures and information campaigns alone reducing transport emissions. The truth is there is huge scope to reduce emissions by choosing a vehicle with great carbon performance. But by and large we don't: partly because there are some trade-offs with size and performance, partly because our car is a major part of our self-image, partly because of the dearth of truly energy-efficient vehicles on the market, and partly because many of us don't care.

The US campaigner and engineer Amory Lovins, who runs the Rocky Mountain Institute, has for two decades been campaigning for and developing hypercars – vehicles that dramatically improve fuel economy through using multiple new technologies like light-weight carbon-fibre technology, downsizing and small engines.

Improving the carbon efficiency of vehicles is the major plank of the UK's policy to reduce transport emissions, though you wouldn't know this looking at the Department for Transport's website – which is almost silent on the subject. There are good websites providing information on emissions from vehicles (see Box 4.3).

Green consumers are faced with a bewildering range of 'low-carbon' motoring options. It's an exciting time underneath the bonnet of the car, with several new technologies vying against one another to meet government targets to improve fuel economy. Just to give a quick taste, till now the Japanese car makers Toyota and Honda have dominated the hybrid market with models like the Prius and Accord; the US has stuck with the traditional engine designs but modified them so they can use biofuels; and European manufacturers are currently focused on enhanced fuel efficiency through incremental changes in design and materials. All of these are driven by policies in their home markets. The next ten years will be an interesting time as the different tactics are tested in the marketplace.

Before we look at the different options here is a bit of policy background. In 1998 the EU Commission asked car manufacturers to 'volunteer' to reduce the average emissions of cars sold in the EU by a quarter to $140gCO_2/km$ by 2008.[15] We are making slow progress towards this target. In 2006 emissions

---

Box 4.3 *Information on carbon efficiency of vehicles and driving distances*

CO_2 emissions for different models of car

- www.smmtco2.co.uk/co2search2.asp includes details of emissions from older models of car – good if you're looking for second-hand vehicles.
- www.vcacarfueldata.org.uk/index.asp is the official website for current models of car. The same data is used by government to set emission-related taxes.
- www.whatgreencar.com/ is an excellent website set up by the consultant Ben Page.

Driving distances

- www.distance-calculator.co.uk/ has point-to-point distances and road distances.

---

across the EU were 160gCO_2/km; those in UK were a lamentable 167gCO_2/km – still miles off the target. In the UK the improvement occurred chiefly by selling a higher proportion of diesel cars.[16] But to make matters worse, the average weight of new cars has risen by 3 per cent over the last two years – so more energy is expended lugging metal over the road.

So as a consumer what things should you look for when deciding which model of car to buy and what are the trade-offs?

Diesel vs petrol

Diesel engines have always been standard in large vehicles like buses and commercial vehicles. But technological improvements made by European engine manufacturers, such as better turbochargers (cars with TDI in their name), electronic fuel injection and particulate filters, have helped overcome diesel's sooty and sluggish image, and they are now common in cars.

Diesel cars have much better carbon performance per km than petrol-engine cars. Emissions from my diesel Octavia are 20 per cent lower than the equivalent petrol model, and the diesel Peugeot 307 and new Ford Mondeo's are both 27 per cent lower than their petrol counterparts. Part of the reason diesel has better fuel efficiency (roughly 15 per cent) is because diesel is denser so contains more combustible material per litre. But the main reason is that the diesel engine is just better at converting the energy in the fuel into motion.

Counting against diesel is its cost. The fuel retails at between 5p and 10p per litre more than petrol. The vehicles are up to £1000 more expensive to make. But because of the much better fuel efficiency the average driver will save about £650 per year in fuel costs, quickly recouping the higher purchase costs.

So for the climate conscious, buying a diesel vehicle should be a no-brainer. However, only about 30 per cent of cars sold in the UK have a diesel engine. Use of diesel cars is much higher in continental Europe, reaching 50 per cent in France, mainly because diesel has a lower level of duty per litre than petrol and hence the higher *apparent* cost of diesel at the forecourt is less. If forecourt prices were displayed in pounds per kilometre travelled this appearance would change immediately.

The other major problem with diesel engines is they emit greater quantities of local air pollution, especially particulates which causes respiratory problems. However, new vehicle emissions standards in Europe mean that new diesel vehicles will be fitted with filters to trap these emissions. Such filters can remove at least 85 per cent of the particulates.

Alternative fuels: Road fuel gases, biofuels and electricity

With the price of oil hovering around the US$140 per barrel mark in summer 2008 (though it has come down since) there should be a strong incentive to move to vehicles with lower fuel bills – ideally less exposed to the wildly fluctuating prices on the oil market. Biofuels, compressed natural gas (CNG), liquefied petroleum gas (LPG) and grid electricity are the main alternative fuel sources. (The price of CNG and LPG does vary with crude oil prices since LPG is made from oil and CNG is made from natural gas, the price of which is linked to the price of crude.)

A major consideration with alternative fuels is the availability of suitable refuelling points. There are few places for gas-powered vehicles to refuel at present; similar problems exist for biodiesel and bioethanol. Electric vehicles do not suffer from any difficulty in refuelling points since any electric socket will do the job, though you will need a dedicated parking space, either a garage or a drive. Without off-street parking your options are limited as you are not legally allowed to trail an electric wire over the pavement.

CNG and LPG are available in selected fuel stations. Both of these fuels offer significant benefits over petrol and diesel in terms of local air pollutants; their CO_2 performance is better than petrol but not too different from diesel. The cost of adapting standard petrol vehicles is around £2000. At present the government charges a low rate of fuel duty on the gases (equivalent to just 6p/L compared to 48p/L for petrol and diesel), hence the fuel costs are very low. If they catch on, don't be surprised if the government increases the tax back up again.

A radically different approach is the development of the electric (battery-powered) vehicle. This technology is actually quite old (it has been used in the UK's fleet of 16,000 milk floats for years). The main issue inhibiting the electric car's development is the inability of conventional batteries to store large amounts of energy, severely limiting the vehicle's range. In the movie *Iron Man*, Tony Stark cannily develops a minute arc reactor, about the size of an iPod nano, from some scrap metal which he finds lying around his cave in Afghanistan. The arc reactor propels him several miles from the clutches of the Taliban. Sadly life doesn't always mimic art – batteries take about 100 times more weight than fossil fuel to store the same amount of energy. Several electric passenger vehicles have come on the market, and then been withdrawn again because of poor sales or low profitability.

Electric vehicles will be an attractive proposition in London as they are exempt from the congestion charge and some boroughs offer free parking. The only model on the market is the G-Wiz. Smart is trialling one. Perhaps the most renowned electric vehicle – star of the documentary *Who Killed the Electric Vehicle?*[17] – was General Motors' EV1, which was launched in California in 1998 in response to the state's mandate that a proportion of cars sold in the state should be zero emissions. The car was withdrawn in 2003 and all cars had to be returned to GM. The car embodied many state-of-the-art technologies to dramatically reduce energy use, including aluminium frame, regenerative braking, low-resistance tyres, very streamlined shape and heat pumps to control the internal temperatures. The car could certainly move, it was capable of accelerating from 0 to 60mph in 8 seconds – and only a speed inhibitor prevented the speed from exceeding 80mph; more Ferrari than milk float.

One of the most interesting electric vehicles available at the moment is the Tesla Roadster.[18] This can accelerate from 0 to 60mph in just 3.9 seconds and has a range of 220 miles. The car is basically a battery pack with wheels; a third of its 1.2 tonne weight consists of 7000 laptop-style batteries. If you want one it'll set you back about €100,000 and you have to wait your turn. According to the US Department of Energy's methodology for computing fuel efficiency, it manages a startling 293mpg, prompting one motoring journalist to write 'If you like sports cars and you want to be green, this is the only way to go.' The first one was delivered ahead of schedule in February 2008.

Battery-powered cars use motors to convert stored energy into motion instead of engines – which is about twice as efficient as the internal combustion engine. This means they are spared the weight and much of the paraphernalia of the internal combustion engine like spark plugs, cooling oil, pistons, etc. – and radiators, since they produce little waste heat. They are also easier to maintain having fewer mechanical parts. You would think that they were much less carbon efficient than petrol engines because of inefficiency of electricity production (only 40 per cent of the energy in fossil fuels becomes electricity) but this isn't so – because the internal combustion engine is even less efficient than power stations at converting energy into motion. Electric cars use no power when stationary, and are well suited to stop-start driving since they can recover energy through regenerative breaking. Their CO_2 emissions depend on the source of energy used to make electricity. Using today's current fuel mix their CO_2 emissions per km are around 35–40 per cent below petrol.

Figure 4.8 shows the gulf in this 'energy density' between hydrogen at one end and batteries at the other. Low energy density means that more weight of fuel has to be carried to travel reasonable distances between refuelling. Petrol stores 47MJ/kg, LPG around 50MJ/kg (but requires heavy steel casing material to store the liquefied gas); the best current batteries, lithium-ion, store only 0.23MJ/kg; older lead-acid batteries store only one-sixth of this. Bioethanol only contains about two-thirds the energy of petrol. On the other hand, electric engines are lighter than internal combustion engines which partly compensates.

The nano-wire lithium battery being researched in Stanford University, if successful, would be an amazing breakthrough,[19] allowing a tenfold increase in energy storage from conventional batteries – though still not quite enough to power *Iron Man* at supersonic speeds.

Two intermediate technologies that overcome the all-electric car's need for heavy and expensive batteries are the widely available hybrids and the less well-known plug-in hybrids. Hybrid vehicles are akin to electrical vehicles, but the bulk of the energy is stored in a fossil fuel. The smaller nickel-cadmium battery (the type that was used in laptops a few years ago) is charged from a small internal combustion engine which is run at a fixed and highly efficient speed or by regenerative breaking which recovers the car's momentum when

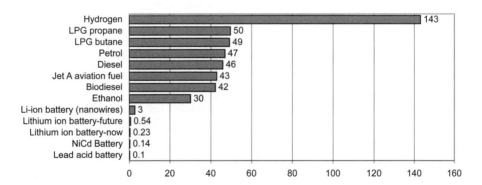

Figure 4.8 Energy density of different fuels (MJ/kg fuel)

Source: http://en.wikipedia.org/wiki/Energy_density, original data from US Department of Energy and 'Aircraft fuels', in *Encyclopedia of Energy, Technology and the Environment* (1995) ed. A. Bisio and S. Boots, Wiley, New York, 4 vols

it slows down. Hybrids cost more than normal cars because of the two sets of drive system – the Toyota Prius costs about £5000 more than the standard version of the car, but will save about £400 per year in petrol. There are a number of hybrid passenger cars on the market in the UK: Toyoto's Prius, Honda's Accord and Lexus's hybrid SUV and saloon. All of these are based on petrol engines.

Hybrid technology is well suited to larger vehicles too. Anyone who has ever cycled behind a bus in London will appreciate how much time buses spend speeding up and slowing down – offering scope for savings from regenerative breaking. London is presently trialling the introduction of cleaner designs for its buses including hybrid electric-diesel engine models. The buses have a measured 40 per cent improvement in CO_2 emissions; far better than using alternative fuels like LPG or CNG, and better also than biodiesel. It's a surprise that hybrid technology has not been used in buses earlier.

Plug-in hybrids are basically exactly what the name suggests – hybrids with a plug. The length of flex allows the batteries to be recharged from house-hold electricity, rather than the on-board petrol engine. The advantage of the plug-in hybrid is it has much greater range than an electric car – since it's not as handicapped by poor energy density of batteries. But at the moment there are no plug-in hybrids on the market. The weakness of plug-ins is that you have to bear the cost of two engines and two power stores, and have two sets of engine to go wrong, undermining both their economics and their fuel efficiency. But I have friends, whose views I respect, who swear by them … so who knows?

The last two types of alternative fuels are bioethanol and biodiesel. The CO_2 in the exhaust gases from using bioethanol and biodiesel is from the crop that *fixed* the carbon using carbon dioxide from the atmosphere only a few months previously, so does not add to the stock of CO_2 in the atmosphere when viewed across the whole year. However, the emissions of carbon dioxide from cultivating the crop, processing and drying the fuels do count and are quite substantial.

Figure 4.9 shows the total emissions from making and using the different fuels. Using bioethanol made from wheat and biodiesel made from oilseed rape reduces CO_2 emissions by 15 and 45 per cent, respectively. Quite a respectable number, except that CO_2 emissions are not the whole story. These figures ignore emissions of other greenhouse gases produced from agriculture like nitrous oxide emitted from the fertilizer use. I did some work for the biofuels lobby in the late 1990s and at the time I worked out the emissions of nitrous oxide from applying fertilizers to the rapeseed. This added another $10gCO_2e/km$ to the oilseed rape figures, and probably the same for the bioethanol from cereal.

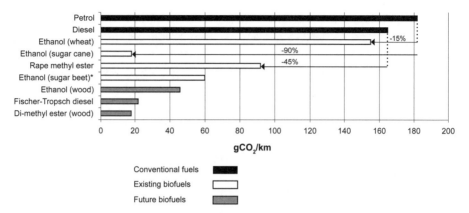

Figure 4.9 Total life-cycle CO_2 emissions from producing and using conventional transport fuels and existing and new biofuels

Note: * No data on fossil energy input.

Source: UK Petroleum Industry Association (2005) Future Road Fuels; sugarcane from International Energy Agency (2007) Energy Technology essentials (ETE02), January.

Biofuels made from wheat grown in *temperate climates* are fairly lack-lustre in their carbon savings. If you take account of nitrous oxide emissions from fertilizers they may offer no savings over petrol. Temperate biodiesel is better than temperate bioethanol, generating carbon savings of about 45 per cent; but yields are quite low, typically producing about 1000L of biodiesel per hectare of cropland. Both the fuels are supported by substantial subsidies in the form of reduced rates of fuel duty. The best type of biodiesel in terms of the environment is the use of recovered cooking oil; but the quantities of this waste oil are fairly limited.

The greatest saving is from ethanol made from sugar cane; the Brazilians have been making this for decades. The yield of ethanol made in Brazil is high, at around 3000–6000L of bioethanol per hectare, because of excellent growing conditions. Brazil's current ethanol production of 8 million tonnes of oil uses 1–2 million hectares of land. But there has been criticism of bioethanol imports because the land used for its cultivation might be at the expense of food production or rainforest. Sugar cane is also a very thirsty crop; I've read claims that it takes 3 tonnes of water to produce 1kg of sugar.

The great white hope in the biofuels world is the development of second-generation biofuels. Conventional biofuel technology uses a subset of the energy locked up in crops – typically just the carbohydrates: starch and sugar. Plants use these to store and transmit energy; biochemically they are easy to ferment into alcohol (basically bog standard brewing). Enthusiasts hope second-generation biofuel technology will use a greater proportion of the crop than the existing technology. About a third of the dry weight of a plant is cellulose. This is also a carbohydrate but it is much tougher. It makes up the rigid cell walls and it's hard to get energy from it: animals and most microbes lack the enzymes to digest cellulose. But bacteria living in herbivores' digestive tracts and fungi living in termite mounds are able to exploit the energy from cellulose. Researchers are trying to persuade these bacteria to perform this alchemy for us too.

An even more tricky substance to get energy from is lignin. Lignin (bound to cellulose) makes up about 30 per cent of the weight of wood, and gives wood its distinctive strength and toughness. The conversion of lignin to auto-fuel is very difficult – the process essentially converts a material that's good at standing up for hundreds of years into a highly engineered liquid capable of being precisely injected within a car engine. Whether this transformation is done by microbes or in high-temperature bio-refineries, it is still going to require a lot of energy and capital.

Maybe second-generation biofuels are a diversion to delay making changes to car design or use. There are other arguments for being sceptical that second-generation biofuels will rescue conventional cars – lignin and cellulose perform an essential ecological role. The straw from a crop is a store of carbon, a habitat for insects and other soil fauna. Humus produced from the slow breakdown of cellulose and lignin gives soil its texture and water-retaining properties. Greatly increasing the amount of photosynthesis we appropriate for driving might make the soil itself unfit for cultivation. The third issue remains one of scale. Each vehicle currently uses about 1000L of fuel a year, which is coincidentally about the yield of biodiesel from one hectare of oilseed rape. The UK's land area is 25 million hectares, which means meeting UK cars' energy needs under current technology would need the whole land area of the UK. Even if second-generation biofuels double or triple useful yields of biofuels we are talking about an immense use of land. The production and use of fertilizers necessary to generate the high yields is also a source of GHG emissions.

European policymakers have set ambitious targets to increase the amount of renewables we use. As part of its policy to achieve this, the UK has created an obligation on the oil companies – the renewable transport fuel obligation – to include biofuels in the fuel they sell. However, the way the regulation has been crafted means that the oil companies can cry off if no sufficiently 'sustainable' source of biofuel can be found, and there is every chance the government will, correctly in many people's view, backtrack on renewable transport fuels. Table 4.1 compares the different alternate fuels in terms of their environmental performance, fuel and vehicle costs and the ease of accessing suitable fuelling points.

Table 4.1 Comparison between different alternative fuels

	Petrol	Diesel	Battery	CNG	LPG	Biodiesel, including blends	Bioethanol
Models and extra cost			Few models: G-Wiz; Th!nk; Tesla	Conversion costs approx £2000	Conversion costs approx £2000	5% blend requires no adjustment; 30% or higher model-specific	5% blend requires no changes; 85% blend requires vehicle modification
Duty (p/L or p/kg)*	0.4835	0.4835	0	0.1081	0.1221	0.2835	0.2835
Number of refuelling stations			Home electric sockets + 50 charge points	22	1306	170	23
Other benefits			100% discount London Congestion Charge £15–20 discount in road tax				
CO$_2$ reduction	0	15–25%	35–40%	10–15%		60%	25% or more
Other air pollutants			no tailpipe emissions	no particulates; 80% lower NO$_x$ emissions			
Conversion cost				approx £2000	approx £2000		extra £500
Other issues			low range	loss of space in boot for fuel tank in dual fuel models		fuel competes with food crop production	

Note: * Duty on CNG and LPG is paid on a per kg basis. There are around two litres of gas per kilogram.

Source: Largely, the Energy Saving Trust website, www.energysavingtrust.org.uk/

Cars in the same class of vehicle can vary greatly in their carbon emissions because of styling, weight and energy-efficient design

Buying carbon-efficient cars does not necessarily mean buying small cars. Good engine design and aerodynamics and use of light materials can make a huge difference in the emissions performance. Figure 4.10 uses just some of the data on the excellent *What Green Car?* website created by Ben Lane. The two bars give the best and the 50th best vehicle for several different classes of car. As you can see it's quite possible to reduce your emissions by between 30 per cent and 60 per cent by selecting smaller vehicles of the same class.

According to the Department for Transport's figures, it would be possible to reduce emissions and improve fuel economy by 25 per cent simply by consumers choosing the lowest in class, rather than the average vehicle.[20]

The very best vehicle in terms of emissions performance is the G-Wiz electric car. However, it is quite unlike the standard car – for instance its range between recharges is currently 48 miles, and its maximum speed is 50mph. It's the only car I know of which advertises the maximum incline it can climb. Instead of refuelling at the pump you plug it into a mains power source; it needs eight hours for a full charge and two hours for an 80 per cent charge. But the car is amazing in terms of reducing GHG emissions, cheap as chips to run and as a further bonus for Londoners it is exempt from the congestion charge. Assuming it's recharged with the 'average' UK electricity mix, it emits just 62g/km – just two-thirds of the next lowest emitting. Other plug-in electric cars are soon to be introduced to the UK market. The car that looks like a spelling mistake, Th!nk, is launching an electric model – which will also have very low emissions. Smart are presently trialling an electric car. As well as being low in terms of CO_2 emissions, electric vehicles emit no local air pollutants from their exhaust; and because power plants (even coal power plants) are required to scrub their emissions, they emit fewer particulates and less sulphur than internal combustion engines.

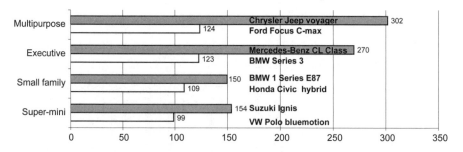

Figure 4.10 CO_2 emissions from the best in class (white) and the 50th best car (grey) for different classes of vehicle (gCO_2/km)

Source: www.whatgreencar.com/

Another interesting new trend in car developments is the simultaneous inclusion of several energy-efficiency technologies. The best current example of these incremental improvements is Volkswagon's new Bluemotion range of cars. The smallest of the range is the new Polo 1.4L diesel engine – they've made changes to the gearing, the aerodynamics, fitted low rolling-resistance tyres and reduced the weight so its emissions are now just 99g/km – lower than the Prius.

Table 4.2 is taken from the recently published King Review[21] and explains the scope and cost of the new engine technologies to reduce emissions. Further improvements in design, such as making the bottom of the vehicle more aerodynamic, could improve carbon emissions a further 10 per cent, the use of low-roll tyres another 2–4 per cent. The King Review assumed in combination these could reduce emissions by 30 per cent. All of the technologies listed below would pay back the extra production costs within three years of purchase. At current forecourt prices a car owner spends about £22,000 in fuel over the lifetime of the vehicle. There really is no excuse not to introduce *all* these technologies quickly.

Table 4.2 New engine and transmission efficiency savings, and indicative production costs

Technology	Efficiency saving	Cost per vehicle (£)	Annual savings in fuel (£)
Direct injection and lean burn	10–13%	200–400	161
Variable valve actuation	5–7%	175–250	88
Downsizing engine capacity with turbocharging or supercharging	10–15%	150–300	183
Dual clutch transmission	4–5%	400–600	66
Stop-start	3–4%	100–200	51
Stop-start with regenerative braking	7%*	350–450	103
Electric motor assist	7%*	1000	103
Reduced mechanical friction components	3–5%	Negligible	59

Notes: Direct injection ensures fuel is burnt more efficiently; stop-start: engine switches off when vehicle is at rest; electrical motor assistance: battery supplements engine during acceleration.
* Figure quoted is for the whole drive cycle; savings are much greater for urban driving.

Source: HM Treasury (2007) The King Review; annual savings are my calculations taking the mid-point improvement in efficiency.

The take-home messages for people who need a car is to go for a small, energy-efficient diesel engine car; it will reduce fuel cost and emissions by 15–25 per cent.

Biodiesel and bioethanol still have major unresolved issues about the competition for land and it's quite possible that sustainability standards, soon to be set by the EU, will make it difficult to use imported biofuels from countries where they can be grown efficiently. Technological improvements in biomass processing might improve yields and hence improve the economics. But this does not change the underlying competition with food production. The present range of fuel–electric hybrids is pretty limited and, to date, manufacturers have only used the technology on their classier models – but this might change with the proposed launch of a diesel micro-hybrid engine. It offers great advantages in vehicles that operate chiefly in urban conditions. The alternative road fuels also offer carbon savings over diesel but they need to be weighed up against the difficulty in getting fuel. To my mind the great hope is battery cars which do away with the internal combustion engine altogether; unlike the other great white hope – hydrogen powered cars (with or without fuel cells) – these are already on the market now.

In theory policies and technologies exist to improve fuel efficiency but the data on what's happening in real life is more ambiguous

Government is regulating cars to make them more fuel efficient – is it working? The information from government statistics is mixed on this. Data gathered on the fuel efficiency in the field (reported in Table 3.4 of their flagship publication *Transport Statistics Great Britain*) suggests that fuel consumption has been pretty stationary for ten years averaging 31mpg for petrol and 39mpg for diesel. The information on fuel efficiency from new cars, using a fairly arcane banding methodology, suggests that performance has improved by about 10 per cent over the past ten years. I have asked Department for Transport (DfT) statisticians to explain but so far the department has been hazy about this discrepancy.

GHG emissions from the manufacture of cars and the extraction and refining of fuels are much smaller than those from fuel use, so it makes sense to replace inefficient cars with more efficient ones

Making cars and refining crude oil are both energy-intensive industries in their own right. How significant are these emissions compared to those from driving? This question is particularly important if you're considering whether to eke out another year or two from an elderly car or to taking it to the car equivalent of the knacker's yard.

Analysts who look at the environmental impacts of vehicle production disaggregate it into four stages: the production of the raw materials (steel, batteries); vehicle production and assembly; distribution; and disposal. About three-quarters of these emissions arise from the production of the raw materials,[22] principally because the manufacture of steel and aluminium is so energy intensive. Metals make up two-thirds of the weight of the car. The rest consists of oil, glass, rubber, plastics and a small amount of electronics. Traditionally a very high proportion of cars have been sent to the car-breaking yard and about 98 per cent of steel and aluminium is successfully recovered. Since the introduction of the End of Life Directive an even higher proportion of cars will be recycled as manufacturers have been made responsible for the safe disposal of new vehicles.

A report funded by Camden Council calculates the total CO_2 emissions arising from producing a car are $4.2tCO_2$.[23] This is equivalent to emissions of *28g/km* over the life of the vehicle if it lasts for 150,000km.

In reality the picture is much more complicated because hardly anyone buys a brand new car and drives it 15 years to its grave. Instead the car exchanges hands through the second-hand car market. As a result there is no guarantee just because you've sold your climate time bomb to buy a hybrid that it'll necessarily enhance the quality of the stock of vehicles; it might just add another vehicle to the total number clogging up our roads.

Emissions from making and distributing the fuel arise from the extraction, shipping, refining of the crude oil, and the distribution and retail of the petrol or diesel. The Camden study quoted above calculated these emissions to be around $12.5gCO_2$ per MJ of energy for petrol and slightly more for diesel. This works out at about 15g per passenger-km.

Should I scrap my old car or keep it for another year?

So if you are driving a car with poor energy performance is it worth selling or scrapping it and buying a more energy-efficient model? My friend Tony drives a ten-year-old car and is considering whether to scrap it and get a more energy-efficient model. (He actually asked if he should sell it, but the idea he could find someone willing to pay money for the pile of trash seemed too unbelievable to entertain.) At first blush it seems mad to scrap a car that's still working. How can that save the environment? But, given that an average car emits $28tCO_2$ over its lifetime but only $4tCO_2$ in its construction, maybe it's not such a stupid idea at all, especially if the new car is *much* more energy efficient. Box 4.4 explains why I advised Tony to scrap his ten-year-old car.

Box 4.4 *Tony ought to scrap his car and buy a more fuel-efficient one instead*

Tony drives 12,500km a year in his ten-year-old car. It emits 160gCO$_2$/km. He's considering scrapping it and buying a new model that emits just 100gCO$_2$/km. Both cars are around average size and their production gave rise to 4.2tCO$_2$ emissions during manufacture.

Tony's car now has 125,000km on the clock, and he's wondering what to do. 'I'm sure it's got a good few years left. If I scrap it won't there be some carbon penalty from making a new car? Perhaps I'll keep it another year or two.'

I told him to get a new car. I went through my reasoning with him. If he bought the new car the improved fuel efficiency would save 60gCO$_2$/km driven (equivalent to 0.75tCO$_2$ per year). But he had to take account of the premature scrapping of his old car. It would have conked out some time in the future – for the sake of this analysis I assumed this would occur in six years' time once it had done 200,000 km – the car equivalent of three score years and ten. At the time the car finally ascended to the celestial car park in the sky, emissions from its manufacture would be 21gCO$_2$/km if averaged over its total mileage. If Tony scrapped the car now, after it had been driven just 125,000km emissions from the manufacture averaged over its present mileage would be 34gCO$_2$/km. Premature scrapping gives rise to a penalty of 13gCO$_2$/km. – much smaller than the improvement in fuel efficiency of the new car.

I did a quick model to show that the emissions released during the manufacture decline over the lifetime of the vehicle as its cumulative mileage rises. Figure 4.11 shows shows this. There's a spreadsheet on the book's internet site which allows you to play about with some of the assumptions.

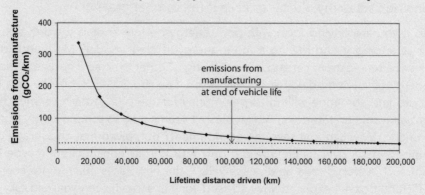

Figure 4.11 Decline in the embodied emissions of vehicle from vehicle manufacture with age

Source: Modelled by author;[24] assumes 12,500km per year and 4.2tCO$_2$ emitted in manufacture.

As it happened the new car was so much more efficient than his current one he could have scrapped the car anytime after 4.5 years and saved carbon. If Tony scrapped the car any earlier, he'd be shooting the environment in the foot.

'You should scrap it, mate, and get the more energy-efficient model. That way you're increasing the number of low-carbon vehicles in use. It sends the manufacturers a message. And while we're talking about improving the stock of low-carbon goods – you should buy lots of copies of my book and give them to your friends ... and have lots of ethical children.' He told me to stop there, as I was beginning to sound weird.

The second-hand car market: An economical environmental view

But what if Tony had put his old car on the market instead of scrapping it? If he'd sold it to someone who did much fewer miles than him and who drove an even less fuel-efficient car the emissions would be lower still.

This is easier said than done. The second-hand car market is far from perfect. If you put a perfectly good car on the market because you want a more energy-efficient one, you'll get a terrible price as others will assume there's something else wrong with it – the economist Akerlof describes these fears of potential buyers as 'being sold lemons'. He dressed the idea up in equations and called the phenomenon 'information asymmetry' and got himself a Nobel Prize in economics. In the case of Tony's ten-year-old car the fear is not so much being sold a lemon, but a time bomb which might seize up at the traffic light, or attract a swingeing bill at the next MOT. The economically rational thing to do would be for Tony to sell the car for a low price, but ask for a second instalment a few months afterwards once the new owner had confirmed the car truly was roadworthy.

But would this really save carbon – doesn't it just increase the number of cars in the UK? The issue about the impact of the premature injection of an extra second-hand car onto the used car market is fiendishly difficult to analyse. Would it cause some *wannabe* car driver to trade in his bus pass for car keys and thereby increase the number of vehicles in the UK; or would it result in an old gas guzzler being scrapped. If it is the latter, then the purchase of a Polo would result in even higher carbon savings by precipitating the removal of a less efficient car. In the nursery rhyme when there are ten in the bed, and they all roll over, one falls out. Is that what happens in the second-hand car market, or do we squeeze ever more cars onto the roads?

The economist in me says it'll be a bit of both. The number of UK vehicles has been rising fairly steadily for the past two decades. However, the numbers of new car purchases peaked in 2003 at 2.8 million per year.[25] Since then sales have dropped to 2.5 million per year. The average age of vehicles has risen slightly, but it's hard to see from the data whether older cars are being scrapped any sooner. I am told by friends who are economists at DfT that they are planning to do some analysis on this later in the year. On balance it looks like selling my car early could well reduce my private emissions, but could increase emissions for the UK since the number of cars will rise slightly.

Replacing a car journey with lower-carbon public transport or bicycle

A man who, beyond the age of 26, finds himself on a bus can count himself as a failure. (erroneously attributed to Margaret Thatcher)

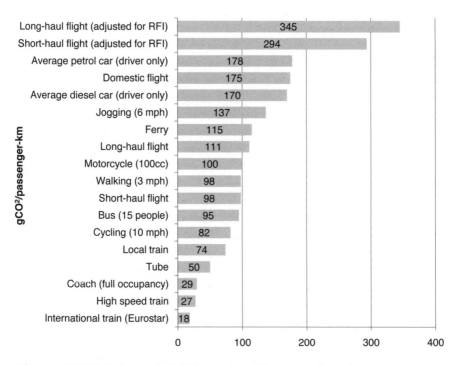

Figure 4.12 Emissions of GHG from the different modes of transport on a per passenger-kilometre basis at average load factor for a modern vehicle

Note: RFI = radiative forcing index: amplification of aviation's greenhouse effect from NO_x and contrails and cirrus clouds (author's adjustment).[26]

Sources: Data from Defra (2008), except jogging, cycling and walking (author's calculations).

Rather disappointingly I cannot find any evidence Margaret Thatcher ever said those words, though the decline in bus patronage during her term in office suggest her ministers could well have believed it.

Buses, cars, trains and planes – the different modes of transport – differ in their greenhouse gas emissions per passenger-kilometre. There is considerable scope for reducing emissions by changing the mode of transport. It is hard to compare the modes on a equivalent basis but Defra and DfT have made a valiant effort,[27] which is reproduced in Figure 4.12. There is a range of figures within each mode. Figures vary, depending on the assumptions about how many people a vehicle typically carries; an optimistic assumption can artificially make it look more carbon efficient than it deserves. Another big source of variation is the age of the vehicle. The newest model might be much more efficient than the commonest model in operation. There are also significant differences between a vehicle's hypothetical fuel efficiency and its performance in the real world. In the real world, cars and buses get snarled up in congestion and planes in holding patterns above busy airports are worsening their emissions figures.

Fully loaded cars are as efficient as trains and buses

According to the most up-to-date information the CO_2 emissions from a person driving alone in a car are three to five times worse than most public transport options. But with two people in the vehicle it is as good as the typical bus, with four people as good as a tube.

Buses are significantly worse than the coach, tube and the train because of their low occupancy rates; the average bus carries 15 people despite having seating for 45 or more. The coach data from National Express rather cheekily assumes full occupancy – optimistic perhaps but coaches do have high occupancy.

Aviation has by far the worst emissions per kilometre travelled, especially if you take account of the greenhouse effect of cirrus cloud formation, contrails and NO_x emissions. The figures for flying are based on the planes and loading factors typically found in long- and short-haul flights. The note to Table 4.12 explains the source of the adjustment for the radiative forcing index. The international train journey assumes that half the journey takes place in France. Because of the very low carbon emissions from French electricity, emissions are very low.

If you want to check the different transport options (and emissions) for any particular journey, try logging into Transport Direct's journey planner, set up by the Department for Transport, www.transportdirect.info/web2/.

If you use your car infrequently dispensing with the car entirely might be a potential option

If you live in a city it might well be possible to dispense with your car altogether. A quarter of London households have done so already. You can still hire a car as and when you need to. The website www.vroomvroomvroom.co.uk has a database of the locations and costs for the major car hire companies, and claims to offer discounts over the turn up price. The prices quoted for London are around £120 per week, with unlimited mileage. You have to pay more for additional drivers. You can also book through ebookers, Carrentals ... and many others.

If you are interested in hiring a car for just a few hours, to do the shopping or for visiting friends, pay-as-you-go car clubs are becoming increasingly common. You typically pay an annual membership fee of £100 per year for a household, and the cost of car hire is £4–10 per hour depending on the company and model. By September 2008 membership of clubs had doubled in 12 months to around 50,000 at 1500 on-street locations. According to the comparison website www.carclubs.org.uk, car clubs best suit people who drive irregularly and so less than 8000 miles a year. Joining and hiring is all conducted online and the cars use mobile technology to find out if you've made a valid booking. You can give as little as a minute's notice. However, none of the operators give a guarantee that a car will be free at the time you want it.

Another option is to informally share a car with neighbours. This might be as little as simply becoming a named driver on the other person's insurance document and contributing to the cost of maintaining the car. This might also suit you if your close family live nearby.

Walking and cycling for short distances are a great way of keeping fit, but the extra food you need to eat can be a significant source of emissions

I used to cycle to work, but it made me so hungry that I had to eat a fried breakfast and I don't think it saved me any money.
(Siân Berry, Green Party London mayoral candidate 2008, interview in *Sunday Times*)

He got on his bike and looked for work ...
(Norman Tebbit, cabinet minister under Margaret Thatcher)

Yes I have got the labels on the two quotes above the right way round: Norman Tebbit extolling the virtue of commuting to work by bike, Siân arguing the contrary view.

Chris Goodall's fascinating book includes a worrisome and counter-intuitive assessment of the greenhouse effect from walking.[28] Provocatively he argues that the agricultural production of the calories used to fuel exercise emits as much greenhouse gas as driving. At the time this struck me as bizarre. Surely shum mistake? How can propelling one tonne of metal through traffic release as much greenhouse gas as walking 60kg of flesh the same distance? After three billion years of evolution was our biochemistry really so bad at converting energy into motion, or was this just another manifestation of the energy we waste in making food?

To work out my numbers I assumed walking for an hour takes 140kcal[29] (roughly a bowl of cereal and milk) more than just sitting down and reading; jogging and cycling take an extra 394kcal per hour. The former figure represents around 5 per cent of a person's daily intake. As we saw in the last chapter, our field-to-fork emissions are about $2.25tCO_2e$ per year or $6kgCO_2e$ per day. The extra emissions from a one-hour walk are therefore about $175gCO_2e$. So Chris Goodall, by neglecting the emissions from basal metabolic activity, has been unfair on walking. Cycling is much more efficient than walking, in the sense that less energy needs to be expended to travel the same distance, and cycling slowly is incredibly low-carbon. The analysis is also slightly unfair on human-powered transport because its carbon footprint includes the entire life-cycle emissions while we have not included the emissions from making the cars and buses or from extracting and refining the fossil fuel. But these are not so large as to affect the thrust of the argument.

I am not trying to argue against cycling or jogging, far from it. Aerobic exercise is necessary to stay healthy. Doctors say we need to get our hearts and lungs going for about 30 minutes at least five times a week to stay healthy, and it seems eminently more sensible to expend this energy getting around rather than working out in a gym. But if Siân does need to top up on her food when she cycles she's best advised to chew on some nuts rather than the bacon and eggs option.

Education trips

For many people getting the kids to school is a major headache. The school run accounts for about 5 per cent of total personal travel – about 10 per cent of it is by walking or cycling. Its politically high profile is arguably more than is strictly fair. It accounts for about a sixth of traffic at 9.00am on school days – and the reduction in traffic during the school holiday is so evident. (Often because *the parents* choose to take their holidays then, rather than any change in the school run itself.)

The travel-to-school journey is unlike other trips in that children under 17 cannot legally drive so they either have to be driven, walk, cycle or take public transport. In the case of children under 11 their unaccompanied travel options are even more restricted. According to the 2006 National Travel Survey only 14 per cent were 'allowed to cross busy roads alone' (down from 19 per cent in 2002,[30] showing us the increased infantilization of our children or the rising paranoia of their parents). It should come as no surprise that 95 per cent of under-11s in 2006 were accompanied on their journey to school.

Figure 4.13 shows that walking is the most common means of getting to school for both primary and secondary pupils. Buses start becoming important for secondary students who live too far away from school to walk and who can't get a lift to school from their parents.

Places in state schools, especially in urban areas, are allocated according to preference and distance between school and home. Lack of school spaces does make for some curious journeys. Another friend drives his children three miles to school, because the school they have been allocated is neither the closest, nor in the right direction to go to his job. He then drives back home – leaves his car and then walks past the oversubscribed school he would rather his children attend on his way to the office. But this is unusual. Most children end up being allocated to schools close to them. The average distance children travel to their primary school is 1.5 miles and to their secondary school 3.5 miles. This makes walking and bus not just feasible but often the most sensible options. Cars are usually favoured *because the parents are dropping their children off en route to work* and they would be driving anyway.

About 7 per cent of pupils attend independent schools. Transporting children to independent schools raises different issues to state schools. Travelling distances are typically further, the schools are often highly concentrated in leafy suburbs or polite Home Counties towns. Getting children to school, especially young children, can be a logistic nightmare for parents. One solution is to organize a private-sector bus – not only does this save carbon, it also

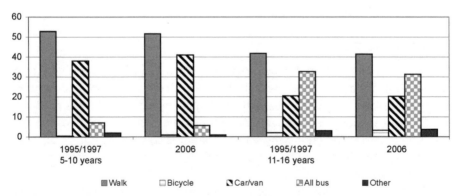

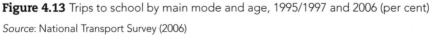

Figure 4.13 Trips to school by main mode and age, 1995/1997 and 2006 (per cent)

Source: National Transport Survey (2006)

reduces the nuisance from traffic for residents living near the school and frees up time for the parents. But it doesn't come cheap. A friend of mine who has a son enrolled in an independent school six miles from her home has managed to organize 14 other parents to chip in to share a private bus. The economics are finely balanced. If one or two drop out the bus company will withdraw the service.

The First Student bus company, a division of FirstGroup plc, is trying to establish a Yellow Bus service, similar to the US system, in the UK (anyone who has watched the Simpsons knows what I mean). They now operate 13 Yellow Bus schemes across the UK. The manager of First Student, Linda Howard, says it's often difficult to get the critical mass of parents to agree to pay between £4 and £8 a day per pupil for the transport costs. She says it's important to get the head teacher's backing. The school can provide information on the addresses of other nearby parents to make the task of finding a viable number of parents easier; it can also coordinate extra-curricular activities so that children all finish school at the same time.

Ultimately emissions can only be reduced by moving around less

One of the main underlying reasons for the increase in transport emissions has been our hypermobility. This is almost the exact opposite of the carbon consciousness I described in Chapter 2. We now take for granted our ability to go to school, university and work vast distances from the place we think of as home. Relationships muddy things further, uniting people from different regions, countries or continents, creating demands to travel unsustainable distances year after year. As we become wealthier those demands are impossible to resist.

When my brother was born in Wales in the 1970s our relatives in India didn't get to see him till he was five. My own young children, who are a generation removed from India, have been there three times and received visits from itinerant Indian guests countless times.

Often people find themselves in this situation by accident and eventually the lust for distance becomes a trap. Box 4.5 describes a familiar situation for the world's expatriate workforce.

We will return to the how to change aspirations for travel in the final chapter.

> **Box 4.5 *How we drift into high-carbon travel patterns***
>
> Brian has worked in an international organization for the past ten years. He has a prestigious and responsible job and loves his work. But his oldest child is now nearing secondary school age. He and his wife Liz want their children to experience the UK's education system at secondary school and university. Liz also wants to resume her career when the children are much older. But Brian cannot find a job in the UK comparable to his current role. He has the option to either find a less prestigious role or to relocate his family in the UK and to commute back to mainland Europe every week by plane. A generation earlier he might have put his children in boarding school, but he and Liz would never countenance this, and the children aren't interested either.
>
> He is now very seriously considering the commuting option. He will return to the UK every Friday evening, as his employer permits him to work from home on Mondays. He is aware and uncomfortable about the carbon emissions. The travel will emit around 20tCO$_2$ per year assuming the family stay with him in the long holidays.
>
> He and Liz hope they can make this work. It's not a situation they ever wanted, and they recognize the strain it will put on Liz looking after three children all week. Would they have left the UK if they had known it would come to this?

My Own Travel Patterns

My travel needs are fairly typical for an urban person with kids. Most of my routine mileage is 'social' involving picking up and dropping off my children at their Mum's house. We meet halfway in Northampton on Friday and I drive all the way to Birmingham on Sundays. I do this every fortnight clocking up 600km for the round trip, making a whopping 15,000km a year car travel. In terms of carbon dioxide it's not as bad as it could have been. I bought the car just two years ago specifically for its fuel efficiency at driving on motorways; I chose not to get a hybrid because most of my driving is on the open motorway where the diesel engine has really low emissions. Like most Londoners living near the tube, I rarely use the car otherwise, cycling most places.

Table 4.3 shows all my non-holiday and non-business travel in 2007.

Aside from holidays I travelled over 21,000km last year: 80 per cent was by car, 17 per cent by bicycle and the balance two train journeys. Surprisingly I made no private use at all of buses or taxis (and very little for business either). My emissions from driving were lower per kilometre than from cycling because I never drive alone. We filled the car with five on our trip to a festival; four of us shared the trip to a friend's stag night (I chose to drive figuring, correctly, my liver would thank me). The travel was dominated by my trips to Birmingham and back to pick up my children, resulting in an average loading of 2.12 across the year.

Table 4.3 My routine personal trips in 2007

Trip	Mode	Distance (km)	Frequency	Distance travelled (km)	Loading	Personal emissions (kgCO$_2$e/yr)
Northampton return	Car	200	25	5000	2	328
Birmingham return	Car	400	25	10,000	2	655
Stag night	Car	450	1	450	4	29
Day trip/long weekends	Car	900	1	900	2	59
Green festival	Car	420	1	420	5	28
Shopping (car)	Car	20	1	20	1	1
Friends	Car	95	1	95	2	6
Entertainment/theatre	Car	20	1	20	2	1
Commuting	Bike	18	180	3240	1	212
Parents and friends	Bike	10	30	300	1	20
Shopping (bike)	Bike	4	20	80	1	5
Commuting	Tube	20	10	200	1	13
Social	Train	500	1	500	1	33
Total car				16,905		1107
Total bike				3620		237
Total others				700		46
Total				21,225		1390

Notes: Emissions factors for the 'actual' for my car 131g/CO$_2$ for motorway driving and 187gCO$_2$/km for city driving; other emissions factors are as shown in Figure 4.12. I have credited emissions from cycling according the average emissions per kcal before I made the dietary changes outlined in the previous chapter. They would be half this on my changed diet.

Most of my routine trips within the UK will be difficult to decarbonize. Most are to towns and villages within three hours' drive of London which I had never considered going to by train because they are hard to access by public transport especially at weekends, and because several of us are going together. The exception was the few days we spent at the Hay-on-Wye book festival which has good public transport links. Unfortunately the same was not true of our accommodation which was tucked up in the Black Mountains 30 miles away from Hay. (It did cross my mind that if the world were in the least bit environmentally optimizing, the whole festival would relocate to Hampstead. This would instantaneously save several hundred tonnes of unnecessary carbon not just from the avoided travel, but all the throwaway plastic raincoats which are standard issue in Hay – surely the wettest and most inappropriately named town in the UK.) The travel patterns are themselves the product of some choice editing on my part. Mindful of my goal of reducing my carbon emissions this year I alienated my favourite cousin by not attending her marriage in New Jersey (she reciprocated a few weeks later by skipping mine). I also cut back on those sneaky lastminute.com weekends to mainland Europe destinations – which I used to enjoy from time to time.

Actions I Took to Reduce my Transport Emissions

The bulk of my non-holiday emissions arise from driving my car to Birmingham and back. My options to reduce these are (a) changing my driving habits, (b) increasing the occupancy rate of the car, or (c) trying public transport. And I've got to do something about my flying.

Changing driving habits

How much difference do better driving practices really make? I start with some pretty bad habits. There's a significant gulf in what I know to be right, and what I do. Normally I tear down the motorway driving at the prevailing speed in the fast lane. It's been an embarrassingly long time since I tested my tyres' pressure. In my favour, I don't carry much unnecessary junk in the car – a mere 5kg (the bizarre treasure trove consisted among other things of two wall clocks, an old electric fan and an ancient water cooler, giving the vehicle a car boot sale feel).

I experimented through a series of trips back and forth to Birmingham changing the speed I drove. Table 4.4 shows how the fuel economy changed when I reduced my maximum speed first to 60mph and then 55mph. I also tried blowing my tyres up correctly. They are meant to be inflated to 44psi, but in my usual dilatory style I found I had let them drop to around 31psi. My car has a fuel-efficient engine. I've always driven at a fairly steady, albeit

Table 4.4 Fuel economy from keeping maximum speeds to 60mph and 55mph, and from pumping tyres to full pressure

	Distance	Time taken	Fuel eff	Emissions
	(km)	(hrs:min)	(km/L)	(gCO$_2$/km)
Unrestricted speed, tyres low	99	01:19	20.9	125.9
Unrestricted speed, tyres low	102	01:11	20.5	128.5
Unrestricted speed, tyres low	190	01:54	18.6	141.6
Unrestricted speed, tyres low	184	02:00	20.9	125.9
Speed restricted to 60mph, tyres pumped	190	02:27	24.8	106.2
Speed restricted to 55mph, tyres pumped	187	02:35	26.8	98.2
Unrestricted speed, tyres pumped, light traffic	99	01:21	19.5	135.0
Unrestricted speed, tyres pumped, heavy traffic	101	01:46	22.4	117.6

Note: Trips to and from Birmingham or Northampton on motorway in a diesel Skoda Octavia May–June 2008.

over-fast, speed. Normally my emissions hover between 126 and 142g/km. I was a little sceptical whether keeping my maximum speed low and maintaining better tyre pressure would make much difference.

The results were a fascinating confirmation of how much difference slowing down on the motorway makes. On the day I carried out my 60mph test, I set the on-board computer to display the vehicle's fuel efficiency. Normally I would regard 59mpg (diesel) as pretty good. By the time I inched through the stop-start traffic in North London and finally reached the motorway I was doing 45mpg; it slowly started climbing up as I got into fifth gear and held it at a constant 60mph. That weekend the Shell tanker drivers had gone on strike and the country was gripped in fear that petrol would run out as it had a few years previously. The chat show hosts had wheeled on mellifluous-sounding pundits who told Britain not to panic. As a result long queues had formed at every petrol station I passed. Our corner shop had the customary run on toilet paper that defines periods of national neuroses. The efficiency on my dial rose to 60mpg, where I assumed it would stay, but it just kept going up. By the time I got to the M1/M6 junction it had reached 66mpg and I idly tried to work out the asymptotic average fuel efficiency I would reach by the end of the trip. I figured it would end up at 68mpg. Near the M6's first junction there is a big dip where I took my foot off the accelerator and cruised for half a mile. The dial hit an average of 70mpg and I think I let out a small whoop. By the time I reached my ex's house I'd managed to average just over 70mpg. On the way back I held the speed to between 55 and 60 and I got an even more amazing fuel economy of 76mpg – which translates into emissions of 98gCO$_2$/km for the vehicle, and just 49gCO$_2$ per passenger-km. This is awesome – it's going to be a difficult figure for public transport to beat.

I asked the kids how they felt about driving in the slow lane and being overtaken by 15-year-old camper vans hauling caravans. They said they found it easier to read and they felt less carsick – it certainly seemed as though there was less fighting but I think that might have been because they were in a good mood after their summer fête. I am not sure how much *I like* cruising in the slow lane though. There's a bit of Jeremy Clarkson in me, and being overtaken by a caravan seems to be an assault on my masculinity – I have issues I need to work through. But driving slower really works – emissions 25 per cent down.

Alternatives to the car

Not every hitchhiker is an axe murderer, so why don't we hitch any more?

Plan B is trying to share the ride to Birmingham with someone else. Surely there must be hundreds of people travelling from North London to Birmingham on Fridays and Sundays who would share the ride with me; it would be even better if they would share the fuel cost with me. Perhaps having a stranger in the car would inhibit my children from waging their low-level guerrilla war for space too: 'Dad she's put her feet on my side of the seat.' 'Dad he started it by being born.' And who knows? I might even edify my guests with podcasts of *Start the Week* and *Money Box*. Though judging from the reaction of my children they might find it as much fun as Vogon poetry.[31]

But how does one get hold of hitchhikers? Years ago slip-roads were garlanded with people waving cardboard placards bearing the names of obscure corners of the UK. But it's all changed now. I've only had one encounter with a hitchhiker recently. Five of us were in the car on the way to Wales. We were a little lost so I slowed down to ask him directions. He broke the sound barrier in his delight at finally finding a lift. But the car was already full and I couldn't bear to talk to him, so I speeded up. It would have felt like asking a beggar for some change to feed the parking meter.

Hitchhiking pretty much seems to have died out in the 1970s. The received wisdom is that people have become more worried about safety and richer – therefore less needful of lifts from strangers. But for me the issue has been the improvement of in-car entertainment: FM radio, CDs and iPod – who needs the hit-or-miss conversation with a stranger to be entertained on long trips.

In place of hitching we have car-share websites where you enter your trip details into the database, and the system speed-dates you to someone else making the same journey. Well at least that's the idea. I enrol on all the free car-share databases: PickupPal, Freewheelers, Shareajourney, Nationalcarshare and Liftshare. Diligently I log in every day and review the results. In which alternative universe is London to Birmingham en route to a journey between Cornwall and Wales? PickupPal deluges me with emails along the line of 'Getrude is making a trip from south London to Dudley before Wednesday – quick make her an offer.' One website gave me a long list of trips many of which had taken place a year or more ago. It reminded me of the window of a local estate agent which still displayed a photo of our house – stamped with 'Sold' in red – two years after we'd bought it. I emailed back a dozen potentials but only got one grateful response back, saying thanks for the offer but that she only travelled on Tuesdays.

At present the competing sites have too few customers to generate a reasonable probability of finding a match. Some of the databases feel clunky and lack the sophistication to filter out unsuitable matches. One of them plaintively reminds us of its cash flow problems by asking for a donation every page. I felt very tempted to yelp à la *Dragon's Den* 'I'm out', but I'm very conscious my plan C for halving my transport emissions doesn't look too great either. So for now I conscientiously delete my dead trips as I make them, and enter in new ones as and when my ex and I agree how we share out the children's weekends. Perhaps there needs to be some box on the website where I can reassure would-be hitchers about the wholesomeness of my children, and the breadth and variety of the music they'll experience if they take a lift with me.

The only road left is the train track

The last remaining option is public transport. My main worry is that the door-to-door journey will take longer. My Friday round trip takes about five hours. It takes the same time on Sunday even though it's twice the distance because the traffic is so much faster.

The time taken for the train journey is more complicated to explain. There are two competing train lines on the Birmingham–London route: the fast Virgin West Coast service and the slower Chiltern route. The usual fare for the Virgin service is astronomic but is much reduced for off-peak tickets. The Virgin train has amazingly low emissions of just $27gCO_2$ per passenger-km. The diesel Chiltern emits more like $74gCO_2$ per passenger-km. There used to be a third company, Silverlink, but it lost its franchise last year and was kicked off the track.

Box 4.6 *Rural transport needs*

I suppose I have two stereotypes about country people and transport: they're either ultra-Greens who power their vehicles from reclaimed organic chip-fat, or they're stockbrokers who drive massive Range Rovers to their office in the City. I asked my friends Ann and Tony who live at Ann's family farm in Sussex with their two under-fives to put me straight. Ann and Tony both work part-time and have to juggle school drop-offs and part-time management of the farm with their other careers. Like most rural people the question they pose themselves is not whether or not to drive but how many and which model. Tony drives a five-year-old Nissan about 200 miles a week to his office and Ann an ancient Skoda as far as the local station two times a week.

Don't they need four-wheel drives for when it snows, or the roads ice up? They'd only ever been caught out by the snow once. According to Ann, the four-wheel drives are more quintessential than essential, about as necessary in the Sussex countryside as a pair of Nikes in the school playground.

Did they really need two cars? Sadly yes. They could arrange most things around just one car. The nearest supermarket is five miles away – but with a big freezer, they only need to go every fortnight, otherwise they top-up shop from the village, buy all their vegetables from local farmers, and when they can get their act together (i.e. when it's not Tony's turn to do the shopping) substitute the modem for the motor and get home delivery. Even the school journey is catered for. The school has organized a walking bus to pick up school children from a street corner. The facility runs all year round no matter what the weather and the kids love it. However, Ann and Tony's farm is a little too far from the village itself, so they have to drive to one of the pick-up points.

It was the commute that has forced them into buying two cars. Ann's journey to the office in Buckinghamshire takes two hours and necessitates a seven-mile drive to the train station, a 60-mile train journey topped off with a bus ride. She tries to work from home as frequently as she can but has to go in about twice a week. Both the cars have been chosen for their fuel economy: the small one emits just $120gCO_2/km$, the larger one $160gCO_2/km$. She's thought about her transport needs carefully – cycling to the train station would lengthen an already over-long day, travelling to work with colleagues is no good because of the eccentricity of her journey. She even considered sharing with some fellow commuters just as far as the train station but it's proved too difficult to agree a fixed return time. Anyone missing their lift back would have to fork out £20 for a taxi.

Tony has also considered buying a newer, more fuel-efficient car, but was worried by wasting the embodied energy in the car, which still has at least five years' life in it. Despite Ann's attempts to use public transport, her trip emits around 15kgCO$_2$ per day or around 1.5tCO$_2$ a year. Tony's daily emissions are a little under Ann's despite his long car journey, because he travels less than half as much as she does. Ann would very much like to work closer to her home, but so far had not found a job nearby.

I suggested they swap cars since Tony drives so much more. This would reduce their overall emissions around 400kgCO$_2$per year and save them money too. Another option was for Ann to try the lift share, perhaps in combination with a fold-up bike for days where the times were not going to work out. Tony says he likes my idea of swapping cars – he hadn't realized it could save so much carbon, though he finds the smaller car's pedals too small for him. We both look at his tennis racket-sized shoes. 'You've got mutant feet', I empathize.

My ex and I agree the times to see the kids many weeks in advance so I can in theory access cheap tickets. However, the speed of the Virgin train drops to that of Chiltern on Sundays – as a result of the work on the West Coast mainline which commenced at about the same time the druids applied for planning permission to build Stonehenge.

If I travel with my children (the return trip on Friday and the outward trip on Sunday) I get a mind-bogglingly good discount with the Family and Friends saver card. (I sense a great opportunity for some entrepreneur to hire out children to accompany adults without sufficient children.) The cheapest options are for me are to buy myself an adult return on Chiltern line on Friday, returning Sunday evening, and also a Family and Friends saver for the Virgin train for the journeys with my kids. I can take my laptop to work on the train, and also some material to entertain the kids. The Virgin and Chiltern tickets cost £31.50 (for all three of us!) and £18, respectively. Carbon savings are given in Table 4.5. In terms of the carbon savings, I have included not just my own emissions but also savings from my ex's car (she drives a larger car, a third of the distance I drive) since she no longer needs to drive to Northampton on Fridays. The tailpipe emissions from conveying the children between our homes come to 2.9tCO$_2$ per year; there are also life-cycle emissions from making the diesel and the car equivalent to a further 0.9tCO$_2$ per year. Using the train will save 2.5tCO$_2$ per year, half for me and half for the kids, if I sell my car and use public transport. Table 4.5 suggests there are some huge carbon savings from taking the train, even if I drive the car much slower.

This leaves me with a car that used to do 10,000 miles a year and now has no *raison d'être*. Do I really still need it? It sits there outside my house, or more accurately at some random spot in the neighbourhood which happened to have a parking bay free, and provides target practice for pigeons to hone their defaecation skills. I do some quick sums to work out how much the car

Table 4.5 My total annual emissions for bringing children to London by car and public transport

	CO_2 emission (kg/yr)	
	By car	**By public transport**
Ex-wife's car	891	
My car	1965	
Virgin train (3 passengers)		608
Chiltern train (1 passenger)		555
Bus		90
Total	2856	1253

Notes: Emissions for ex's car 178g/km.

Table 4.6 Annual running costs for keeping my Octavia or trading to a new Polo Bluemotion

	My Octavia	**New Polo Bluemotion**
Average annual depreciation – 2 yrs	1350	3500
Insurance	700	700
MOT	400	200
Car tax (from C→A)	120	0
Repairs	250	200
Fines	120	120
Resident's parking charge	70	70
Fuel costs	1200	900
Total annual cost	4210	5690

Notes: Depreciation from the What Car? website (www.whatcar.com/) depreciation index. Annual present fuel spend on my car (15,000 km @ 8p/km for diesel) = £1200. Saving of £300/yr from downsizing car, @ 25 per cent of my current fuel bill. Reduction in car tax for moving from band C to band A = £120/yr. Camden resident's car parking charge = no change (remains at £70/yr). Insurance costs = no change, about £700, the same as my old car.

is costing me. It's something I assumed I needed – I never really questioned whether this was true before. Table 4.6 betrays exactly how much my car has cost me these last two years; the second column is the cost of owning a VW Bluemotion to show what the economics of a new energy-efficient car might look like. If you want some information on running costs for different cars take a look at www.emmerson-hill.co.uk/downloads/Motoring_Costs_April_2008. pdf, which the RAC have developed to represent the running costs of a new privately owned car for three years.

I stare at the numbers feeling shell-shocked at the realization it's costing me £3000 per year to keep the car on the road – equivalent to £120 per fortnightly trip to Birmingham. If I took the train, my ex and I would save money from my savings on diesel alone, forgetting about the fixed costs.

Then I think back to all the time I've spent doing things *for the car* these the two years I've owned it: trips to the garage to get a burst tyre replaced; repairs following my accident last year; the annual service; purchase of replacement registration plates when the old ones got nicked; cleaning up after the break-in and the associated nuisance of replacing the CDs; time on the phone trying to appeal (unsuccessfully) all the parking fines; shopping around for insurance; and contending with Camden's resident's parking permit procedures, which appear to be premised on the idea that securing a parking space on my street should be as fraud-proof as a passport application. In *Car Sick*, Lynn Sloman calculates that the average person spends 250 hours on the myriad tasks associated with owning a car: 'washing it, taking it to the garage for repair, filling with petrol, looking for the keys, de-icing it in winter, finding a parking space …'.[32] I am not sure I'd go as far as Lynn but I've probably taken a day to conduct all my car-related business. As well as reducing my emissions from the journey back and forth to Birmingham by about 60 per cent it'll also save me money. I'll spend somewhat longer travelling than I am used to, but with my laptop and iPod I should be entertained. The idea to sell the car starts to take hold.

I ask my wife what she thinks. She shrugs – apart from trips to see her mum who lives about five miles away, she barely uses it either. My parents, who live six miles away, are happy to share their car if I make a contribution to the costs and take it in for service. We are also fortunate to have four different car clubs operating in the borough: Citycarclub, Zipcar, Whizzgo and StreetCar. The idea of not having to MOT, insure and service my car is enticing. Whizzgo and StreetCar both have bays within two streets of me. Membership is around £75 a year for my wife and I to join, and renting a car costs a further £6 an hour or £50 a day from Whizzgo – the closest club – and a bit less from StreetCar. There are some pretty lethal penalties if you overrun your allotted time.

I put the car on eBay and Gumtree, and stick adverts in the windscreen. Not a single person expresses any interest – the recession and the fact Skoda have slashed the prices of their new cars has meant the bottom has fallen out of second-hand cars. I blame Akerlof. If he hadn't started that stuff about lemons none of this would have happened.

Reducing emissions from driving by downsizing to the smallest car you can

Giving up your car entirely is not going to be a viable option for everyone. One of my relations has recently accepted a job working three days a week in an office 20 miles from where she lives. She plans to use the family car to commute since the journey takes too long by public transport. She drives a huge seven-seater Caravelle which she bought to transport her four young children. Her weekly commute will be 120 miles; and the cost of diesel in the Caravelle about £25 per week. The car emits a Hummer-esque 220gCO$_2$/km – equivalent to 2.2tCO$_2$ per year for her commute. She had already looked into and discounted public transport as the office is several miles from the nearest train station. She didn't think the family car was particularly practical, but the cost of diesel, even after the recent increases in prices, was easily affordable.

I was curious to see what her low-carbon options were. Her best option, if she wanted to reduce carbon emissions, seemed to be to buy a small vehicle just for the commute – a new G-Wiz would set her back about £6500, cost just £2.50 per week in electricity costs and emit a quarter of the emissions. However, the range was an issue as she wasn't confident she would be able to access a charging point in the evenings since she only has on-street parking. A second-hand Smart car was quite cheap (circa £5000). While its emissions reductions weren't as pronounced as the G-Wiz, it still managed a respectable 60 per cent cut relative to the Caravelle. She wasn't interested in any of the new low-carbon diesel cars as they were too expensive. I managed to convince her to take a test drive in the Smart but she remains unenthusiastic about owning a second car and the added hassle of maintaining it.

Bringing It All Together

Here is my estimate of how much the actions described will reduce my emissions and cost me (see Figure 4.14).

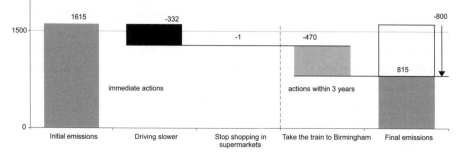

Figure 4.14 Changes to reduce my greenhouse gas emissions

Driving slower

I have already reduced my speed to a little under 60mph. This saves 25 per cent of energy use, and reduces my diesel bill by the same.

Taking the train to Birmingham

I am using the train for some of my journeys to and from Birmingham. The cost of the train and bus tickets for the three of us at the saver rate is £60 per trip; the cost of diesel for my ex-wife and me is £48. Taking the train saves around half the emissions from driving. It also lets me sell the car, which will save me £3000 per year. My car is on the market, but still not sold. If I rent a car from central London for a fortnight in summer it'll cost around £400, the car club will probably cost around £150 a year too.

Stopping shopping in supermarkets

I've started using a box scheme so I no longer use the car to go to the super-market. The savings from this are fairly minimal – perhaps £4 a year, but the higher cost of the food is significant and discussed in the food chapter.

Working from home

My emissions from my cycle journey to work have dropped by 60 per cent as I've started working freelance from home and go and see clients just one or two days a week. I have excluded the emissions saved from eating less food, as I am still trying to do the same exercise else how. Any savings arising from making my diet less carbon intensive are credited in Chapter 1.

Notes

1   Office for National Statistics (2006): Environmental accounts detailed 91 industry disaggregations of emissions for 2004. These can be accessed as Excel spreadsheets at www.statistics.gov.uk/statbase/explorer.asp?CTG=3&SL=&D=4261&DCT=0&DT=32#4261 (accessed July 2009).
2   Department for Transport (2009) UK Air passenger demand and CO_2 forecasts, www.dft.gov.uk/pgr/aviation/atf/co2forecasts09/co2forecasts09.pdf (accessed July 2009).
3   Department for Transport (2008) Transport Statistics Great Britain 2008. The Stationery Office, UK www.dft.gov.uk/pgr/statistics/ (accessed July 2009).
4   Department for Transport (2008) Public Attitudes Towards Climate Change and the Impact of Transport, www.dft.gov.uk/pgr/statistics/datatablespublications/trsnstatsatt/atttoclimchangemay2008 (accessed June 2009).

5   Green Car Congress (2006) *Fuel consumption at high speeds (based on Autobild trials)*, www.greencarcongress.com/2006/05/fuel_consumptio.html (accessed July 2009).

6   Energy Saving Trust, Eco-driving website, www.energysavingtrust.org.uk/Cars-travel-and-driving (accessed July 2009).

7   Boulter, P.G., Hickman, A.J., Latham, S., Layfield, R., Davison, P. and Whiteman, P. (2001) *The Impacts of Traffic Calming Measures on Vehicle Exhaust Emissions*, Transport Research Laboratory, www.trl.co.uk/online_store/reports_publications/trl_reports/cat_traffic_and_the_environment/report_the_impacts_of_traffic_calming_measures_on_vehicle_exhaust_emissions.htm.

8   Rye, T. (2002) 'Travel plans: Do they work?', *Transport Policy*, vol 9, no 4, pp278–298.

9   Pers com Lynn Sloman.

10 Cairns, S., Sloman, L., Newson, C., Anable, J., Kirkbride, A. and Goodwin, P. (2004) *Smarter Choices: Changing the Way We Travel*, University College London, Transport for Quality of Life Final Report to the Department for Transport, The Robert Gordon University and Eco-Logica, London.

11 Cairns, S., Davis, A., Newson, C. and Swiderska, C. (2002) *Making Travel Plans Work: Research Report*, report by Transport 2000, ESRC Transport Studies Unit UCL and Adrian Davis Associates for Department for Transport.

12 Department for Transport (2007) *Public Experiences of Car Sharing*, Department for Transport.

13 Ruiz, Y., and Walling, A. (2005) *Home-Based Working Using Communication Technologies*, Labour Market Division, ONS, London.

14 Cairns et al, see note 12 above.

15 Transport and Environment (2007) *Reducing CO_2 Emissions from New Cars: 2006 Progress Report on the Car Industry's Voluntary Commitment*, September, www.transportenvironment.org/ (accessed June 2009).

16 Train, B. and Owen, N. (2005) *A Study into the Passenger Car CO_2 Reductions for the Department for Transport*, Ricardo Consulting Engineers, www.dft.gov.uk/pgr/roads/environment/research/yintocostsoffuelsavingte3844.pdf (accessed June 2009).

17 Interestingly the kid's classic and similarly titled movie *Who Framed Roger Rabbit?* was about the car industry's earlier homicide of the tram system in California.

18 Much of the funding for the company was provided by the PayPal co-founder Elon Musk; Google and eBay billionaires muscled in refinancing calls. With this parentage it should come as no surprise the stereo can be linked to an iPod – a major but not unique difference between the Tesla and my own Skoda.

19 Stanford News Service, 'Stanford's nanowire battery holds 10 times the charge of existing ones', http://news-service.stanford.edu/pr/2007/pr-nanowire-010908.html (accessed June 2009).

20 HM Treasury (2007) The King Review of Low-Carbon Cars. Part I: The Potential for CO_2 Reduction, p69, www.hm-treasury.gov.uk/d/pbr_csr07_king840.pdf (accessed June 2009).

21 HM Treasury (2007) The King Review of Low-Carbon Cars. Part I: The Potential for CO_2 Reduction, www.hm-treasury.gov.uk/d/pbr_csr07_king840.pdf (accessed June 2009).

22 Assumes the car emits $170gCO_2e/km$, carries 1.6 people, and is scrapped after being driven for 225,000km.

23 Lane, B. (2006) *Life Cycle Assessment of Vehicle Fuels and Technologies*, report by Ecolane Transport Consultancy for the London Borough of Camden.

24 Assumes new vehicle is 60g/km more efficient, that both vehicles embody 4.2tCO_2 to make, and the car is driven 115,000km by age nine years.

25 Department for Transport, *Vehicle Licensing Statistics 2007*, www.dft.gov.uk/pgr/statistics/datatablespublications/vehicles/ (accessed June 2009).

26 Sausen, R., Isaksen, I., Grewel, V., Hauglustaine, D., Lee, D., Myhre, G., Köhler, D., Pitari, G., Schumann, U., Stordal, F. and Zerefos, C. (2004) 'Aviation radiative forcing in 2000: An update on IPCC 1999', *Meteorologische Zeitschrift*, vol 14, no 4, pp555–561. This publication concludes that data on the effects on non-CO_2 gases is only 'fair' in quality, and proposes a total 'multiplier' of 1.9. The effect of cirrus clouds is only poorly understood, which could add a further one- to fourfold increase. These clouds are short-lived.

27 Defra (2008) *2008 Guidelines to Defra's GHG Conversion Factors: Methodology Paper for Transport Emission Factors*, Defra, London.

28 Goodall, C. (2007) *How to Live a Low-Carbon Life*, Earthscan, London, p194.

29 NHS Choices, 'Healthy eating self-assessment', www.nhsdirect.nhs.uk/magazine/interactive/calories/index.aspx. Sedentary calorific need from the President's Council on Physical Fitness and Sport, www.fitness.gov/exerciseweight.htm (accessed June 2009).

30 Department for Transport (2006) *National Travel Survey*, Table 6.9.

31 In Douglas Adams's *Hitchhiker's Guide to the Galaxy* the hapless Arthur Dent is made to listen to Prostetnic Vogon Jeltz's execrable poetry when he stows away on the Vogon spacecraft.

32 Sloman, L. (2006) *Car Sick: Solutions for our car-addicted culture*, Green Books, Dartington.

Keeping Your Home Warm

Heating the average home emits $4.7tCO_2$ and costs £800. Reducing this requires thought and planning. Some of the changes are initially expensive, but will save money for decades. If done well they can increase the resale value of the house. You'll need to manage the process carefully and supervise builders carefully. Over time you can halve your energy use by focusing on just five things. The suggestions below are banded as costing: (a) less than £50, (b) up to £500 and (c) over £500.

1   Learn about your heating controls, and use them.
    (a)   Reduce the temperature on the main thermostat; install thermostatic radiator valves in seldom-used rooms; learn to use your timer and consider updating it if it doesn't have the functions you need.

2   Reduce draughts – the source of 20 per cent or more of heat loss.
    (a)   Use draught excluding strips around doors and windows. Use a chimney balloon to plug up chimneys. Fill any gaps between floorboards and the holes in the floorboards.
    (b)   Professional draught exclusion isn't more effective, but it does look better.

3   Improve the heating system – this can reduce energy use by 20–50 per cent.
    (c)   Replace your boiler now if it's not a condensing boiler. You might qualify for Warm Front grants worth up to £4000 to finance the costs of new heating systems if you are on Income Support or Pension Credit, or have young children.

4   Insulate windows, roof, floor and walls – the source of 80 per cent of heat loss.
    (a)   A hot water cylinder jacket costs about £10–15. DIY window film costs about £10 for enough to cover around five windows and makes a noticeable difference. Thermal lining for curtains costs £15–35 depending on the size of window.
    (b)   Cavity wall insulation has to be fitted professionally; it's free from energy suppliers if you are on benefits, otherwise it costs around £250. You can fit loft insulation yourself or have it done professionally. Costs around the same as cavity wall insulation.
    (c)   Solid wall insulation is expensive: often in excess of £3000. Under-floor insulation beneath the ground floor costs around £500 depending on the material used, and can be done DIY. Double-glazing costs anything from £300 to £3000 per window depending on size and style.

5   Renewable heat sources – solar thermal, biomass and ground source heat pumps – are not cost-effective for most homes yet.
    (c)   In homes off the gas network, especially homes that are presently heated with electricity, renewables might save money and dramatically reduce carbon dioxide emissions.

Plan the energy-efficiency changes alongside other major works. It only makes sense to fit some of the larger insulation measures at the same time as other home improvements, like rewiring or the replastering of a wall.

Introduction

'I'm sorry to say this, but this is doing absolutely nothing for you,' says Phil McGrory, lifting up a limp, thin layer of fibreglass insulation as he shines his torch around the loft of Neil and Colette McLoughlin's semi-detached house in Hoo, Kent. (Guardian, June 2005)

To save energy, officials shut off the heating system in the town hall, leaving themselves and 100 workers no respite from near-freezing temperatures. On a recent frosty morning, rows of desks were full of employees bundled in coats and blankets, nursing flasks of hot tea. (Guardian, February 2006)

It'll come as no surprise that the first quote is a British one. It could easily be my house. Like many people I venture into my loft two or three times a year to pick up and return the Christmas decorations, or forage for our oversized suitcases the day before we go on holiday. That horrible fibreglass insulation will make me sneeze and will scratch my hand, but in a detached frame of mind I will note the insulation is in place and assume the matter is sorted.

The second quote – as much *Tenko* as *Zen and the Art of Home Insulation* – shows the Japanese capacity to withstand suffering and deal with having an OECD-scale demand for energy services but almost no indigenous fossil fuels of its own.

One big misapprehension I want to debunk is that energy efficiency is simple. It's not. *It is rocket science* in the superficial sense that many of the materials used are high-tech: one leading brand of insulating materials is marketed as *space insulation*. But also in the deeper sense, there is a theoretical science underpinning energy efficiency. Before you jump into action it's useful to understand how heat is being lost from your home and try to prioritize the actions that save most money first. Upgrading your boiler could save you more money than double-glazing the windows even though it might be ten times cheaper.[1] Cheaply reducing a house's CO_2 emissions needs good project management skills to ensure that tasks are correctly scheduled – where possible integrated with normal renovation and maintenance activities – and effort to commission and manage contractors so work is carried out to a high standard. You have to pay attention to detail. This means making sure the insulation is fitted properly, because small defects make the whole thing flop, just like NASA's 1999 mission to Mars which spectacularly crashed when one set of engineers gave their advice in the metric system and the other in English system.

Before starting I need to get some ideas. We are taking a train to an open eco-house day in Brighton. My son is intently sketching what he imagines an

Box 5.1 *Peter and Sigrid's low-carbon eco-conversion*

Peter and Sigrid have reduced the energy use of their end-of-terrace Victorian home by 72 per cent. When they came to the UK their dream was to build a passive solar home, within cycling distance of the city centre and their work. Unfortunately greenfield sites in Brighton were too costly, so they decided to buy a run-down Victorian home to eco-upgrade. The project took five months to plan and a further eight months to execute.

So what did they do? What didn't they do! Insulated the floor, walls, roof and windows; installed solar water heating to supply hot water and heating; and installed a wood fuel heater for the living room. They also did the more conventional changes like installing a gas condensing boiler, thermostats and energy-efficient bulbs throughout.

But as Peter puts it '... the first thing to do is insulate, insulate, insulate'. They installed under-floor insulation, first putting a waterproof membrane beneath the joists, then the insulation on top. They live in a conservation area so they weren't allowed to install external insulation. Instead they put 5cm of wood wool beneath the accessible plaster. This reduced the heat loss from the walls by 40 per cent. They put in new high-performing Austrian tilt and turn windows which they bought for a steal.

The house has three different heat sources – a high-efficiency gas condensing boiler, which they only need between October and March; four solar panels, each with 15 tubes, to catch enough sunlight to supply their hot water needs and some of their central heating needs; and a wood stove in the lounge which they use on cold winter's nights – more romantic than practical. They considered installing a ground source heat pump but were quoted over £8000 just to drill the hole in their back garden. Instead of radiators, their home is warmed with under-floor heating in the kitchen and wall radiant heating in other rooms (basically hot water pipes tucked underneath the plaster). Each room has its own thermostat. It's an unusual system but they say it was cheap and easy to install as long as it's done the same time as the replastering. The radiant heating system can utilize relatively cool water just 35–40°C, rather than the much hotter temperatures needed by small radiators. This makes it better suited to the solar water heating unit – which isn't able to produce temperatures hot enough to warm radiators in winter.

With such a wide-ranging conversion it should come as no surprise that they had to get four different planning permissions. Isolating just the cost of the eco-renovation elements alone, Peter said, was difficult as they did so much renovation at the same time, but he paid £13,000 for the insulation (mainly the 23 windows and 2 doors), and a further £7500 for the microgeneration. They probably spent a similar amount in labour. The biggest challenge was to find contractors who were prepared to learn about new techniques and materials.

eco-house house might look like. Maybe it's his school or maybe it's something he's picked up off me, but he seems to have a few ideas of the required components. The house has a solar panel, wind turbines and flowers growing prettily in the front gardens, and more incongruously a 40m swimming pool with a crocodile doing front crawl.

Only one of the homes on show is a Victorian house like ours, and it is owned by my friend Sigrid and her husband Peter. They've managed to shave 70 per cent off their emissions; way beyond my own ambitions. Box 5.1 goes into more detail about their home.

The Present Situation in the UK

Figure 5.1 shows how much CO_2 we release keeping out the elements – around 4.7 tonnes of CO_2 per home or 2 tonnes per person. I have tried to include emissions from producing the heat (or cooling) and also from building the homes.

Figure 5.1 sets out my estimate of the emissions associated with heating and building homes, based on figures from the UK's environmental accounts, supplemented with other government statistics. Interestingly, the transport of

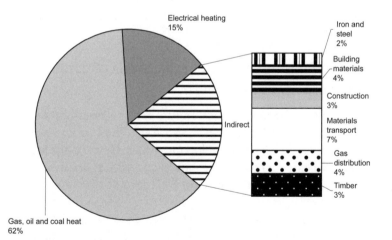

Figure 5.1 GHG emissions from constructing, warming and providing hot water to homes, 2004

Note: 100 per cent = 120MtCO$_2$ or 2 tonnes per person or 4.7 tonnes per household.

Sources: ONS, *Environmental Accounts* 2004; BERR, *Construction Statistics Annual*, 2007 edition, www.berr.gov.uk/files/file42061.pdf; BERR, *Digest of United Kingdom Energy Statistics, 2008*, Table 5.2, for household electricity as a ratio of total electricity sales; Department for Transport: *Road Freight Statistics 2006*.

construction materials causes greater emissions than their manufacture even though the manufacture of cement is infamous for its carbon intensity. Gas is the main fuel used in central heating, with oil used in rural areas. Electricity is important in smaller houses, and to provide top-up heat in a room.

The government has been tightening the energy-efficiency standards for new homes. All homes constructed after 2006 have to be fitted with gas condensing boilers; well-insulated walls, ceilings and floors; and double glazing. The standards are being further ramped up between 2010 and 2016 – culminating in zero-carbon homes.

The bigger problem is old homes, especially those built before the 1930s with solid walls, single-glazed windows and no under-floor insulation. There are two camps about what should be done about old homes. There is the Vogon viewpoint which argues we should raze old homes and replace them with new ones, and the vegan view which argues for the cultivation of the existing stock to improve its energy performance. I've always found the Vogon argument other worldly. For one thing it alienates the sizeable constituency of people who want to reduce greenhouse gases, but *also* care about the built heritage; second, it's plain wrong since it takes so much less energy to improve a home's energy efficiency than to build a new one. About a quarter of the emissions from homes are associated with building and maintaining new homes. Since we are adding less than 1 per cent to the housing stock each year (a much smaller number are also being torn down), the average new build embodies the equivalent of about 40 years of the emissions of the average existing home.

Rising household numbers and better levels of comfort mean we use more energy to keep warm

Figure 5.2 shows that the demand for energy used to keep homes warm has risen almost 30 per cent between 1970 and 2004. The top and bottom lines show two of the reasons why. Population growth and fewer people per house mean we have 35 per cent more households, and almost universal ownership of central heating means our homes are 6°C warmer then they were in the 1970s.

Figure 5.3 reminds us there has been a big change in the fossil fuels we use to keep warm in our homes. Demand for oil and electricity has been fairly stable. These fuels are used for homes in the countryside and many flats. The big switch has been from coal to gas. Coal deliveries to homes fell sharply as the gas network was extended and town gas was replaced by plentiful natural gas. Because gas emits so much less carbon than coal for the same amount of delivered energy, carbon emissions have been coming down even though more heat is being delivered.

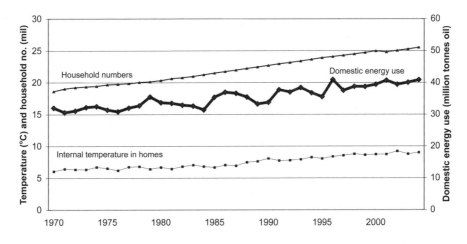

Figure 5.2 Change in domestic heating energy use, household numbers and internal temperature between 1970 and 2004

Source: Berr (2008)[2]

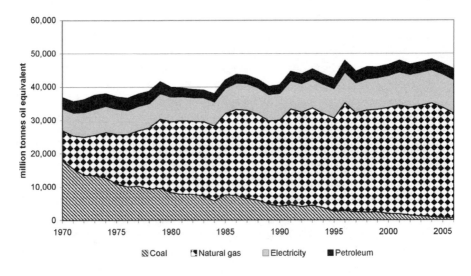

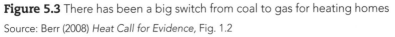

Figure 5.3 There has been a big switch from coal to gas for heating homes

Source: Berr (2008) *Heat Call for Evidence*, Fig. 1.2

But the use of electricity has remained fairly stable over time. Homes use electrical heating either because they are far from the gas grid, or to save the cost of connection and gas safety checks. Electrical heating, while fine for topping up fossil fuel-based heating, is a high-carbon and expensive way of keeping homes warm. A unit of electrical energy can be four times more expensive than a unit of gas energy. Box 5.2 shows how electrical heating and fuel poverty can be linked.

Box 5.2 *Two million elderly and vulnerable people struggle to afford to keep warm in winter*

I cycled to Angie's home on a cold December evening. She lives in a ground-floor flat in a Victorian house, which she bought almost 30 years ago. I broke out into a sweat as soon as I got inside. I measured the temperature as being a not unreasonable 19°C. 'I'm sixty-eight years old and feel the cold', she explained. 'I wasn't like it was when I was younger.' Angie had her gas cut off 18 months ago because she fell into arrears with her gas bill following her debt problems. She keeps just one room at a time warm using an oil-filled radiator, which she wheels between the living room, her bedroom and the kitchen. Her electricity bill averages £70 per month; which takes quite a large chunk of her £500 per month income. She was on an Economy-7 tariff.

Keeping warm in winters is a major headache for her, and a cause of ill-health. I mention that, because of her age, her gas supplier should never have disconnected her. She should have been offered a social tariff or a pre-payment meter. But either she didn't understand this or it was never explained to her. She now has the difficult job of finding a new gas supplier to take her on even with a poor payment record. I suggested she speak to the Citizen's Advice Bureau or lodge an appeal to the Energy Ombudsman, as she might have been unfairly treated. We both agree we'll have to do the best we can under the circumstances.

Her house has no insulation except for the thin carpet on the floor. Her solid brick walls are leaching cold and she would be happy if someone fitted internal or external insulation but both options are too expensive for her. Luckily there is another flat above her, so she doesn't have a roof to insulate. She keeps the curtains drawn in winter to stop the draughts from the windows – but I can see them twitch every now and then as the outside gusts seep through the ill-fitting sash windows. A couple of panes in the back window are cracked. The most affordable options would be to install Gapseal in the floorboards and some draught-proofing around the windows. She might also want to stick some plastic film over the windows. All of these together shouldn't cost more than £50 and her tenant might be willing to install it for her, especially if she paid him a little.

I suggest she discard her oil-filled heater and buy a cheap fan heater. It'd be much easier to carry from room to room, cost around £10 and warm the room faster than the oil heater. She might also get an electric blanket to keep warm at night, rather than keep the entire room warm – this would cost another £15. I also told her to come off her Economy-7 tariff. It was likely she could get a cheaper rate using the standard tariff.

The flat has damp at the rear. I think it is rising from the floor but I have no suggestions to help her. Unfortunately because she owns the flat she's not entitled to the government's Decent Homes subsidy which she could claim if she was a social housing tenant.

I leave her house feeling sorry on her behalf. She has a well-located and valuable flat, which with some money and attention would make a great home, but it's difficult to see how she will ever be able to restore it, or even afford to keep properly warm under the current rules. Her income is desperately low, with no prospect of an increase, but she is asset-rich and so qualifies for no benefits. I hope she and her tenant may be able to improve their living conditions.

Energy-efficiency measures are usually the most cost-effective way of reducing your emissions … and they save you money

Figure 5.4 shows how heat is lost from an uninsulated home.

The walls are usually the home's largest surface so it's no surprise they are usually the largest source of heat loss. The roof accounts for about a quarter of losses, but this can be cheaply remedied by improving the loft insulation. The floor and draughts both account on average for 15 per cent. The figure underlines the limitations of double glazing – since only about 10 per cent of heat is lost from the window, the maximum savings from double glazing are also limited.

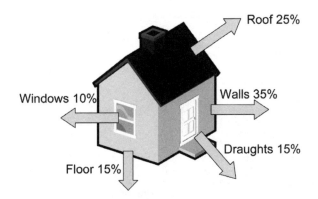

Figure 5.4 Sources of heat loss in an uninsulated home

Source: Communities and Local Government (2006)[3]

The figures are only averages; nearly all homes have already undertaken some improvements – 90 per cent of UK homes have some loft insulation, and half the homes with cavity walls have them insulated.[4]

Age is an important determinant of a home's energy efficiency. Many of the older homes, though great on charm and period features, were built to lower thermal standards, and are further losing heat from their sagging floors and ill-fitting doors and windows. Another major source of variation that we rarely talk about is simply quality of workmanship. One energy auditor I spoke to said the house with the best airtightness he had seen was an old 1950s home which had simply been built very well. Many brand new homes' performance doesn't live up to the claims on the tin. Our high, regulated standards are not being backed up with effective enforcement.

The UK government has devised a standard methodology to work out the cost of heating and lighting a house of a fixed size – this is called the Standard Assessment Procedure (SAP). It's intended to tell you how much it will cost to heat and provide light for a home. An average home with a SAP rating of less than 20 would be expected to cost £1200 to heat and light, a SAP rating of 50 costs £400 and a SAP rating of 80 around £200.[5] Figure 5.5 shows how the energy efficiency, as measured by the SAP, varies with the vintage of homes. About 5 million homes were built before 1918 and lack cavity walls, as do a proportion of houses built between the 1918 and 1945.

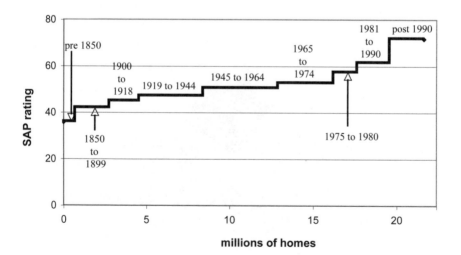

Figure 5.5 Home energy efficiency (SAP rating) and age of house
Source: Data from the English House Condition Survey 2005, analysis by author.

Understanding your House's Energy-Efficiency Performance

Before planning how you are going to reduce your house's emissions, it's worth assessing how it is performing at present. There are many ways of assessing your house's energy efficiency. You can use:

- gas (and power) use data from your gas (and electricity) meter readings;
- complete a web-based questionnaire from the Energy Saving Trust (EST) or energy supplier;
- pay for an Energy Performance Certificate (EPC) inspection; or
- you could go for a full-blown energy survey that considers in detail the type of insulation materials, the airtightness of the house and the size and orientation of windows.

Which one is for you? If all you are interested in is simply knowing how much emissions your heating causes, then utility bills (using 'actual' as opposed to 'estimated' figures) give an accurate estimate of your CO_2 emissions from heating. You simply multiply your energy use measured in kWh by 0.194 if you have gas heating, 0.265 for oil heating and 0.422 for electrical heating to convert to $kgCO_2$. Older gas meters are calibrated in cubic feet so you have to convert to kWh. Box 6.2 in Chapter 6 to will help you do this.

But if the purpose of the survey is to help you understand the opportunities to reduce your emissions, you need to understand how your heating system and insulation work. All the surveys take information about your house, and then apply standard assumptions about how the typical household uses their home, to work out emissions.

I tried several of the surveys to see what they had to say about my house. The Energy Saving Trust's online *home energy check* asks about the house's size, age and lighting and then emails back a six-page report on the energy costs and CO_2 emissions. The report also suggests a list of improvements and the energy and carbon savings you might expect to achieve. The format of the report is as a mock Energy Performance Certificate to show what kind of rating the house might achieve. The energy suppliers provide similar online reports. The British Gas website was easy to use and asked many pertinent questions about the number of double-glazed windows, size of house, details of what times of the day the house was heated on weekdays and at weekends.

I also asked London's Green Concierge Service to assess my home. For a fee of £199 they carried out a full Energy Performance Certificate (EPC) survey, recommended the most cost-effective measures in my house, provided contact details for firms who will supply and install the measures, and provided indicative prices. In a second meeting they talked me through the results and then provided a year's support to research the implementation of the recommendations. I also paid extra for a pressure test to assess the house's airtightness to understand losses from draughts. They go around the house showing the holes in the house's envelope. They can also take a thermal image of the outside of the house showing where heat is escaping from the house. But this only works on winter nights.

The most comprehensive result, without a doubt, was from an internet-based SAP survey available on the insulator manufacturer Knauf's website (http://tools.knaufinsulation.co.uk/sap2005_981/project_add.asp). And it was free. You don't need a degree in physics to fill it out, *but it would help*; I would strongly recommend you have the SAP2005 manual on hand (http://projects. bre.co.uk/sap2005/) to help answer the more technical questions, and maybe skim the manual's initial few pages to understand some basic concepts, since Knauf's interactive help feature wasn't fully working when I tried it. It took me over an hour and a half to fill in - and I had to supply a lot of information about the house (dimensions of each floor, area and orientation of the windows, materials used to build the house envelope, U-values[6] for the materials). There are some fairly esoteric parts of the SAP methodology where you can just use their default values. The information in Table 5.2 will provide some further defaults. The most painful way of assessing your house's thermal performance is using the SAP manual on the Building Research Establishment (BRE) website. It took me several days to get my head around it – I'm still not convinced I got it right. (But nor am I convinced many energy assessors understand it either.)

Table 5.1 shows how different reports' results compare with my true energy use from my gas and electricity bill.

The most striking fact is our household uses much less energy than any of the 'modelled' figures suggest. The formulae used by the internet sites and the SAP methodology use standard assumptions about the price of gas, temperature and occupancy. This is because they provide an understanding of the performance *of the house*, rather than *of the household*. The reason my energy bill is so low is not because the house is marvellously energy efficient, it's because during the week we only heat the home for about five hours per day and we keep the temperature at 17°C – rather than 18.9°C assumed in the SAP figure. The second most striking thing is how much the results differ. British Gas and EST both score my house well, which is about as justified as giving the CEO of Lehman Brothers a generous 2008 bonus. But even the SAP-based calculations vary hugely *and they really shouldn't*. I can only assume it's because of the judgements needed to fill in the form (Has the extension got the same type of floor as the rest of the house? Dunno. OK – I'll put 'yes' in the spreadsheet then) and partly because people doing the

Table 5.1 Assessments of energy use in my home

	Utility bill	Internet based		RD-SAP	SAP2005	
		EST	British Gas*	Green Concierge	SAP2005 by hand	Knauf SAP
Current rating		C	D	E	F	F
Potential rating		B	C	E	E	F
CO_2 emissions (tCO_2/yr)	2.7	3.8	7.4	6.3	9	8.6
Cost of heat and light (£/yr)	445	880	1790	985	1302	1518

Notes: RD-SAP: (reduced form standard assessment procedure). Rating refers to the A–G ratings found on EPCs. * British Gas estimate includes all household appliances and not just lighting.

measuring don't always get it right. Even so, the divergence between £985 and £1518 is hard to understand.

The British Gas survey asked the amount of hours we heated the house, but mystifyingly it made no use of the data in its calculation. The company must have the country's best database if they ever choose to give up selling gas and start selling energy services instead. Most of the websites also suggested things you could do to improve the energy efficiency. Only the Green Concierge's seemed to get this right. It advised replacing our boiler with an A-rated one to increase the SAP from 43 to 52. This would move us from the bottom of the E band to higher up the E band. They also suggested other 'worth doing' measures that were not immediately cost-effective: double-glazing with low-E glass and argon-filled windows (+5 improvement in SAP rating, £73 saving per year in gas bill), solid wall insulation (+11, saving £171), solar PV (+2, saving £32) so potentially bringing our SAP rating to 70 which is on the lower end of the C label and lowering our annual gas bill by £335 per year. A 'C' rating would be a very good show for a house as old as ours – comparable to my Mum putting in a six-minute mile. None of the other surveys suggested we update our ten-year-old boiler to a gas condensing one, several leapt into advocating solar PV, ignoring cheaper options. None recommended improving under-floor insulation which is the source of Siberian-style draughts in winter.

There are two consequences that concern me about this information. First, because they so massively overstate our house's true heating costs they will also greatly overstate the benefits. We only spend £350 a year on gas so there is no way we are going to make the claimed savings from installing the measures they recommend, yet the cost of installation will be the same. Would installing them increase the value of the house? John Doggart, who runs a charity, the Sustainable Energy Academy, provided me some reassurance by digging out a recent article which showed that house prices in Australia rose by 6 per cent when owners improved the energy efficiency by 60 per cent. He argued the introduction of the Energy Performance Certificate, which provides unbiased and standardized information on the energy efficiency of a house to prospective buyers, should have the same effect in the UK. If this is so, an eco-conversion would increase the value of the average house price by about £21,000. That could pay for quite a lot of energy efficiency even if my wife and I don't personally get that much benefit from reduced energy costs. I'd like to believe the Australian evidence and there are some things in life you have to take on trust. And it's not as though there are too many safer investment options out there just now.

My second worry is that the simplified energy-efficiency programme used to calculate the EPC does not credit many sensible energy-saving measures people undertake, like draught-proofing the house, investing in under-floor insulation, decent controls and thermostats. If you do these things you will need to make sure that the energy assessor is aware these have been under-taken. It also means you'll need to have the assessor carry out a full (and more expensive) SAP calculation rather than the cheap and cheerful Reduced Form SAP which is usually carried out when houses are put on the market.

My recommendation is to first use your utility bills to calculate your heating emissions and costs. But then to understand how heat is lost from your house, it's worth going through the Knauf tool to properly understand the opportun-ities in your home. If you wish to pay for advice, make sure you obtain an airtightness test to find out where the air gaps are and also have a thermal image to help locate failures in your insulation. These can only be taken on winter evenings. I wouldn't bother with the quick-and-dirty websites – they're too unreliable. I'd also ignore the advice they give. If you're reading this book you've already gone beyond that stage.

Options for Reducing Energy Use

The estate agent who sold us our home described it as a charming Victorian mid-terrace in a North London conservation area. It has three bedrooms on the first floor, two receptions and a kitchen (extended in the 1970s). While writing this book we had the loft converted, adding two extra bedrooms and another bathroom. I've spent the past few weeks fretting about how I am going to halve the emissions from my home. I have good reason to be careful. It is our main store of wealth and we cannot afford to make changes to the house that reduce its value or make it difficult to sell.

There is a lot of talk about home energy efficiency providing win–win, low-hanging fruit, five-pound-notes-lying-on-the-floor benefits to everyone. Economists in government tell ministers that eco-refurbishing homes is the policymaker's holy grail: creating jobs, saving money and also saving the planet. I used to say this kind of thing myself. I still believe it, but realizing this potential takes research and time. The situation has improved in London with the creation of the Green Homes Concierge which gives project management support and recommends suppliers. Elsewhere there is a network of exemplar Superhomes organized by the Sustainable Energy Academy,[7] two of which are located in Camden.

But the problem isn't just the house. It's me, my wife and our middle-class sensibilities. Sheepishly I realize that since we have owned our home we have probably made its energy efficiency worse, not better. We cleaned out and opened up the chimneys. We have replaced the tatty lino floor with stone tiles. The old flooring, despite its gender-bending vapour emissions, was at least warm underfoot, betraying its superior insulating properties compared to the tiles which bleed heat away. Even the paintwork has deteriorated during our watch so the sash windows rattle in their frames and the thin Ikea curtains flutter in the weakest of breezes. The only energy-efficient feature I can point to is the 150mm of loft insulation the previous owners put in. Lately I have been getting bad attacks of cognitive dissonance. This ailment is making me spend all my time checking the energy efficiency of the fittings the builder used in our loft conversion. I find myself constantly ruing the fact I hadn't done more research and more forcefully insisted they go beyond the minimum regulated standards. (I understand most car ads are read by people who've just bought a vehicle, to obtain reassurance that they haven't been ripped off.)

We are lucky that we are well-off enough to be unconcerned about how much we spend on heating. Yet we are cold most of the winter, stoically tolerating the mild discomfort to help the environment. A little sheepishly I realize I have no idea how much our gas supplier direct-debits from my account every month. I look back at the energy bills for the last two years. Our gas energy consumption is just 12,000kWh per year: three-quarters for our winter heating and the rest for hot water. Altogether our gas bill at today's gas prices is £350 a year, just £260 of which is for space heating, not much for a house as big and old as ours. We spend just a third of what Angie spends: because we use gas rather than electricity, work in offices where our employer pays for our warmth and because we aren't frail.

So how do we go about cost-effectively reducing our bills and CO_2 emissions? There are four basic ways:

1   reducing the temperature of our house;
2   reducing draughts;

3   increasing the amount of insulation; and
4   replacing fossil fuels with renewable energy sources.

Reducing the temperature of your house

If you are smart you might be able to do this without anyone in the house noticing. The trick, of course, is to lower the temperature in rooms that are not being used, or to turn the heat off when the house is empty.

According to the government's Energy Saving Trust, making proper use of heating controls can lop off 15 per cent of energy use.

A good set of heating controls includes a timer to ensure the heating only operates when you are up and about in the house, a thermostat which monitors the temperature in the 'core of the house' and only fires the boiler when necessary, and thermostatic valves on individual radiators to maintain rooms at different temperatures.

Modern programmable room thermostats set the time the heating turns on and off, and ensure room temperature does not rise above a defined level. They usually also have a frost setting, which overrides the timer and turns the heat on if the room temperature drops below 5°C, to stop the pipes freezing. The price of controllers varies from £15 for the simplest models, to up to £180 for the most sophisticated ones.

So what do you get for your money? Cheaper mechanical controllers may have a clock dial with pins or tabs to programme in times for the heating to turn on and off. More sophisticated digital models have a touch-sensitive screen and are more flexible, allowing you more 'on/off' changes per day, and have different settings for different days of the week. This means if you fancy lying in on weekend mornings you can set it so the heating doesn't come on till the middle of the morning. Expensive controllers operate the boiler wirelessly so they can be located away from the boiler, in the room where the temperature is most likely to be stable. All new room thermostats detect the room temperature electronically, so they can immediately assess the temperature to the nearest 0.1°C. They normally tolerate temperatures exceeding and undershooting the stipulated temperature by around half a degree to avoid the boiler being constantly switched on and off, which is inefficient and increases wear and tear.

Thermostatic radiator valves (TRVs) are used to set different temperatures around the house. They allow rooms like the hall or the guest bedroom to be kept a bit cooler. The valve detects the temperature mechanically instead of electronically. Because of the time delay in mechanical regulation – it takes time for the metal switch to heat up and its shape to deform – the temperature will constantly be overshooting and undershooting, making the room's

Box 5.3 *Reducing energy bills in rented accommodation*

Duncan rents a room in a ten-year-old purpose-built flat. It is double-glazed throughout, and has flats both above and below. I wasn't surprised to find it lovely and warm when I came to interview him, despite being the middle of winter. There were three cycles in the hallway – his two flatmates must be pretty environmentally aware too. I wondered how much scope there would be to reduce their energy use.

He had his rent statement to show me how they paid for their energy. 'We don't pay for the utilities directly. Our landlady just takes off a fixed sum every month - £25 a month for gas and £39 a month for electricity. I'd prefer if we used the meter, that way we'd have an incentive to save, but the landlady thinks it's simpler as she constantly has people moving in and out.' I walked around the flat and measured the temperature in a couple of rooms. It was 22°C in the hall. The kitchen where we were sitting was much cooler because the window was wide open. Did they always keep the hall so hot? 'I'm not quite sure. It's a bit difficult with a flat share. No one knows when one of the others are in, so we're not very disciplined about heating. Jackie's doing a PhD so she's at home quite a bit.' I asked if I could take a look at the thermostat just to see what temperature they had set it at. Duncan grinned. 'I don't actually know where it is, Jackie'll know.' Jackie did know where it was – she had whacked it up in the afternoon, without thinking, because she'd been cold. Neither of them knew how long the kitchen window had been open, perhaps all day, maybe it had been Jackie's partner Salim when he had come back from work. He'd gone out for the evening now.

Despite the high energy efficiency of the home there was a lot Duncan and his two flatmates could do to reduce their energy use. First, I suggested they speak to the landlady and ask if they could pay their energy utility bills themselves, instead of her picking it up through the rent. They were all on six-month assured tenancies so were likely to be here a reasonable time. At least they'd have the incentive to economize. Second, they should agree some house rules like the last one to leave the house had to close the kitchen and living room windows. They could also do with some radiator controls in the bedrooms as they seemed unnecessarily hot. Feeling a bit shamefaced, Duncan said he'd be happy to buy them and fit them so long as the landlady paid for them. He told me that under the new rules landlords had to prepare an energy performance certificate before they could put the property on the market; so it was in her interests to improve the energy efficiency.

LIMERICK COUNTY LIBRARY

temperature oscillate. The most sophisticated room controls use 'zonal' technology. Digital thermostat/transmitters are located in each zone to measure the temperature and send a wireless signal to the radiators they control. Each radiator can be independently programmed with its own on/off times and temperature. For instance the living room and kitchen might come on at 6.00pm and the bedroom at 10.00pm. The manufacturer Honeywell makes such zonal systems. They cost around £60 per thermostat/transmitter and you'll also need to upgrade each radiator valve too so it can work using the wireless technology. The Heatmiser system (www.heatmiser.co.uk) is particularly sophisticated and allows you to control the home heating system through the internet, or through your mobile phone. You can maintain different temperatures in different rooms; the user interface looks fairly straightforward to use. Heatmiser's most basic thermostat costs around £45. If you've got a big home it might be worth installing these systems.

It can sometimes be counterproductive buying a heating control system more complicated than you need. There's no point in a voice-activated system if you'll never have the time to learn how to use the function, or to set it up properly. A plain mechanical system might be enough if you keep regular hours and have a small flat which you keep at a uniform temperature.

Turning the room thermostat down by 1°C reduces the average heating bill by 9 per cent

I think people will use less energy and I hate to go back to the Jimmy Carter days in the US but maybe it's two jumpers instead of one. I think people will change the temperature they keep the house.

(Jake Ulrich, MD of Centrica, at least at time of writing)

Jake Ulrich's above career-limiting pronouncement, while no Gerald Ratner,[8] was certainly a creditable performance. The press were keen to pounce on another British Gas fat cat. Even the usually po-faced civil servants at Energywatch got themselves worked up enough to indignantly declare: 'The remarks demonstrate how out of touch they [British Gas/Centrica/boardrooms in general] are with the daily struggle their vulnerable customers face to keep warm. … Comments like this don't help anyone.'

But Jake may be right. As well as reducing heating we are not using, we can also reduce the temperature of the room we *are* using. On an average winter day increasing the temperature on the thermostat by 1°C adds about 9 per cent to the heating need (see Annex 2 at the end of this chapter for accurate data on the relationship between different desired indoor temperatures and heat demand).

I was in the pub speaking to a friend of mine who astounded me by declaring he was so concerned about climate change he hadn't turned the heating on all last winter. 'The temperature in the house often dropped to 9°C', he explained excitedly. 'But I coped by putting on ski gear. Did you know the string vest[9] was designed for cold weather explorers? But nowadays you can get ski gear made out of Gortex which lets you sleep in it in the snow. It only weighs 200g/m², resists moisture and is easy to wash.' I looked at him slightly at a loss for words. 'But don't your fingers get cold?' 'You can get Gortex mittens too', he added cheerily.

How hot does the room need to be, to stay healthy? The World Health Organization recommends that the living room (where we tend to slob around) be kept at around 21°C. The rest of the house can be cooler – 19–20°C. But this isn't set in stone. Our core body temperature is 37°C; the skin is usually cooler, hovering between 32 and 34°C. Someone eating and metabolizing 2000kcal a day is generating 100W of heat. Younger people, especially if they're active, will be generating their own heat. Michael Phelps's 12,000kcal diet times three would be equivalent to a fan heater! Home temperatures below 16°C are regarded as cold, and below 12°C as unhealthily cold. Shorn of his Gortex underpants, my friend in the pub would soon get hypothermia.

The upshot of this is that healthy people can live within a reasonably wide range of summer and winter temperatures, without risking ill-health, by dressing appropriately. Even if wearing Quechua skiwear around the house is not for you, there's a lot that can be achieved by turning the thermostat down a notch and dressing appropriately for the season. You'll feel less cold in the house by just putting on your warmest pair of socks, a thick jumper and getting up and walking around every now and again. That way you can retain heat generated by your own metabolism. At night-time there's really no need to have the heat on at all. It's healthier and less carbon intensive to let the air temperature fall and to use an electric blanket to keep warm. My blanket uses 50W to warm up and 10W on its overnight setting. If you use an electric blanket every night between December and March, its electricity use will emit just 9kgCO$_2$. This logic works in summer too; stripping off the tie and shirt collar helps the body to stay cool.

Reducing heat loss from the house

Cutting down on draughts is the cheapest way of reducing heat loss

Heat loss through draughts (convection) is the second most important loss of heat from the house, but it's probably the simplest to reduce. The rate at which air escapes from a house is measured in terms of the volume of air lost, per unit area of envelope each hour. It can also be expressed in terms of air changes per hour (ACH) The performance of houses range from 2 to 25m³/hr/m². The average air exchange for UK buildings is 11m³/hr/m² while best practice is 3m³/hr/m². The demanding German Passivhaus environmental standard is 0.6m³/hr/m² – so airtight it needs mechanical ventilation to ensure moisture and odours are removed. Poor airtightness represents sloppy building – badly fitting doors and windows, cracks in the brickwork or unwanted holes in the floor. There is some depressing data that suggests that the airtightness of newly constructed buildings is no different from those built 100 years ago.[10] Performance depends on how carefully the houses have been built and how well workmen fill holes after they've done work. The main sources of unwanted air loss are: open chimneys, draughty loft hatches, doors and windows, badly fitting entrances to attics and cellars and holes drilled through the envelope – for drainage, wiring and flues.

These draughts matter. Research in the US suggests that air leaks from fireplaces in a home can add US$500 or 30 per cent to the energy bill. UK figures are probably lower as our winters are much milder but they are still responsible for a fifth of the heat loss.

There needs to be *some* circulation of air to prevent the house from becoming damp, to replace the CO_2 we breathe out and to get rid of odours and dust. The usual recommendation is that the air should be replaced around once an hour (at normal pressure), but I have heard experts advise that replacing the air only once every three hours is enough so long as we make sure we ventilate the kitchen when we are cooking and the bathroom and the toilet to clear smells and steam. There are other things we can do to stop the build-up of moisture, like cooking with the lid on the pan and lowering the flame!

The airtightness of a house is measured using a *pressure test*, which is quite fun to watch, resembling the type of manoeuvre that would get Mulder and Scully drooling. During the test all the windows and external doors are closed and air is pumped into the house to increase the inside pressure. The speed at which air leaks through the gaps is then measured. Figure 5.7 is taken from an analysis of over 200 homes that were tested for their airtightness. It shows that cracks in the walls are the largest source of air loss, but gaps in suspended timber floorboards are second worst. The goods news is that measures to reduce draughts also reduce conduction losses. But to reduce draughts effectively needs good quality control; it's no good just installing cavity wall insulation or sealing the timber floors; it has to be done well. One result from the study showed that the infiltration *got worse* when contractors installed radiators because of the holes they drilled for the water pipes, which weren't properly sealed.

So what can we do to reduce draughts? Fireplaces first: cast-iron period fireplaces can be fitted with a hinged flap which creates a reasonable seal. (I went through about two winters not realizing our fires had the flaps!) If your chimney doesn't have one you can trace the design and take it a shop making reproduction fireplaces to see if they will make one. Another option is buying

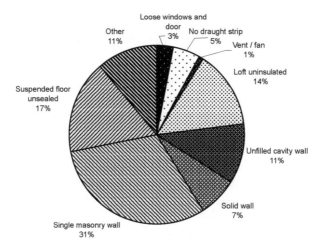

Figure 5.6 Sources of unwanted ventilation in the average UK home in the Warm Front programme

Source: Warm Front Study Group[11]

a chimney balloon, which is an inflatable cushion made of plastic which you install about a foot above the hole. They cost £20–25 depending on the size of the chimney breast. Their design should include a small gap to provide the chimney with some air flow and avoid problems with damp (and you have to remember to take them out if you're going to use the fire). The standard way of reducing draughts from doors and windows is to line the side of the frame with rubber or brush draught excluders. These can be bought from DIY shops for about £10 for a 20m strip which is sufficient to cover four doors. Brushes are useful for the bottom of the door.

Another major source of draughts is leaky floors. Older homes with wooden floors are open to the atmosphere from below – usually the floorboards are nailed onto wooden joists which are held off the soil on load-bearing brickwork. Air bricks maintain a flow of air under the timber to prevent the wood from becoming damp and rotting. The usual way of filling in the gaps between the floorboards is to squirt in rubber sealant, perhaps with sawdust mixed in, depending on the width of the gap. However, this doesn't last all that long. There are other products that can be used, such as Gapseal, which is a tape you push into the gap and, it is claimed, will stay in place better. The irksome holes left by builders when they sink pipes and wires through floorboards and walls have to be dealt with one by one with sealants.

If you manage to reduce the losses to very low rates you might need to install mechanical ventilation

Very airtight houses need mechanical exchange of air, especially in the bathroom and kitchen. Heat exchangers are a technology to avoid losing heat at the same time. They consist of fine tubing that allows the hot, damp, stale air to wind around the cool, dry fresh air, recovering around 80 per cent of the heat.

Firms like Ventaxia make mechanical ventilators with heat exchangers suitable for kitchen and bathroom walls. They cost around £250 each and consume around 4W of power when operating in trickle mode and 17W when the fans are really going for it – which you need when you've just had a shower and need to clear the room of water vapour. They're quite noisy too. According to my calculations each heat exchanger consumes about 50kWh per year causing emissions of 20kgCO_2e per extractor fan; you'll probably need about three around the house.

The people who made the low-carbon BedZed[12] estate in South London claim the electricity used by powered heat exchangers neutralizes any savings in carbon from the heat recovery. I think they're being harsh on mechanical heat exchangers – my back-of-the-envelope estimate suggests the CO_2 emitted to replace the one interchange an hour to be around 100kgCO_2. But I agree their savings are marginal and it's just more things in the house that could go wrong. The BedZed people recommend using a passive heat-exchange system, which recovers over 70 per cent of the heat from the air. The ingenious design uses the rising warm air exiting from the top of the house to pull cold air through a heat exchanger. The system gives BedZed its distinctive, brightly coloured cowls; it's also used in the new bits of the House of Commons. The 'passive heat recovery' requires no electricity to drive it – a rare example of wind power actually delivering the goods in an urban environment. The cheaper option is of course just using the windows, which we have chosen to do.

The third type of heat interchange is radiation.[13] Heat is gained by a building when high-energy radiation from the sun streams in through the windows. You can feel the heat on your face when you sit in the sun. Low-emissivity glass contains traces of metal which is opaque to low-energy (long-wavelength) radiation so stops heat from leaking back out of the window to the outside environment. Pilkington have developed low-E double glazing that is widely used in UK windows. Firms will take thermal photos of your house so you can see where heat is escaping from the outer envelope; patchily insulated walls and roofs show up well. Or you can make your own infrared camera.[14]

You need to insulate to reduce heat loss from conduction

Poor insulators let heat out by conduction through the envelope of the house (the walls, floor, windows and roof); they include materials like metals, glass, slate and stone. Dry organic materials like straw, wood, plastics and cork are

Table 5.2 Selection of U-values for new-build houses and materials used in existing homes

		U-values
		(W/m²K)
Walls	New build	0.35
	Solid brick external insulation, best practice	0.6
	Cavity wall – filled	0.54
	Cavity wall – unfilled (60mm gap, bricks 105mm each)	1.44
	Solid brick and plaster	2.1
Floor	New build	0.25
	Concrete floor	0.45–0.7
	Floor exposed to outside air from below	1.2
Roof	New build	0.16
	250mm loft insulation	0.2
	150mm loft insulation	0.35
	100mm loft insulation	0.4
	Uninsulated	2.3
Windows	Double-glazed with argon and low-E glass (6–16mm gap)	1.5–2.3
	New build	2
	Double-glazed with argon in gap (6–16mm gap)	2.6–2.9
	Double-glazed (6–16mm gap)	2.7–3.1
	Single-glazed	5
Door	Wooden door	2

Note: New build: the standards for new homes under current building regulations. Older homes were built to lower standards.

Sources: HM Government, *The Government's Standard Assessment Procedure for Energy Rating of Dwellings*, 2005 edition; Thierry Salmon and Stephane Bedel (2007), *Energy Saving House*, Centre for Alternative Technology publication; Energy Saving Trust, *Energy Efficiency Best Practice in Housing*, pamphlet (2004).

good insulators, inert noble gas like argon, or better still xenon or krypton are very good insulators – but the best is a vacuum. Many of the materials used to insulate homes are really vessels for tightly trapping air. Annex 1 at the end of this chapter shows how well different materials conduct heat. The use of vacuum insulation is common for hot drinks flasks; it's becoming available for fridges but it's still too expensive for construction. The force of the atmosphere on a 1m^2 panel is like a 7 tonne weight.

Walls consist of layers of different materials of different thicknesses and conductivities. The wall's overall effectiveness at insulating is given by the 'U-value'. Table 5.2 gives the U-values for a number of barriers that make up a house's envelope. The lower the number, the better.

Eco-renovation is the art of saving the planet without ruining the neighbourhood

Andrew Hazel, 46, will have to spend £450,000 knocking down the extensive building work he has carried out ... demolishing a large section of the listed structure and adding a kitchen with modern windows. Judge said: 'Fixtures intended to improve the property had been added without consideration or sympathy – like painting a moustache on an old master or adding a drum and bass track to music written by Mozart.'

(*The Daily Telegraph*, September 2008)

In the case of changing the appearance of your home, beauty is not in the eye of the beholder, but in the eye of the planning committee. Under present regulations eco-renovation of older homes has to balance reducing heat loss, maintaining the heritage and keeping the costs affordable. And because for many people their home is their main store of wealth they only make changes to the house that enhance its market value and avoid those that detract from it. This is particularly important when the property market is flat and buyers are biding their time for the right deal.

So how do we go about reducing the heat loss through conduction? The trick is try and make the building envelope – the ground floor, walls, windows, doors and ceiling – a continuous skin of well-insulated material. The word 'continuous' is important. Any break – or thermal bridge – acts like a leak in a water tank, draining heat from the inside.

The largest surface is usually the outer wall. There is a huge gulf in performance between an uninsulated cavity wall / solid wall and modern walls. Uninsulated walls lose four or five times more heat than their modern equivalents. If you're reading this book you'll already be well aware of the benefits of cavity wall insulation. It costs just £250 per house and energy companies will install it for you. It's free for people in 'priority groups', and even if you have to pay for it yourself the payback period is one to two years. It's not even particularly disruptive – holes are drilled on the external side of the wall and foam is blown into the cavity between the walls. It's a complete no-brainer. There can be problems filling the cavity completely either if the gap is too thin or if there are obstructions preventing the foam from spreading. There are still about 9 million homes with unfilled cavities that could be filled. The effectiveness of cavity wall insulation can be visualized using thermal imagery. Pictures of adjacent houses with and without cavity wall insulation on a winter evening look starkly different. The images also reveal patches which the installer failed to fill properly.

For the 30 per cent of homes that do not have cavities – which means most homes built before 1930 – the two main options are external insulation or internal insulation, also called dry-lining. In the former panels of insulation material are fixed onto the outside brickwork of a house. The panels consist of 5–10cm of insulant which is then finished off either with white render or brick. A 10cm-thick panel can reduce the U-value to a tenth of its original value. The cost of having the insulation fitted will be between £90 and £150 per square metre depending on the finish. Firms like Wetherby have developed a range of external insulating panels.

Internal insulation works on a similar principle: the internal plaster is stripped down to the brickwork. Firms like Kingspan sell panels of insulants that can be screwed either to the wall directly or to wooden batons fixed to the brick. The insulating material has an aluminium vapour-proof membrane to prevent moisture from the house wetting the insulant. The material costs around £40 per square metre. The panels reduce the size of the room by 5–10cm.

The advantages of external insulation over internal insulation are that it avoids the loss of valuable internal floor space (easily 5m² in a medium-sized detached home) and avoids the aggravation of removing and reinstalling objects affixed or embedded in the wall like radiators, power points, coving and skirting. Internal insulation covers a smaller proportion of the envelope as the ceiling, floors and the void between floors cannot usually be reached. A slightly more technical advantage of external insulation, but one argued by the guru of such things, Bill Dunster, is it's better to have the thermal mass of the bricks on the 'warm' side of the insulant to moderate the temperature of the house over the day and night period.

An important advantage of internal insulation is that it avoids changing the external look of the house, particularly important in a line of terraced houses, or a block of flats. Development control offices see this as a major issue in conservation areas. In conservation areas homeowners will often not have the option of using external insulation on the front of the house, though there is nothing to stop local residents grouping together in their conservation area committee and agreeing a common approach and look to the outside walls in a row of houses. This is something being discussed where I live.

An alternative to full-blown internal insulation is a product called Sempatap which is marketed by an unsavoury-sounding company Mould Growth Consultants – which hints at the origins of the firm. A couple of people have mentioned insulating wallpapers to me – one rather optimistically describing it as magic wallpaper – which I suppose it is, in the sense it can only be an act of wizardry that could persuade people to part with money to buy the stuff. It only has a marginal effect on energy efficiency, reducing the U-value of a solid wall by around 0.5 from around 2. If we are trying to save the planet we really need to do better than this stuff.

An uninsulated roof is a large source of heat loss. Luckily the majority of UK homes have some form of insulation in their loft. Building regulations now specify the equivalent of 270mm of mineral wool in the lofts. The same resistance to heat flow can be achieved with thinner layers of new materials, which are also easier to fit. Homes that have had their roof insulated some time ago will find it doesn't conform to today's standards. Back in 1982 standard practice was just to fit 50mm. While it's worth topping this up, you shouldn't get too euphoric about the savings. BRE have done research indicating the 50mm of loft insulation gives 55 per cent and 100mm 80 per cent of the performance of 300mm of roof insulation.[15] More productive than piling more and more blankets onto a bed that's already pretty warm is finding the spots that have been left out. Awkward to reach corners are worth checking, as is the top of the loft hatch door, and areas above bay windows.

An interesting research project reviewed the quality of installation of cavity wall and loft insulation fitted in social housing through the Warm Front programme; it found that on average a fifth of the cavity wall and 13 per cent of the loft remained uninsulated.[16] It's important to check for defects because of incorrect fitting.

Single-glazed windows are poor at retaining heat

A single-glazed window has a U-value of around 5; possibly the worst performing part of the building's envelope. Old windows, as well as being poor insulators, are often poorly fitting and a source of draughts. Building regulations mean that new windows have to have a U-value of at most 2, which in practice means ditching single panes of glass and using 'sealed units' which consist of two panes of glass held apart by a spacer bar and filled with an insulating gas.

Windows built to Germany's Passivhaus standard outperform building standards significantly: they are triple glazed, argon filled, and use low-emissivity (heat-trapping) glass. I got a German manufacturer to provide us quotes for casement windows with U-value of 0.7, rather better than our wall – which is a pretty amazing feat of engineering. Window frames are also conductors of

Box 5.4 *Window frames: Wood, aluminium or uPVC?*

Windows frames in new homes are usually made from uPVC. And no wonder; mass-produced from moulds in their hundreds, they cost little make, are lighter than metals so easy to handle and cheap to transport. They are also cheaper to maintain than timber – needing just an occasional wipe down rather than a regular paint.

But uPVC gets a bad rap from most environmental groups. They hate uPVC for a whole bunch of reasons. Half the weight of uPVC is chlorine which is energy intensive to produce. As a material, uPVC is difficult to repair and cannot be recycled, so has to be disposed of when it is damaged or reaches the end of its life. But some of the complaints against uPVC are unfair. It doesn't contain the infamous gender-bending plasticizers used in other PVC polymers. And while the incineration of uPVC creates hazardous dioxins, the modern incinerators in which waste is burnt are strictly regulated so they render these dangerous gases harmless.

The other big issue is how long the different materials last, and their relative energy intensity of production. A life-cycle analysis performed by researchers at Napier University in Scotland suggests that the production of a 1.2×1.2m timber window emits 0.11kgCO_2e, the production of an equivalent uPVC, 1.4kgCO_2e and aluminium, 11kgCO_2e.[17] (Recycled aluminium emits just 0.7kgCO_2 per window.) But this is all small beer compared to the loss of heat through a single square metre of glass which leaks out something like 50kgCO_2e per year. It's more important that the windows are affordable.

How about longevity and repair? The researchers sent out a questionnaire to local authorities asking about their durability. They found that aluminium were the longest lasting and easiest to maintain, lasting an average of 43 years, timber around 40 years and uPVC just 24 years. But timber windows are the most expensive to maintain needing to be painted every five years. One problem with uPVC is its weakness. This means the window frames have to be much thicker to hold the glass in place, shrinking the effective area of glass. As a result uPVC isn't a great choice for small panes. Aluminium-clad timber is a recent innovation on the market. Aluminium is used on the outer face of the window, making them easy to maintain, but the inside uses wood's excellent thermal properties and better interior look.

So it's a difficult call. For the economical environmentalist, uPVC has a lot going for it since it can be significantly cheaper and easier to maintain than wood. But the most important consideration will probably be on the value of the house, especially in conservation areas where 'cheap-looking' uPVC may detract from the home's value.

heat and it makes a difference whether they made from wood, aluminium or uPVC. The pros and cons between the three materials are given in Box 5.4.

A cheaper option is to have secondary glazing on the inside of the house. This doesn't have particularly great thermal properties – secondary glazing will be air filled – so U-values might be reduced from 5 to 3. But it does provide good sound insulation, prevents draughts and is normally tolerated even in conservation areas.

English Heritage forbids listed buildings from being fitted with double glazing, but allows secondary glazing to be installed because secondary glazing is seen as a reversible transgression of taste and the character of the building can be restored once we have got climate change licked! For a peek into the way English Heritage, local authorities' planning departments and the sustainability team interact, take a look at a report *Conserving Buildings Saves Money* produced by Camden[18] which shows the excruciating knots different public authorities tie themselves in resolving conflicts between competing policy objectives.

Retrofitting sash windows in older homes can be an expensive job as sash windows are a complicated bit of engineering, often made to bespoke sizes. As well as the numerous individual glass panes in a normal bay window, there is also the delicate system of counterbalances using lead or cast iron weights to hold the windows at the required height. If your home has traditional rattling wooden sash windows and you wish to improve the energy efficiency and restore them to their former glory, your options are:

- Refurbish and update the windows and fit draught-proofing. This might cost about £300/window. This won't change the U-value – it'll stay at around 5, but you'll get rid of the draughts.
- Replace the single pane sash windows with 'sealed units' inside the existing box. This costs around £1000 per window. However, thicker double glazed panes often have a hard time squeezing into the old boxes, making this approach more difficult. The sealed unit is also much heavier than a single pane of glass so you'll need new weights in the box. It's possible to get the U-value down to about 1.5 and also remove the draughts.
- Entirely replace the sash with brand new box and windows. There are many companies that will be delighted to do this for you. Costs are around £1200–1500 for replacement with wood, about £300 cheaper if you go for uPVC. The uPVC windows use springs instead of weights to hold the weight of the glass up.
- Replace the traditional sash windows altogether and go for casement windows. There is a variety of highly energy-efficient products on the market. Windows meeting the Passivhaus standard can be

imported from Germany. They are cheap – around €500 for the standard design, and about double this for one that looks like a sash window from the outside, and you will need to pay £400 to a local installer.

The technology is changing briskly as the building standards tighten and consumers become savvy. Using low-E glass on the inside pane is fairly standard. The choice of the filler gas can affect the performance significantly: dry air no longer meets building standards, so argon is usually used in sealed units; heavier noble gases like xenon and krypton are better insulators but a lot more expensive. Annex 1 at the end of this chapter gives information on the conductivities of the different gases. The last thing to look out for is whether the spacer bar holding the two glass panes apart uses warm edge spacer materials, i.e. materials other than aluminium. This use of smarter materials can cheaply improve the window's performance.

The current building regulations specify windows with a U-value of 2.0. It is easy to outperform this, probably at no extra cost. But just because something is possible doesn't necessarily mean it's worth doing. The value of the energy saved from installing the best double glazing is fairly marginal – a 1 × 1m single-glazed window lets through heat worth less than £10 every year. The difference in thermal performance between OK double glazing (U-value of 1.7), and amazing double glazing (U-value of 0.7) will annually save at best £2 in energy costs. The issue for the economical environmentalist isn't really about getting the most energy-efficient double glazing, but about getting something that is good enough, and, more importantly, allows the house to be marketed as low energy and enhances the value of the property. Box 5.5 shows the kind of debate we went through at home.

Box 5.5 *Sash or cash?*

'Could you pass me the Coco Pops?' I glare at my wife over the breakfast table. All is not well in the Vaze household. '... please.' She stares at me with pursed lips. 'This isn't about Coco Pops ... it's about those sash windows isn't it? You think I don't care about climate change just because I think PVC casement windows are ugly.'

Luckily we have avoided the above scene – but the issue of whether to retain wooden sash windows or install cheaper PVC casement windows divides us. This probably sounds somewhat heretical, and our neighbours will no doubt strike us from the virtual Christmas card list, but neither of us particularly cares for sash windows. They're less practical and harder to clean than the modern tilt and turn designs and they cost a fortune to install. Where we disagree is in our second guessing of how removing these 'period features' will effect the ultimate resale value of the house. As with so many housing choices, we have half an eye to when we sell up and move somewhere else.

Our home is in a conservation area, but not one with an 'Article 4 designation'. Our designation means we can replace the windows without getting permission from the council. If it did have an Article 4 designation the development control Tsar could insist we replace like for like. I spoke to the development officer just to make sure we could go ahead and do what we liked. She put a lot of pressure on me saying I should stick with timber sash windows, and gleefully said at the end our postcode was soon to be re-designated as Article 4, putting us within her bailiwick.

The difference in price between different styles of window can be staggering. The Chinese company Zehao, a subsidiary of the Austrian firm Zech Fenstra which has been making windows for over a century, sells energy-efficient PVC casement windows on the web for £70 per window – a local joiner might fit it for around £175. I have never been quoted less than £1200 (including fitting) for each of my wooden sash windows. Our living room's three-window bay alone will cost in the region of £5000. What kind of statement are we trying to make to people living in conservation areas who can't afford to replace their draughty windows with the handcrafted replacements – that they have to take out a second mortgage on their house, live in the cold, or move out of the area? With people like Angie it can quite literally be a matter of life and death. Each year around 20,000 more elderly people die in winter than in summer. Affordable insulation is not the only answer to this situation, but better windows and walls can be part of the answer.

It's the sash-ness rather than the wood-ness that costs the money. Our quotes for PVC sashes were around £1000 each, just 15 per cent less than the wood windows. But it's difficult to work out why the prices are so high. The pricing is mind-bogglingly opaque. The salesmen that traipsed through my home were prepared to evangelize about the most obscure minutiae about the finish, but became evasive when I asked for quotes on a room-by-room basis, or heaven forbid, particular windows. Why are they asking ten times more than the no-frills alternative. Is it all the extra ironmongery and carpentry required to make the sash window's counterweights? Or is it cynical market segmentation working on the assumption anyone living in a conservation zone is rich enough to afford the cost?

Flooring can be the cheapest part of the envelope to sort out, especially if undertaken at the same time as rewiring the house or installing under-floor heating

The last fold of the building's thermal envelope is the floor. This accounts for around 15 per cent of energy loss, because of their large surface area and the fact that the ground is itself a much better conductor of cold than the atmosphere. New houses need to achieve a U-value of 0.25 and modern houses' foundations consist of several layers to get the necessary strength, thermal insulation and watertightness to prevent heat loss and ward off damp. Typically the insulant is fitted on top of the concrete. Firms like Jablite, Knauf and Kingspan ('Kooltherm' range) make a range of products that meet very high thermal standards.

Older homes have suspended floors, with a void beneath the floorboards and the bare earth below that. The trick is to get insulation stuck tightly between the timber joists. This material is quite cheap, costing around £800 for a 50m² ground floor. You have to be sure the insulation is pressed right up to the floorboards. If you don't do this, air enters through the air bricks making the insulation almost redundant. The cost and complexity of this job depends entirely on the ease of access to the void between the joists. If the void is tall the insulation can be inserted from below. If the void is short the floorboards have to be lifted. The best time to do this is when the floorboards have to be lifted anyway – perhaps if the electric wiring is being replaced.

The right heating system

The average house uses 20,000kWh of heat per year. The most cost-effective way of making a substantial cut in emissions is by installing a gas condensing boiler which converts nearly all the energy in the fuel into useful warmth rather than discarding it into the atmosphere through the flue.

Building regulations require all new gas and oil boilers to be either A or B rated; in practice this means they have to be a good-quality gas condensing boiler. These are designed to extract energy not just from the heat of the flame, but also the heat trapped in the water vapour that is produced from the combustion of fuels.

Updating a long-in-the-tooth boiler is possibly the cheapest and most dramatic reduction you can make in energy use in the house. Most people only update their boilers when they break down. This results in ancient, and dreadfully inefficient old specimens still clunking along using far more gas to heat the water than a modern equivalent. Boilers should be replaced as soon as you've got the funds to do so. To understand this, look at Box 4.4 about why you should scrap a gas-guzzling car; it's the same logic.

Defra are so worried by people failing to update their boilers that they set up a website where the performance of many new and defunct boilers can be looked up. The website, www.sedbuk.com, sounds like the alien from Battlestar Galactica but has a lot of useful information. Good-condition non-condensing boilers are typically 78 per cent efficient, old, lighter boilers about 65 per cent and old, heavier boilers just 55 per cent. The newest A-rated boilers have an efficiency of 91 per cent – reducing gas use by between 15 per cent to 40 per cent. A small new boiler will cost around £2000 to buy and install, so it should pay back within four to eight years.

Gas condensing boilers have a mixed reputation and are regarded by some plumbers as being unreliable and expensive to maintain. This might have been true a decade ago but the technology has come on a lot since then. The then Energy-Efficiency Minister Larry Whitty made it compulsory to install gas condensing boilers and at the same time embarked on a Soviet style re-education programme to teach plumbers how to install and service the devices properly. The evidence of how gas condensing boilers operate in the field suggests they are working well. A recent study by academics from Leeds Metropolitan University shows the measured performance of boilers in 44 new homes to be 85–89 per cent, not quite the 91.3 per cent it says on the tin, but this is nowhere near as low as some of the horror stories that plumbers sometimes regale you with.[19]

Fuel switching and renewable energy sources

The other change you might be able to make to the heating system is to make sure you are using the most carbon-efficient sort of fuel. Most people rely on fossil fuels to provide the majority of their heat – principally gas. It hasn't always been like this. As recently as 1970 coal and coke made up half the heating fuel used by homes.[20] The demise of solid fuels has been rapid as the gas network has permeated through the cities and suburbs of the UK and as tighter clean air regulation has outlawed the use of dirty solid fuels. Gas supplanted dirtier fossil fuels in most homes long ago. There is some scope to further 'fuel switch' from electrical heating to gas – but this is probably quite limited since most people are forced to use electricity for heat because they are not able to connect to the gas network cost-effectively. Figure 5.7 shows the relative environmental performance of the different heat sources. The line for 'exhaust heat' shows the emissions associated with the heat lost through the flue. Heat pumps are explained below.

There are three main types of renewable heat that people can use in their homes: solar water heaters, biomass stoves or boilers which either burn wood chip or logs and ground/air/water source heat pumps which take heat from the outside and use it to heat a refrigerant which brings the heat inside. We

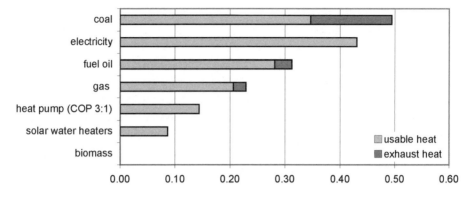

Figure 5.7 CO_2 emissions per kWh of heat from different fuel sources

Source: Guidelines to Defra's GHG conversion factors for company reporting.

can also avoid the need for artificial heating by designing and orientating windows and glass doors to capture heat from sunlight.

Not surprisingly, renewable heat sources like solar hot water, biomass and ground source heat pumps emit the least carbon. They are not necessarily carbon free. Ground source heat pumps and solar water heaters both use electricity to pump fluid to the roof and the outside environment.

Prices of fossil fuels have been rising and in summer 2008 the prices were 2p/kWh for gas, 7.7p/kWh for electricity and 5.1p/kWh for fuel oil. Wood fuel is sold by the bag and retails for the equivalent of 3.8p/kWh for an 80L bag of wood chip and 4.45p/kWh for wood pellets.[21]

Solar water heating is already commonplace in southern Europe

In the UK solar water heating is by far the most commonly used renewable energy source and was installed in 90,000 homes in 2007;[22] there are also around 2000 ground source heat pumps installed in the UK. No official figures are given for biomass heating. These technologies will become more common after 2016 when the government's zero-carbon homes policy kicks in and developers will be obliged to use these technologies in all new homes.

The three different renewable heat sources differ markedly in how much energy they can typically produce, when they produce energy, the temperature of heat generated and hence its usefulness.

Solar hot water systems are used to produce hot water for bathing and washing. On a warm summer's day when they're at their most effective they will probably produce more piping-hot water then you can use. They are not well suited to space heating because they produce little heat in winter when you need space heating. At UK latitudes, a December day has only a tenth of the energy of a mid-June day, because of shorter days and because the sun is much lower in the sky, though as I indicate in Box 5.1, if you adapt your central heating to use low-temperature heat, solar thermal can make a contribution even in winter.

Solar water heaters consist of a 'collector' mounted on a house's south-facing roof. There are two basic models. The *flat plate* system consists of black pipes through which flows the working fluid. These pipes are sandwiched between a glass plate on the top to stop heat escaping and an insulating material below. The *evacuated tube* system consists of rows of glass tubes each with separate absorber plates. These get much hotter than the plate systems. The newer evacuated tube models allow the tubes to be rotated so they can be orientated towards the sun on flat as well as pitched roofs. The working fluid might contain water mixed with ethylene or propylene glycol. The glycol acts as an antifreeze and increases the boiling point of the fluid, allowing it to heat up to much higher temperatures and improves its efficiency at harvesting the sunlight. Solar water heaters can supply 70 per cent or more of the hot water needs in summer. In winter they make only a modest contribution. According to the EST, over the year the panel will produce around 40 per cent of the hot water. The pumps used to propel the fluid around the pipework also consume power, which reduces the carbon saved by 10–20 per cent. A friend of mine used a small photovoltaic panel to power the pump. (However, the installer didn't site the PV panel correctly so it was shaded for much of the day and didn't generate enough electricity to power the pumps! You have to keep an eye on the contractors.)

The solar water heater needs a hot water cylinder to store the water that is produced in daylight hours, and also a heat exchanger to transfer heat from the working fluid to the water in the tank. It can be quite a nuisance fitting a solar water heater in an older home, partly because you have to find the space to site the hot water cylinder and associated pipework and partly because of the cost of running the pipes up and down the house and possibly also erecting scaffolding. You can buy solar panels installed from B&Q with the hot water cylinder and heat exchanger for about £5000 for a 2 × 1m panel. It's much cheaper if you can arrange the installation yourself. The value of the gas saved is around £70 per year or more if gas prices keep on increasing, or something like 300kgCO_2 per year.

Ground and air source heat pumps make a lot of sense if you live off the gas grid

Ground source heat pumps (GSHPs) are a novel technology in the UK, but are well established in other countries. It is an amazingly counter-intuitive technology that takes a little time to get your head around. The best analogy I can come up with is Guinness's tipping point advert in which a falling domino sets off a chain of collapse through tyres, mattresses even cars, liberating the energy from the standing objects to trigger bigger and bigger discharges of energy as they fall. Similarly GSHPs do not create heat, they simply transfer existing heat from outside the house (making the outside colder) to the inside, using the condensing and boiling of refrigerants to move the heat. Heat pump-based systems use hot water cylinders to store hot water for showers and baths, because they cannot suddenly generate large amounts of heat.

Ground source heat pumps need a reasonable-sized garden for burying the pipes, and also an appropriate point of access for the digging equipment. In many terrace houses there is no feasible way of getting the machinery into the back garden, which is a bit of a showstopper. The cost of digging the trench can be in excess of £5000. In Sweden, where about 10 per cent of homes use ground source heat pumps, they make use of pile drivers as big as a two-storey building to bore a deep shaft to house the vertical coils. With a ground source heat pump you can expect around 5 units of heat (at 35°C) out

---

Box 5.6 *Renewable energy sources are most cost-effective if you use electricity or heating oil*

Tony lives in a farm-worker's cottage with his family. The building is listed by English Heritage which limits the changes they are allowed to make to the windows and outside walls. The stone floor in the kitchen and hall make it easy to keep clean, perfect considering the amount of mud and water they pick up from outside – but a lot of heat is lost through the floor of the cottage, especially in the winter. They warm the house with an oil-fired central heating system and small wood stove in the living room. The stove takes time to turn on so they mainly use it on winter weekends, so at least one room can be kept warm. They get fuel either from the farm or buy it in from nearby farms. They currently spend £1200 per year buying oil and servicing their boiler. It emits around 7 tonnes of CO_2 every year.

Tony has looked into various options to make his home still more carbon efficient and bring costs down. He's got plenty of space in the garden to lay or sink the pipes for a ground source heat pump and the cost of laying the pipes was considerable but affordable. The new Ecodan range of air source heat pumps by Mitsubishi is also an option. If the air source heat pump performs as well as the sales brochure claims and they schedule it so it runs more intensively at night on an Economy-7 tariff, it's possible they might get their extra electricity costs down to £400 per year and emissions from the electricity will be just 3tCO_2 – quite a marked saving. But what is presently putting him off is the cost of installing under-floor insulation and heating which will require the lifting of their tiles – this will cost several thousand pounds but, once the switch is made, will save money for decades.

for every unit of electricity you put in. They are no good if you want to heat water to 65°C to use in a radiator and are currently using gas central heating, as you'll only see a heat gain of 2.5 – which is not worth having economically nor environmentally given the high cost and carbon content of electricity compared to gas. For this reason most people advocate using GSHP with under-floor heating which can warm a house using much lower-temperature water than radiators. Ground source heat pumps are a no-brainer if you only use electrical resistance or storage heaters.

Air source heat pumps (ASHPs) are similar to GSHPs, the only difference being that the outside air rather than the soil is used to warm up the cold refrigerant. The temperature of the deep ground tends to be fairly constant throughout the year, making it well suited to heat pumps. The outside air in winter is neither warm nor a good conductor of heat which is why air source heat pumps are less efficient than ground or water source pumps. Mitsubishi has recently launched an air source heat pump in the UK market which it claims produces 3.6kWh of heat for every kWh of electricity it uses. The units cost up to £2300 for the house-size units. If substantiated, this makes the technology around 30 per cent more efficient than gas condensing boilers, and fairly affordable. ASHP make sense if you are off the gas grid, don't want a ground source heat pump and have to use expensive fuel oil or bottled gas for your heating. One big benefit of collecting heat from the outside air is that it avoids the need to dig trenches or shafts. Air source heat pumps have big fans to transfer the heat from the refrigerant to the atmosphere, which means noisy outdoor motors. According to the Green Company the level of noise is 37 decibels at a distance of 5m away, which is a little quieter than people talking.

Biomass makes little sense in cities, requiring road transport of large quantities of wood, but it makes sense in rural areas, especially if you have reliable access to local wood

The other renewable source of heat is biomass. Obtaining heat from wood dates back to the days of the Flintstones, but that's not to say the technology hasn't changed quite a lot since the Neolithic times. Stringent air quality regulations mean that the boilers are designed to minimize emissions of local air pollutants like soot. Boilers are also much more efficient, able to convert around 80 per cent of the energy in the wood into usable heat, unlike old-fashioned chimneys which made a much more direct contribution to global warming. Larger units also have mechanical apparatus to automatically feed wood chips or pellets into the flame, avoiding the need to chuck in logs every hour. On mainland Europe the use of biomass is well established, especially in Austria, Germany and Scandinavia. The same isn't true in the UK, where there are only a handful of companies with much experience in installing biomass boilers. It's important to pick a business that knows what it's doing. There are many horror stories of boilers being installed which are either too big or far too small for the property, or without adequate thought being given to whether there is a reliable and affordable source of fuel nearby. Having to drive 30 miles to buy a sack of pellets rather undermines the whole rationale for purchasing the device.

Wood fuels are currently cheaper to buy than electricity or fuel oil, but not as cheap as gas. If you're living in a city subject to smokeless zone restrictions, you are restricted in the models that you can buy.

There are a number of decisions you have to make before going for biomass. First there is the choice of whether you want a simple stove just to heat a single room (or to heat a room and cook on too if you are buying an Aga) or one with a back boiler to provide energy for central heating and hot water needs. A simple wood-burning stove costs around £1000 to buy and another £1000 to install. It can stand in the living room looking decorous and produces more than enough heat to keep the living room and hall warm. The fuel is relatively inexpensive and many models are fairly catholic in their appetite accepting wood and other solid fuels. They are around 80 per cent efficient at converting wood into energy; not as good as condensing technologies but much better than they used to be. Then there is the choice of fuel: logs, wood chip or pellets. Wood pellets are small tubes 0.5–1.0cm long that look like rabbit food and are made from compressed sawdust and wood. They are made to strict standards for size and moisture content which extends the life expectancy of the stove and means they deliver a predictable amount of heat. Automatic loading systems need wood pellets or wood chips.

Fetching and storing the fuel is a significant issue. A tonne of wood pellets occupies 1.5m^3 and in heating a big house you can get through 200kg a week or 2–3 tonnes of pellets in a winter. The fire also produces a small amount of ash which needs to be cleaned out every two weeks.

Biomass offers the opportunity to entirely decarbonize heating needs in the home. It still requires energy to grow, process and transport. One review of life-cycle analyses undertaken by the Scottish government suggests that life-cycle emissions of GHG from wood chip are only about 5 per cent those of gas,[23] because of the low level of processing and transport needed to make heating fuels – compared to say transport fuels.

Grants for domestic renewable energy in the UK are a bit hit and miss. Local authorities sometimes offer a grant. Central government does too from time to time. In 2008 BERR made a fresh injection of £10 million into the Low Carbon Building Scheme which has been administered by the Energy Saving Trust since 2006 and the Building Research Establishment more recently. The grant is paid in arrears to a maximum of 30 per cent of the value of the installation on a list of approved products. If there was ever a contest to design a

Table 5.3 Pros and cons of the different micro-generation heat technologies

Heat source	Solar water heating	Ground source heat pump	Air source heat pump	Biomass stove	Biomass boiler
Suitable for	Houses/flats with SE–SW-facing roofs	Homes with space in gardens for loop/borehole, under-floor heating recommended	Space for external unit (0.5m² footfall), some external noise, under-floor heating	Needs access to fuel source, need to adapt flue	Space for storing wood chip/pellets, local fuel source, need to adapt flue
Type of heat provided	Hot water only: 70% summer, 10% winter	Central heating only: warm water up to 40°C	Central heating only: warm water up to 40°C	Room heating	Central heating and hot water
Installed capital cost (£)	3000–5000	6000–12,000	6000–8000	2000–4000	5000–14,000
Installation issues	Need hot water cylinder and possibly new boiler	Hot water cylinder, borehole cost c£8000	Hot water cylinder, under-floor heating, external fan	Need to adapt new flue	Need wood store and new flue
Fuel costs	Very low power needed to pump water	COP[a] 1:3.5 to power compressors and pumps 2p/kWh[b]	COP[a] 1:4 to power compressors, pumps and air fan 2.3 p/kWh[b]	Ranges from 4p/kWh wood – 5p/kWh pellets	5p/kWh pellets
Central government grants	Lower of £400 or 30% of cost	Lower of £1200 or 30% of costs	Lower of 30% of cost or £900	£600 or 20% of cost	Lower of £1500 or 30% of cost
Carbon saving per house (tCO₂/yr) if replacing gas	0.3	1.7	1.5	0.2 if replaces 10% of space heating needs	3

Notes: [a] COP – coefficient of performance: ratio of electricity needed to heat produced; assumes heat is extracted at 40°C for under-floor heating; [b] Economy-7 tariff can halve electricity cost.

Source: Various; costs are from BERR website.

grant programme to ossify the industry and increase uncertainty this would win first prize. It has always been dogged by difficulties. For about a year money was allocated on a month by month basis, but this was grabbed faster than touts making a beeline for Rolling Stones concert tickets. In March 2007 funds ran out 75 minutes after midnight – evoking visions of bleary eyed environmentalists, their RSI-gnarled fingers all hitting the return keys to send out their completed application forms in record times. Much of the earmarked money was never actually spent because homeowners found they could not get clearance to install the equipment in the short window of time they had to spend the money.

Table 5.3 summarizes the strengths and weaknesses of the different options. Most of these technologies are much easier to install in new-build than existing homes.

Another low-carbon technology that gets some people very excited is micro-CHP using the Sterling engine, or in the longer term using fuel cells. I personally have never seen the attraction. The idea behind micro-CHP is that the household makes its own power from gas, and uses the low temperature heat that is unsuitable for power generation to supply its hot water needs. Small-scale power plants extract less than half of the energy available in natural gas leaving a third of perfectly usable heat, which could be used to meet our hot water demands. All sounds very promising until you see the mismatch between a house's heat and power needs. A typical home will only use about 1kW of power at any moment of time, but needs 10–15kW of heat during winter and barely anything the rest of the year. As a result there is only one micro-CHP that is anywhere near market ready: the fleetingly available Whispergen. It is essentially an inefficient boiler which does some moonlighting as a power plant (output of around 9kW of heat and 1kW of electricity). This lopsided configuration is costly – some £3000, compared to £600 for a similar boiler. It'll also be hard to find anyone able to fit it – the installer will need to be proficient in both gas and electrical fitting.

Research is also under way on fuel cell-based micro-CHP which produces much more power. No costs are available yet for this technology, and mismatch and seasonality of heat demand will be a problem for this technology too. I am a big fan of CHP but not at the micro-scale.

My Actions to Reduce the House's Emissions

Where is heat being lost from the house?

The first step was to work out where energy was being lost in the house to try and work out my priorities. The EPC audit and some subsequent measurement had given me quite a lot of data to play around with. I worked out the heat loss through conduction and convection (from the pressure test results). The house is quite draughty, but I was pleasantly surprised to find the pressure test measured the air loss to be 15.5m³ per m² area per hour – not that much worse than for a new home. Table 5.4 shows where heat is being lost from the materials that make up the envelope of my house.[24] If you are interested in calculating your own figures you can use the information in Table 5.2 which has some of the U-values of different types of wall, floor, window and roof. Annex 1 gives the U-values of possible replacement materials.

Table 5.4 Sources of heat loss in my house

	Area (m²)	U-value (W/m²/°C)	Heat loss (W/°C)	Proportion of heat loss
Walls	72	2.1	152	32%
Windows	20	4.8	96	20%
Door	1.4	2	3	1%
Floor	52	1.2	62	13%
Pitched roof	68	0.7	46	10%
Total conduction heat loss			360	75%
* Draughts			118	25%
Total	214		478	

Note: * Draughts derived from the worksheet in the SAP procedure manual.

The penultimate column in Table 5.4 gives the amount of heat loss over the average year, assuming 2500 degree-days (illustrative figures given in the Annex to this chapter) of heating need a year and a boiler efficiency of 80 per cent. The fact we are getting by with so much less reiterates either how cold-toughened we are (not true) or how little time we spend indoors at home (more like it).

The heat loss by source is fairly similar to that shown in Figure 5.4. All that number crunching and measurement reveals is that we are basically Mr and Mrs Average. The biggest source of heat loss is the solid brick wall, entirely by dint of its large surface area. Due to the 'L-shaped' extension, two-thirds of the wall area is at the back of the house. The windows are not particularly large but they have appalling energy efficiency, and are the source of much of our draughts too. The roof is well insulated with little scope for further improvement. About a quarter of the heat is lost from draughts.

My priority is to get the best reduction in CO_2 emissions, without hurting the value of the house. We have savings, so as a rule we will finance any improvements that either save money in the long term, or which add to the value of the house. And I don't want to give up too much of our internal space.

We have 32m length of external wall so a 10cm thick layer of internal insulation will take out 3.2m² which is equivalent to £20,000 of floor space given the bonkers prices of homes in North London (at least at the start of the 2008, if not at the end). It'll also make our already narrow bathroom and kitchen even more squashed.

There are a couple of changes that are relative no-brainers: installing an A-rated gas condensing boiler and draught-proofing the house. Double-glazing the windows and insulating the walls (from the outside) are both expensive but could make a real difference. Over the course of the time I wrote this book we also converted the loft which offered a great opportunity to install solar thermal.

Renewable technologies

Because we were converting our loft while this book was being written, it seemed the ideal time to install solar water heating on the roof – the scaffolding would be there, and we could design the rooms to accommodate the hot water cylinder. It looked as though we were eligible for grants from BERR and also Camden.

I got a local company in to provide a quote. The solar technology sounded pretty amazing – it would fit on the flat part of our loft conversion, the design of the tubes allowed the heat collecting surface to be tilted towards the south irrespective of the direction of the roof. Because it was on the flat part of the roof, it would not be visible from the road and therefore raised no issue with the conservation zone rules. The 2m² of vacuum tube was capable of collecting 900kWh which would meet about 9 per cent of our current gas consumption.

The solar supplier gave us a very reasonable-sounding quote. The cost of the panel, the pipework to transfer the heat carrier between the water tank and the collector came to £3000 inclusive of VAT. The Low Carbon Building Programme was offering us a grant of £400 and Camden a further £1000. The savings from avoiding gas use would be around some £30 per year; so quite a long payback.

We then got in touch with a plumber about the costs of fitting the hot water cylinder and the associated pipework to link the cylinder with the boiler in the kitchen. We had an inkling of what was ahead of us when he walked us through the house with that 'it'll cost'cha' look about him. 'Your problem is the layout of the kitchen where your combi-boiler is located, relative to the positioning of the panel, and the hot water cylinder.'

'But the scaffolding will already be up so that will reduce the cost of installing things', I say plaintively. He looks at me as though this comment was about as relevant as being told that Genghis Khan had issues with anger management. A few weeks elapsed and the plumber failed to send me a quote. I called and it turned out he'd lost our details and would have to come and measure up again (this was a recurrent theme, for many of the trades). We had the same hand-wringing exposition about the unsuitability of our home's layout … we'd have to drill through your bathroom tiles, don't know what you might find when you start drilling, you see. A few days later we got the quote. The cost of an upgraded boiler, cylinder and pipework was £4500, on top of the solar system. So the cylinder and pipework needed to transfer the hot water from the panel down to the boiler was the most expensive part of the package; and there were no grants or reduced rate of VAT for this cost.

In the end my wife pulled the plug on the idea; it was the space require-ments for the cylinder that finished us off. With a footfall of around $1m^2$, with lots of ugly piping needed to link the expansion vessel, antifreeze/water reservoir, etc., she declared this town just wasn't big enough for her and the cylinder.

We drew a blank with the other solar technologies too. Heat pumps were unsuitable because of the lack of access for the ground loop and because we do not have under-floor heating. We live in inner city London so biomass was a non-starter as far as I was concerned. So we ended up giving up on all the renewable heat technologies.

Boiler

The Green Concierge looked up the efficiency of my existing boiler for me. It was a ten-year-old Worcester Bosch that worked fine and as far as I could tell would carry on working for some years yet. Plumbers who came and inspected it salivated whenever they saw it. It had a great reputation, was reliable, would never break down, etc., etc. But it would have to go. With a seasonal SAP rating of just 70 per cent, it performed nowhere near as well as the best A-rated gas condensing boilers and their SAP seasonal ratings of 91 per cent. The other advantage with the new boiler was that it had better controls – including a room thermostat, which the old one lacked.

The plumber also fitted a couple of thermostatic radiator valves in rooms where these were absent. The whole thing came to £2000 including VAT and would probably reduce emissions by 25 per cent. Energy is needed to make the boiler. I am not aware of any life-cycle analysis of the emissions arising from this, but it weighs 40kg, the production of a tonne of steel emits $2.2tCO_2$, so roughly 100kg of CO_2 would be emitted from my new boiler (though the recycling of the old boiler would save carbon too). I comforted myself that the replacement of the boiler would redeem its own carbon emissions of produc-tion in about two months.

Draught exclusion

The next recommendation was draught-proofing our doors, windows and loft hatch. I have tried putting DIY foam draught excluders in previous houses before. I found they kept the draughts out fairly well, but they made the doors harder to close and lock. They also started peeling off after a few years. Our next-door neighbours had got the professionals in. A groove was chiselled around the door and some wonderfully discrete brushes slipped in. It cost them a fortune though.

A friend had had her house in Birmingham professionally draught-proofed for just £200. I phoned the Green Concierge to find a firm to do the same for me. The firm uses a patented silicon-based sealant which is applied around each door and window. Once dry the seal cleverly allows the window to open and close – forming a close bond, but without actually sticking the two surfaces together. The product had a good write-up from researchers in the Building Research Establishment (BRE).[25] The BRE had tested the product in houses similar to ours, and it had reduced air loss by a third. However, the company was not proposing to deal with the gaps in the floorboards, or the other losses of air in the house which I suspected were much more important. I said I looked forward to their quote. But I more or less gagged on my cornflakes when it arrived. It was four times bigger than the figure suggested on their website. Surely they must have got a decimal place wrong. I called to sort out the error, but the lady who (wo)manned the phone said: 'The price is correct.' I spluttered we're talking about taking a few tubes of sealant and applying it around the windows, loft hatch and doors. They were taking us for a ride because we lived in a posh neighbourhood. Nor was she impressed when I pointed out the quoted savings in emissions of $237kgCO_2$ in an average three-bedroom house sounded optimistic. I made the figure more like 170kg once we installed a gas condensing boiler. This is equivalent to around £30 of gas per year – giving a payback of more than 40 years. She sighed, sounding as though she bore a pained expression, as though she hated smarty-pants.

If it wasn't for the fact it couldn't be bought directly from the manufacturer but only through registered installers we wouldn't be having this conversation at all. I muttered something about Office of Fair Trading and abuse of monopoly and hung up.

Draught-proofing of doors and windows is usually regarded as a DIY activity. I have a pathological aversion to DIY, or more specifically to DIY shops. But it looked as though we'd have to go down that route too. Our local one (a half-hour drive – giving rise to emissions around $3kgCO_2$) did not disappoint. It was full of men with a disconcerting proclivity to debate the merits of different gauges of wood, and pensioners with all the time in the world blocking up the aisles. It wasn't helped by the fact only one member of staff in the 2500m² shed actually knew anything about the products.

Three of us stood around the customer information desk for half an hour waiting for Sanjay, a man who made Godot look punctual. To hold the terrible silence at bay we made polite conversation about the merits of different gauges of wood. I got home three hours later; twice the time I expected. The materials I bought: 10m of white rubber seal and a brush for the front door. This only cost £16 and took about half a day to install ... and reinstall so my wife could open the door. I decided not to bother with the windows as we would get them double glazed. Blocking the chimneys was straightforward using chimney balloons which cost around £20 each. I only needed to buy one as the other three chimneys were already fitted with thick cast iron flaps which I had never noticed before; the howling gales we had endured through last winter had been avoidable if I had bothered to bend down and look into the chimney. The tedious holes in the back wall that generations of builders had excavated were cemented easily enough. The last major loss of air was between the floorboards. I bought 160m of a product called Gapseal for £35. This is pushed into the cracks between the floorboards and it expands to fill the space. It works very well and was probably the most effective change I made.

So we managed to sort out all the leaks in the house for around £85. I estimate that heat loss from leakages will cost me around £70 per year after the gas condensing boiler is installed, so this should make good economic sense as well as saving up to 460kgCO_2e per year, depending on how the house performs in the airtightness test.

Not bad going.

Windows

Our house has seven single-glazed sash windows which are large and bright but leak out heat like colanders; they are all either draughty because they no longer close properly, or not draughty since they've been painted over and don't open at all. We have a further seven casement windows fitted in our 1970s extension. These are also single glazed and two of them are rotting and need to be replaced. We decided to retain them for now – and deal with them in a year or two when we've saved up enough to extend the kitchen.

Double-glazing the windows won't save me much money. My calculations suggest they account for maybe 30 per cent of heat losses; but that's barely £85 of gas per year. The best windows would reduce this to £20 a year, which is a fantastic drop. But the cost of replacing our 16 windows runs into well over £15,000 – way over the top to save just £65 of gas every year. An economical environmentalist has to focus on how changing a house's windows will effect the resale value of the house; the value of the energy saving is more or less irrelevant. If we wish to eventually market the house as an *eco-conversion* the least any purchaser will expect is double glazing. I've spent a few afternoons showing people around a local eco-refurbishment of a Victorian home. The double-glazed wooden sash windows were easily the most popular change. People were almost drooling at the way they fitted so snugly in the box, how they retained their character, that their vertical movement up and down the box was so stately and elegant. I will never be able to fathom such people, but I will one day have to sell my house to them; I better take note of what they like. The quality and authenticity of the finish was of critical importance to them. They buy homes in the conservation area because they care about these things.

The other advantage of double-glazed windows is that it provides sound insulation. Sound doesn't much bother me usually but we have a barmy moped rider who insists on racing up and down our street at three in the morning; anything to blot him out of my sleep would be welcome.

The Green Concierge provided us with the names of two installers. We got both companies to measure us up. We also found an architect who imported some Passivhaus windows from Germany. Last, we got a quote from our local joiner, asking him to make up some double-glazed panes, and use the existing boxes which were still in good condition.

The local joiner gave the best price for the sash windows so we decided to go with him. The quote for the six windows was £6500, undercutting the Green Concierge recommendations by about £4000. We were all set to go with the Passivhaus triple-glazed casement windows in our four extension windows. The U-value was an eye-watering 0.7. But then sterling went into freefall against the euro, greatly increasing the cost of the imported windows; and the recommended fitter came in with an expensive quote. So we instead went with the Green Concierge recommendation. These ten windows represent about half of our glazed areas. The other half was either in our recent loft conversion, or would be done when we updated the kitchen.

But the local joiner worried me. We'd already experienced difficulties with him. He was reluctant to give us the names of any of his local clients, excusing himself by saying he only ever worked as a subcontractor so never knew the end customer himself. Reluctantly he owned up to installing windows in the neighbouring street, but the Data Protection Act conveniently forbade him from telling us which house. 'I understand', I said soothingly. As soon as he'd gone we walked up and down the street till we spotted the house. I can be an undercover economist too. 'Is your mummy home?' we asked the incredibly well-spoken 13 year old. 'We're not trying to sell you double glazing, honest.' When the joiner came to do the final measurement, I walked around the house with him listening as he kept sucking air through his teeth and nodding his head gravely. 'No', he exclaimed, 'the boxes aren't wide enough to take the thicker panes.' My eyes rolled. 'I'm not trying to be funny, but this is the fourth time you and your colleague have been to our house. Didn't you by chance notice this before you quoted us a price? OK, how much will the new boxes cost?' His revised price was still quite good, but there was still the matter of finding someone who would vouch for the quality of his work.

While waiting for him to furnish some pukka credentials, I googled another company that claimed they could install new panes in existing window frames by using a revolutionary approach to double glazing which replaced argon with krypton and xenon as the filler gases and used warm spacer technology. As a result their panes had reasonably good U-value (but nowhere near as good as the Passivhaus casements) and were skinny enough to fit in existing boxes, bringing their price down. I told him to come and give us a quote, and also the difficulties in parking around Camden, so he would have to come in the afternoon; 'No worries man. I'll bike over, or come by tube. Vans emit so much CO_2.' I was in love – professionally speaking. He gave a quote for £7000 and we decided to go with him.

Walls

Our walls are our home's largest source of heat loss. Other people I have spoken to who have performed eco-conversions on old solid wall homes have installed internal insulation to avoid changing the external look. Normally they go for a depth of 5cm, which is less insulation than ideal, but neces-sary to avoid losing too much internal space. Their walls were in a poor state of repair, which meant they had to strip the plaster in any event. The inside walls of my own house are in good condition and the cost and nuisance of replastering would be prohibitive. Nor can we spare the space in some of the smaller rooms.

As a result I was keen to install external insulation, at least on the large back wall which is in any case not visible from the street. We obtained a quote from a company that specialized in external insulation. The salesman was a bit bemused at the idea of retrofitting a house such as ours. 'We normally do social housing – or new build', he said sagely. 'You'll never get planning permission.'

Their cheaper quote was £8000 for a white render finish on all our external walls; they also offered a brick slip finish but this was substantially more. They claimed the insulation could reduce the wall's U-value from around 2.8 to 0.3, making it comparable to new build. Such a measure would shave a third off my conduction losses and save around £120 per year in gas. This is much more cost-effective than double glazing.

I spoke to the planning department informally, showed them the mater-ials I planned to use and photographs of my own home and those of my neighbours. Their response was surprisingly un-negative, almost deadpan, belying their unstated fear that applying external insulation to the back of the property would turn the Conservation Area into Sodom and Gomorrah. I reproduce their email:

As previously expressed I am concerned that the proposed insulation would have a detrimental impact on the dwelling and terrace and fail to preserve the character or appearance of the Conservation Area. The brick sample shown in the attached pictures would result in the external appearance of the building that has a different brick bond, gauge, colour and texture and mortar mix and depth than the remaining buildings in the terrace. ... The Council welcomes all attempts to improve the energy efficiency of properties within the borough however there needs to be a balance between sustainability and preserving the character and appearance of the area. You may wish to consider using the render style insulation on the rear of the property.

The last sentence gave me some hope. I phoned to find out what they meant by the statement. The duty officer argued weakly that solid brick walls were actually pretty good insulators, and was unsure why I was making a fuss. This is when I got a little impatient and said something to the effect that some of us were more concerned with saving the planet than pacifying the local NIMBYs, she should go and read the council's own CO_2 reduction targets. It was probably around then we agreed the issues between us weren't about to be resolved over the phone, and I would have to complete a planning application form.

Incidentally the planning application form produced by Communities and Local Government (CLG) is ten pages long, and the application fee is £150. It makes the HM Revenue and Customs tax return seem a model of bureaucratic restraint. There are boxes to fill in about foul sewage, flood risk, biodiversity and geological conservation, trade effluent, industrial processes ... the list goes on; all this to apply 10cm of material to the back of a house visible to six other homes and a few US spy satellites. One wonders why the take-up of energy efficiency remains so low.

Floor

The surface area of our floor is about three-quarters that of our walls. As a result we lose something like 15 per cent of our heat through the floor. After speaking to other eco-renovators I wanted to undertake one sizeable job for myself, using my hands rather than my Visa card. Of all the jobs the floor seemed the easiest. From reading websites like www.greenbuilder.com, all I had to do was lift the floorboards, nail some netting to the underside of the joists and either stuff the gap with insulating wool, or cut some blocks of insulating material. Box 5.7 shows you how far I got with the idea.

Box 5.7 *DIY eco-renovation of the floor*

After visiting Peter and Sigrid's house and talking to two other people who had done eco-conversions of their own home, I was determined to install a major energy-saving measure – and do it myself. Gavin Killip had lopped off 65 per cent of his house's emissions by insulating his house himself for £7000.[26] He told me: 'It was no harder than putting up an Ikea wardrobe – just a bit more nerve racking when you stop and think you're tearing chunks out of a £250,000 house. But if I hadn't done it myself I couldn't really understand or write about the process.'

I can do Ikea, I said, goading myself into the kind of eco-religious ecstasy that whirling dervishes probably get into after their 50th spin. I sped around the house to find a DIY project I could try out. The boiler was out: it would kill us if I screwed up. The windows and walls were way beyond my ability. I finally settled into the living room and stared triumphantly at the timber floorboards we had recently had sanded and varnished. I put a piece of tissue paper over the gap between the timbers and inferred a slight flutter in the paper. 'I'll start with insulating beneath the floorboards', I yelled to my wife before rolling up my sleeves. How on Earth were they held down? There were no screws visible. 'I think they're glued to the joists.' I'd just learned the word 'joist' five minutes ago on the maiden outing of our 1990 edition of the *Reader's Digest* DIY guide, which Mum and Dad had bought me when I bought my first home, two decades ago.

'Are you sure you want to do this? Why don't we just get someone in to do it?'

'What do you mean?' I said indignantly. I felt my own confidence flutter – with the mechanical competence of Homer Simpson and the attention to detail of Bart, was I really going to pull this off?

My wife bent down and saw something I'd missed. 'Look they're nailed down.' She pointed to a small black mark on the wood which I had taken for staining. 'So they are … the nails look ancient.' I went to the hardware store, demanding a crowbar so I could manfully lift up the floorboards. The assistant handed me a skinny, wide floor chisel. 'This should do the trick.' It took me a further two hours to locate a floorboard far enough away from its neighbour that I could slide the chisel under, but in a few minutes I had lifted my first floorboard. All the nails snapped as I pulled the floorboard up. I peered into the void. 30cm below the floorboards was soil and rubble. The joists looked black and charred like they'd come out of a forest fire. I put the floorboard back – it had taken me just over three hours to lift it. Not bad – it'd get easier once I had established a production line. We had a couple of people over for lunch in an hour's time, and it was my turn to cook.

After the main course our guests and I gravely crowded around the floorboard; there were three lawyers, a sociologist and an engineer and myself. The hole was again opened and they appreciated the void below, floored by rubble, bits of glass and sweet wrappers. 'Didn't know the Victorians ate KitKats', one of us commented. This was the closest any of us had ever got to messing around with the structure of our house, despite living on the planet for 240 years between us. 'Should we get back to pudding ... it's tiramisu. I think I'll get someone in to do it', I finally conceded.

Bringing It All Together

So what did all this achieve? Figure 5.8 shows the changes I have either already made or plan to make over the next few years. The figures are calculated as though we used the 'standard' amount of heat, i.e. that we kept the house warm all day and heated it to 18.9°C. We only use a third of this so the information below differs from that produced in earlier chapters which is based on our true pattern of energy use.

Figure 5.8 assumes we have double-glazed *all* our windows and installed solid wall insulation – something we are still debating. The graph shows the potential saving we expect to achieve, rather than the actual savings. Ultimately we can reduce our energy use by around two-thirds.

So how much did it all cost and was it worth it? Table 5.5 shows the savings in CO_2 and money that would arise every year, again assuming we used *the standard amount* of energy; it excludes the costs and carbon savings for the four downstairs windows we have decided to leave for a few years and for

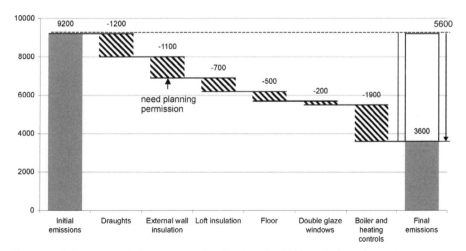

Figure 5.8 Summary of the proposed reductions in GHG emissions from changes, $kgCO_2/yr$

Table 5.5 Reductions in energy spending and emissions from my house, using standard assumptions for heating demand

	% saving where installed	Emissions from heat loss		Carbon saved	Saving	Cost
		(kgCO$_2$)		(kgCO$_2$)	£/yr	£
		Before	Installed			
Walls	66%	2100	1200	900	120	7800
Windows	67%	1300	1000	300	50	9500
Door	0%	0	0	0	0	0
Floor	75%	900	400	500	60	2200
Roof	72%	1000	300	700	90	0
Air flow	75%	1600	400	1200	160	85
Heat gain[a]		1200	1200			
New loft wall		0	100	−100	−20	0
New loft window		0	100	−100	−10	0
Total room heating	68%	5800	2300	3500	440	19,585
Hot water	0%	700	700	0	0	0
Boiler losses	23%	2800	200[b]	2600	480	2000
Total heat and water	78%	9200	2000	6100	930	21,585
Gas bill (£/yr)	78%	1190	260			

Notes: [a] Heat gain: heat provided by waste heat from electricity use, people and sun.
[b] Boiler losses after treatments are so low, because of the better boiler and lower use of gas.

which we have no quote. Over the course of the year we also had a loft conversion which increased our floor area by a half, but curiously reduced our heat need because it was so much better insulated than our old loft. The net effect of the new roof and walls was to save £60 per year on gas.

Table 5.5 shows that £21,600 of spending would reduce our emissions (and gas bills) by 78 per cent from 9.2tCO$_2$ to around 2tCO$_2$. This is a huge saving, which lasts for as long as the windows and wall remain in good repair. The different rows of the table give some indication of the relative cost-effectiveness of the different changes. The windows are the most expensive change and won't recoup their value for two centuries at present energy prices. Draught-proofing is at the other end of the spectrum where the investment will be recouped in six months.

Overall, the gas bill is reduced by £930 per year at a cost of £21,500 – a payback period of 23 years; a return of 4.3 per cent. Altogether they'll change the house from its 'E' rating on the EPC to a 'C' rating. The house will also feel nicer. In particular, the under-floor insulation makes the downstairs more bearable in winter.

There are two flaws in the above table. The first is that our household uses much less energy than the standard assumptions and our savings will be correspondingly lower. Instead of being £260 a year they'll be more like £80 a year – implying a rate of return for the package of 1.4 per cent. Not a figure that would normally get a hedge fund manager's mouth salivating. Is this worth doing? Some of our grandparents, who lived through the depression, squirrelled away their savings under pillows, a zero per cent return. This wasn't necessarily because they had gone ga-ga – but maybe because the failure of banks in the 1930s has left such a strong impression on them. Putting some of your savings into your home today might also be a good hedge against risk. The years 2007 and 2008 have seen the failure and nationalization of many banks, share prices and dividends collapse, the yield on fixed income bonds wilt to zero per cent in real terms (at the time of writing the UK government's National Savings was offering just 3 per cent for its five-year bonds, the same as inflation). If you believe, as I do, that the price of gas (which is how the return in investment in energy efficiency is paid out) will rise faster than the rate of inflation, then economically speaking it *is* worth investing in the above package, despite the miserable rate of return. Believe it or not, it's actually higher than other risk-free investments.

The second flaw is that the investment might not be risk free and that reality might disappoint. The figures are based on the energy-efficiency measures delivering the thermal improvements claimed by the manufacturers. In reality many might underperform because of poor workmanship or unforeseen issues. That is what construction is like. I'll keep my website posted on how my gas bill changes.

The other great unknown is how these changes will affect the property price. Here I am optimistic. Many people have been interested and admiring of our efforts to improve our home's energy efficiency. The new EPC will help give these efforts official recognition, even though I'll probably have to pay for a full SAP assessment rather than the standard off-the-shelf measurement. Homes in energy-efficient developments like BedZed trade at a premium relative to similar-sized houses in the same postcode, because of the cachet in more sustainable homes. Eco-renovations, I hope, will have the same cachet.

But overall it's hard to say the process has been easy. While we were undertaking the eco-improvements we also had our loft converted. The two experiences couldn't have been more different. The latter process was streamlined and efficient. A succession of professions and trades: architects, party-wall surveyors, fitters, plumbers, electricians, roofers and decorators seamlessly came and did their thing. Hardly any time was wasted. So in three months the loft was converted and ready for use for a price we thought reasonable. Some of the work was done off site, such as reproducing the downstairs banisters using sophisticated equipment that used laser-cutting technology to copy our downstairs pattern. We were delighted with the results.

The same could not be said for the eco-renovation; throughout, there was a significant level of project management skill needed to ensure tasks were scheduled in the correct order and done to a good standard. Some of the measures are unnecessarily complicated to implement because of the difficulty of finding contractors willing to do the work and obtaining consents from the council. The process of collecting the quotes took the best part of six months. Over that time we had umpteen reschedules and no-shows. Our experience of trying to install double-glazed windows was the most extreme. The window fitter we almost selected was hesitant about providing references that we could actually call on and see. Three firms came to measure up, but never followed up with a quote because they lost the measurements (two of whom I insisted come again). One had to remeasure the windows three times (and the first tentative quote he proffered us, bless him, was for 15 windows rather than the 10 that we actually wanted fitted). How many other people would be prepared to go through with this?

The government has spoken about installation of energy efficiency as being a high priority. There is certainly space in the market for an enterprising company to provide an integrated service to install a similar suite of draught-proofing and energy-efficiency measures, fit new boilers and update controls, and perhaps also the micro-generation technologies. And the fuel-poor need this even more. A lot of draught reduction in particular could be achieved cheaply for some of the most vulnerable. This could be a profitable and useful business model for the construction industry to look into over the next few years.

Notes

1   Differences in cost-effectiveness bedevil rocket science too. Two probes were sent to explore Mars in 2003: the *Beagle 2* developed by UK academics cost just £66 million, while NASA's rovers *Spirit* and *Opportunity* cost US$820 million (however, the NASA ones landed successfully and continue to send pictures today; the *Beagle 2* failed during descent).
2   BERR (2008) *Heat: Call for Evidence*, p13, www.berr.gov.uk/files/file43609.pdf (accessed June 2009).
3   Communities and Local Government (2006) *Review of Sustainability of Existing Buildings*. www.communities.gov.uk/publications/planningandbuilding/reviewsustainability (accessed July 2009).

4   Utley, J.I. and Shorrock, L.D. (2006) *Domestic Energy Fact File*, Building Research Establishment, Watford.
5   Boardman, B., Darby, S., Killip, G., Hinnells, M., Jardine, C., Palmer, J. and Sinden, G. (2005) *40% House*, Environmental Change Institute, Oxford University.
6   The 'U-value' is the amount of heat a conductor lets through. It is expressed in heat flow per unit temperature difference between the inside and outside surface per unit area.
7   See www.sustainable-energyacademy.org.uk/pages/inspired/list.php (accessed July 2009) for a map of 22 super-homes locations in England and Wales.
8   to Gerald Ratner – *verb*; to torpedo your career, for instance by describing your company's products as 'total crap' in front of a large audience.
9   In 1955 the UK army's directorate of physiological and biological research conducted in-depth field research on the subjective comfort of different designs of vests for soldiers working in the Canal Zone in Egypt. The clear winner was the Sherpa with its looser wide-knit mesh. Fortunately Nasser nationalized the canal in July 1956 sparing soldiers further sartorial indignity.
10 Johnston, D., Wingfield, J., Miles-Shenton, D. and Bell, M. (2004) 'Airtightness of UK dwellings: some recent measurements', Leeds Metropolitan University COBRA 2004 conference, www.rics.org/NR/rdonlyres/7D1AE22D-C1BA-43CF-88E0-35F30BD9409A/0/airtightness.pdf (accessed July 2009).
11 Hong, S., Ridley, I. and Oreszczyn, T. (2004) 'The impact of energy efficient refurbishment on the airtightness in English dwellings', in 25th Air Infiltration and Ventilation Centre Conference 15–17 September, Prague, Czech Republic.
12 Dunster, B., Simmons, C. and Gilbert, B. (2008) *The ZEDbook: Solutions for a Shrinking World*, Taylor and Francis, Oxford, p167.
13 One particularly dark day I was sitting in the pub with one of the ministerial advisers speculating on how the UK could deal with our piles of nuclear waste and the difficulties of keeping our homes warm. Several drinks into the evening we thought we had a win–win solution. It was so simple – just mix intermediate-level nuclear waste into clay and fire it into bricks. With a bit of lead screening and sufficient dilution the bricks should be safe, cosy warm and, more importantly, so widely distributed that no terrorist would ever contemplate seizing them to make a nuclear bomb. The next morning we agreed the less said about the idea the better.
14 It's like it says on the can, www.metacafe.com/watch/746423/infrared_goggle_hack_for_under_10/ (accessed June 2009).
15 Shorrock, I.D., Henderson, J. and Utley, J.I. (2005) *Reducing Carbon Emissions from the UK Housing Stock*, Building Research Establishment, Watford.
16 Tadj Oreszczyn, Imperial College and one of the Warm Front study group, pers com.
17 Asif, M., Daidson, A. and Muneer, T. (no date) *Life Cycle of Window Materials*, School of Engineering, Napier University
18 London Borough of Camden (2005) *Conserving Buildings Saving Energy*, www.camden.gov.uk/ccm/content/environment/file-storage-item/green-building-guides.en (accessed July 2009).
19 Wingfield, J., Bell, M., Miles-Shenton, D., South, T. and Lowe, B. (2007) *Lessons from Stamford Brook – Understanding the Gap between Designed and Real Performance*, Leeds Metropolitan University.

20   BERR (2008) *Digest of UK Energy Statistics*, The Stationery Office, Annex 1.1.5.
21   Various sources: U-Switch for gas and electricity, John Willoughby's website for coal (and so much else) www.johnwilloughby.co.uk.
22   BERR (2008) *Renewable Energy Strategy Consultation*, Chapter 4 'Heat', www.decc.gov.uk/en/content/cms/consultations/cons_res/cons_res.aspx (accessed July 2009).
23   Galbraith, D., Smith, P. and Mortimer, N. (2006) *Review of Greenhouse Gas Life Cycle Emissions, Air Pollution Impacts and Economics of Biomass Production and Consumption in Scotland*, www.scotland.gov.uk/Publications/2006/09/22094104/0 (accessed June 2009).
24   Building Research Establishment (2005) *The Government's Standard Assessment Procedure for Energy Rating of Dwellings*, version 2, Building Research Establishment, Watford.
25   Building Research Establishment (2005) '*Airtight sealant process*' *remedial sealing – further BREDEM calculations prepared for Adrian Brown Airtight Solutions Ltd*, www.airoseal.com/?page=documents&action=view&id=19&PHPSESSID=f4fcb46a564a353897374b461ed9b8b2 (accessed July 2009).
26   Gavin Killip's two-bedroom Oxford house is described in greater detail as a case study in his 2008 report for the Federation of Master Builders, *Transforming the UK's Existing Housing Stock*, Environmental Change Institute, Oxford.

Annex 1: Heat Conducting Properties of Different Materials (at Atmospheric Pressure)

Material	Thermal conductivity (W/m²K)
Xenon	0.00565
Krypton	0.00943
Argon	0.0172
Air	0.025
Phenolic	0.025
Expanded polystyrene	0.033
Mineral wool	0.033
Cork	0.033
Wood	0.04 to 0.4
Cement	0.29
Solid brick	approx 0.5
Water	0.6
Glass	1.1
Soil	1.5
Concrete	1.7
Steel	12 to 45
Aluminium	237

Source: Wikipedia http://en.wikipedia.org/wiki/List_of_thermal_conductivities (original sources: *CRC Handbook of Chemistry and Physics*, ed. David Lide; and Saloman, T. and Bedel, S., (2002) *The Energy Saving House (New Futures)*, Centre for Alternative Technology, Machynlleth.

Thermal conductivity is the rate at which a thickness of material will transmit heat. It depends on the surface area of the material, the temperature difference between the inside and outside of the surface, the thickness of the material, and on the heat retaining properties of the materials making up the envelope.

Annex 2: Desired Temperature of House and Number of Degree-Days of Heat Needed to Maintain Desired Temperature (for England)

Desired temp. (°C)	Degree-days	Desired temp. (°C)	Degree-days
1.0	0	11.0	1140
1.5	30	11.5	1240
2.0	60	12.0	1345
2.5	95	12.5	1450
3.0	125	13.0	1560
3.5	150	13.5	1670
4.0	185	14.0	1780
4.5	220	14.5	1900
5.0	265	15.0	2015
5.5	310	15.5	2130
6.0	360	16.0	2250
6.5	420	16.5	2370
7.0	480	17.0	2490
7.5	550	17.5	2610
8.0	620	18.0	2730
8.5	695	18.5	2850
9.0	775	19.0	2970
9.5	860	19.5	3090
10.0	950	20.0	3210
10.5	1045	20.5	3330

Source: Building Research Establishment (2005), see note 24 above, Table 10.

Degree-days is an expression of how hard the heating system must work to create the internal temperature given the temperature outside. It depends on the expected outside temperature each day subtracted from the desired temperature added for every day of the year.

Our Friends Electric

Electricity use in the house accounts for under a tonne of CO_2 per person. Government policy is to reduce the amount of carbon emitted from electricity production. However, the carbon content of electricity has not decreased since 2000, so the economical environmentalists will have to reduce use of electricity to cut their emissions.

- Install low-energy light bulbs throughout your house, now. Don't wait till they stop working. It just wastes your money for even longer. There are models on the market that work with small light fittings and with dimmer switches. Though more expensive, these will eventually save money too.
- Drying your clothes in a tumble dryer takes a lot of energy. Try using clothes that need less frequent washing and hang them outside to dry, or in a well-ventilated room.
- When you buy appliances or electronic items look out for the Energy Saving Trust's recommendations. This is a better guide than the EU energy label. There are also a couple of websites with information on standby and in-use energy consumption. Energy-efficient models don't cost any more than standard models.
- Replacing your desktop with a laptop can make a significant difference if you use your home computer for four to five hours a day.
- Buy a TV with a small screen – if you double the width of the screen its energy use quadruples; go for LCD in preference to plasma.

It should be possible to reduce the electricity bill from £200–£300 by half depending on the opportunities in your house.

There are a number of green tariffs available on the market. Paying more for 'green' electricity won't actually increase the amount of green electricity being produced since the biting constraint limiting the amount of renewable electricity being produced is the speed at which new renewables can be built (or get permission to be built) rather than demand. Some of the green tariffs improve the economics of renewables, even if they do not directly result in new build of renewables, so you can at least draw some comfort you are doing some good.

An economical environmentalist would not install micro-renewable technologies in their homes just yet, but if you've got a few thousand lying around and you want to help stimulate the industry then biomass CHP might be an option for you, as might solar PV. Micro-wind has so far been not been successful and cannot be recommended.

Introduction

The title of this chapter is a corruption of Tubeway Army's song *Are 'Friends' Electric?* This was, I think, the first song I danced to – and I can still recall Gary Numan rapping his depressing lyrics, while I swayed like a zombie at the local youth centre's spectacularly unsuccessful disco. This period marked the start of my obsession with music and the media through which it is transmitted. Over the years I have changed my allegiance from vinyl to CDs and now to iTunes – with a brief but unsatisfying fling with cassette tapes.

As the technology used to access music has changed, so too has the carbon cost of doing so. Superficially this is a success story for dematerialization – bulky records and record players, replaced with CDs and midi then micro hi-fi units, replaced by a virtually dematerialized iPod and replaced finally by a fully virtual iTunes library. But another story that could be woven from this example is one of growing wealth, faster obsolescence and over-consumption. Being so bulky, I have never owned more than one turntable at a time. I now have five devices capable of playing CDs in the house and can access my iTunes library or amplify my iPod over six different devices. It's just so cheap to buy multiple gadgets, why bother carting a machine around the house or setting aside space just to listen to music.

This chapter is about the carbon emissions from electrical devices. We all know about the sensible advice to replace tungsten light bulbs with low-energy light bulbs, to turn devices on standby off at the wall, and to buy A-labelled appliances. This is all good advice, but will it be enough to halve our emissions?

Electricity purchases seem to be one place where you can buy your way out of environmental guilt by buying renewable electricity off the grid or investing in wind turbines or solar electricity. But are these really cost-effective?

This chapter does not tackle the carbon rucksack of electrical goods. That is left to the next chapter. These might not show up in your electricity bill but for some goods they're more important than direct operational emissions. Once we take account of the energy used to mine the rare earth metals and purify the silicon so to make microprocessors, we find the manufacture of electronic goods attracting Ryanair-style excess baggage fines.

Carbon Emissions from Electricity Generation

The electricity generators' decarbonization of the grid is occurring too slowly to halve our emissions anytime soon

The average household use of electricity causes around $2tCO_2e$ – a little under a tonne per person – to be released at power plants. These emissions have fallen by about a fifth since 1970. All good news then – let the government and power companies keep on doing more of the same?

Sadly it's not so simple. The fall took place between 1970 and 1999, due to the switch from coal-fired electricity to gas and nuclear. Since 1999 emissions have climbed by 20 per cent. You can see the change in Figure 6.1. The dotted line shows the amount of carbon dioxide released when a kWh of electricity is produced. This has dropped from 0.95kg/kWh in 1970 to about 0.40kg/kWh in 1999 mainly as a result of the so-called dash-to-gas when government allowed power companies to build gas-fired power stations. But emissions intensity has been rising since 1999 because the country's nuclear reactors are spending more of their time being repaired and less time running. And as the price of gas has risen, the big electricity generating companies have

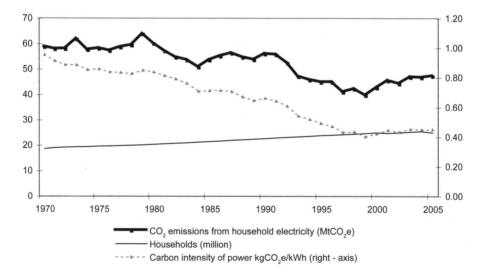

CO$_2$ emissions from household electricity (MtCO$_2$e)
Households (million)
Carbon intensity of power kgCO$_2$e/kWh (right - axis)

Figure 6.1 Emissions of CO$_2$ from household electricity use, and other drivers

Source: Emissions data from NETCEN, electricity use from Berr, carbon intensity calculated by author.

cranked up output on their existing coal-fired plants, because the price of coal has remained cheap. The controversy around E.On's planned new coal-fired power station at Kingsnorth is just another manifestation of the relative cheapness of coal compared to other fossil fuels. The EU's carbon trading schemes make coal power more expensive but carbon prices are too low to seriously hurt coal's price advantage.

Nuclear power is being hailed as an important part of the solution to climate change. Maybe it will be but we need to do a lot else besides

Ten years ago I parked the issue of nuclear power. Today, I believe without it, we are going to face an energy crisis and we can't let that happen.

And Madam President, that means a policy for safe, sensible and balanced use of nuclear power. It's we who are not merely friends of the Earth – we are its guardians and trustees for generations to come. The core of [our] philosophy and the case for protecting the environment are the same. No generation has a freehold on this Earth. All we have is a life tenancy – with a full repairing lease. This Government intends to meet the terms of that lease in full.

Both the above quotes are speeches made by prime ministers at their party conference. Both speeches were made in the twilight of their political leadership. The first was made in 2006 by Tony Blair, the second in 1988 by Margaret Thatcher. In the intervening 18 years only one nuclear power station was switched on in the UK – Sizewell B. This was commissioned by Margaret Thatcher as the first in a suite of ten new nuclear power stations; the remaining nine were never built.

As I write this it's been announced that the French power utility EDF has purchased the UK's main nuclear reactor operator British Energy *and more crucially its ten sites*. They plan to build four new French-designed nuclear power stations with a combined capacity of around 6GW which will meet more than 10 per cent of UK's current electricity demand. We are pinning a lot of hope on nuclear generation reducing our emissions of carbon dioxide at source. We may be right but we have a poor track record on successfully building nuclear power stations.

Leaving aside the issue of safe disposal of nuclear waste, the uncertain economics of new build and the real risk that EDF will screw up its costings and will eventually confront the UK government with a begging bowl to pay for 'unforeseen' costs, there is the tardiness of the building of new nuclear power plants. The soonest the European Power Reactor (EPR) design could be approved for use in the UK, be built and have all the safety checks completed is likely to be 2021[1] – and that's with a fair wind behind it.[2] But we don't have a fair wind behind us – we lack trained and experienced personnel to regulate and oversee the construction, and there are long waiting lists to build crucial parts of the reactor vessel. We are not the only country eyeing up nuclear power as a low-carbon, and strategically reliable alternative to fossil fuels. If we really only have a decade to save the planet – as this book is contending – then new nuclear can play no part of it … unlike Cinderella, it arrives at the ball hours after midnight. Prince Charming has already taken off in his carriage with someone else. The argument I am making against relying on nuclear is not on environmental or economic grounds – you have to show up on time to make history.

We have pursued renewable electricity policy for 15 years, with limited success

There is the potential, we believe out there, using the resources that are around the UK to generate maybe all of the electricity that households need in the UK from renewable sources, from off-shore wind sources. So we should explore whether we can maximize that potential because it is obviously in the nation's interests and the world's interest for us to make sure that more of our energy comes from clean sources.

(John Hutton, former Secretary of State for Energy, 2007)

Apart from nuclear, there are two other technologies to reduce the amount of carbon in grid electricity: carbon capture and storage, and large-scale wind. Both could be rolled out within a decade but it remains to be seen whether we have the political will to do so. In the UK, renewables still make only a relatively unimportant contribution to electricity generation, accounting for around 5 per cent of power production.

The problem isn't the economics of wind power. Though the subsidy paid for new wind farms has been reduced, investors have identified 300 wind projects in the UK which could generate 7000MW of power, according to the British Wind Energy Association.[3] This is the same amount of installed capacity as five nuclear reactors. Yet less than a third of these wind farms are going forward. Instead they are snarled up in the mire that is our planning and consents process. Small on-shore wind farms spend several months (or even years in planning) and often get turned down. Once they pass through this hurdle they then have to wait in a queue for National Grid to link them to the system.

The process isn't much better in other countries. The International Energy Agency declared in September 2008 that:

Administrative hurdles, obstacles to grid access, poor electricity market design, lack of information and training, and social acceptance issues have significantly hampered the effectiveness of renewable support policies and driven up costs in many countries ... irrespective of the type of incentive scheme.

At the moment there are 9300MW of renewables waiting to be connected to the grid across Europe.

How is all this electricity used?

So if emissions from electricity are not about to halve any time soon through actions by government or the electricity generators, can households reduce their demand?

The amount of electricity used by different electrical appliances is given in Figure 6.2. Household usage of electricity has more than doubled over the past 30 years, almost negating the substitution of gas and nuclear for coal over the same period. The fastest growth at the moment is in information and communications technologies (ICT), which have come from nowhere to over 10 per cent of emissions. But lighting, fridges and consumer electronics

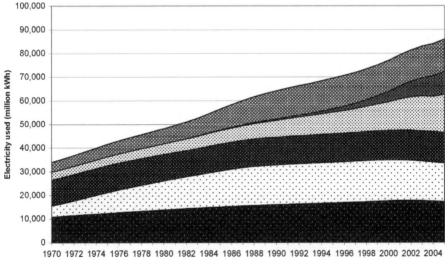

■ Lighting ⬚ Cold ■ Cooking ▩ Consumer Electronics ▨ ICT ▩ Washing machines and dishwashers

Figure 6.2 Electricity usage by households for appliances, lighting and other goods

Source: Market Transformation Programme, www.mtprog.com

remain the most important electricity users in the home, grabbing about a fifth of consumption each.

People today have a wider range of gadgets and more of them: when you buy a flash new TV the old one is often relegated to the kid's bedroom, and new appliances are so often bigger and more power hungry than the generation before. Table 6.1 shows how the ownership of some common labour-saving devices has increased over time.

Table 6.1 Increased penetration of common household appliances

Labour-saving device	Increase in household ownership 1970–2004
Dishwashers	1 per cent in 1970 to 26 per cent in 2004
Microwaves	<1 per cent in 1977 to 84 per cent in 2004
Tumble dryers/washer dryers	<1 per cent in 1970 to 55 per cent in 2004
Vacuum cleaner	80 per cent in 1970 to 100 per cent in 2004

Source: Energy Saving Trust (2007)[4]

Luckily for us, we do not have to spend the void in our lives created by the penetration of labour-saving gadgets twiddling our thumbs – instead we can … watch daytime TV. Incredibly the average person in the UK now spends 13 hours and 38 minutes per day watching TV/DVD or listening to music.[5] My mind boggles – that only leaves ten and a half hours to do everything else. The ownership of consumer electronics has rocketed. By 2006 the UK's 25 million households owned 63 million TVs, 70 million phone chargers and 43 million DVDs/VCRs.[6] There are now more TVs in the UK than there are people; many homes have become *de facto* multiplex cinemas for their inhabitants. By way of comparison, in 1970 there were just 16 million TVs and 10,000 VCRs. Such high penetration of goods brings about social changes too; watching TV is less Cosby family, and more a David Bowie-style solipsism à la *The Man Who Fell to Earth*.

New technology has reduced the size of the components and offers the opportunity to miniaturize – but this hasn't happened; instead technology has been used to aggrandize products. In the 1970s a 26-inch TV was considered a behemoth. Nowadays, nothing less than 50 inches would raise an eyebrow. The largest TV in the high street today is a mammoth 60-inch plasma for £2000. Though it's counter-intuitive to associate the development of these big beasts and miniaturization, in an oblique way they are miniaturization's illegitimate child. The depth of the old-school cathode ray televisions was related to the screen size. The move to *flat screen* LCD and plasma technologies decouples the depth from the size of the screen. There are many similar stories of technological advance becoming manifest as more power-hungry gadgets. This happens for car engines (despite speed limits staying the same), fridges and computers, and even our weekly food intake.

The Energy Saving Trust published a list of the range of products found in the average home now compared to 30 years ago. I have reproduced the whole list in Table 6.2. The average household has gone from owning about 20 electrical items to 50, often with more than one model of each (in our house we have three electric blankets, three CD players, two laptops, four mobile phones). Electric sockets begin to resemble old fashioned telephone exchanges, sprouting wart-like multi-plugs and extension leads snaking around the room.

But owning more and more gadgets doesn't necessarily mean that much more energy consumption. An electric juicer does no great CO_2 damage sitting in a kitchen cupboard and labour-saving devices like electric blankets or microwave ovens save carbon if they displace a more carbon-hungry item. Also, as we acquire more gadgets, we use them for less time. On average the house's *primary* TV is used for 6.5 hours a day, the *secondary* set(s) for 2.5 hours.

But even if the energy they use directly is limited, resources are taken to make, transport and dispose of these gadgets. Around 400kgCO_2 is emitted making a 1m^2 plasma TV,[7] but it emits just 350kgCO_2 each year if used for 2.5 hours a day. As we accumulate more goods, use them less and throw them away more readily, the production and disposal phase become more and more important relative to the in-use energy consumption.

Table 6.2 Typical energy-using products in an average household

1970s	2000s
Television	Televisions
Vacuum cleaner	Video players
Electric bar heaters	DVD player/recorder
Hi-fi music system	Portable music players
Hairdryer	Mobile phones
Electric kettle	Hairdryers
Washing machine	Hair irons
Iron	Electric toothbrushes
Electric blanket	Wireless telephone/answering machine
Radio	Slave portable phone handsets
Sewing machine	Electric kettle

1970s	2000s
Cooker	Smoothie maker
Cassette player	Magimix
Fridge	Ice-cream maker
DIY appliance	Digital radio
Toaster	Mini hi-fi systems
Occasional lamps	Washing machine
	Tumble dryer
	Dishwasher
	PlayStation/games console
	Cappuccino maker
	Digital clock/radios
	Electric lawnmower
	Strimmer
	Microwave
	Electric oven
	Electric hob
	Extractor fan
	Large fridge-freezer
	Drinks cooler
	Portable fan
	Vacuum cleaner
	PC computer
	Monitor
	Printer
	Scanner/fax
	Digital camera
	Set-top box
	Electric shaver
	Steam iron
	Juicer
	Home security system
	Broadband connection
	Halogen bulb light fittings
	Personal care products
	Power tools
	Electric blanket

Perhaps the most pernicious effect of technological change has been to make the old seem second-rate or tired-looking. The electricity needed to illuminate a room has increased not because we are becoming more night blind, but because the solitary light bulb stuck in the middle of the ceiling has become a 1970s cliché, we now expect light-installations recessed into our ceilings that appear to have come straight out of the Tate Modern. In my lifetime there have been four waves of technological change in television sets: the introduction of colour, then remote controls, then flat screen and now digital. Each time the older models seem shabby and out of place – not even fit for the bedroom.

Options for Reducing Carbon Dioxide Emissions from Electrical Appliances

The basic opportunities for reducing carbon dioxide emissions from appliances are:

- behaviour change in terms of turning appliances off;
- using renewable electricity, either generated domestically or bought in from outside providers;
- selecting appliances that consume less power; and
- changing appliances less frequently, to reduce embodied emissions.

Switching things off when they're not being used

> ... consider groceries in a hypothetical store totally without price markings, billed via a monthly statement. ... How could grocery shoppers economize under such a billing regime? (W. Kempton and L. L. Layne, 1994)

Turning off mobile chargers has been stigmatized as a poster boy for 'top ten tips to save money and save the world'. While it is patently not true that rigorously remembering to turn off your phone charger at the socket every night (saves around $25kgCO_2$ per year) will save enough carbon to fly you to the US and back (takes around 3.5 tonnes CO_2 if you include the radiative forcing), you can save a useful sum of money and CO_2 at the same time. As the quote above makes clear, households have dreadfully little usable information on their energy use. The first step is understanding how much energy is used.

There are two types of energy monitor on the market. The first monitors the whole house's electricity use – and spits out the results in terms of energy,

Box 6.1 *Converting gas and electricity meters' output into English*

My gas meter measures energy use in a unit known as the 'cubic foot'. To anyone who thought the EU, in a fit of Napoleonic standardization, had outlawed such things they need only take a peek under their staircase at the gas meters. In the high-tech world of energy measurement, feudal measurement units live on. (Reputedly, the foot was calibrated around the shoe size of Henry I of England. The average British foot is around 9.4 inches which suggests he had abnormally large feet, or was very bad at measuring.)

To convert cubic feet to something that makes sense is not straightforward.

[gas use in ft^3]	× 2.83	× 1.02264	× 39.25	/ 3.6
	To hundredths of cubic metre	Loss of gas in transmission	Energy content (in kJ of 1/100 m^3 of gas)	Convert from joules to kWh

The upshot of the formula is that to convert a gas meter's cubic reading into kWh you multiply by 31 if it measures cubic feet or by 11 if it uses hundredths of a cubic metre. Since the average unit of gas costs about 2.6p/kWh at the time of writing each unit saved is worth either 82p/ft^3 of gas saved, or £28/m^3. It's worth checking that your meter and gas bill agree on the unit of measurement. There has been a spate of complaints about people being overcharged because of this simple misunderstanding.

Electricity meters normally already measure in kWh – the same unit the tariff is set in. But they have their own quirks – especially the cascade of dials used on old meters to record each digit of energy use. Adjacent dials revolve in opposite directions – just in case your brain was feeling on top of it. Digital meters are more straightforward.

Some households have Economy-7 tariffs. The standard cost of electricity on the Economy-7 (around 14p/kWh) is a little higher than the best rates on other tariffs (10p/kWh), but the cost of power at night-time (midnight to 7.00am, or 1.00am to 8.00am) can be less than half the standard rate (around 5p/kWh). So it makes sense to go for Economy-7 tariffs if you are able to ensure that at least 40 per cent of electricity usage is at night-time. This means turning your dishwasher, washing machine and other power-hungry appliances on after midnight. If you use storage heaters you should definitely go for the Economy-7 tariff. Night-time electricity is generally lower carbon too since it is generated from a higher proportion of 'always-on' nuclear and intermittent wind than in the daytime when power consumption increases and the more flexible fossil fuel power stations are powered up.

carbon or money either instantaneously or over a period of time. It consists of two parts: the sensor and the portable display. The sensor uses a transponder to detect energy use; this is clipped to the electricity cable between the electricity meter and the fuse box – it takes five minutes to install. The sensor wirelessly transmits information on electricity consumption to the mobile display unit. The Owl, Eco-eye mini and Efergy wireless monitors all cost around £40 when you include the various bits and bobs. The more stylish Wattson costs about three times more but is capable of linking up to your computer to store historic data, so you can keep a running total of your annual power bill. Those with aesthetic sensibilities say it looks as elegant as the iPod. Whether this functionality justifies the price I don't know.

The whole-house meter is interesting for the first few days of use. My kids and I walked around excitedly switching things on and off to see how much (or little) power they sucked from the grid. You won't pick up a small ticket energy user – the device is not discerning enough to isolate the battery charger and energy-efficient light bulb from the white noise fluctuations in energy use of the fridge and the pump on the central heating. But nonetheless, it was a great educational tool to show how the toaster, fan heater and grill gobble up energy. It's particularly useful for casting an eye over as you leave the house for work just to make sure you haven't left an electric heater or some lights on.

The other type of monitor is the plug-in electricity meter that sits in between the plug and the socket. These are cheaper, costing about £10–15 and give the instantaneous read-out of power, current, voltage and cumulative energy use. These can be used to measure the power consumption of small energy users like phone chargers and standby power use of TVs and PCs. It doesn't work on appliances that don't have plugs (lights, main cooker circuit) or where the plugs are inaccessible (some built in appliances) so complements the wireless monitor, though only the real enthusiast will want to buy both.

Do they encourage people to reduce their emissions? Research undertaken by Defra suggests direct immediate feedback can reduce household energy use by 5–15 per cent,[8] somewhat lower than the claim by some of the products of 25 per cent, but still a respectable payback of less than a year for most households. The research also shows that more informative bills – that let you see this quarter's energy use compared to the same time last year – can also induce people to hunt out and reduce energy use by up to 10 per cent. And these are free.

While we're thinking about high-tech devices, it's worth mentioning *standby power savers*. The commonest sort is for use with PCs. The device looks like a fancy multi-plug with a master socket which the PC is plugged into and slave sockets for the printer and monitor. The device detects when the PC is powering down and then depowers the peripherals – equivalent to turning them off at the wall. The adverts claim you can reduce standby power use by 35W if all eight slave plugs are used. This is worth having – even if you're not the plugged-in-cyber-sicko with all eight peripherals sockets in use (I manage five – so I've got no reason to be smug).

You can also buy variants of this device with a remote control that cuts off the power to a TV or DVD. Note these still draw a small amount of power (about 0.5W) so they can receive the remote control signal to fire up again. Such devices need alkaline batteries (used in the remote control), which are probably one of the most ecologically disastrous forms of energy storage ever designed – well, perhaps not as bad as burning whale blubber. Four AA batteries give rise to 0.5kgCO_2.[9] The pretty obvious point I am making is that walking over and turning something off at the wall is the most low-cost and effective way of reducing standby energy use. If you want to buy these gizmos they cost £20–25. There's a range available from www.mygreenerhome.co.uk.

Is buying electricity on a green tariff a big con?

This is not a straightforward question to answer. When people sign on to a green tariff they pay their electricity supplier (electricity-industry speak for the company that sells you power) as much as 40 per cent more than the cheapest supplier. What happens to this money? Does it increase the amount of renewable electricity stations being built or does it just go into the supplier's pockets as more profits?

To answer this question properly it's necessary to understand the industry structure and the way the government subsidizes renewable electricity production. You can skip the next paragraph if your reaction to the previous sentence is whoa … too much information!

The electricity industry is dominated by six big companies that build and operate power generation plants (generators) or sell power to customers (suppliers). There are also several smaller supply companies that only generate or only supply, several of these are environmentally minded. Since April 2002 government has required a proportion of electricity sold by suppliers to be renewable – this is the principal means of supporting renewable electricity in the UK. A renewable power plant is awarded certificates called ROCs by the energy regulator, Ofgem, for the amount of renewable electricity produced. These ROCs are tradable and can be sold to any energy supplier, independently of the power itself, to demonstrate to Ofgem that they have met their obligation to source a proportion of their power from a renewable generator. Most of the money earned by renewable generators comes from selling these ROCs. They also get revenue from selling their electricity on the open market for the going price (which fluctuates like crazy), or on long-term contracts for a stable price close to the market price. Unfortunately the building of renewable electricity power plants in the UK has not kept up with the targets the government has set the industry. In practice the suppliers have to pay Ofgem a modest fine (currently about 4.5p/kWh) to buy themselves out of any unfulfilled obligation. So effectively there is a subsidy of around 4.5p/kWh for any qualifying renewable power.[10]

The complaint against most green tariffs is that all they are just a means of suppliers charging extra for something they had to supply anyway, they're in no way increasing the amount of green power they sell.

But not all the green tariffs are cons – behind the chicanery there are actually some businesses trying to make a difference. This is where it gets complicated. There are four types of support given by electricity suppliers that go beyond their licence obligations:

1 Sourcing their power from green generators. This is cheap and easy since the electricity is bought near the wholesale price, and handy for the renewable generator, who can go to the bank waving a contract to show they have a guaranteed source of income.
2 Investing in new green generating capacity. This is time consuming and tricky, but not intrinsically more expensive since wind is fairly competitive nowadays. It probably still adds 1p/kWh to each unit.
3 Offsetting carbon emissions from the generation using permits from the carbon market (more about this in Chapter 7). It costs roughly 0.5p/kWh for permits from the European Union's Emissions Trading Scheme (EU-ETS), cheaper still from the UN Kyoto Protocol permits.
4 'Retiring' the ROCs to avoid their being used to greenwash another supplier's non-renewable supply. This very expensive and altruistic act costs about 5p/kWh and increases the support being paid to new renewables.

If you are interested in paying for green electricity there are three independent supply companies of interest. The oldest kid on the block is Ecotricity which was founded by Dale Vince in 1995. It has about 40,000 customers and is a major investor in renewable generation meeting around 30 per cent of its supply from its own generation. It has two green tariffs: New energy, which matches the local electricity company in terms of price but invests in building new wind power generation (Type 2). The remaining 70 per cent of the power is what they call brown power and is bought off the grid. Their other tariff, the New energy plus, supplements the 30 per cent own-generated green electricity with green electricity bought in from the market (Type 1 supplemented with Type 2). The company will buy any electricity you generate from solar panels or domestic wind for 10p/kWh.

Good Energy, founded by Juliet Davenport, who used to run Unit E, has a different model with just one tariff, 100 per cent renewables bought from wind farms and hydro schemes (Type 1 from the list above, but also Type 4 since it retires 5 per cent more ROCs than it legally has to). Good Energy tries to source its power from smaller independent generators, including micro-generators, to whom it pays around 10p/kWh in exchange for the ROCs they produce.

The newest company, Green Energy, also supplies 100 per cent 'Green power' but their cheaper tariff makes use of a high proportion of combined heat and power (about two-thirds) and a third renewables (Type 2). Electricity from CHP is 15–20 per cent lower carbon than gas-fired electricity since about 80–85 per cent of the energy content of the gas is successfully exploited.

British Gas has also launched two green tariffs under the 'Future energy' banner. Their model is to source their power from renewables (Type 2), but they also spend some money – about £20 per customer – on a green renewables fund for schools. Their *zero carbon* gas and electricity tariff is an interesting beast which retires 12 per cent of the ROCs to stimulate investment in new UK

Table 6.3 Prices and costs for standard and green electricity providers

	Standing charge	Charge for initial units	Charge for later units	Carbon emissions	Annual cost
	(£/yr)	(p/kWh)	(p/kWh)	(gCO$_2$/kWh)	(£)
London Electricity (EDF)		19.9	12.1	0.54	469
British Gas: Standard		18.6	9.0	0.382	345
British Gas: Zero carbon		28.8	12.4	−0.06	491
Ecotricity: New energy		19.9	12.1	0.316	469
Ecotricity: New energy plus		20.4	12.6	0	486
Good Energy	46.5	16.3	16.3	−0.025	583
Green Energy: Deep green	53.7	15.3	15.3	0	559
Green Energy: Light green	53.7	14.1	14.1	0.136	518

Source: Company websites; www.electricityinfo.org/ for CO$_2$ emissions; data for October 2008, London for the use of 3300kWh per year, representing 1.45tCO$_2$/yr.

generation plant and also offsets domestic gas and electricity use by buying Kyoto Protocol emissions permits (Type 3). Speaking as a geeky analyst, this is the best tariff for stimulating new UK generation and also investing in pukka low-cost emissions reductions globally, so it gets my thumbs up.[11] They claim the cost will be just £84 plus VAT per year more than their standard plan but I couldn't get this to happen on their website. At the moment British Gas only offer a dual fuel tariff, which means you have to buy gas from them too. The tariff does not offer to buy ROCs off you so is not suitable if you are planning to install a PV panel or wind turbine.

Table 6.3 gives information about the costs of renewable electricity and the amount of carbon they save. I have awarded Good Energy and the Zero carbon from British Gas negative carbon emissions because not only do they source all their electricity from renewable generators, they also retire 5 per cent and 12 per cent of the ROCs, respectively – preventing them being sold on to someone else so they can relabel their power as green.

For more information on switching to green tariffs look at websites like uSwitch or my own favourite, the *Green electricity marketplace* set up by a couple of former Friends of the Earth – Scotland campaigners, www.green-electricity.org/tariffs.php.

Domestic renewables

If you wish to generate your own renewable electricity your basic options are installing solar photovoltaic panels, a micro wind turbine, or micro-hydro if you're lucky enough to have a stream flowing through your garden. Another option for a street or block of flats is have a small biomass-fuelled CHP system to provide communal power and heat. This is not uncommon on new estates in local authorities that have imposed the so-called 'Merton Rule' which makes it obligatory for new developments to source a proportion of their energy from on-site renewables in order to get planning permission.

None of these technologies is cheap. In fact the words 'domestic renewable electricity' and 'good value' usually only find themselves in the same sentence when prefixed by 'not' or 'bit of a joke'. Solar panels cost upwards of £5000–£8000 per kWp of capacity (the unit kWp refers to the peak amount of power the panel produces on a summer afternoon). Domestic-scale wind turbines start at around £4500/kW installed cost but come down to around £1000/kW if 15 or so homes club together and buy a 75kW turbine communally.

Should you buy micro-renewables? The main argument for spending money on domestic renewables is not economic (unless you are unable to connect to the electricity grid for some reason) but because you wish to stimulate the technology and bring down future prices. This is not a bad argument. Figure 6.3 shows how the cost of producing renewable electricity has declined

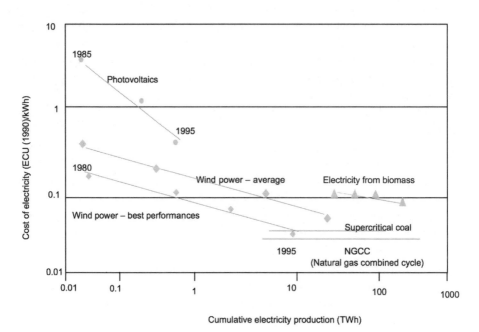

Figure 6.3 Learning curve data for selected energy technologies

Source: IEA (2000) *Experience Curves for Energy Technology Policy*, p21

over time. Each tick on the cost axis is ten times less than the value above. The Government has announced that from 2010 small-scale renewable electricity will be eligible for support through the feed-in tariff in common with many mainland European countries. Depending on the level the tariff is paid at it could significantly improve the economics of domestic micro-renewables.

The Energy Saving Trust recommends you make sure you've done every-thing you can on improving energy efficiency first – this includes the energy efficiency of household appliances – before thinking about micro-renewables. This is good advice. It is even worth thinking outside the box and spending extra money doing slightly wacky things like using a gas-heated washing machine, or binning your old fridge and buying the most energy-efficient new one, before installing renewable electricity.

That said, let's look at how they work, and whether they are for you.

Solar photovoltaic electricity

Solar photovoltaic electricity is relatively simple (at least by today's standards) semiconductor-based technology. Sunlight falls on the module, generates a direct current that is used by a stand-alone electrical device like a calculator or recharger, stored in a car battery for later use or converted, using an inverter, into AC current. Conversion into AC allows it be used in normal household devices or fed back into the grid. The conversion from DC to AC loses about a quarter of the energy. The inverter is a notoriously unreliable piece of kit prone to breaking down or being knocked over by a spike in the grid. PV modules are highly reliable devices needing little maintenance, if used for stand-alone use or combined with a simple battery.

Solar is touted as a complement to grid electricity by the PV industry – there are two main options here, either installing building-integrated PV tiles or as panels that sit on top of your roof or porch. If you install PV tiles when the house is being built or when it is being refurbished you can avoid some of the costs of roofing materials. Grants from the Department of Energy and Climate Change (DECC) can contribute up to £2500 or 50 per cent of the cost whichever is the lowest – but you have to use a professional installer. Installed costs are around £8000/kWp in London. It is now also possible to get money back from suppliers for any electricity you export. The government has also announced its intention to create feed-in tariffs to buy electricity from domestically produced electricity. Let's see how generous they make the offered price.

Let's look at how the technologies perform in practice. In 2006 the DTI undertook a thorough evaluation of 28 different schemes fitted between 2000 and 2005.[12] On average the panels generated 800kWh of power per 1kWp panel – which would save around £80 per year of electricity at prices then. The astute among you will have spotted there are 8800 hours in a year, so the panel only produces about 10% of its peak rating through the year. Electricity prices will have to rise very markedly to make this a worthwhile investment. The evaluation found that if the panels lasted 25 years the average cost of electricity produced would be 47.5p/kWh if you take account of the cost of buying and installing the panel.

Common problems included unreliability of the inverter. If you are not able to use the electricity being produced (i.e. if you are not at home in daylight hours) you have to sell it onto the grid for whatever price, if any, your supplier is prepared to pay. The Renewable Obligation has been changed to the advantage of domestic electricity production, allowing your supplier to claim the ROCs (remember the subsidy the government pays renewable generators) on your behalf. To receive this subsidy, you have to measure how much electricity is being produced from your panel using a meter that Ofgem is sure is tamperproof and give this information to your electricity supplier, who can claim around 10p/kWh on your behalf. To date, most electricity suppliers have resisted paying for the electricity supplied them by micro-generators. I have been in meetings with them and challenged them about this; it felt like I was asking turkeys to chip into the secret Santa fund. Good Energy and Ecotricity are honourable exceptions and will pay you the full value of the ROCs you supply them so long as you buy your top-up electricity from them.

Britain is not a particularly sunny country; because of the UK's latitude the sun is low in the sky. The amount of energy in the sunlight varies from around 2.25kWh/m²/day in north Scotland to 2.75kWh/m²/day in London. By way of comparison, southern Italy receives around 5kWh/m²/day[13] – greatly improving the technology's economic viability.

Because electricity made by domestic solar panels is usually not stored but is exported to the grid, the time of production is as important as how much is produced. Peak production is around noon and the early afternoon. If you are only at home in the evenings and weekends you'll have to think carefully about whether you will make use of the power produced – the fridge might draw 100W, what else do you use in the daytime – washing machine, dishwasher? The sunshine is also highly seasonal. In December you'll only be getting around 0.5kWh/m²/day compared to 5kWh/m²/day of insolation in June.

On the plus side for solar is the amazing way in which prices have come down. The price of photovoltaic technology fell by 90 per cent in the period 1985 to 1995 to around 40 USc/kWh. There are forecasts suggesting the price will come down to 10 USc/kWh by 2020 in countries like Spain – achieving the status of 'grid parity', which is its holy grail in the sense that it becomes competitive with the electricity it displaces. If prices do come down like this then it does start to look more cost competitive if you've high daytime electricity demands, especially in summer.

Wind power

From Figure 6.3 above you can see that large-scale wind is ten times cheaper than solar PV, which explains investors' enthusiasm for wind. Wind turbines are an established and fast-growing industry.

But the fact it works well on the large scale doesn't make it well suited to domestic customers. Wind comes into its own in areas where the wind speed is above 6m/s most of the time, and where the direction doesn't keep switching. Power production peaks when the wind is between 12 and 25m/s, but the output tails off sharply at lower wind speeds; so much so that at 10m/s you get 75 per cent of the peak output and at 8m/s just 50 per cent. Urban areas where the winds are gusty are pretty useless for wind.

If you are interested in the average wind speed for your area, there's a UK wind speed database set up by DECC.[14] You can use it to look up the feasibility of putting up a wind turbine on your plot; it's accurate to 1km² grids and gives wind speeds at 10m, 24m and 45m above the ground.

There has been an extensive assessment of the performance of micro wind turbines through the Warwick wind trials.[15] The trial has tracked the actual performance of 30 domestic wind turbines over the length of the UK from Aberdeen to Cornwall. The turbines had a capacity of 0.4–1.1kW with the majority being small 0.6kW turbines.

The results have been diabolical. On average the turbines have only been generating power for 2 per cent of the time. If you exclude turbines that were broken or shut down this still only rises to 2.7 per cent. Compare this to a large commercial wind farm which generates power around a third of the time. The actual observed wind speeds have been a third of the national wind speed database's prediction, and the power generated lower than expected, even for the low wind speeds. On average the turbines only produce 0.2kWh a day – worth about 2p/day, and consume around 0.06kWh a day. From the evidence of these trials you'd be mad to go for micro wind turbines.

Maybe there's hope from a radically different approach in the cities. Proponents of urban wind power argue we're looking at wind turbines in cities all wrong, they should be viewed side-on rotating around a vertical axis, since this is quieter and puts less stress on the building. One of the most elegant such designs – the iPod of the renewables industry – is the quietrevolution. It is 5m tall; its blades are sculpted into DNA helices and it looks more like an art installation than a piece of electricity generation kit. The manufacturers claim it works at wind speeds of 4–13m/s and phlegmatically handles gusts. It's not cheap, costing about £35,000–40,000 for a 6kW system, which it is claimed will deliver an output of 10,000kWh per year – perhaps enough juice for two or three homes if the wind keeps around 6m/s. On noise, the main source of objection faced by small wind turbines in obtaining local planning permission, the clue is in the name of the product. The shape of the turbine makes the quietrevolution much quieter than other small wind turbine. Anyway, RWE has sunk £7 million in the company to trial the design in different sites. Lead times, if you want one, are six months.

Should you install micro-generation or buy a green tariff?

If you want to make a statement about 'green', there is no doubt that getting a PV panel or maybe a quietrevolution wind turbine is the loudest statement of eco-bling – much more impressive than under-floor insulation and more visible than conscientiously switching the TV off at the socket every night. But at the moment it doesn't make economic sense unless you're going to be in the house a long time and don't mind waiting decades.

If you simply want to accelerate the development of the renewable sector, careful selection of your energy tariff might be a better idea. The better green suppliers like Ecotricity, Good Energy and the zero carbon tariff on British Gas are sinking new money into wind. Box 6.2 describes a wind farm opened in England. Its construction cost per kW was less than £1000, compared to closer to £3000 for small wind and £8000 for solar PV and, more importantly, its yields are much higher.

Box 6.2 *Helping onshore wind*

Scout Moor wind farm in Lancashire was developed by the independent company Peel Power. At the time of writing it is the biggest wind farm in England – though just a minnow by international standards. The farm's 26 turbines have a capacity of 65MW, and they produce enough power for 40,000 people – about half the needs of the nearby town of Rochdale. The term 'wind farm' conjures up images of a grove of turbines with cows mooing at its roots. And this isn't too wide of the mark. When the blades reach their zenith they each stand 100m tall – twice the height of Nelson's column – but their trunks are surprisingly delicate, just 4m in diameter. This lightness of footfall means the land used by wind farms often continues being owned and farmed by the landowners, with the farmer earning a rent or a share of the proceeds.

The economics of large wind farms like Scout Moor look pretty good. It cost £1000/kW to build, including the spending on the 12km of new road. This is much less than the cost of a domestic unit and it produces electricity for a much greater amount of the day (around 30 per cent). And they can be built quickly. Spain increased its wind generation from 2GW in 2000 to 15GW in 2007. On a windy day in April 2008 wind accounted for 32 per cent of all Spanish generation.

The main problem facing turbines is getting planning permission. Scout Moor straddles two local authority boundaries and is visible from a third; getting the scheme through all the planning enquiries was a major cost, and required two years of process. Peel Power commissioned market research company Mori to sample local people's views – 70 per cent of the local community supported the development. Richard Dibley, the site's manager, explains that opposition was from a small number of highly organized individuals, not the community at large.

Another complaint about turbines is the emissions arising from their production. Building the turbine and its huge subterranean foundations certainly consumes a lot of resources. But a study by Vesta, the Danish manufacturer, claims the carbon debt is paid off in seven months – so over its 20-year life the turbine will earn its carbon back 35 times over. Not zero carbon, but not far off.

So if you want to reduce your emissions, do what you can to support the building of new wind farms – choose a tariff that encourages new build and campaign locally to support wind farm developments to counter the anti-wind protestors.

Rage against the machine: Choosing energy-efficient gadgets

The amount of electricity used by appliances is reduced by buying the most energy-efficient model. This is much easier than it used to be because of the energy labelling and some excellent websites that have up-to-date information about the best-performing makes and models for a whole range of goods. The EU Commission has played a major role through its energy-labelling directives and will be doing more through another landmark piece of legislation, the Energy Using Products Directive which will ban some of the poorest-performing products over the coming years.[16]

The labelling issue is complicated by the fact that there are several competing official energy-labelling systems operating in the UK. The three main ones are given in Box 6.3.[17]

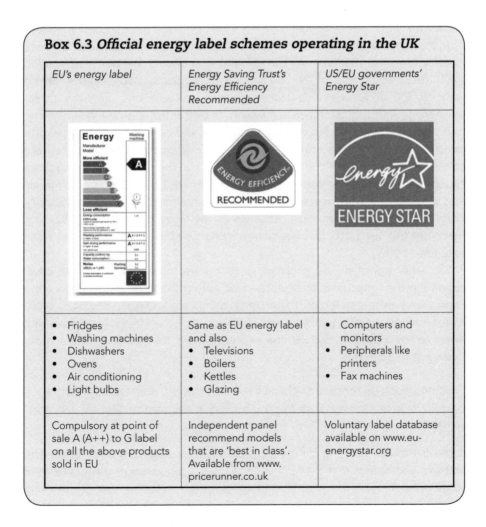

Box 6.3 _Official energy label schemes operating in the UK_

EU's energy label	Energy Saving Trust's Energy Efficiency Recommended	US/EU governments' Energy Star
• Fridges • Washing machines • Dishwashers • Ovens • Air conditioning • Light bulbs	Same as EU energy label and also • Televisions • Boilers • Kettles • Glazing	• Computers and monitors • Peripherals like printers • Fax machines
Compulsory at point of sale A (A++) to G label on all the above products sold in EU	Independent panel recommend models that are 'best in class'. Available from www.pricerunner.co.uk	Voluntary label database available on www.eu-energystar.org

The Energy Saving Trust (EST) is my favourite – it seeks to identify the best in class and gives information on how the product is superior to others. The only downside is the label is little used in the high street, so you need to check on EST's website (www.energysavingtrust.org.uk/Energy-saving-products/) before you hit the shops. The other option is buying the goods you like over the internet. EST has teamed up with the price comparison website www.pricerunner.co.uk to help you do this.

The Energy Star is the oldest energy label, established by the US Environmental Protection Agency in 1992. It's now been endorsed by the EU too but it's clunky to use, with key information (like energy use) often missing from the database.

The most important and ubiquitous of the energy labels is the EU Energy label. It is illegal for goods covered by the scheme to be displayed in stores without it. Products are marked on a scale of A to G, with A being the best and G the worst. But of course nothing is that simple. The first problem arises from the scheme's success; manufacturers have withdrawn the most inefficient models from the market – so the remaining products are bunched around the highest labels. Out of the 350 models of fridges available on the Kelkoo website, 300 are A rated or better and none is worse than C. Similarly, three-quarters of washing machines are now A or better for energy efficiency. The performance bands are fixed in the regulation and cannot easily be strength-ened to create further incentives to innovate. Washing machine are even more confusing as they have a clutch of letters ('ABA') on their labels signifying three separate criteria energy consumption (kWh per wash), washing performance and spin drying performance. The label also contains information on capacity, noise and water consumption. Because of the large proportion of washing machines that are now classified as A for energy efficiency this too has been extended to A+.

Another (more minor) problem is that some manufacturers have been grooming their machines to beat the test, rather than actually incorporating expensive new technologies. In particular dryers are finding it difficult to score well. I have heard of a tumble dryer which has an eco-setting that takes eight hours to dry a load of clothes; the express, where the heater element is on, takes just two hours.

So how much difference is there between the different energy label bands? Is it really worth swapping an old inefficient model for a better model?

Table 6.4 shows how the different product bands vary from each other. The first thing to note is that they convey the energy efficiency of devices relative to the size of machine rather than in absolute terms, for instance fridges and

Table 6.4 Actual energy used by product for the different bands (numbers of models available of each band in the UK, 2008)

Units	Fridge-freezer	Washing machines	Tumble dryers	Dishwashers	Ovens	Light bulbs	
	Relative energy use adjusted for compartments and volume	kWh per kg of cotton washed at 60°C	kWh per kg, cotton cycle	kWh for 12 place-setting wash	Energy used in medium (50L) oven (kWh/load)	Energy use per lumen of light	
A++	<30						LEDs
A+	42 (112)						
A	55 (433)	<0.19 (350)	<0.51 (3)	<1.06 (314)	<0.8 (142)	20–50	CFLs
B	75 (62)	0.23 (45)	0.59 (22)	1.25 (22)	1 (146)	75	
C	90 (1)	0.27 (38)	0.67 (75)	1.45 (3)	1.2	90	
D	100 (0)	0.31 (7)	0.75 (10)	1.65 (1)	1.4	100	Halogen
E	110 (0)	0.35 (0)	0.83 (0)	1.85 (0)	1.6	110	Tungsten
F	125 (0)	0.39 (0)	0.91 (1)	2.05	1.8	125	
G	>125 (0)	>0.39 (0)	>0.91 (0)	>2.05	>1.8	>125	
savings (£)	39	11		23		50	
savings (kgCO$_2$)	142	45		90		200	

Notes: Numbers of models for each energy band from Kelkoo price comparison website. Savings (£) and (CO$_2$) from the Energy Saving Trust and refer to the saving from replacing a product bought new in 1998 with an A or A+ purchase today. Assumes electricity costs 14p/kWh. Light bulbs: LED = light emitting diode; CFL = compact fluorescent light bulb; assumes switching tungsten for CFLs.
Source: www.energy.eu/#energy-focus and various EU directives http://europa.eu/legislation_summaries/consumers/product_labelling_and_packaging/l32004_en.htm

ovens are rated *per volume capacity*. So a big A-rated fridge might use more energy than a small C-rated fridge. Manufacturers' tendency to supersize their fridges and TVs will go uncensured by the labelling system. The second point to notice is that the gaps between the bands differs across appliances. Compact fluorescent light bulbs are up to 80 per cent better than tungsten bulbs, the best-rated fridges on the market are more than twice as good as the worst models, but the best tumble dryers are only about 40 per cent better than the worst, so there's less to be gained from shopping around.

Opportunities to reduce emissions from different appliances

Figure 6.4 shows emissions for the principal different electrical devices around the house in 2006. The total emissions come to $1360kgCO_2$/yr per household – somewhat lower than the numbers in Figure 6.1 because it excludes electrical heating and minor electrical devices.

The largest source of emissions is lighting using standard tungsten filament bulbs. They emit 15 times more CO_2 than CFLs because of their inefficiency and the large number in the average house. Household use of TVs and fridge-freezers each emit a little over $150kgCO_2$ per year. The rapid growth in home ownership of computers means they use almost half as much electricity as TVs. Washing machines are still the most emitting of kitchen appliances. The prodigious energy needed for drying clothes means tumble dryers are not

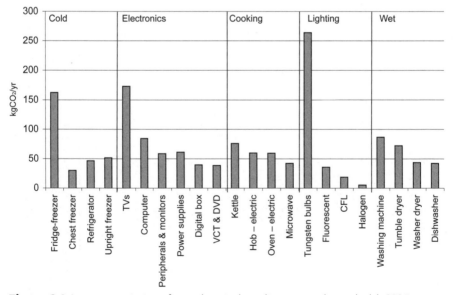

Figure 6.4 Average emissions from electrical appliances per household, 2006

Source: Market Transformation Programme (2006) www.mtprog.com, various tables in the annexes

lagging that far behind washing machines despite being only half as common as washing machines.

The following discussion helps you reduce electricity use for the principal energy-using devices. Fridges and cooking appliances have already been covered in Chapter 3 on Food.

Light bulbs

Lights use about 20 per cent of the power used in the home but only 5 per cent of the energy is actually converted to light. The average house has 25 bulbs dotted around, far more than the number of rooms due to the move away from having just one tungsten filament bulb per room to several halogen spotlights. As Table 6.4 indicated, even though halogen lights are intrinsically 10–15 per cent more efficient than tungsten bulbs this efficiency is undermined by our tendency to fit racks of many small bulbs, which in aggregate use more energy than the tungsten bulbs they replace. The real saving arises from fitting energy-efficient CFLs – which only use one-fifth of the energy of the tungsten bulb. The average home has only one energy-efficient compact fluorescent light bulb. There are several reasons cited for their low rate of uptake: their high upfront cost (but they save £40 over their lifetimes because of their lower electricity use), their bulkiness making them unsuited to some lampshades, their unsuitability for use with dimmers and their tardiness at becoming fully bright.

But a lot of these criticisms are no longer true. Technology is moving on quickly. The price of the bog standard CFL has fallen to £3, so it should payback for itself within a year. Manufacturers like Megaman and Osram now offer a wide range of shapes and sizes of CFL, and Megaman (www.megamanuk. com/) have brought out a model that works with a dimmer switch.

The leaders of the EU countries are so confident that tungsten lights have had their day that in March 2007 they announced the banning of tungsten filament bulbs by 2020. Box 6.4 documents the industry's enthusiastic response (not).

Even more efficient than CFLs are light emitting diodes. They light up immediately, last for 35,000 hours (around 15 times longer than a tungsten light), work with dimmers and are tiny. But they're expensive to produce. At the moment the cost of an LED bright enough to light a room is something like US$100 per bulb, but researcher Tim Sands at Purdue University is currently working on a radically different way of making the diodes and hoping for a 90 per cent reduction in price.[18] To date, they are mainly used in torches and bike lights where the amount of light being demanded is modest, and where batteries rather than grid electricity are supplying the energy. Even so you can buy a range of LED light bulbs from Ryness which consume a mere 2W and provide the equivalent light to a 35W tungsten bulb. The price of a bulb is £15 – or you can buy ten for £130.

Box 6.4 *How many lobbyists does it take to stop a light bulb being changed?*

In March 2007 the leaders of the European nations agreed to phase out tungsten light bulbs. This was a brave decision – perhaps the first banning of a technology purely on poor energy-efficiency performance. In some ways it's a no-brainer – low-energy compact fluorescent lights (CFLs) are a mature technology and have been around for 30 years; they use just a fifth of the electricity used by tungsten light bulbs. Though they cost more to buy, they last ten times longer. The Energy Saving Trust says they will save £40 over their lifetime, and almost 80 per cent carbon savings.

So everyone is a winner? Well not quite.[19] Some of the manufacturers of tungsten light bulbs found they were backing the wrong technology. General Electrics had poured US$200 million of investment into high-efficiency incandescent light bulbs. In a hurriedly issued press statement, appearing two days after Australia announced its ban on tungsten light bulbs and a few weeks before the EU did the same, GE claimed they were 're-inventing Edison'. In their brazen press release they boasted about a technological breakthrough that would be ready in three years, be less energy efficient than CFLs and last nowhere near as long! Edison must have spun in his grave, ruing the fact he ever created General Electric.

One of the main criticisms against compact fluorescent light bulbs is their alleged poor light quality. This might have been true some years ago. But in a Pepsi taste test-style exercise, the Energy Saving Trust invited 761 shoppers to take the light bulb challenge and see whether they preferred the light from the tungsten light bulb or the newest CFLs. In the experiment 53 per cent of shoppers either could not spot the difference or preferred the CFL.

Australia announced the phasing out of tungsten light bulbs by 2010, Canada by 2012. The UK's excruciatingly hand-wringing response was for ministers to announce they had asked retailers to voluntarily withdraw tungsten light bulbs from the shelves by 2012 – if they'd be so kind. So has the tungsten light bulb really been phased out in Europe? Who knows? There's barely been a peep from the Commission as the manufacturers plead their cases. Instead there's been a flurry of lawsuits as some manufacturers demand stronger tariff protection against Chinese CFL imports while they try to reorganize their own production plants; others who've already offshored their CFL production are launching counter-suits.

What's the take-home message? Perhaps that banning energy-inefficient products works, and politicians should be more bold. It edits out needless choices that consumers are too busy to think about. Who has the time to peer at the packaging on the back of a DVD player to find out its standby energy consumption? It also drives forward technological development. Would CFL manufacturers have invested in developing dimmable CFL lights if there hadn't been a guaranteed market for these innovations? Banning of poor-performing old technologies – bring it on.

Washing machines

Washing machines are the largest user of electricity in the house after lighting and fridges, though tumble dryers are fast catching up. Modern machines are becoming dramatically more energy efficient as manufacturers design them to become much more economical in their use of water, using as little as 50 litres of water per wash. This is illustrated in Figure 6.5, based on a German report by the excellent Oko-Institut. The last point on the graph shows the effect of replacing the standard size washing machine with a bigger model. Water consumption has dropped by three-quarters from 40L/kg of washing in 1970 to just 10L/kg in 2004. We'll cover whether to junk your existing machine and buy a new one in the next chapter.

Some tips to reduce your energy use:

- Fill the machine to its weight capacity.
- Use 30°C instead of 40°C for most clothes. This can reduce washing machine energy use by 40 per cent.
- If you have a large family buy a 7kg rather than 5kg machine (so long as you fill it).
- Use biological washing powders (as long as you aren't allergic to them); enzymes get damaged by excessive heat.
- Use the fastest spin cycle your clothes can stand: 800rpm leaves clothes with 70 per cent residual moisture, 1000 with 60 per cent, 1200 with 53 per cent, 1400 with 50 per cent and 1800rpm with 42 per cent. The energy needed to tumble-dry falls from 4kWh to 2.6kWh over the same range of spin speeds.

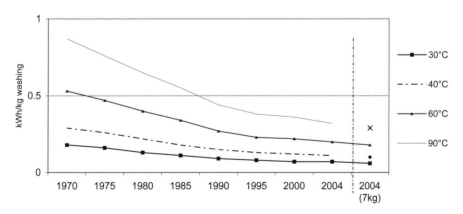

Figure 6.5 Energy used to wash 5kg of washing, by age of washing machine

Source: Oko-Institut[20]

- If you are buying a new machine choose a direct drive – it shows a modest improvement in energy efficiency and is less noisy as the motor is attached straight to the drum, rather than via a belt

Tumble dryers

It takes a lot of energy to evaporate water – that's just a fact of life. So drying a load of clothes in a tumble dryer will take twice as much energy as washing them. The cheapest 'solar' alternative is a washing line. Another alternative is the Rotamate – an outdoors rotary washing line with an umbrella to protect washing from brief showers which you can buy for £13 from eBay – featured on the TV show *Dragons' Den*.[21] If you dry your clothes indoors be aware that energy is still needed to evaporate the water; it's just that it'll be drawn from the room, so the house will be cooler and damper as a consequence.

If you have to use a tumble dryer it's probably not worth rushing out and buying a new one. The best machines on the market use about two-thirds the energy of the worst – so not a huge gain. An A-rated dryer requires about 2.5kWh per load of clothes so emits around $1kgCO_2$, costing around £0.25 in electricity per load. So to save money and carbon avoid using it. Here are a few tips:

- It's best to dry your clothes outside or in a well-ventilated indoor room.
- New electric dryers have sensors to switch them off when the clothes are dry, saving energy.
- Choose a gas-heated dryer – gas dryers cost about half as much to run and emit much less CO_2 – there are now a few on the market (White Knight). However, they cost about £100 more to buy and install (since they need a Corgi-registered engineer). You might get a payback after around eight years.
- Make sure you dry the same sort of fabric together (cotton, nylon) to avoid needlessly heating up nylon clothes that are already dry.

There was an attempt in 1999 to sell a heat pump-based dryer which would have been very energy efficient but it never caught on. It might be worth keeping a eye open to see if they are reintroduced.

Televisions

In 2005 televisions used about 8 per cent of the electricity in homes.[22] No eco-labelling scheme has been agreed, which is a shame because they are major energy users ranging from 50 to 1000W when they in use and 1 to 4W on standby. The TV market is also rapidly changing – with quite a fast turnover.

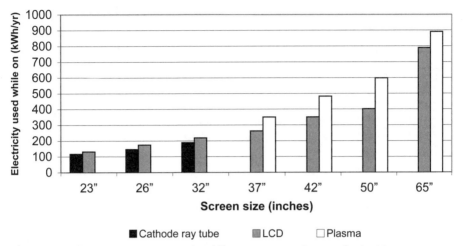

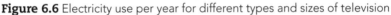

Figure 6.6 Electricity use per year for different types and sizes of television

Source: Fraunhofer Institute for Reliability and Microintegration (2007) *Energy Using Products Directive Preparatory Studies: Televisions (Lot 5)*, Final Report on Task 5 'Definition of Base Cases'.

Sales of liquid crystal display (LCD) TVs overtook those of cathode ray tube TVs in 2006; but sales of plasma remain modest because of their expense. Figure 6.6 shows the variation in the annual in-use energy consumption assuming four hours' viewing per day for the three different technologies.

The take-home message is to buy as small a screen size as you possibly can if you want to save energy. There is a tenfold difference in energy use between the respectably sized 23-inch screen and the mammoth 'in-house movie theatre' 65-inch screen. There is not a huge amount of variation between the technologies – the bad press received by plasma is deserved but not because of the poor energy efficiency *per se* (it's about a third worse than LCD) but because people who go for plasma go for a *large plasma*. Standby use of power by TVs is fairly fixed at around 20kWh per year irrespective of size. So even if you have a small TV and only watch it for four hours or so a day, leaving the TV on all the time can add 20 per cent to its electricity consumption.

Most new TVs integrate the old Freeview box so you don't need a separate digital decoder. This integration should save around 60kWh (25kgCO$_2$e) of energy use per year if you used to have an always-on Freeview before. Sky boxes take more power.

Computers

A home computer has come from nowhere to be a major user of energy. US research shows that a home PC uses around 140kWh of electricity per year,[23] resulting in emissions of around 65kgCO$_2$ per year. This is consistent with UK research which showed that mean power consumption while the computer is active is around 80W, around the same as that used by TVs. Newer machines use fast processors and video chips, which need heat sinks and fans to keep them cool – and there is an Olympian battle between Intel and its rivals striving to be faster, higher, stronger – which unfortunately means more energy hungry too (like the athletes).

In terms of reducing energy use there are a number of options. Laptops are more efficient than desktops, partly because they have smaller monitors and partly because their chipsets are designed to economize on energy use to prolong battery charge.

Windows has some powerful built-in tools for saving power when the PC is not being used: sleep (standby) and hibernate. (A screen saver does not save any power at all and shouldn't be used.) However, hardly anyone uses Windows power management facilities properly, which is a shame. In a test of 60 households (Market Transformation Programme (undated))[24] researchers logged the use of PCs for two weeks. They found that computers were in active use for six hours, operating in reduced power for 12 minutes (i.e. hardly anyone used it) and were switched off for 18 hours (though not at the mains, so the power supply unit carried on drawing some power).

So here's a quick recap on the power management options the clever people in Microsoft have designed into Windows. The *sleep* setting can be used to turn off the hard drive and monitor but carries on using some juice to ensure the software and documents running remain stored in RAM (memory). Power consumption is slashed from 80–100W down to about 6W in sleep mode. It takes two or three seconds for the computer to get going again. The *hibernate* setting is even more parsimonious in its energy use. It stashes whatever is held in memory onto the hard drive and switches off completely. No power is consumed in hibernation, but it does take a minute or more for the computer to start working again – and your hard drive needs to have enough free space to cache whatever happens to be in memory. You can play around with the options in the control panel to specify the amount of time of inaction before it goes into standby/hibernation, and also the various components that power down (hard drive, monitor). Windows Vista has got rid of hibernate, except when a laptop is running low on battery, when the computer automatically assumes brace position before power loss.[25]

A SavaPlug might be worth buying too if you're not able to switch the machine off at the wall. The plug ensures that when the main PC is powered down, two subsidiary devices (e.g. monitor and printer) switch off completely too.

Mobile device rechargers get a bad press for their energy use. But they're actually only minor power users. In my house, which is not exactly short of mobile phones and iPods, their combined standby energy is 5 per cent of

> **Box 6.5 *Websites for information on green electronic goods***
>
> There is a lot of useful material around on the internet which is worth checking before buying a new appliance. Most of the websites also act as price comparison sites with links to websites if you want to buy the goods too.
>
> - www.kelkoo.co.uk allows you to search appliances by their energy label band.
> - www.sust-it.net/ has information on the actual energy consumption of many brands and models both 'in use' and in standby settings, submitted by the manufacturers. It is particularly good for electronic goods, outside the scope of the official energy labelling schemes.
> - www.ecoelectricals.co.uk/ is a similar website, though with a more restricted range of goods.
> - www.whitegoodshelp.co.uk/about.html gives techie advice on fridges, washing machines, dryers and dishwashers.
>
> The UK's long-established consumer champion Which? also often has information on energy use for products, but it's a bit patchy. Good Energy Shop, a spin-off from Good Energy, the electricity supplier, has decent reviews of the products written by professional environmentalists.

total electricity use. If you always forget to turn your recharger off at the plug it might be worth investing in a solar charger (around £30) which is an elegant way of utilizing solar power cheaply without all the losses from converting DC current to AC and then back again in the recharger.

Greenpeace have launched a fairly useful review of the environmental performance of different brands producing electronic goods.[26] The information is mainly drawn from corporate reports rather than testing appliances but it does set out companies' commitments on energy efficiency.

What I Did and Didn't Do

We used around 2000kWh of electricity in our house last year (emitting around 875kgCO$_2$). This is well below the UK average since most of our lights were already fitted with low-energy bulbs, and we make a point of switching things off at the wall. It's going to be a challenge to reduce our emissions further, given that we start from such a low base already. I need to start by looking at how we use electricity in the house.

Our house has 34 electrical devices. This is just the gadgets that are connected to sockets most of the time – it excludes all those gathering dust in the attic and cupboards: the drill, the hair dryer, the electric toothbrush and hair clipper, which are used a few times a year.

I used a plug-in meter to measure the power consumption of all our electrical devices and multiplied it by my estimate of how many hours a year each device was in operation and in standby (see Figure 6.7). A couple of devices proved difficult to measure: the electric oven and grill because they are wired into the mains circuit instead of plugged in, and the washing machine because the wire is hidden behind the built-in cupboards. These were measured using the Owl meter.

Lighting accounts for around a quarter of our electricity use. This is despite the fact most of our bulbs are already energy efficient. The principal exception is in our kitchen where there is a rack of six 60W spotlights that is on for about three hours a day. This accounts for around 80 per cent of the lighting energy need.

We have three computers in the house – a desktop and two laptops (one from my wife's work). An energy audit neatly captured how sad our lives are – we spend an inordinate amount of time on the home computers catching up on emails and tending to other commitments: and since the launch of BBC's iPlayer I watch a lot of TV on the PC too. The laptop and the desktop are in use about the same amount of time – each for four or five hours a day. The base unit of the PC uses more than four times more power (90W compared to the laptop's 20W). Once you add on the PC's peripherals – especially the monitor – the whole rig consumes seven times more power than the laptop. We also have a Wi-Fi hub which is on 24/7 – though it only consumes 9W it uses the same amount of electricity as my laptop over the course of the day.

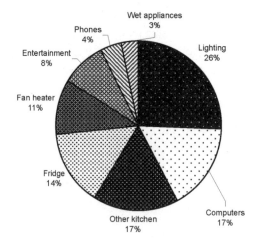

Figure 6.7 Electricity energy use in my house

I thought an assessment of electricity use for entertainment – TV, DVD and music centres – could provide us a few moments of smugness. We own a 20-inch LCD TV made by LG, which we turn off at the socket at night. It uses 50W when on, and a mere 1W in standby. However there are three other devices attached to the same plug point – DVD, digibox and a cheap music centre. I bought the music centre one Christmas; I don't recall ever switching it on. Its baleful screen is constantly blinking 'Hello' at us or listing its bog-standard features as though we cared. Whoever designed it could be electrocuted on the electricity it wastes. It consume 25W in use and a jaw-dropping 14W even when switched off (which is all the time). It uses £10 of electricity a year even though it's never turned on. We have another music centre in the kitchen which we listen to over breakfast; this was an equally cheap and cheerful load of trash. It consumes 3W, whether on or in standby but suffers total amnesia if you turn it off at the socket – forgetting the time and all the pre-programmed stations. As a result we tend to leave it on all the time.

We also have four phone chargers for our mobiles (my ten-year-old daughter has a hand-me-down) and my wife's Blackberry. They consume between 2 and 7W of energy; the least efficient gobbles up 60kWh a year (£8 per year of power) if it's always left on. The difference between the different phone chargers is interesting. It only costs a few pence more to design an energy-efficient charger ... why are we so slow to make manufacturers do this? The South Korean manufacturer HTC's charger uses much less in standby than the one-would-expect-environmental Finnish Nokia. The parsimony of the South Korean gadget's use of electricity, and that of the LG television, appear to be driven by the South Korean government's standby power consumption regulations which have now been in force for ten years and are ingrained in the manufacturers' psyche. It knocks the spots off our own grandly titled but toothless programme – the Market Transformation Programme – which has been kicking along for years too!

The small individual use of power by standby adds up. Altogether our electrical phone chargers and entertainment goods used 200kWh of electricity in standby and just 100kWh in use. This is even though we were already in the habit of switching most appliances off at the plug at night!

We also use a 2kW fan heater in winter, just to warm a single room when there's only one of us in the house. We use it barely 100 hours a year but it still accounts for 10 per cent of energy use. However, this remains a much more energy-efficient way of keeping a single room warm than turning on the 25kW gas central heating.

We have two wet appliances: a washing machine and an iron. They both consume around 35kWh a year. I've never much seen the point in ironing and have tended to dress casually at work keeping a suit and shirt at hand for important meetings. Slightly ironically, my last ever meeting as a civil servant was with Adair Turner, the recently installed climate tsar. I respectfully donned my suit and made my obsequious presentation to him; a couple of days later he coincidentally gave an interview on climate change on the radio urging people to dress down at work.

Bringing It Altogether

We are not exactly profligate electricity users, but we still managed to reduce emissions by 42 per cent. Here's what we did:

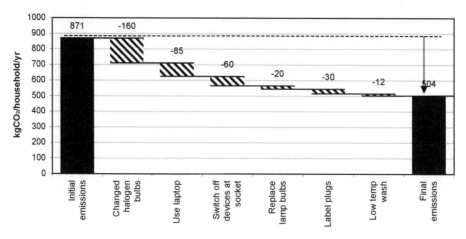

Figure 6.8 Summary of the GHG impacts of the changes in household electricity use ($kgCO_2e/yr$)

Changed the 60W halogen spotlights in the kitchen to 7W Megaman reflector bulbs

These cost £10 each so £60 for the room and saved around $160kgCO_2$ per year and around £40 per year in electricity. I also saved the cost of continually replacing the halogen bulbs which were constantly blowing and cost around £30 a year to replace.

Stopped using the desktop and worked entirely from my laptop

This cost nothing and saves around $85kgCO_2$ per year of electricity worth £22 per year.

Got anal about switching things off at the socket and not leaving them in standby

This is very boring and irritates my wife and you might not wish to do this but it saves a further 60kgCO_2 a year (£15/yr) at no cost, in addition to the savings from isolating the seldom-used devices. I also got a SavaPlug for free from a conference, which I've linked to the desktop, but this does the same thing and saves no further electricity. The main negative point is having to find Radio 4 every morning on our amnesiac kitchen radio. I'll try and get Mum to buy me a wind-up radio for Diwali.

Replaced the remaining five tungsten filament light bulbs in our lamps and toilet with CFLs

These cost £5 each from B&Q so £25 for the whole lot. Together we use them for about four hours a day – so they save around £8 per year in electricity and about 32kgCO_2. It also saves on the cost of the light bulbs – probably £1 a year.

Labelled the plugs and changed the configuration of plugs on our sockets to isolate low-use appliances when not in use

This stopped my power-sapping living room hi-fi system being switched on every time the TV was on. It costs nothing and saves 30kgCO_2 per yr (£7/yr) of electricity and stops the witless fluorescent messages.

Turned the washing temperature down from 40°C to 30°C and started using biological washing powders

The ASDA research says this reduces energy use by 40 per cent. I have no idea whether this is true or not but have credited a 12kgCO_2 per year saving.

Changed tariff from Ecotricity to British Gas zero carbon

This was a difficult choice and I have agonized about whether it was the correct one. In terms of pure global carbon emissions savings British Gas have got the most attractive tariff through their purchase of Kyoto carbon offsets. They also retire the highest proportion of ROCs, which in my view is the best way of stimulating new development of renewables within the UK. I also like the fact they've set up a fund for installing renewables in schools as I think getting kids to experience, feel pride and become accustomed to renewables is very important. But I also like Ecotricity's commitment to getting their hands dirty actually commissioning and building new renewables. The extra cost of changing tariff is £22 a year. It is dual fuel so also neutralizes our modest gas emissions, but more about my views on offsetting in the final chapter.

In the longer term the other thing to do is buy the most fuel-efficient fridge on the market when it's time to change the old one. I'll also want to switch to LED spotlights in our dining room which still uses tiny halogen bulbs. This can wait till when we extend the kitchen.

Notes

1   Though EDF's UK chief claims they can be built by 2017.
2   See Tom Burke's article, 'The lousy economics of nuclear power', in the September 2008 edition of *Prospect* for more information on the prospects for new nuclear power stations.
3   British Wind Association (2008) *Wind Energy in the UK: A BWEA State of the Industry Report,* www.bwea.com/pdf/publications/Industry_Report_08.pdf (accessed July 2009).
4   Energy Saving Trust (2007) *The Ampere Strikes Back: How Consumer Electronics are Taking Over the World* www.energysavingtrust.org.uk/Publication-Download/?p=4&pid=1085 (accessed June 2009).
5   Energy Saving Trust (2007) *The Ampere Strikes Back: How Consumer Electronics are Taking Over the World,* www.energysavingtrust.org.uk/Publication-Download/?p=4&pid=1085 (accessed June 2009).
6   BERR (2008) *Energy Consumption in the UK, Domestic Data Tables,* www.berr.gov.uk/whatwedo/energy/statistics/publications/ecuk/page17658.html (accessed June 2009).
7   Fraunhofer Institute for Reliability and Microintegration (2007) *Energy Using Products Directive Preparatory Studies: Televisions (Lot 5),* Final Report on Task 4 'Technical analysis', Fraunhofer Institute for Reliability and Microintegration, IZM, Berlin.
8   Environment Change Institute (2006), *Effectiveness of Feedback on Energy Consumption,* Environment Change Institute, Oxford University.
9   Daniel-Ivad, J. (2007) *Environmental Impact of Batteries: Green House Gas Emissions and Solid Battery Waste from Alkaline Batteries,* Pure Energy Visions Inc, Toronto.
10 The picture has now become more complicated as the government has reformed the renewable obligation to give more ROCs for immature technologies, which need higher subsidy, and fewer for mature technologies like wind, which were making a killing from the 4.5p/kWh extra.
11 This view was not shared by the Advertising Standards Authority, which forced British Gas to pull TV advertising in January 2008 because they found advertising implying it was zero carbon was misleading.
12 Department of Trade and Industry (2006) *Domestic Photovoltaic Field Trials,* Building Research Establishment, Contract Number S/P2/00305.
13 Starr, M. and Palz, W. (1983) *Photovoltaic Power for Europe: An Assessment Study,* Springer, Dordrecht.
14 BERR, UK Wind Speed Database, www.berr.gov.uk/energy/sources/renewables/explained/wind/windspeed-database/page27708.html.
15 Encraft (2008) *Warwick Wind Trials Interim Report August 2008,* www.warwickwindtrials.org.uk/resources/Interim+Report+August+2008.pdf (accessed June 2009).

16 They are starting rather ignominiously with banning mercury street lights, which actually save quite a lot of energy!

17 The Carbon Trust also runs a scheme for identifying some low-energy investment goods for relief from capital gains tax.

18 Purdue University (2008) *Advance brings low-cost, bright LED lighting closer to reality,* www.purdue.edu/uns/x/2008b/080717SandsLighting.html (accessed July 2009).

19 Thanks to Matt Prescott (www.banthebulb.org) for these insights.

20 Oko-Institut (2005) *Eco-Efficiency Analysis of Washing Machines,* Oko-Institut, Freiberg, Germany, www.oeko.de/new/dok/318text.php (accessed July 2009).

21 But the entrepreneur famously blew off the approaches from two of the Dragons.

22 Energy Saving Trust (2007) *The Ampere Strikes Back: How Consumer Electronics are Taking Over the World* www.energysavingtrust.org.uk/Publication-Download/?p=4&pid=1085 (accessed June 2009).

23 Williams, E. (undated) *Environmental Impacts of Microchip and Computer Production,* United Nations University, Tokyo.

24 Market Transformation Programme (undated) *Monitoring Home Computers,* www.mtprog.com (accessed June 2009).

25 It's possible to rejuvenate the hibernate setting in Windows Vista by going to the Command prompt and typing in 'powercfg -h on' (no speech marks). It's a bit buggy so might not be worth it just to save 6W.

26 Greenpeace, *Guide to Greener Electronics,* www.greenpeace.org/raw/content/international/press/reports/Guide-Greener-Electronics-10-edition.pdf (accessed June 2009).

Waste Not, Want Not

Emissions per person from making, packaging and transporting goods release around $8tCO_2e$ per year. Their disposal causes a further $0.25tCO_2e$ per year. To make a substantial reduction in this figure it's not enough to recycle – we actually have to consume less. An economical environmentalist will need to reduce his throughput of goods but retain the use of the goods. This might be from extending the goods' life, gifting and re-using items, and mending them. Only once these opportunities have been exhausted should we recycle them. To reduce emissions:

- Buy fewer new belongings, especially objects with high embodied energy like electronics. It is worth stepping back and considering whether you actually need to replace items which break down or get lost. Maybe you could be happier having less clutter and fewer possessions. This can save money and simplify your life.
- Encourage re-use of things you no longer need by giving them to charity shops or using sites like Freecycle. CD and games exchanges will also swap goods. Borrow books, CDs and DVDs from public libraries and friends.
- Go virtual: newspapers, music and video can now be enjoyed without buying physical goods. The energy used by internet providers is much less than the energy used to make and transport the physical goods.
- Buy goods that are easy to repair and maintain, and keep them for longer. The environmental benefit of recycling materials in complex physical goods is trivial compared to the energy used to make and transport the goods.
- Recycle packaging, but make sure you segregate the waste as per the council's instructions. Be an active citizen locally. Much more can be done to improve the value and market value of recycled materials collected by local authorities. Push for the collection of segregated wastes, especially plastics and glass.

Our economy, I think, is still ... the fundamentals of our economy are strong.
(John McCaine, 15 September 2008, the day Lehman Brothers filed for
bankruptcy and the financial crisis really got going)

Why should I part with my children's inheritance investing in this?
(Theo Paphitis, *Dragons' Den* panellist)

Introduction

Economics is known as the dismal science. But economists have been known
to tell jokes. One joke they tell at the expense of environmentalists goes: 'The
Stone Age didn't finish because people ran out of stones.' It's not a joke that
will necessarily make you laugh out loud but there is truth behind the irony:
markets have been good at inducing us to invent our way out of resource scar-
city. But does this mean resources will never become scarce? Whatever their
skills as stand-up comics, economists *are* dismal scientists. It's virtually impossible to use controlled scientific experiments to predict how the economy will
behave. Instead economists rely on theoretical models; the veracity of these
are statistically tested from historical and cross-sectional data. John McCaine
– at the time he spoke surely one of best-briefed men in the world – reminds
us how spectacularly wrong economic advice can be.

The second quote is by the sometime venture capitalist Theo Paphitis,
rationalizing his reluctance to commit resources on a business venture he is
less than enthusiastic about. Financial capital is scarce and all businessmen
know it needs to be retained for superior future uses. Palpably there is only
a finite amount of high-grade mineral ores in the Earth's crust; the rate of
extraction of fossil fuels in many countries is already in decline. Though no
one speaks about 'peak iron ore' or 'peak halibut' – these phrases somehow
sounding more clumsy than 'peak oil' – there is evidence that we are running
up against constraints. The price of metal ores surged by 60 per cent between
2007 and early 2008; so too did food prices. The metal markets are under
similar demand and supply pressures as the oil and food markets. Before
the current recession got going the news was about how China was wining
and dining unsavoury African dictators to guarantee access to the world's
best mineral ore deposits – precisely what the US did to the Saudis only two
generations earlier.

This chapter is about subjecting our handling of natural material resources
to the Paphitis principles. The materials we use are not available in infinite
quantities and there are benefits aside from carbon emissions from using them
more wisely. The chapter is also about rethinking whether buying and owning
more stuff really brings us happiness. There's a growing body of psychological research looking at the pleasure we *really* derive from purchasing new
goods.

The Scale of the Challenge

How much carbon is emitted by making and disposing of stuff? This is a very difficult question to answer and as far as I can tell no one has yet produced a complete answer. As a result of the credit crunch we are used to thinking of the interconnectedness of the financial world pretty well – the consequences of housing defaults in the US are still rippling through the banking system.

The production, manufacture and disposal of goods is no less intertwined. The laptop I am working on is made by a firm in the US, where the microprocessor and video chips are also made, the screen was made in the Far East and the machine itself assembled in Ireland. It was purchased using a Visa card in sterling, but the manufacturer might have hedged its exposure to exchange rate changes in the Forex market in London. So trying to work out the CO_2 emissions in a good we need to think about energy used in extraction, production and transport, and the business service and component industries too.

It is not possible to follow this web for all the products we buy individually. But we can get an estimate of how much emissions go into making stuff at the macro level. According to the ONS environmental accounts,[1] emissions from UK businesses and government were 570MtCO$_2$e in 2004. Household purchases make up half of the final demand, the other half is government, investment and exports. We also have to add the emissions arising in producing our (net) imported goods. Research funded by Defra calculates the embodied emissions from imported household goods to have been 370MtCO$_2$ in 2004. Net emissions have been rising fast, from 4 per cent of UK emissions in 1990 to 21 per cent in 2004.[2] The upshot of this is that the embedded emissions from making the goods used by UK households is around 8tCO$_2$ per person.[3]

Throwing stuff away also causes greenhouse gas emissions. Government data suggests the average household throws away around a tonne of material per year. To this could be added a further 2.5 tonnes of sewage. These waste products are a climate change issue because energy is needed to dispose of waste, putrescent waste like food gives off methane in landfill sites and sewage treatment works, and plastics give rise to carbon dioxide when they are burnt in incinerators. So how much greenhouse gas is emitted from disposing of stuff? According to the ONS environmental accounts around 15MtCO$_2$e of methane is released from landfill sites (covers not just households but also business waste), and a further 0.7MtCO$_2$ of carbon dioxide emissions from sewage treatment works. Emissions from our wastes are around 0.25tCO$_2$e per year.

But for a household to reduce its emissions from waste we need to understand which products and which waste streams give rise to the most emissions. And there is no getting away from it – we buy a lot. A two-person household buys around 4400 products a year, weighing 2.4 tonnes with 180kg

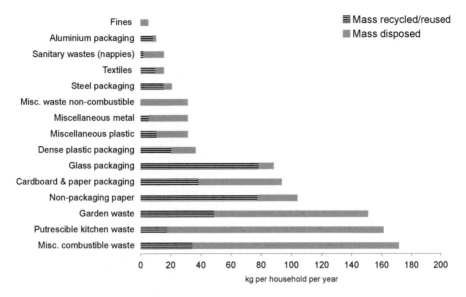

Figure 7.1 Mass of materials recycled and thrown away per household, 2007

Notes: Misc. combustible waste: mainly wood, but includes combustible DIY materials and furniture; fines: dust, ash; misc. non-combustible: rubble, brick and animal litter.

Source: Open University annual waste survey based on 207 households, undertaken on behalf of Defra.

of packaging. Smaller households buy more goods per person, larger households less.[4]

To understand this we have to hold our noses and dig into these figures a bit more. Since 1994 intrepid Open University (OU) students, armed with nasal plugs and heavy duty gloves, have provided a detailed breakdown of their weekly waste disposal habits[5] – a fact worth pointing out to your children next time they complain about *their* homework. Their data is captured in Figure 7.1. About a third of the solid waste thrown out is packaging. The much-maligned plastic shopping bags account for only a few per cent of all the waste leaving our homes; wine bottles figure rather more significantly than the paper and plastic packaging – these are students after all.

There is scope to reduce the amount of emissions arising from disposal if we increase the amount recycled, especially the recycling of energy-intensive goods like metals.

The different types of waste vary in the extent they are recycled. It is hard to recycle garden, kitchen and 'misc. combustible waste', and this is borne out in the OU data. We are much better at recycling newspaper and magazines (75 per cent), glass (90 per cent) and metals (around 80 per cent), in large part because of the much better-developed facilities to collect these materials. But if we want to reduce our emissions it's not enough to know UK-wide totals. We need to make choices about where to focus effort. Should we cut back on clothes shopping or the mobile phone? Figure 7.2 gives my estimate of the greenhouse gas emissions embodied in the creation and disposal of materials. The data are mainly from an analytical report published by Defra alongside the new Waste Strategy.[6] A slightly different approach is taken for food, where I have used the calculations from the earlier food chapter to work out the average emissions in food. This is part of the reason the embodied emissions are so high. I don't have equivalent embodied emissions data for other goods. Defra's data on embodied emissions in plastic are much higher than most other commentators'.

The figure suggests that the emissions arising from making the materials we use are around 2.6tCO$_2$e per household per year and those from disposal (chiefly methane from landfill gas) around 0.24tCO$_2$e per household per year. This figure is much lower than the 8tCO$_2$e per person (17tCO$_2$e per household) mentioned at the start of the chapter, because it only includes the energy used in producing the raw materials. A washing machine is more than just an ingot of steel and a few kilograms of plastic – energy has gone into reordering the plastic and metal to make it into a washing machine. Such ordering of matter takes energy and creates commercial and industrial waste. To demonstrate how significantly we understate the reality, it's worth looking at life-cycle analyses of some famously high-emitting finished goods: PCs, mobile phones and clothes (see Figure 7.3). For each of these, the carbon dioxide produced is 20–100 times the weight of the goods themselves. By way of comparison,

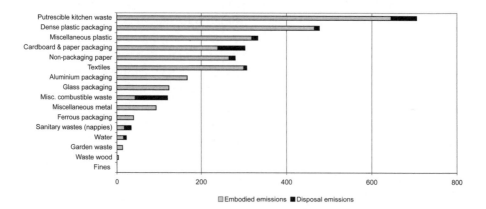

Figure 7.2 Greenhouse gas emissions from manufacturing materials and from their disposal (kg per household per year)

Sources: Embodied emissions from Defra (2007);[7] disposal emissions from ERM and Golders Associates (Annexes A and B)[8] assume 100-year global warming potential from future waste options; nappies, Environment Agency; water and sewage from ONS environmental accounts[9].

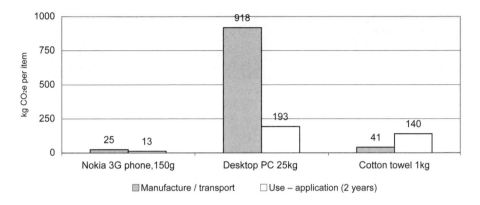

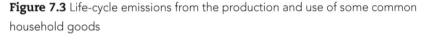

□ Manufacture / transport   □ Use – application (2 years)

Figure 7.3 Life-cycle emissions from the production and use of some common household goods

Source: Nokia (2005),[10] Kuehr and Williams (2003),[11] Blackburn and Payne (2004)[12]

the CO_2 emissions needed to make the raw materials are only around half to twice the mass of the material being produced.

How come this huge discrepancy? Let's look at PCs first. One estimate suggests 1.7kg of fossil fuels and chemicals are needed to make a single 2g memory chip.[13] Microprocessors, graphics processors and memory chips are highly engineered components: high-energy lasers operating in sterile, dust-free fabrication plants scratch out narrow gullies for electrons to flow down – their widths measured in nanometres. The study goes on to calculate that the manufacture of a PC and monitor emits a whopping 918kgCO_2e. I have to pinch myself to comprehend that number – this is the same amount as my wife and I emit in a year from all the electricity used in the house.

The huge amount of emissions required to make consumer electronics is reinforced by looking at the share of energy used in the manufacture of three items. For phones, manufacture accounts for two-thirds of energy use, for desktop computers over four-fifths, but for cotton towels (assuming they are washed at 40°C and tumble-dried 100 times in their lifetime) just a fifth – and cotton is notorious for the large amounts of fertilizer, water and pesticide used in its manufacture.

Options for Reducing CO_2

The government has developed of notion of the *Waste Hierarchy* (see Figure 7.4). This is the sequence of actions people should take to reduce the amount of waste, especially packaging, they produce. Luckily it accords well with the sequence for reducing greenhouse gas emissions too. (Incidentally the world's

Figure 7.4 The waste hierarchy

second coolest Hawaiian, and sometime surfer, Jack Johnson renders the hierarchy into one of the better environmental songs '3Rs'; – worth checking out on YouTube).

If our objective is to reduce greenhouse gas emissions as opposed to reducing waste it's worth adding another option – *electronification* – to the hierarchy, by which I mean substituting material goods for electronic goods and energy from waste. Electronification is already a major trend – more music is bought off the internet than in CD format; newspapers are read off the screen instead of from squashed dead trees; we can watch TV shows and movies from iPlayer or video on demand rather than buying the DVD or videocassette; and phone conferencing facilities, like BT's MeetMe, and videoconferencing are making it much simpler to reduce travel. Electronic is not the same thing as carbon free; BT, which owns most of the UK's data cabling emitted 680,000tCO$_2$ in 2008 – equivalent to 10kg per citizen – but small compared to the emissions of all the newspaper and DVDs avoided.

But before forsaking paper and plastic for electronic databases, it's worth considering how much emissions are caused by the big websites, especially those with banks of servers holding vast amounts of data, or undertaking searches on our behalf like Google and Apple. A Harvard academic, Alex Wissner-Gross, has calculated that viewing a simple website generates 0.02gCO$_2$ per second, a complex website with graphics and sound (like iPlayer) about ten times that figure, and a Google search which is distributed over many competing servers up to 7gCO$_2$ per search. (The latter figure is disputed by Google who claim a figure of just 0.2gCO$_2$) This implies an hour-long TV show would emit 0.7kgCO$_2$ – this rapidly mounts up. If you watch around ten hours of TV on iPlayer a week we are talking a third of a tonne CO$_2$ per year from viewing habits alone. But there are good reasons to believe that these emissions will come down, unlike those from conventional media. The major websites are all investing in technologies and approaches to reduce their emissions, and there is huge scope for them to do so successfully. Simply moving the servers to a country like Iceland, which is cold and flush with renewable electricity, will simultaneously reduce the electricity needed to keep the buildings cool and utilize the country's surplus geothermal power. So I am making a strong plug for going electronic, even though the emissions are significant.

Energy from waste fits halfway between the 'recycle' and 'incinerate' options but is presently socially excluded from the hierarchy. There are two types of energy-from-waste plant: electricity only (fairly common) and combined heat and power (almost unheard of in the UK but common in continental Europe). Waste is a poor fuel, having a low and unpredictable calorific content, which means it doesn't burn at a particularly high temperature. We're only able to convert around 25 per cent of its energy content into power; it's not too bad at producing heat suitable for warming homes, and plants in Denmark manage to recover 50–60 per cent of the energy either as heat or power.

While there has been some success in reducing the amount of waste going to landfill and a corresponding increase in the amount recycled and inciner-ated, there's a glass ceiling preventing us scaling the higher echelons of the waste hierarchy. The amount of matter being thrown away is still growing, and a sale at John Lewis is still more likely to have them queuing round the block than one at Oxfam.

Reducing waste

'I've got a better idea: don't buy these ships, buy better ships.' 'But Sam we want these ships. This is as little we've paid for a fleet of ships.' … 'Buy ships that won't break up. There's a broader liability to think of.'
(Paraphrased conversation from 'In the shadow of two gunmen, Part II', *West Wing*, series 2)

Reducing our production of goods means either buying less or buying more durable goods and using them for longer. As the writers of the script imply above, buying better, more reliable goods is more expensive in the short term and can be hard to justify. Making do with less will be considered at the end of this chapter. Let's see about the cost and benefits from reducing waste for a few different types of goods.

How to avoid buying so many personal computers

Computers first, as they take a huge amount of energy to produce. In a quick survey of people around me, they give two main reasons for chucking their PCs – first, because the PCs have started to slow down and, second, as successive incarnations of software became more bloated their hard disks or memory could no longer cope. The reason why a PC gets slower over time is not because of the onset of arthritis in its cables or memory chips, but because the hard drive becomes fragmented and because it's running loads of unnec-essary programs which have insinuated themselves into the start-up routine. (You might also have a virus but you don't need a book like this to tell you to get it sorted.) You can defragment the hard drive using standard utilities in Windows. If you've got unwanted programs starting up, here is a link to a page that explains how to remove unnecessary programs launching at start-up that I find useful and unbiased: http://reviews.cnet.com/4520-10165_7-5554402-1.html. Windows probably also gets slow because the registry file has become corrupted. The jury is out on whether the bloated registry files really do make that much of a difference on modern versions of Windows. I have read that some of the packages purporting to clean up the registry mess up the computer.

In terms of software, you need to be fairly ruthless in suppressing packages like Adobe's Acrobat reader updating for no good reason. Just to give you some idea of the rate of inflation in memory requirement: version 7 (released in January 2005) took just 90MB, version 8 (released November 2006) took 170MB and version 9 (released in July 2008) – took 405MB of hard drive space – it's like the Weimar Republic all over. It's worth asking yourself whether this quadrupling of size is justified by the additional functionality, especially if you have to upgrade your computer just to fit the bigger packages. This book and graphics have been put together using the 2003 versions of Word and Excel. Even if you need to upgrade the base unit, do keep the monitor as it accounts for around a quarter of the production emissions.

Electronic goods

Defra's Market Transformation Programme undertook work to understand the weight of appliances being sent to disposal. These are probably largely *in addition* to the waste reported in Figure 7.1, since the large bulky items in Table 7.1 will often either be taken away by retailers as they install the new one or be put in a neighbourhood skip and therefore end up in a commercial waste site. The tonnage below represents some 2 million fridges and 2 million white goods being chucked a year – or roughly around 10–15 per cent of the stock.

The frequency with which we replace electronic goods is important. A painfully detailed life-cycle analysis of a number of TVs[14] showed that a 23kg LCD TV with a 32-inch screen emitted 146kgCO_2e in production and 32kgCO_2e in disposal (though nearly all of this can be recovered if the TV is recycled). My back-of-the-envelope calculations suggest the average TV lasts for just six years, and probably with half its life as a secondary TV. The upshot of all this is that thinking twice about upgrading our appliances can save significant amounts of carbon dioxide. By way of comparison, for every extra day you keep the TV described above beyond six years you save 80g of CO_2, equivalent to around 50 carrier bags.

The Swedish white-good manufacturer Electrolux has undertaken quite a detailed analysis of the environmental effects of its manufacturing. In 2005 it produced 40 million fridges, vacuum cleaners, washing machines and ovens weighing 3 million tonnes. About half of this by mass was metals, about a sixth

Table 7.1 Mass of different appliances and hazardous waste sources from homes

	1000 tonnes
Fridges/freezers	104
White goods	290
TVs	196
VCRs, DVDs, computer base units	14
Household hazardous waste	17
Paint	43
Varnish	7
Lighting domestic	8.5
Lighting commercial	9.5
Total	385

Source: Market Transformation Programme (2006);[15] paint: Oko-Institut (2005);[16] varnish: ONS (2007).[17]

was plastics and the rest packaging and miscellaneous materials; a third of the weight of a washing machine is concrete to stop the machine from vibrating. Electrolux is making much greater use of recycled materials, including recycled plastic, in the manufacture of its goods.

Nonetheless, the manufacture of appliances is an important source of emissions in the home. Life-cycle analyses of fridges and washing machines undertaken by the Oko-Institut suggest their production (mainly from making the metals, plastics, etc.) gives rise to around four times their own mass of CO_2.[18] This is roughly equivalent to twice the energy they consume in a year.

So should we replace old, relatively energy-efficient models with newer more efficient ones? This is the same question we posed when we thought about replacing an old banger with a new car. In the Oko-Institut paper they suggest that a new A+ 40kg fridge, or a 95kg fridge-freezer will use about half the electricity of a similar model from 2000 and save €18 or €25, respectively, per year. But because the purchase price of the fridge is about the same as the price of its lifetime electricity use it's unlikely to be cost-effective to scrap the fridge early on financial grounds; but it does make carbon sense after a couple of years – highlighting the cheapness of electricity once again. If it breaks down, however, it's probably wiser to have it recycled rather than fixed. If you are determined to reduce your personal emissions it's worth thinking about whether you can sell your old fridge to someone with a really clapped-out old one.

Consuming fewer clothes

According to the ONS we spend an average of £1200 per year per household on clothes; which in spite of the ubiquity of high street fashion stores still represents a 15 per cent reduction in our real expenditure compared to spending 20 years ago.[19] Altogether this represented 1.1 million tonnes in weight or 17kg of clothes per person (women spend twice as much as men).[20] Another estimate for 2004 based on Customs and Excise trade data puts the figure even higher at 55kg per person, of which 35kg is clothes.[21] Both represent a substantial amount of clothes – 100–200 items per person per year. The table below shows the weight of different garments from my wardrobe so you can get some idea of how much clothing 55kg represents. Until the credit crunch crunched it was still growing. In 2007 we bought 20 per cent more clothes, by weight, compared to the year before. Given the limited amount of wardrobe space most of us have, many of these clothes end up in the 9000 or so charity clothes banks, and from there who knows – who wants to buy second hand when you can buy a brand new T-shirt for less than a fiver, and a pair of jeans for just £10?

Table 7.2 Weight of some clothes from my wardrobe, per garment

	Weight (g)
Jeans	500
Jumper	400
T-shirt	200
Socks/underwear	50–100

So what are the environmental implications of the huge throughput of all this fabric? At the global level textiles are around half and half natural (largely cotton) and synthetic. Each kilogram of fabric emits around $6kgCO_2$ during its cultivation and production and around $0.5kgCO_2e$ in its disposal (assumes 50 per cent re-used and 90 per cent of waste incinerated). Figure 7.5 shows how this varies for three fabrics. There is surprisingly little difference between cotton and viscose. Both are made from natural materials, but viscose is man-made from the wood pulp. The production of nylon fibres is about the same in this life-cycle analysis. The use phase shows the use of energy to wash and dry the two garments 25 times. The cotton is assumed to be washed at a high temperature, tumble-dried and ironed. The viscose on the other hand is simply drip-dried. But overall we can see the purchase of textiles accounts for around $200kgCO_2/kg$.

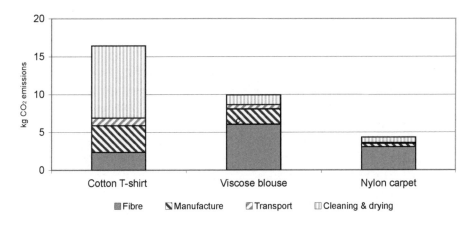

Figure 7.5 Emissions of CO_2 from the production and use of different materials (per kg textile)

Source: Adapted from Allwood et al (2006)[22]

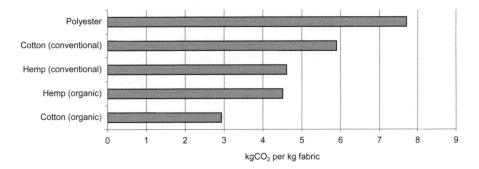

Figure 7.6 CO_2 emissions from the crop cultivation and fibre production for different textiles

Note: Several of the results represent averages of a number of studies; there is a wide spread for each fibre.

Source: Stockholm Environmental Institute and Bioregional (2005)[23]

Figure 7.6 shows the effect of using different materials. This shows that natural fibres emit between a quarter and two-thirds less CO_2e than polyester. However, the studies appeared to exclude emissions of nitrous oxide from fertilizer production and use. For arable crops this is around three times more important than CO_2 emissions. There might be some scope for reducing emissions by buying organic natural fibres or switching to clothes which include hemp fibre; but the real trick to decarbonizing is buying fewer clothes.

Hemp is an interesting alternative to cotton. Until the 1930s it was an important source of fibre but it became a casualty of an earlier *war on drugs* and was banned in the US and the UK because of the plant's close resemblance to marijuana. The fibre is harder wearing than cotton, so it should last longer. The plant is tough and, unlike cotton, requires few pesticides or fertilizers. It also lacks cotton's prodigious thirst – the cotton crop has already drained the Aral sea, and looks like it might down the Indus too. The production of 1kg of cotton needs around 10 tonnes of water, the same quantity of hemp needs a mere 2 tonnes. The Australian firm Braintree (www.braintreehemp. co.uk) make hemp clothes (and also clothes made from the softer bamboo and soya fibres).

The CO_2 emissions from washing and drying clothes are much more significant than those from the production of the fibre. Here drip-dry polyester wins hand down.

Furnishings

In terms of choosing materials for furniture and doors, the choice is often between wood and engineered woods like medium-density fibre board (MDF – made from wood fibres), plywood (wood veneer) or chipboard (wood chips or dust). Engineered woods have the advantage of being less prone to warping, but if the veneer is cracked and exposed to the outside they tend to soak up water and swell – an issue in kitchen surfaces especially. Their life-cycle emissions can be 30 per cent higher than wood timber because of the energy used to make the adhesives used to bind the wood under high temperature. The embodied carbon for timber is around $0.46kgCO_2/kg$, that for engineered woods between 0.5 and $0.86kgCO_2/kg$. Bearing in mind a single large wardrobe can weigh 100kg, the embodied energy of a home's wood furnishings can easily be two or three tonnes, and much more if you are buying steel or aluminium. Don't forget emissions from transporting the wood – emissions from local UK wood can be as little as $60gCO_2/kg$, while shipped wood from another continent can require $700gCO_2/kg$.

Many people are snobbish about wooden furniture being superior to plywood or MDF. Wooden furniture is often more expensive – especially if it's handmade from reclaimed pine. But a quick look at the Ikea website suggests prices for either wood or plywood are similar.

Table 7.3 shows the embodied emissions for different materials used for furniture.

Carpets weigh a lot and are carbon rich. Their production takes much more energy than making tiles and more even than the deeply unfashionable PVC. A 100m^2 house with 300kg of carpet packs a 2tCO$_2$e load if nylon carpeting is used. A number of firms now produce carpet tiles for use in homes which

Table 7.3 Energy and embodied carbon in different furnishing and flooring materials

Material	Energy (MJ/kg)	Carbon (kgCO$_2$/kg)
Furniture		
Steel (recycled)	9.5	0.43
Timber (general)	8.5	0.46
MDF	11	0.59
Glue-laminated timber	12	0.65
Plywood	15	0.81
Hardboard	16	0.86
Steel (virgin)	35.3	2.75
Aluminium (general & incl 33% recycled)	155	8.24
Flooring		
Terrazzo tiles	1.4	0.12
Concrete tile	2	0.215
Clay tile	6.5	0.46
Ceramic tiles	9	0.59
Linoleum	25	1.21
PVC flooring	65.64	2.29
Wool carpet	106	5.48
Nylon carpet	67.90–149	3.55–7.31
Miscellaneous		
Ceramic sanitary ware	29	1.48
Glass	15	0.85
Wallpaper	36.4	1.93

Source: GreenSpec at www.greenspec.co.uk/index.html

avoid the need to replace the entire carpet just because of localized wear and tear. Interfaceflor, set up by Ray Anderson, goes out of its way to reduce the environmental impacts from its flooring materials and takes back old carpet tiles and offsets emissions from its production process too.

Refurbishing and re-using goods

Our mission is to build a worldwide gifting movement that reduces waste, saves precious resources and eases the burden on our landfills while enabling our members to benefit from the strength of a larger community.

(Freecycle mission statement)

Freecycle's mission statement above is a far cry from the image most of us have of the re-use industry. In most people's imagination, re-use smells of hand-me-down poverty, seedy pawnbrokers and shifty, snake-eyed car boot salesmen – I blame *Steptoe and Son*. There is amazingly little data about the quantity or value of re-used goods traded in the formal economy (where the goods are transferred through businesses or charities) or the informal economy, where they handed around through friends and family.

The re-use market is dominated by the traditional outlets such as pawn shops which often sell high-end, near-new valuable goods like jewellery, electronics and cameras. Charity shops are enjoying growth too. Year-on-year sales at Oxfam, one of the prominent high street charity stores, rose by 7 per cent to £80 million in April 2008. Charity stores are fairly space constrained and tend to concentrate on clothes, books, CDs, DVDs, records and tapes. Charity shops usually won't handle electrical items or children's shoes. Prices are typically a third or a quarter of the new price.

But the real new boy in re-use arises from the specialist web-based markets and email lists for re-use. People I know who wouldn't be seen dead within eyeshot of a charity shop or pawnbrokers are stealthily on eBay watch lists sharking for a cut-price Brabantia kitchen bin or Tako baby stroller. Not yet liberated from their consumerist instincts, but down-carbonizing despite themselves.

Head to head are web-based www.gumtree.com and www.ebay.com. Gumtree tries to create more of a local community and each website is set up and developed around a city. There are 50 such city-based Gumtree sites in the UK, and it's spread to around 30 countries. On the day of writing, 25 second-hand desktops or laptops had been newly posted on the London website. Gumtree was set up in 2000 as an online community to help people newly moved to London set up shop. It has since been bought by eBay. Somehow the global village thing works and I found a site for the Indian city I was born in with quirky (if you're Indian, that is) headings for *tiffin delivery*, jobs in *Call centres*, etc. eBay has less of a second-hand feel about it these days but it must surely still have the widest selection of second-hand goods and services on it, also including a great selection of reconditioned machines and spare parts. The most explicitly environmental website cum email list is Freecycle (www.uk.freecycle.org) This is an online charitable service for people wanting to give away their unwanted goods to people in their neighbourhood. The goods are free, but you usually have to arrange pick up yourself. The first Freecycle started in 2003 and there are now around 500 groups in the UK with 1.5 million members; I have four groups within my neighbourhood and they're great for picking up furniture, small appliances and almost anything else. There are also a couple of useful social movements like swishing.

Recycling and composting

The UK's new rubbish dump: China … more than a third of waste plastic and paper collected by British local authorities … without any knowledge of the environmental and social costs. (Guardian, 20 September 2004)

Paper price collapse blows hole in Britain's recycling strategy … Britain lacks the capacity to handle the rising amount of paper being recovered for recycling, and its dependence on exports has left it vulnerable to a rapid price collapse. (Guardian, 11 November 2008)

Recycling is regarded as a good thing, and it is probably the one thing that most British people can put their hand up to when asked if they do anything to help the environment. The first headline from the *Guardian* is typical of the moral ambiguity about the way we treat waste. We want to do our bit, but we'd rather not know too much as it reminds us of our decadence and the fact that we are asking poor countries to clean up our mess. The second quote questions the usefulness of recycling and the viability of the market.

There are a lot of different estimates of how much energy can be saved from recycling – that's the nature of results based on life-cycle analysis. Most of the data suggests recycling is a better option than incineration even with energy recovery. Figure 7.7 shows the best estimate I could find of the energy needed to make the materials from virgin and waste sources. The figure has been sorted according to the percentage saving from recycling so materials with the highest percentage savings are at the top. Recycling yields great benefits: 90 per cent reduction for aluminium, 75 per cent for plastics, 50 per cent for steel and paper.

The graph assumes that the recycled material will replace the virgin material on a like-for-like basis. In the real world recycled material doesn't replace virgin material so neatly. We alcoholic Brits throw away tonnes of green beer and wine bottles but have little use for green waste glass. Being bulky and low value the glass can't cost-effectively be sent back to countries where green glass is used. Instead, the collected material is often used in construction with more modest carbon savings.

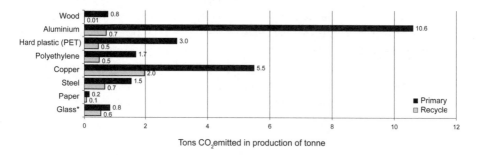

Figure 7.7 Emissions from the production of primary and recycled materials

Source: Fraunhofer Institute and Interseroh (2007)[24], except * Enviros (2003)[25]

Tough EU recycling targets have seen a massive expansion in the amount of waste being sent for recycling. Local authorities have to pay hefty and escalating fees for sending waste into landfill, businesses have obligations to take responsibility for the packaging material they produce and this producer responsibility logic is being extended to vehicles and electrical goods. However, the plant for processing the waste, and the markets for utilizing the materials have not grown at the same speed. Box 7.1 shows the new challenges posed by the gulf between supply and demand for waste paper in the UK. The same story could be told for glass and plastic, and even steel.

It makes a lot of sense to recycle our waste. But it's also important to engage with the local authority politically to ensure that instead of simply increasing the amount of waste collected for recycling, we also maximize the usefulness and value of the waste. In Camden, driven by national recycling targets, the authority is trying to increase the quantity of recyclate being collected irrespective of the fact there aren't enough vehicles or space at the amenity sites to house the separate waste streams. What could be clean resources is being transformed into valueless rubbish. Perhaps rather than going hell for leather to increase quantity, we should instead go for quality. The aluminium, steel and food waste should be our first priority. Going for volume instead of quality risks the materials being too dirty to be economically exploitable and expensively collected and segregated waste ending up in landfill sites – surely the worst of all worlds.

At the local level we cannot just oppose the construction of recycling centres and new waste-handling facilities out of hand. Material recovery facilities and incinerators are now built to high environmental standards. Yet local opposition can hold up the construction of new facilities for a decade – the joke in the waste industry is that incinerators are more fiercely opposed than prisons and nuclear power stations. Other countries – notably Denmark, The Netherlands and Switzerland, not usually singled out as environmental

Box 7.1 *What happens to paper once you put it in the recycling bin?*

In 2007 the UK consumed 14 million tonnes of paper; the amount consumers send to recycling centres has shot up and stands at 8 million tonnes. Recycling paper makes a lot of sense both environmentally and economically under the right conditions. The recycling of paper saves around $1300kgCO_2$ per tonne of paper – by avoiding the creation of paper pulp from wood chips. You can recycle paper around six times before the fibres get too mangled. But it's not the UK paper industry that is seeing the benefit of the cheap, local source of pulp. The UK paper industry has been in decline for years – in 2006 seven more paper mills closed down. UK paper mills aren't able to compete internationally – even when working flat out our mills only make use of 4.5 million tonnes of the waste paper.

In 2006 we exported 3.5 million tonnes of waste paper to China. The Chinese turn it into cardboard and send it back to us as packaging for all the goods they sell us. But isn't energy wasted transporting the paper to China and back again? Not really, the container ships bringing goods from China have to make the return journey: indeed they'd probably end up carrying water or stones as ballast ... so the extra emissions from transporting paper and plastic waste to China are pretty close to zero.

It's a nice circular materials flow and even makes some money out of selling paper to the Chinese, but not as much as we should. The price of paper pulp, like most waste materials, depends crucially on their purity. UK mills pay just £40/tonne for mixed paper. If they are presented with office paper and newsprint separately the waste would command £60/tonne. But things can be worse than this. A lot of waste is collected from homes 'co-mingled' in order to reduce the collection costs faced by Councils. This means a single lorry takes the metals, plastic, glass and paper in one go; and the different waste streams have to be separated out at the materials recovery facility. Magnets suck out the iron, the plastic is blown off, the paper and glass spun around, agitated and sieved to try and cost-effectively separate out the different materials. But the practice of co-mingling degrades the quality of the waste. Consignments of paper are sometimes being rejected because of fragments of glass.

In autumn 2008 the market the price paid for the UK's waste paper collapsed. The dirty and badly separated paper and plastic is proving hard to shift in the economic downturn. With a glut on the waste market, better sorted and cleaner waste from Germany and Japan is a more attractive proposition for Chinese waste importers. It's not enough just to recycle, we have to sort our waste better or we'll lose one of our few remaining resource exports – waste; otherwise it is just going to end up in the incinerator or, worse, in landfill.

pariahs – have examined the evidence for energy from waste and concluded there is a role for it once the higher-value types of paper and plastic have been extracted. Local opposition (and space constraints) limit the number of street-corner recycling points – so instead of the old-style facilities which separate out the different colours of glass and grade of paper, everything is mushed up.

Local authorities are currently experimenting with collecting kitchen and garden waste. If we are to reduce the emissions from waste it is important that communities get this right. Organic wastes can either be composted (not suitable for meat or dairy waste) or put into an anaerobic digester which turns the food into an energy-containing gas and compost. If we can make it work, this has a hugely positive climate change benefit, creating energy from what was previously a source of methane. The main challenge is being disciplined – separating out our waste and allowing facilities to be sited close enough to reduce transport emissions. Just as we wouldn't dream of serving lettuce in its packet, or microwaving soup still in its steel, we need the same common sense when we dispose of kitchen and garden waste. This is a big psychological change but it's not intrinsically difficult.

But the current trends are not promising. At a recent community meeting with the recycling officer the biggest complaint was the authority's lowest-common-denominator approach to recycling. People are not so stupid they cannot understand the need to separate waste properly and the bar should not be set so low there is hardly any environmental point to recycling. It makes good economic sense too, as properly separated waste is an income stream not a liability.

Recycling packaging

Journalists have come out with a new oxymoron, *precycling*, for the practice of shunning packaging. As far as I can make out this involves taking your own shopping bags to the store and your own mug to Starbucks. This is all eminently sensible and might save 5–10 kg of CO_2 a year; while it won't save the world it is, as the poet says, better than a kick in the teeth.

One of the more confusing aspects of recycling is dealing with plastics (see Table 7.4). It is possible to recycle plastics, but to make it cost-effective the council needs to be able to separate out marketable plastic polymers from those that they cannot sell. Plastic bottles all have an encouraging, but misleading, recycling symbol at the bottom. The most valuable plastics tend to be PET and HDPE so it's worth making sure you recycle these. Before the economic downturn clean HDPE waste could fetch over £200/tonne and PET over £100/tonne. Even mixed plastic was worth around £80/tonne. (By way of comparison a tonne of oil was of the order of £500/tonne.) Tetrapac quite rightly is rejected by most local authorities because the Swedish billionaire manufacturers have ingeniously designed one of most difficult to re-use or recycle products: fusing lots of low value paper, a film of plastic and high-value aluminium in a gluey gunge. Avoid products that use it. Confusingly there are now some vegetable-based 'biodegradable plastics' which should be composted but probably get chucked in the recycling, where they could worsen the quality of recycled material.

Table 7.4 Plastic recycling codes

Code	Plastic resin type	Description	Where you'll find it
1	Polyethylene terephthalate (PETE)	Clear or coloured plastic	Soft drink and edible oil bottles; toiletries, cosmetics and pharmaceuticals
2	High-density polyethylene (HDPE)	Waxy, translucent or opaque	Rigid containers, crinkly retail bags, milk and juice cartons, margarine tubs, detergent bottles, motor oil containers
3	Polyvinyl chloride (PVC)	Clear, colourless, white creases, bottles have a seam on the base	Bottles for squash and mineral water; cling film
4	Low-density polyethylene (LDPE)	Flexible, smooth, soft to the touch	Carrier bags, bin liners
5	Polypropylene (PP)	Transparent, clear or opaque, smooth, semi-rigid	Coating on milk cartons, shrink wrap, bottle caps, yogurt and margarine tubs, transparent candy wrapping
6	Polystyrene (PS)	Stiff but flexible, snaps when bent	Foam meat trays, egg cartons and coffee cups; plastic cutlery
7	Mix of plastics		Ketchup bottles

Tetrapak is not that bad

Tetrapak is hard to recycle because it binds paper, plastic and aluminium together. Most paper mills can only handle small quantities of it, and the option of sending it back to recycling facilities in Sweden is bonkers. There are perfectly good plastic cartons available for most purposes. Even so, and it galls me to say it, Tetrapak is not all that bad. It is a lightweight form of packaging; its composition by weight is 80 per cent paper, 15 per cent polyethylene and 5 per cent aluminium. The embodied emissions from making it are low and it allows liquids to be stored and transported at ambient temperature. The emissions from a pack containing 1 litre of milk will be around $80gCO_2$, manufacturing a glass bottle to carry the same amount of fluid causes ten times more CO_2. Incidentally the emissions from the milk itself will be around $1kgCO_2e$.

Voluntary simplicity

I see young men, my townsmen, whose misfortune it is to have inherited farms, houses, barns, cattle, and farming tools; for these are more easily acquired than got rid of. (Walden, by Henry David Thoreau)

You work in a job you hate, to buy stuff that you don't need, to impress people that you don't like. (Anon)

Covetousness alone is a great destroyer of merit and goodness. From covetousness proceeds sin.
(Bhishma, teacher of the Pandava, speaking in the Mahabharata)

The above range of quotes shows that writers, wags and sages have for some time been pointing out that the pursuit of goods is a source of unhappiness. This contrasts starkly with orthodox economics that sees continued growth of consumption as a good thing, albeit with a smaller and smaller growth in satisfaction. Most mainstream economists see climate change as being a case of getting the price of carbon right either by taxing it to include the price of future damage to the environment or capping emissions at the sustainable level. But if consumption doesn't lead to happiness, and there is a strong correlation between the amount of economic activity and CO_2 emissions, why do we need to consume as much as we do? Is it what really makes us happy? Could we be 90 per cent as happy even if we halve the amount of things we own or by choosing different goods? Could part of the solution to the economic downturn be consuming less, and handling this change with equanimity?

The quotes set out the two really big challenges that face us. Can we still be happy with a simpler life without being able to zoom from place to place as and when we feel like it? Can we still feel happy and maintain our self-respect without all our material trappings?

Figure 7.8 shows the results from a fascinating study undertaken by the social scientist Daniel Kahneman (who won his Nobel Prize in economics) and his colleagues.[26] It shows the activities undertaken by 900 working women over a day and how much enjoyment they obtained from different time uses. It adds up to more than 27 hours (and excludes sleep) because women are of course very good at multi-tasking, as they will have you know. I have censored some of the more minor uses of time – including the most enjoyable which goes under Kahneman's rubric of 'intimate relations', which clocked in at 11 minutes per day in case you're curious.

The interesting thing is that the only thing less enjoyable than working is commuting to work. Shopping, which is made possible by all this additional working and commuting, is only slightly more positively regarded than napping and cooking and less positively than watching TV, exercising, eating, praying/meditating, relaxing, socializing and 'intimate relations', all of which are either free or very cheap. Which does raise the question: why do we work so hard, if we don't particularly enjoy it and nor do we enjoy the activity it begets?

The researchers also asked about the amount people enjoyed being with different people. Friends and family scored the highest, spouse and children came in after that, clients and co-workers were lower still; then the boss. Sadly for people in solitary jobs, like writers, the least enjoyable way of spending time, even worse than time with your boss, was time by yourself. Well at least I have my iPod for company. The economist Richard Thaler has tried to dissect the idea of utility from consumption to try and explain our shopping bulimia. He talks about transactional utility which I suppose most of us would think

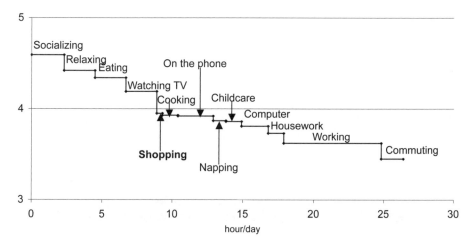

Figure 7.8 Positive state of mind while undertaking different daily tasks

Note: 5 = most positive; 3 = least positive.

Source: Kahneman et al (2004)[27]

of as the excitement of being out in the nice brightly coloured shopping malls, doing our thing with the Visa card; choosing objects, trying on clothes, bargaining, getting a good deal and talking about it afterwards. The object of the shopping trip, the actual good being purchased, is almost incidental. You need only look at my wardrobe or bookshelf to see all the things that seemed a good idea to buy, but which I never had the time to consume. Too little time to enjoy the books and music I have bought.

While this evidence of time use is interesting, it is only half the picture – the issue about consuming less isn't so much about how much we enjoy working and buying things. It's the enjoyment and feeling of self-esteem linked to experiencing, owning or using carbon-hungry goods compared to carbon-lite goods.

To understand this better I'll go over some of the empirical work on what makes people happy. This is among some of the most exciting collaborative work between economists and social researchers. The European Commission has been conducting the Eurobarometer survey since 1973. This has included the anodyne question 'On the whole are you satisfied with life?' for around 40 years. The UK national psyche can be summed up as 'can't grumble'. A third of Brits say they are 'very satisfied', a further half say they are 'satisfied'; the miserable rump makes up just one-sixth. Interestingly, these proportions have barely moved for the last 35 years, as evidenced in Figure 7.9. All the economic upturns and downturns of the last three and a half decades – the oil shocks and winter of discontent in the 1970s, the recession of the early

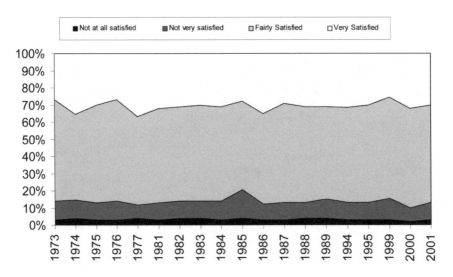

Figure 7.9 Life satisfaction results for the UK, 1973–2001

Source: Donovan and Halpern (2002)[28]

1980s and again in the early mid-1990s have barely caused a flicker. And most disconcertingly for anyone wishing to argue that economic consumption is all that matters, average disposable income and wealth have grown fairly steadily over that time.

Data on international variation in life satisfaction shows that people in richer countries are happier than people in poorer countries but only until income rises to around US$15,000 per head (in 1995 prices). Beyond this it flat-lines: people in countries as diverse as Ireland (GDP of US$15,000 per head) and the US (US$30,000 per head) were on average all equally happy. So national and international data suggests that money does not buy happiness – well, not if you earn more than US$15,000 per year.

There has been some interesting work looking at differences in life satisfaction at the individual level (see Figure 7.10). Here the indication is that income does make some difference; richer people are happier than poorer people.

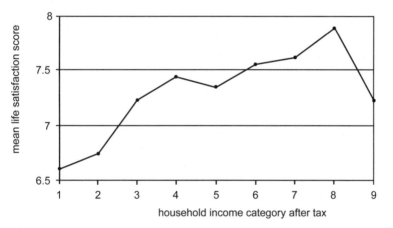

Figure 7.10 Life satisfaction and income in Britain, 2000

Source: Donovan and Halpern (2002)[29]

But income is much less important than other features of our lives. Work by Andrew Clark and Andrew Oswald suggests that having a job, good health and successful relationships are much more significant than income.[30] So how do income and wealth actually bring happiness? Richard Layard put it well when he quoted a study that showed that women were more likely to go out and work if their husband earned less than their sister's husband.[31] Self-esteem isn't about how much you consume, it's about how much more you consume than those you compare yourself with. A simple need for shelter and employment can be met without putting unmanageable strain on the world's resources. But if you introduce desire for esteem then just any old house isn't enough – it has have more features than your rivals.

> Homer: *Aw, twenty dollars! I wanted a peanut!*
> Homer's Brain: *Twenty dollars can buy many peanuts!*
> Homer: *Explain how!*
> Homer's Brain: *Money can be exchanged for goods and services!*
> (*The Simpsons*, 'Boy scoutz 'n the hood')

Homer, unencumbered by his brain, wanted just a peanut. Being paid peanuts, despite the adage to the contrary, was sufficient; it satisfied his need. But his economically conditioned brain made him feel dissatisfied with simply satiating his hunger. A 20-dollar bill gives you more options, more flexibility, more potential consumption. Most environmentalists run through the same conflicts as Homer. If less is more, why is so it hard to feel satisfied with less? Deep down, we don't buy it: economy *is* a false economy. I remember my first favourite TV show was the *Six Million Dollar Man*; having the money to get my own bionic appendages seemed a great idea ... and the loss of humanity a minor price to pay.

Does having a higher income really matter? Sadly the evidence suggests income turns you into an environmental Rambo. Figure 7.11 shows the composition of people's expenditure for different income bands. The highest-earning fifth of UK households spend four times more than the least paid fifth. In absolute terms they buy more of everything: but while their spending on food and rent is less than twice as much, their spending on transport, recreation and eating out is more than six times as much.

The difference is starker when you look at more detailed data.[32] The highest-earning 10 per cent of households earn five and half times more than the lowest-earning 10 per cent of households. But this increased income is spent on the most environmentally destructive types of purchases – the richest tenth outspend the poorest by a factor of seven on petrol, 24 on plane fares and 40 on package holidays. Environmentally benign spending is much more egalitarian: the richest tenth outspend the poorest tenth twofold on telephone calls, fourfold on 'games, toys and hobbies', sixfold on books and gardening. The only exception to this is spending on education, where the richest 10 per cent outspend the poorest 20-fold.

So here we are. Individuals want to earn more than others around them even though it doesn't make them any happier, and the actual process of work is one of the most disliked ways of spending time. Then we blow our extra earnings on things that damage the environment. This is the human condition.

So the upshot of all this is that shopping and owning more and more goods isn't going to bring you happiness, no matter how attractive it sounds in the advert. To be happy:

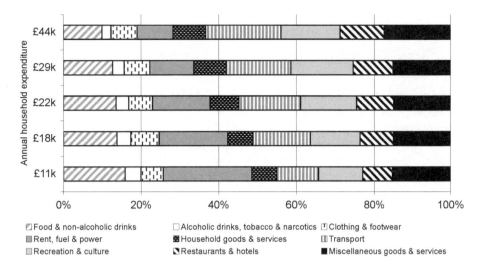

Figure 7.11 Proportion of annual household expenditure on different items for gross income quintiles of population (head of household 30–49 years old)

Source: ONS (2007)[33]

- spend time with friends and family;
- find lower-maintenance friends and hobbies; and
- enjoy what you've already got rather than trying to acquire more.

Low-carbon gifts and celebrations

It's one thing reducing your own carbon emissions but how do you apply these ideas when you are buying for others. What can you give that doesn't hurt the environment, that does not come across as hand-wringingly preachy, and that won't just be politely received before finding its way into the attic (or eBay) a few weeks later?

It's late November as I write this. My son, never one to knowingly under-inform me of his material hopes, has been lounging on the computer clicking through the Toys'R'Us website. He has it all planned out – Bionics Lego (lots of it), a new bike and some models from *Lord of the Rings*.

There are a good many green shops that you can access online. Few of them manage to get around the fundamental contradiction in their business that they are making money from selling you goods, and the environment is often best served by you doing without those goods. One green shopping website sold global warming mugs (that shows the retreating coastlines when you put a hot drink in), climate change calendars (showing 12 aspects of climate change), world music CDs and some rather puritanical looking

Box 7.2 *Christmas without gifts*

Those who say that money can't buy happiness don't know where to shop.   (Anon)

'About Christmas', I say to my son good-naturedly. 'Have I told you I am writing a chapter on voluntary simplicity?'

'What's that?'

I put on a tone of excessive cheeriness, which doesn't fool him. He listens to me gravely and his face becomes increasingly pallid as he's still young enough to believe everything I tell him. His mouth opens and he does a pretty good impersonation of computer having a hard crash – Dad, what you're saying does not compute. 'But can't you see you're just being fetishist about Nike?' I finish triumphantly.

'But Santa was getting me Adidas ...'. Their mother had told me he still believed in Santa Claus and I was on strict orders not to seed any existentialist doubts. Though how he could reconcile Santa with his highly prescriptive wish list from the local toyshop was beyond me. Maybe they still rationalized it that Santa and the toy store were in cahoots. When I tune back into the conversation he says with that glint in his eye as though he was about to unseat me: 'In Star Trek, they use replicators to make things. Why don't we invent one of those?' This was not a stupid question. Like others (see www.blahblahtech.com/2006/10/how-close-are-we-to-star-trek-technology.html), I had noticed there was a disconcerting tendency for copy-cat technologies to be invented a couple of decades after *Star Trek* screened the idea. What a lot of people take to be creativity might actually just be bad viewing habits – look at mobile phones and tasers: even the name is copied from phasers! But how do you explain to an eight-year-old mind that the technological distance between a factory and on-demand matter creation was far greater that the difference between a videocassette and on-demand films, even if technologic -al progress is travelling at Warp 9? I wonder how many people's scientific education allows them to appreciate this.

My daughter sees the connection between voluntary simplicity and reducing climate change emissions straight away. 'I don't want anything for Christmas. It's just a waste of money.' This is what she said last year too, and the year before – which still leaves me in a quandary. Voluntary simplicity is fine to apply to oneself but how is it applied by a parent to an eight year-old child, at Christmas. Being mean at Christmas is virtually a crime. And given the role Christmas plays in bankrolling much of retail and manufacture, this is no surprise. Christmas's most famous villain – the strident bah humbug anti-consumerist Scrooge – is by my estimation actually its most misunderstood hero.

With heavy heart I took the kids to Woolworths to shop for Christmas – the firm had gone into administration that week and I hoped our purchases might help its 40,000 employees hang onto their jobs.

wooden toys which would never satisfy any attention-deficit-syndrome child for more than a minute. No one I like would actually use these things; if they did, I doubt I would like them. Here's a few websites nonetheless:

- www.nigelsecostore.com has a wide range of goods made from recycled materials. It also includes a re-gifting service to give away unwanted presents.
- www.ethicalsuperstore.com has a very wide range of goods, not noticeably carbon friendly, though there are some useful eco-gadgets.
- www.mygreenerhome.co.uk/ has a narrow range of goods, but they have been well vetted for their greenness.
- www.ecoemporia.com/ has a good range of quirky products made from recycled material (old vinyl records, jeans, circuit boards).

Better than gifts made from recycled materials is re-use of goods. In the US there's a movement of re-gifting, where unwanted presents are gifted to someone else. Nigel's eco store (web link above) has a section.

Books, DVDs and games are particularly popular gifts. Here are a few places to obtain second-hand consumables:

- www.readitswapit.co.uk/TheLibrary.aspx and www.bookmooch.com are great free sites to swap and talk about books.
- www.swapitshop.com/new is a website for swapping CDs, DVDs and electronic goods. It has its own currency (swapits) which appear to be fairly credit crunch proof – a Tracy Beaker paperback is 300 Swapits. Before you can really get going you need to put something into the system. It's aimed at teenagers. While there's a whole section devoted to *SpongeBob*, I was disappointed to find no equivalent section on *West Wing*.
- www.dvdexchange-online.co.uk and www.lovefilm.com are online DVD and game exchanges which you pay for by monthly fee. These might provide a low-carbon, low-waste alternative gift for kids who've lost the fascination for wooden toys. The basic rental (two films a month) costs around £50 per year.

There's also a vogue at the moment for swishing, which sounds fun – but I have never been invited so can't say from first-hand experience. It involves throwing a party and bringing along high-quality clothes, jewellery or shoes that you might have worn at a wedding, or a major work do and which you are unlikely to use again. Here's the website: www.swishing.org/ – though there seem to be some alarmingly sexist (anti-men, that is) overtones to the whole phenomenon. While we are on the subject of sexual stereotyping, there's a wonderful franchise www.rentahubby.co.uk for the mythical male of yore that could fix anything.

What I Did and Didn't Do

There's a scene in Neil Stephenson's novel *Quicksilver* where the natural philosopher Isaac Newton, while researching his bestseller *Optiks*, detaches his eyeball, sticks a pin in his eye and renders himself blind for a few days by staring into the sun. What some people do to get published! I relate this story to my wife as I clear some space on the kitchen floor and tip out the contents of the recycling bin, so I can weigh what we threw away last week. I am also trying to put the sacrifices she is making in some kind of context. 'Kitchen bin next', I say cheerily. 'No you don't. I don't ever recall reading about any *Mrs* Isaac Newton', she says in a no-nonsense tone. I sniff inside the bin: 'Good point. There are some good secondary data sources I guess I could use.'

Much less work has been done on quantifying the embodied emissions in household goods, for the simple reason it's hard. An everyday item like a shirt is often made from a mixture of cotton, polyester and plastic buttons. Each of these three materials could be sourced from several different countries, which are liable to change depending on prevailing prices. The emissions from freighting goods long distance can be a fairly significant proportion of emissions, especially if there are multiple journeys for raw materials and finished goods. Emissions from transporting goods from Shanghai to UK via the Suez Canal are 0.45kgCO_2/kg of product – assuming the ship is just half full on the return leg of the journey.[34] If the raw materials are themselves imported from sub-Saharan Africa, Australia or North America (the sources of many metal ores and coal), the embodied transport emissions can easily be around 1kgCO_2/kg of good. The final column of Table 7.5 gives the embodied emissions from producing the goods. In the case of plastic goods, transport emissions might be half the embodied production emissions.

Table 7.5 lists all my routine purchases over the last year or so. The embodied and landfill emissions are around $1.25\text{tCO}_2\text{e}$. These will underestimate the true emissions because they leave out transport and production emissions and waste after the production of raw materials.

The main thing that strikes me about Table 7.5 is how few things I have actually replaced over the past 12 months, apart from clothes. Like many people, we had a big purchasing splurge in the first 18 months after buying our home, fitting out the larger space. Most things are replaced when they break down. By far the largest source appears to be my laptop (which I had to buy again when my old one got stolen from a hotel – serves me right for taking it on my

Table 7.5 Number, mass and approximate embodied CO_2 emissions from a year's purchases (except food waste)

	My annual purchases	Unit weight	Unit emissions factor	Emissions
		(kg)	(kgCO$_2$/kg)	(kgCO$_2$)
Books	30	0.4	3.0	36
Newspaper – local and free	50	0.2	3.0	30
Newspaper – national	60	0.4	3.0	72
Newspaper – weekend	30	1	3.0	91
Magazines	30	0.2	3.0	18
Writing pads	2	0.5	3.0	3
Wooden chair	1	4	0.7	2.8
Luggage	2	1.2	3.0	7
Vacuum cleaner	1	6	2.1	12
Mobile phone	1	0.25	*	25
Laptop	1	3	*	500
iPod speakers	1	0.2	*	20
CD/DVD	20	0.05	2.4	2
Clothes				
Socks/underwear	20	0.05	19.2	19
T-shirts	5	0.2	19.2	19
Shirts	5	0.3	19.2	29
Towels	2	0.4	19.2	15
Trousers	4	0.5	19.2	38
Coat	3	1	19.2	58
Shoes	3	1	19.2	58
Food packaging				
Wine bottles	60	0.8	1.4	67
Steel cans	100	0.06	1.9	12
Aluminium containers	50	0.02	16.1	16
Plastic PDPE	50	0.2	10.2	102
Total				1254

* No unit emissions are quoted as it is assumed the emissions are related to the complexity of the circuit design rather than their mass.

honeymoon). Guiltily I realize I have been buying a new machine every couple of years, taken in, but ever disappointed, by Moore's law which promised every new machine would have twice the oomph of the previous incarnation. Books/ publications and clothes are both around 250kgCO$_2$. The average household spending on clothes is £1000; my spending is broadly in line.

Leaving aside the laptop, emissions from the packaging material accounted for about a quarter of the total materials flowing into the home. Nearly all of this was for food and drink. I already recycle all that Camden lets me, so to the extent they are able to find places to take the waste, a high proportion of the embodied energy in the packaging and paper should be retrieved. Unfortunately the economic downturn has resulted in a sharp fall in the demand for waste and the company that the borough uses to dispose of its waste is having the same problem as other waste authorities. The problem arises not because making steel, plastic and aluminium from virgin material is better economically; it's not. Waste is sold on flexible short-term contracts which the steel producers and paper mills can get out of, while the virgin material comes on firmer long-term contracts which are expensive to renege on, irrespective of the underlying economic rationality.

As well as the emissions from the production of goods, there are also the emissions from methane produced in the landfill site. We've already discussed emissions from food wastes in an earlier chapter. Most of the other waste streams do not give rise to methane in landfill sites. The exception is paper. My annual purchases are around 100kg of paper and wood products a year, giving rise to around 70kgCO$_2$e of greenhouse gas in the landfill site (over a 100-year period). The vast majority of the waste paper is newspaper and peri-odicals; we subscribe to one weekly and half a dozen monthly publications. The assortment of cards from taxi-cab companies, fast food joints and estate agents (which have stopped now) and all the other junk mail cause a lot of clutter but only make up around 2kg of paper a year – though I could swear I used to get a lot more financial junk mail a few months ago – maybe they're feeling chastened about pushing their credit cards on me now.

A year's snapshot picture like this is always a little misleading, since in practice there will always be one-off items that need to changed every few years, like the roof or buying a new car. Each year the average household spends £175 on household appliances, £1200 on purchasing a car and £400 on repairing their house. Our own spending this year bears no resemblance to the average. Our big lumpy purchase was building a loft conversion to give the kids more space when they come to visit. The loft conversion added a bathroom and two extra rooms, which the kids might describe as bijoux if they had the vocabulary. Table 7.6 shows my calculation of the emissions involved. The figures miss out emissions from transporting the materials to the site and

Table 7.6 Estimated emissions from constructing a two-bedroom loft conversion

	Size	Mass per unit	Mass	Emissions factor	CO_2 emissions
		(kg/unit)	(kg)	(kgCO₂/unit)	(kg)
Rolled steel joists	15m	23	345	1750	604
Glass (five windows)			250	850	213
Timber	1m³	590	590	−3200	−1888
Carpet (nylon)	50m²			10	500
Ceramics			100	1480	148
Paint (double coat)	120m²		20	1.06	21
Plasterboard/plaster	70m²	44	3080	380	1170
Tiles	50m²	21	1028	460	473
Insulation	0.8m³	200	160	1000	160
Pipes (plastic)			30	2400	72
Wires			20	3800	76
Total			5623		1549

Sources: Emissions factors: Hammond and Jones, Inventory of Carbon and Energy database;[35] typical masses: Stephen Biddle (structural engineer), pers com, extracted from British Standards for students of structural design.

taking away the construction waste. We seemed to have had a succession of white vans coming to and going from our house, gobbling up my parking permits as quickly as the local authority issued them. All told we generated around 50 trips between Essex and North London, which works out at roughly 250kgCO₂. The emissions from the loft conversion were much less than I expected, certainly if you take account of the fact we'll stay in the house for a few years longer as a result. But I really wish I'd got the fitters to use some lower-carbon alternatives. If they had substituted more timber for cement and steel I could have sequestered carbon dioxide instead of emitting it. We had discussed this before the work commenced, but the idea got quietly dropped when they got the measure of me and realized I didn't know the first thing about construction, and it was just going to add time to the project. As it was, the project got finished on time and to budget and we all liked the quality of the work; but it could have been much lower carbon so easily.

Christmas was tough. The main gifts were bikes for the two children. Christmas Eve was a bit blurry and I vaguely recollect watching celebrity chefs being evicted from the Australian outback while ballroom dancing. Still reeling from this state of mind I revealed the two bikes to my children: my son inherited his older sister's uni-sex model, while I bought her a second-hand one from eBay.

Bringing It All Together

This is a list of actions I have taken to reduce my emissions.

Making a conscious decision not to buy items I don't really need

Last year my kettle and camcorder both broke down. Normally I would have bought new ones straight away, but we hardly ever use the camcorder and we already had an old-fashioned kettle for the stove. Surely we didn't need to replace the broken items. Emboldened, I also decided not to buy a new game station for my children. The embodied emissions of the three goods are probably comparable to that of a medium-sized TV – around $100kgCO_2$.

Duncan has succeeded in living a remarkably uncluttered life. He doesn't own a mobile, or an iPod – though he thinks his parents are likely to give him an iPod for Christmas, despite his hints to them not to. I asked what he'd do if he won £10,000 and without hesitation he rattled off the charities he'd donate the money too. His place in Green heaven is reserved.

Extending the life of items I already own

I made a solemn promise to stop replacing my computer so frequently. This should save around $250kgCO_2$ and £200 per year and also the hassle of transferring all my files from one machine to another (which I suspect takes many hours longer than the few moments per day a faster processor delivers).

Angie doesn't have a computer – but she does use the internet in the library to read emails and use the internet. This remains the cheapest option for her. For Duncan the best option might be to buy a netbook like the Acer Aspire or the Asus Eee which fits in his flat and lets him keep in touch with his friends and browse the internet. It costs less than £300.

I've also started to rehabilitate my old clothes. All I did was invest in some heavy-duty cleaning products and starch to remove cycle grease, grass stains, etc. from my clothes. Before, mildly damaged clothes used to sit in the wardrobe for ages until I finally threw them out. Angie didn't believe me when I said I hadn't sewn a button on a shirt in almost ten years; she even repairs her socks! Three items have been restored, saving about £100 and 20kgCO_2. Be careful about repairing electronic goods – I paid £200 to get my camcorder fixed and it broke down again a few weeks later.

Replacing purchased physical products with electronic or rental products

I've pretty much stopped buying CDs. I used to have a 50-CD-a-year habit, and it's now down to 2 or 3. Downloading individual songs on iTunes costs just £0.79, albums are usually £7.99 while the physical albums from Amazon are often around £10 once you include shipping costs (though retail stores can be cheaper for the more popular items).

I've also stopped accepting free newspapers, buying daily newspapers and halved weekend papers. I read news on the internet now. The two measures together save around 200kgCO_2e and £200 per year. I've also started frequenting the library for books, CDs and DVDs. I was never a big buyer of DVDs, and my book purchases haven't gone down – I just have a larger pile of books I want to read … so minimal savings.

Being more systematic about re-use: buying and donating second-hand gear

I had always been in the habit of giving away old books and CDs to charity shops. But large items of furniture and electrical items were harder to donate as shops and door-to-door collections refused them. Instead they'd sit in a corner and eventually get thrown away. This year I Freecycled an electric racing car set my son had grown out of to a delighted mother, just before Christmas, and donated a surplus sofa arising from the union of my new wife's and my possessions. There were numerous no-shows for the sofa – many of the would-be recipients decided the cost and hassle of organizing a large taxi to retrieve it was too much; but we eventually found a grateful owner and probably saved its weight in carbon – around 100kgCO_2. I also started to shop in second-hand shops once again and Abebooks – something I haven't done since I was a student.

Angie acquired her TV for free informally; her son scavenged it from the streets. Duncan has always been in the habit of buying second-hand clothes. He showed me shirts he uses for work, a suit and trousers he'd got from second-hand shops. He also got his hi-fi from an emigrating friend.

Purchasing goods that are easier to repair

I've made a promise to buy simpler, more durable goods, even if they cost more. So far this has meant buying some hemp/cotton socks and T-shirts which are meant to be more durable. It's too early to say whether they really are longer lasting. The cost of the hemp T-shirt was several times more than the cheapest mass-produced item.

We have also tried to buy better-quality white goods – this means brands like Miele that have a reputation for reliability and where there is more chance of finding spare parts a few years later. In the case of our desktop computer it is the CD-ROM drive that is currently playing up. This is cheap to replace, or it's easy to buy an external drive which avoids the need to install. Our desktop (already three years old) should last us another year or two. This saves the equivalent of around £300 and 200kgCO_2e.

Being an active citizen locally – pushing for greater segregation of wastes especially plastics and glass

The environmental benefits of recycling would be much improved if different grades of paper and colours of glass were collected separately. Instead of doing this some local authorities are co-mingling disparate waste, reducing its value and in some cases making it valueless. So press for the reintroduction of bottle banks and paper banks on street corners, and use them.

What hasn't worked: Buying goods made from recycled materials

It's all very well recycling but the recovered materials also need to be used, to make the materials recovery profitable and worthwhile. Environmental benefits are maximized if recycled materials can be utilized locally *and substitute for virgin material of the same sort.* I have recently bought glasses and containers made in Cornwall from recycled glass. The carbon savings will be less than 1kg and the cost of the glass quite high.

Notes

1   Office for National Statistics (2006): Environmental accounts detailed 91 industry disaggregations of emissions for 2004. These can be accessed as Excel spreadsheets at www.statistics.gov.uk/statbase/explorer.asp?CTG=3&SL=&D=4261&DCT=0&DT=3 2#4261 (accessed on July 2009).

2   Wiedmann, T., Wood, R., Lenzen, M., Minx, J., Guan, D. and Barrett, J. (2008) *Development of an Embedded Carbon Emissions Indicator – Producing a Time Series of Input–Output Tables and Embedded Carbon Dioxide Emissions for the UK by Using a MRIO Data Optimisation System,* Report to the UK Department for Environment,

Food and Rural Affairs by Stockholm Environment Institute at the University of York and Centre for Integrated Sustainability Analysis at the University of Sydney, June, Defra, London, Table 2 on p20. The modelled estimate in this report looks at product groups imported by UK households. It assumes that production overseas gives rise to similar emissions per unit value as production in the UK.

3   570MtCO$_2$ – emissions from the economy (except by the gas and petrol sectors) + gross embodied emissions of 375MtCO$_2$. This is halved to reflect the final demand of just households.

4   Incpen (Industry Council for Packaging and the Environment) (2004) *Towards Greener Households Products, Packaging and Energy*, www.incpen.org (accessed June 2009).

5   The Open University mainly has mature students so there is actually a wide variety of ages and family types among them.

6   Defra (2007) *Waste Strategy for England 2007. Annex A: Impact Assessment,* Command Paper 7086, Table A.28: 'Emission factors for waste treatment processes (kg carbon dioxide equivalents / tonne of waste processed)', www.defra.gov.uk/environment/ waste/strategy/strategy07/pdf/waste07-annex-a.pdf.

7   Defra (2007) as above.

8   ERM and Golders Associates (2006) *Carbon Balances and Energy Impacts of the Management of UK Wastes,* (Annexes A and B) Defra R&D Project WRT 237.

9   ONS environmental accounts (2005) as above in note 1.

10 Nokia (2005) *Integrated Product Policy Pilot Project – Life Cycle Environmental Emission from Mobile Phones*, Espoo, Finland.

11 Kuehr, R. and Williams, E. (2003) *Computers and the Environment*, Kluwer Academic Press, Dordrecht.

12 Blackburn, R and Payne, J (2004) 'Life cycle analyses of cotton towels: Impact of domestic laundering and recommendation for extending periods between washing', *Green Chemistry*, vol 6, ppG59–G61.

13 Kuehr, R. and Williams, E. (2003) *Computers and the Environment*, Kluwer Academic Press, Dordrecht.

14 Fraunhofer Institute for Reliability and Microintegration (2007) *Energy Using Products Directive Preparatory Studies: Televisions (Lot 5)*, Final Report on Task 4 'Technical analysis', Fraunhofer Institute for Reliability and Microintegration, IZM, Berlin.

15 Market Transformation Programme (2006) *Product Overview – Waste*.

16 Oko-Institut (2005) 'Eco-Efficiency Analysis of Washing Machines', Oko-Institut, Freiburg, Germany, www.oeko.de/publications/reports_studies/dok/659.php?PHPSE SSID=0d16p8cdt2gk3dmtcubedcvaq3 (accessed July 2009). This analysis is based on a washing machine weighing 70kg – which by mass is made from 20kg concrete, 25 kg steel and a mixture of others metals and plastic. The production of its materials emits 285kgCO$_2$, manufacture 27kgCO$_2$ and transport 2kgCO$_2$. An analysis of fridge-freezers, 'Environmental and economic evaluation of the accelerated replacement of domestic appliances', suggests the emissions from producing a 40kg fridge to be around 150kgCO$_2$.

17 Office for National Statistics (2007) *Family Spending – A Report on the 2007 Expenditure and Food Survey*, www.statistics.gov.uk/downloads/theme_social/Family_ Spending_2007/FamilySpending2008_web.pdf (accessed July 2009).

18 Oko-Institut (2005) 'Environmental and economic evaluation of the accelerated replacement of domestic appliances', Oko-Institut, Freiburg, Germany.

19 Office for National Statistics (2007) *Family Spending*.

20   UK Trade Info, 'Top 30 products quarterly: Value and net mass' data set.

21   Allwood, J., Laursen, S., de Rodriguez, C. and Bocken, N. (2006) *Well Dressed: The Present and Future Sustainability of Clothing and Textiles in the United Kingdom*, Institute for Manufacturing, University of Cambridge.

22   Allwood, J., Laursen, S., de Rodriguez, C. and Bocken, N. (2006) *Well Dressed: The Present and Future Sustainability of Clothing and Textiles in the United Kingdom*, Institute for Manufacturing, University of Cambridge.

23   Stockholm Environment Institute and Bioregional (2005) *Ecological Footprint and Water Analysis of Cotton, Hemp and Polyester*, Report prepared for Bioregional and WWF.

24   Fraunhofer Institute and Interseroh (2007) *Recycling for Climate Protection*, http://cms. interseroh-gruppe.de/interseroh-prod/INTERSEROH-Gruppe/common/documents/ Hilfsdateien_Infoservice_EN/Recycling_for_climate_protection_Brochure_10_2008.pdf (accessed June 2009).

25   Enviros (2003) *Glass Recycling: Life Cycle Carbon Dioxide Emissions*. Report for British Glass www.britglass.org.uk//Files/Enviros_LCA.pdf.

26   Kahneman, D., Krueger, A.B., Schkade, D.A., Schwarz, N. and Stone, A.A. (2004) 'A survey method for characterizing daily life experience: The day reconstruction method', *Science*, vol 306, no 5702, pp1776–1780.

27   Kahneman, D., Krueger, A.B., Schkade, D.A., Schwarz, N. and Stone, A.A. (2004) 'A survey method for characterizing daily life experience: The day reconstruction method', *Science*, vol 306, no 5702, pp1776–1780.

28   Donovan, N. and Halpern, D. (2002) *Life Satisfaction: The State of Knowledge and the Implications for Government*, PM's Strategy Unit, Cabinet Office, www.cabinetoffice. gov.uk/strategy/seminars/life_satisfaction.aspx (accessed June 2009).

29   Donovan, N. and Halpern, D. (2002) *Life Satisfaction: The State of Knowledge and the Implications for Government*, PM's Strategy Unit, Cabinet Office, www.cabinetoffice. gov.uk/strategy/seminars/life_satisfaction.aspx (accessed June 2009).

30   Clark, A. and Oswald, A. (2002) 'A simple statistical method for measuring how life events affect happiness', *International Journal of Epidemiology*, vol 31, no 6, pp1139–1144.

31   Layard, R. (2005) *Happiness*, Penguin Books, London.

32   Office of National Statistics (2007). *Family Spending – A Report on the 2007 Expenditure and Food Survey*, Table A8 'Detailed household expenditure by gross income decile group'.

33   ONS (2007) - see previous note.

34   The distance by sea from London to Shanghai is 10,400 nautical miles via the Suez Canal; 1 nautical mile = 1.852km and sea freight emissions are around $0.015tCO_2$ per tonne-km of freight. The distance to Singapore is 8400 nautical miles, Mumbai 6300 nautical miles and New York 3340 nautical miles.

35   Hammond, G. and Jones, C. 'Inventory of Carbon and Energy database', University of Bath, www.bath.ac.uk/mech-eng/sert/embodied/ (accessed June 2009). The emissions factor for timber has been altered to net off (44/12 =) $3.7tCO_2$/tonne timber for sequestering recently captured carbon dioxide. The emissions for plasterboard in the database might be too low as they seem to underplay the process emissions of carbon dioxide in cement production.

Travel and
Leisure

- Reduce the amount you fly. Planes allow us to travel distances that would have seemed stupendous to people living just a century ago. Flying less is something we are all going to have to come to terms with over the next few years if we are to reduce our emissions.
- Spend more of your holidays at home or as close to home as possible. The UK has great food, culture and attractions.
- Trips in western Europe can often be undertaken as cheaply as no frills flying, by booking tickets in advance. Travelling by ferry/car, especially for a whole family, is cheaper than flying.
- Reduce long-haul flights to an absolute minimum or give them up entirely. If you are going to go, organize as long a leave as you can to really see the country.
- There are some good websites to help locate hotels and leisure facilities that are trying to reduce their emissions.
- Try and apply these ideas to your work travel. For most airlines, business travellers cross-subsidize personal travel. Travelling for business also normalizes unsustainable transport habits.

Introduction

What are you, a travel agent? 'Cause you're sending me on a guilt trip.
(Homer, *The Simpsons*)

Homer sums up the way many environmentalists feel about flying. The thought of travel fills us with longing and guilt at the same time. I have to come clean. Like many environmentalists, I love travel. I always have. When I get off the plane and feel the hot Indian or Mediterranean sun lick my face, I have that papal urge to bend down and kiss the ground.

This chapter is chiefly a conversation I am still having with myself to persuade me to fly less. Most of the book is about switching to lower-carbon goods and services that provide essentially the same results – heat, nutrition and light, etc. – but with much lower carbon *from existing technology*. The sad truth is existing technology cannot provide fast, long-distance travel sustainably.

Here are some figures that make the same point. According to the UN's World Tourism Organization, in 2005 international tourist flights accounted for 2 per cent of global greenhouse gas emissions.[1] These arose from 336 million international tourist flights. The figure of 336 million sounds a lot, but it's actually only one international flight per global citizen *every 18 years*. The average UK citizen already flies more than once a year. Even more starkly, 1 per cent of the world's CO_2 emissions arise because of the 22 million long-haul tourist flights; the average global citizen only makes one long-haul flight every 250 years. More than any other type of consumption, flying – especially long-haul flying – is a luxury that our climate system can afford only to the few. Thomas Friedman makes the point in the excellent *Hot, Flat and Crowded* that we have to watch out for India, China and the other emerging economies becoming 'our carbon copies' and importing our unsustainable patterns of consumption.

The title of this chapter is 'travel and leisure'; travel doesn't just mean flying, though flying dominates the emissions from travel and leisure. The chapter also includes emissions from the other modes of transport, accommodation and activities we undertake while on holiday.

Unlike other chapters, this one will discuss business-related travel. I have done this for two reasons – the first is economic – the viability of many scheduled routes depends on business travel. In a sense leisure travel and business travel are umbilically linked by economics. Second, many business travellers have discretion about whether they choose to fly. No one press-gangs academics into attending a conference in Tokyo. The dirty secret is that despite their protestations to the contrary, many international trips are fun and undertaken voluntarily. You get to stay in plush hotels in the most prosperous districts of interesting cities. You might even be able to tag on a few days of sight-seeing afterwards. And you might even be able to turn in a profit; in the public sector it's usual to provide generous overseas allowances to cover incidental expenses and hotel costs. Through work I have visited countries and stayed in accommodation I could never have afforded to go to if I'd have been paying myself. This has been a privilege rather than a chore.

The transition to flying less is something we all need to share

A few years ago I attended an event celebrating the 30th anniversary of the magazine *Resurgence*. The final session of the day was a question and answer session with several prominent environmentalists on the podium. Someone from the audience asked how many miles they had each flown for work and pleasure. This was a great question and the audience went quiet, eager to hear how the environmental movement's jet-set got along without the jets.

The truth is they didn't. It wasn't possible to do so and be effective in their jobs. The three people who gave interpretable answers had clocked up something like 25,000 miles between them. This was more than the average person in the UK. But each had grappled with the issue, accommodating the tension as best they could. One of them flew to continental Europe regularly but did the return leg by train. One chaired an international working group and had no choice but to fly in order to attend meetings in southern Africa. And the other never flew within Europe.

Reducing the amount we travel will require profound change in the way people, and the affluent especially, conduct their lives: necessitating changes in the way we work, our conception of holidays and perhaps also the readiness with which we enter long-distance business and romantic entanglements.

Non-CO_2 greenhouse gas emissions from aviation

Emissions from planes are even worse than suggested by some of the figures quoted above. Exhaust from planes is released into the troposphere (8–13km above sea level) where the climate chemistry is different to that at the Earth's surface. At this altitude emissions of water vapour turn into long streaky clouds which you see in the plane's wake ('contrails') and nitrous oxides (NO_x) which the sunlight turns into methane and ozone. The troublesome bit is adding the greenhouse effects of all these gases together. The different gases don't hang around in the atmosphere for the same amount of time, so the problem is essentially insoluble; it's like trying to work out how much vegetation there is in a field – it depends in which season you do your sums.

At the moment the UK government advises 'The total climate impact of aviation due to Radiative Forcing is estimated to be up to 2–4 times that of CO_2 alone', then adds 'however the science of Radiative Forcing is currently uncertain'.[2] Thanks! This echoes the IPCC's most recent advice which also recommended using a correction factor of 2–4 to assess climate change impacts for the next few decades.[3] Some parts of the aviation industry have exploited this uncertainty to ignore the effects of non-CO_2 GHG emitted from planes at high altitudes. I asked Kevin Anderson, an expert on this subject from the Tyndall Centre, what the number was. 'It depends …' he started unhelpfully, and evaded the question for the rest of the conversation. Later in the chapter I will use the figure of 1.9 because it is recommended by government. The more astute among you might have noticed that 1.9 lies outside the 2–4 range that both the government and IPCC identify as the appropriate uplift – smells a bit like lobbying by the aviation industry.

Emissions from holidays are growing fast

No one concerned about climate change is unaware of the basic fact that the greenhouse gas emissions from planes have been growing quickly. Emissions from planes taking off in the UK were 36MtCO_2 in 2006. This is around 0.6tCO_2e per person. If you take account of the other greenhouse gases effects from planes, this is 1.1tCO_2e each. As well as planes, other bits of the holiday industry are significant energy users. The hospitality sector – restaurants, hotels and pubs – emits a further 12.5MtCO_2 a year, around a quarter of a tonne of CO_2 per person.

Figure 8.1 shows how emissions have risen sixfold since 1970. A generation ago flying was an infrequent delight, but now it is commonplace. In 2006 UK residents made 70 million trips abroad, about 80 per cent of these by plane. Between 1990 and 2006 emissions doubled – growing at 5 per cent a year. For many comfortably off people holidays will be their largest source of greenhouse gas emissions. And most worrying, it's the long-haul flights that are growing fastest of all, at around 11 per cent a year.

Economists describe holidays as 'superior goods'. As people and countries become wealthier they spend a higher proportion of income on travel. In the next chapter we see that the rich are the overwhelmingly big spenders on flying. The top 10 per cent richest households fly 11 times more than the bottom 10 per cent. This is by far the greatest inequity in fuel use between rich and poor households. But because the duration of holidays is constrained by holiday entitlement and head teachers' dictums on unauthorized school absence, more spending doesn't mean longer holidays – it means more short bursts of holidays around bank holidays and summer.

Planes are ideal for quick, last minute consumption. A Boeing 747 consumes 15,000 litres of fuel an hour; if it's configured to carry 500 people, each passenger emits the equivalent of 100kgCO_2 per hour. It is hard to think of any other legal way of emitting so much carbon dioxide so quickly – apart from burning your house down, which will get you into trouble with your

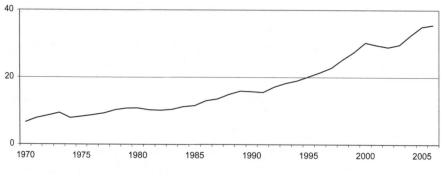

Figure 8.1 Carbon dioxide emissions from aviation (MtCO$_2$)

Source: Defra, www.defra.gov.uk/environment/statistics/globatmos/index.htm

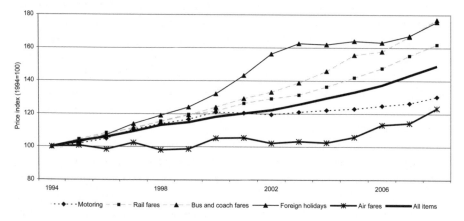

Figure 8.2 Prices for different transport modes, holidays and general rate of inflation

Sources: ONS (2009) *Focus on Consumer Price Indices,* Table 4.10 'Detail prices indices for RPI'; except 'Air fares' from US Bureau of Transportation Statistics Air Travel Price Index, www.bts.gov/xml/atpi/src/datadisp.xml?t=1.

insurance company and your neighbours (and probably contravenes local ordinances on air quality). The real shocker is that on average, for the richest 10 per cent of households, flights account for 40 per cent of their emissions from transport, electricity and heating.[4]

Government policy has done little to tame that urge

But the growth of flying isn't just due to people's innate preferences. It's also because government has done little to curb emissions growth and has often helped stimulate the aviation industry. We're going to get a bit technical now.

Figure 8.2 shows how the prices of different forms of transport have developed over time. The thick line shows the overall cost of living in the UK. The price of flying – based on US data as I couldn't find a UK data series – shows how the costs of flights between the US and international destinations has fallen substantially over the past 15 years relative to the general rate of inflation.

Cheap flights are the result of cheap oil (at least till 2000), open skies policies on EU–US routes and the advent of the no-frills carriers. The price of public transport (trains and buses) has gone up faster than the general rate of inflation, mainly because government has reduced the level of public subsidy, the high costs of rail infrastructure and the failure of the industry to reduce costs through standardizing designs. Motoring costs in the UK have risen slower than inflation because of the dramatic fall in the price of cars since 2002, mainly as a result of competition policy. Aviation is spared the burden of tax and the cost of infrastructure borne by other forms of transport. No tax is paid on aviation fuel, non-EU flights are allowed to sell VAT-free and duty-free goods, and no VAT is paid on aircraft or tickets. But the surprising thing is that the most marked increase in cost has been that of 'packaged' foreign holidays (the same is true of UK package holidays).

How come the price of flying has come down and yet the cost of foreign holidays gone up? The answer is of course that ONS sample '... a range of foreign destinations, accommodation and holiday types, including late-booked holidays'. The reason spending on holidays has risen is people are flying further and living in more opulent accommodation. As people become wealthier they spend an increasing share of their income on holidays.

Understanding Why, Where and How Much We Travel

I blame the telly, especially Judith Chalmers and *Wish You Were Here*. This programme and the travel supplements in newspapers democratized the sangria-and-picture-postcard image of holidays. Not only were these accessible to everyone; more than that, they were the *just reward* for slogging our guts out at work for the rest of the year.

The holiday industry still pushes this line and nurtures our craving for classy, far-flung, exotic holidays on unspoilt beaches, through bankrolling the newspapers' travel section infomercials, often supported by a national government hungry for foreign exchange. In my weekend newspaper this week there was not a single story or advertisement about a domestic UK holiday; instead there were features about Sri Lanka, China and southern Spain. There were even adverts to entice you to Bhutan (population: 600,000; national sport: horseshoe throwing; most famous (and only) culinary speciality: yak ... no disrespect to any Bhutanese intended), despite it being forbidden to travel there independently. Mysteriously no journalist had chosen to write, nor any UK tourist board to pay for an advertisement for any UK destination (population: 60,000,000; great culture and every cuisine under the sun)! Compared to the far-flung, the local seems cheap and jaded. But the reality of flying is different: diarrhoea, delays, drug searches, documentation, just to name a few nightmares that begin with the letter d – no one ever writes about these.

The idea of mass tourism is actually a Victorian one. Thomas Cook was a pioneer in the industry. His early package holidays already incorporated many of the features found today: organized transport, pre-booked accommodation and trips, and carefully crafted brochures to entice the punters. He chartered entire trains to take people from their homes in the Midlands to Liverpool on temperance weekends. His first international tour to Europe was in 1855 via Antwerp and Brussels to Napoleon III's Great Exhibition in Paris. Far from being lager louts the early British package tourists were teetotal culture vultures.

At the same time the working classes made use of the week-long holidays when their manufacturing plants closed down for maintenance, to escape the pollution and drudgery of the industrial revolution in seaside resort towns like Skegness, Blackpool, Brighton and Morecambe. Billy Butlin opened his first holiday camps in Skegness in 1936. This grew to almost 2000 chalets, indoor swimming pools, child-minding services, redcoats and on-site catering. It presented a different vision of a holiday – nothing high minded; just all-inclusive, relaxing and cheap fun.

Why we travel

Figure 8.3 breaks down international trips by purpose. Two-thirds of trips are for holidays and a sixth are to visit relatives. In 2006 business trips made up just 13 per cent of overseas travel and the remaining 5 per cent was for miscellaneous purposes including shopping, international commuting, pilgrimage and education.

The number of times people fly per year varies widely. At one extreme are international commuters and people who own second homes in another country. Around 115,000 British people own a second home outside the UK. There is also a large number of people who live outside the UK and commute to the UK every week. Thomson Travel funded work by the Future Forum which forecast that 1.5 million British people would commute every week from mainland Europe by 2020.[5] With the price of a pre-bought off-peak flight from Barcelona about the same price as a peak-time ticket to London from the commuter belt and the costs of housing so much lower, this is not a ridiculous idea. Box 8.1 explains how three people I have interviewed have found themselves in the situation of being weekly international commuters. Once, on a plane, I found myself sitting next to an agency nurse who worked four nights

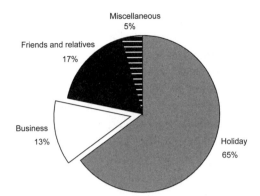

Figure 8.3 Number of UK residents' visits abroad by purpose for all modes of international travel, 2006

Source: ONS International Passenger Survey

Box 8.1 *International commuting and family life*

Joseph bought his house in southern Italy 15 years ago when he worked for a global IT firm. The company used to post him on short-term assignments anywhere in Europe and it suited him to live near to his Italian girlfriend. This worked well for a number of years but his relationship ended and he married Lizzie, an England-based colleague. Lizzie reluctantly agreed to move to Italy. They had two girls and she got a job teaching English to local businessmen.

Joseph secured a great job working for an international organization based in Rome which allowed him to spend more time at home with Lizzie and the girls. Life went smoothly for a few years, though Lizzie was beginning to feel increasingly isolated in Italy, especially after her father became a widower. They decided to move back to England so the girls could attend an English secondary school and Lizzie could resume her career.

But Joseph was unable to find a job in the UK at a similar level to his role in Rome. Reluctantly they decided to buy a house in Sussex and maintain a small place in Rome for his weekday use. His employer allowed him to work one day a week from Sussex but he finds the travelling tiresome. Fridays are particularly stressful since he has to leave work early and still fails to make the children's bedtime. At least financially they were still secure; they had luckily maintained a foothold in the UK property market, and the €100 cost of the weekly flight was easily affordable – but he has to be flexible and prepared to return to any of London's airports. But the arrangement is not ideal as he's away from the family four nights a week. Lizzie was looking forward to being back in England, but being a single mother for half the week is not what she had had in mind. But this is the only way they can juggle careers and education.

Though philosophical, he wonders if he could do it all again; whether he'd have just settled for a lower-status job in the UK so the family could have been together.

a week in London and flew back to his girlfriend on the French–Swiss border every week. The low cost of pre-booked tickets coupled with the high wages and high property prices have so distorted prices that even the relatively modestly paid find themselves part of the international commuter jet set.

But it would be a mistake to assume that it's spread to all levels of society. Four-fifths of the poorest fifth of households in the UK made no flights in the year they were surveyed, on average flying just once every five years.[6]

Where we travel

Figure 8.4 shows about four-fifths of our foreign travel is to Europe – with Spain and France the commonest destinations.

Figure 8.5 shows the number of international trips according to their duration, over recent years. About a fifth of personal international trips are short breaks of three nights or less away from the UK. These have been growing but the real growth has been in the classic one to two week foreign holiday.

The average duration of the overseas holiday is around ten nights long; around 14 nights in North America, and 8.4 days in Europe. The average duration of trips to Belgium is a mere three nights; trips to New Zealand, Australia and, curiously, Pakistan, around 40 days.

We are more likely to visit the UK than another country, but only just. According to data from the national and regional tourism boards we made 100 million overnight or longer non-business trips within the UK in 2007. But these visits were typically of short duration – the average stay a mere three nights.[7] Far more nights of holiday are spent in other countries than in the UK. The south west is the most popular destination for holidays, attracting about a fifth of all visits. People are attracted to the sun, sea and relative warmth of the seaside towns and countryside.

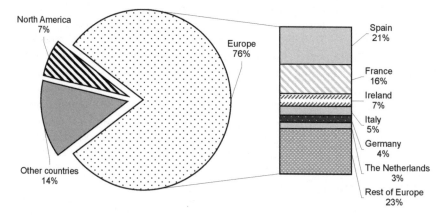

Figure 8.4 Number of foreign visits by UK nationals, 2006 (total of 70 million visits)

Source: ONS, International Passage Survey, 2006

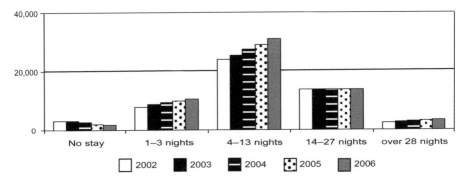

Figure 8.5 Change in the duration of personal (non-business) trips (thousand trips per year)

Source: ONS, International Passenger Survey, 2006, Travel Trends Table 3.13

Believe it or not, the UK is the sixth most popular country in the world for inward tourism, receiving around 32 million visits a year. London is the most popular tourist destination in the UK with around 15 million visits a year, more than the rest of England combined. But we have a huge trade imbalance in foreign travel; twice as many British people holiday overseas as foreigners come on holiday in the UK. Overall, international tourism represents a huge burden on the UK economy – costing us jobs. Private (as opposed to business) spending by British holidaymakers was £29 billion in 2006 (about 3 per cent of GDP). But visitors to the UK only spent £11 billion. But this imbalance ought to be less pronounced in the next few years. Since the recession, sterling has become weaker than pretty much every other currency save the Icelandic Krona, so it is becoming more expensive for British people to holiday abroad.

So when we have time off, we would rather spend it in another country than in the UK. This is despite our country being one of the most popular destinations for the international tourist. In short, we don't appreciate how lucky we are.

Options for Reducing Emissions

In theory there are three broad ways of reducing emissions from travelling. These are to develop technologies to reduce the greenhouse gas emissions from flying, to develop substitutes for flying like ultra-high-speed trains or to travel less.

But surely scientists will invent a low-carbon way of flying

... well they haven't yet. Plane designers have always put a lot of effort into designing planes to be as energy efficient as possible. They'd be mad not to, aviation fuel is one of the largest costs of running a plane. Planes already use ultra-light-weight materials, state-of-the-art IT, clever engine design and carefully engineered fuels, and then cram more fare-paying people into the economy class than would be allowed if they were merely taking sheep to the abattoir. Even so, Boeing's new 747-8 Intercontinental, due to be launched in 2010, is only 15 per cent more fuel efficient than the current 747-400 which came into service in 1988 – pretty pathetic progress compared to that achieved in cars, fridges, etc. According to the UN World Tourism Organization report, the current rate of improvement in energy efficiency arising from technological improvements, air traffic management and operational improvements is 1.3 per cent per year[8] – worth having but much less than the growth in traffic of 5 per cent per year.

There are some other more optimistic assessments of technological potential. Research undertaken for the Committee on Climate Change foresees new technologies which might reduce emissions from new planes by 40–50 per cent by 2030.[9] These would have to utilize dramatically different aircraft designs such as blended wing bodies (where the cabin and wings are merged), which will take a decade or more to design and build. Maybe this will happen – but given that aviation emissions are doubling every ten years, and most aircraft that will be in operation in 2030 have already been built, the typical plane we board in 2020 will be using today's technology.

A couple of people have said to me that it is OK flying long distances because most of the fuel is required in the take-off and landing phases, and planes use little energy once they are airborne. This is an urban myth. As with any dense 500-tonne mass suspended in the Earth's troposphere, considerable energy has to be expended to avoid it crashing down. Figure 8.6 shows how the fuel efficiency per passenger-km varies across different lengths of flight. As the length of trip increases from 1000 to 4000km fuel economy improves as the energy needed to take off is smeared over a larger distance. As the trip length increases further the weight penalty of having to carry so much fuel at the beginning of the journey kicks in and fuel efficiency deteriorates. More than half the take-off weight of a Boeing flying long distance will be fuel! The high-density configuration of Japan Airlines' planes is around twice as efficient as its long-distance configuration. It's leg room rather than length of journey that affects fuel efficiency.

The most pernicious threat is that improved technology and better fuel efficiency will strengthen the 'rebound effect'. This is the phenomenon that for some luxury goods our desire to consume grows as they become more efficient and their price falls, undermining the technical savings. Though it's

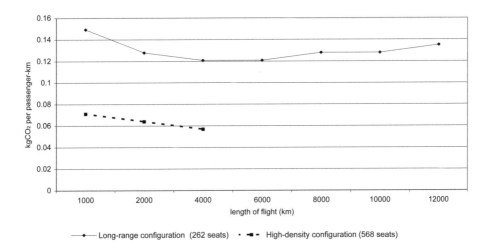

Figure 8.6 Effect of configuration on fuel consumption in Boeing 747-400 aircraft

Source: Japan Airlines, from the IPCC special report *Aviation and the Global Atmosphere*[10]

sometimes difficult to believe it, flying is incredibly cheap and keeps getting cheaper. The price of everything in life goes up, except the price of the London–Mumbai ticket which for the last 20 years has cost me £400.

Biofuels and electricity

Today marks a biofuel breakthrough for the whole airline industry. Virgin Atlantic, and its partners, are proving that you can find an alternative to traditional jet fuel and fly a plane on new technology, such as sustainable biofuel. This pioneering flight will enable those of us who are serious about reducing our carbon emissions to go on developing the fuels of the future, fuels which will power our aircraft in the years ahead through sustainable next-generation oils, such as algae. (Richard Branson, 24 February 2008)

Despite what Virgin want us to believe, today's flight is nothing short of high altitude greenwash. The scientific evidence is now clear – using the finite amount of land we have to grow biofuels is bad for the world's poor, bad for biodiversity and bad for the climate. (Doug Parr, Greenpeace, 24 February 2008)

Can we sustainably reduce emissions by replacing jet fuel with biofuels or electricity? The energy source used by planes has to be energy dense in order to fly long distances without having to constantly stop to refuel. This pretty much rules out batteries whose energy density is a hundred times lower than fossil fuels.

Biofuels are in theory a more practical proposition. Their energy density is poorer than aviation fuel but still OK. The quotes above show it is technically possible for biofuel to be used without the plane falling out of the sky … but as the Virgin press release goes on to make clear, only one of the four engines used biodiesel and even here the biodiesel was just a 20 per cent blend with normal aviation fuel making up the balance, and the plane only flew the relatively low-altitude London–Amsterdam route. (Even so Virgin's is not an insignificant achievement, biodiesel turns into wax in the cold so it's impressive that the propulsion was maintained under the low-temperature in-flight conditions.) The bigger issue is where is all this biodiesel going to come from? At the moment it takes around 1 hectare of land to produce a tonne of biodiesel in the UK. A fleet of ten 747's working flat out will blaze their way through 1 million litres of aviation oil – equivalent to the output of 10 per cent of UK's cropland. It's all very well hoping the planes will be fuelled with algae – but this technology has yet to be invented, and there are other competing uses that algal fuels could be put to – like freight shipping, which emits only around 1 per cent of the emissions per tonne-km of planes.

Biodiesel still causes problems with contrails and NO_x.

Alternatives to jet-engined craft

Instead of using conventional jets to fly between countries couldn't we use some other form of transport? David MacKay's excellent book painstakingly summarizes the different modes of transport that are available for holiday travel. In Figure 8.7, the x-axis shows the energy used per passenger-kilometre travelled. Cars and planes are really not that different in their efficiency – it's just that the plane's high speed allows you to travel so much further in a given time.

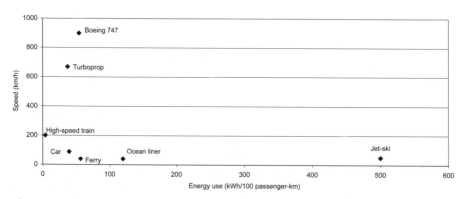

Figure 8.7 Speed and energy use by modes of transport used on holiday

Source: David MacKay (2008) Sustainable Energy – Without the Hot Air, Figure 20.23. The car assumes an occupancy rate of two people. The other data assume the standard occupancy rates (approximately three-quarters for planes, trains and ocean liners). Ferry data from DfT[11]

What does Figure 8.7 tell us? The main message is that only electric trains have successfully combined travelling fast with travelling fuel efficiently. Travelling fast on water is energy hungry – jet-skis and motor-boats managing a paltry 50km/h gobble up fuel at the same rate as a Hummer. Long-distance transport of people on boats is also hugely energy hungry because the liner has to carry not just fuel but also food, drinking water, beds and in the case of cruise liners, swimming pools and entertainment complexes. Hauling around this weight implies a huge carbon penalty.

Within western Europe we are lucky that we have an extensive and easily accessible network of high-speed rail. We are fortunate to be on the borders of this network. The French have the extensive TGV network that attains speeds of 300km/h, and the networks in Germany and Spain are almost as impressive. Japan's jaw-droppingly reliable (average lateness in 2004: 12 seconds), ultra-safe (one derailment in its 50-year history, caused by an earthquake) and popular (6 billion passengers carried so far) 'bullet train', the Shinkansen, motors along at speeds of 300km/h. A maglev (magnetic-levitation) train being used in Shanghai is capable of speeds of 500km/h.

So the future is high-speed electric train? Maybe – but maybe not, too. The problem is the economics, and the location and condition of existing rail infrastructure. To show this: the elapsed time to get to Madrid by train is around 16 hours, as a result of a change in Paris, and the return fare around £160. This compares unfavourably with the plane which takes around six hours (including extra time for check-in and travel to the airport) and costs around £50 on a budget airline, plus another £30 to get to and from the airports. Trains are likely to get faster and lower carbon as technology develops, but they're not getting any cheaper. The Chinese maglev track cost around US$17 million per kilometre. We'll need to multiply that by three for the cost in Europe and by three again for the cost in the UK. It's hard to see how cash-strapped UK and European governments will embark on the necessary investment any time soon. Even the relatively low-tech bullet train bankrupted its developers. For more information on travelling by train or ship within Europe the best website is the curiously named *The Man in Seat Sixty-One* (www.Seat61.com) run by Mark Smith. It's brilliant.

Prop planes are another option. But despite the hype about prop planes from some green websites, models like the Bombardier Q400 75-seater are only about 10 per cent more fuel efficient than jet planes per passenger-km. They travel at two-thirds of the speed of a jet – most customers will find the speed penalty too high a price for the modest improvement in fuel efficiency. I've not found any information whether the prop planes have lower non-CO_2 emissions – but their cruising altitude is within the troposphere so it is unlikely there will be much difference. Prop planes can use higher blends of biodiesel but the same issues about land availability apply.

Travelling less and avoiding travel altogether

New technology and investment in existing technologies are unlikely to permit us to travel as far or as quickly as we have become accustomed. We are going to have to travel less than many of us would ideally like. Many of us, myself included, have become accustomed to one, maybe two, long-haul flights a year, as well as several short-haul flights too. Long-haul holidays, especially with the family in tow, are a major carbon blowout. A return trip to the west coast of the US for a family of four emits $14tCO_2$ if you include the non-CO_2 greenhouse gases. For my own household this is equivalent to our full year's emissions from heating ($2.7tCO_2$), electricity ($0.9tCO_2$) and car use ($2.2tCO_2$) doubled and then some! No amount of changing our light bulbs, diets or trading in our car keys for cycle locks will make such a lifestyle sustainable. Though only a minority of us can afford such lifestyles, many others aspire to acquire similar travel patterns. In our lexicon 'jet set' is a synonym for wealthy and influential.

We need this association to reverse. Though it might seem an odd analogy there are parallels between planes and social vices like smoking. In sections of society smoking has long been regarded as abhorrent – and lighting up was forbidden long before it became *legally* banned. A similar change in mindset might be needed if we are to reduce our demand for travel. The reduction in the consumption of cigarettes hasn't arisen because high taxes put people off (though price has played a part), nor from technological changes in the cigarettes. The change has arisen through changes in our views about smoking – in part due to decades of public health campaigns and policy.

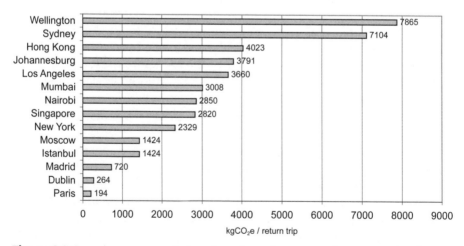

Figure 8.8 Greenhouse gas emissions for selected economy class return trips from London

Note: Includes radiative forcing from non-CO_2 greenhouse gases at 1.9.
Source: Distances from www.landings.com, based on the great circle distance.

Table 8.1 Reasons for wanting to fly and possible resolutions

Reason for wanting to fly	Possible resolutions
Everyone else flies – why shouldn't I?	Only a minority of people can afford to fly. Thankfully it remains the preserve of just the richer parts of the world's population. Friends who are committed to reducing their carbon emissions will support and help normalize low-carbon local travel choices.
Travel broadens the mind	A rushed weekend away does nothing to broaden the mind. There are opportunities to experience foreign cultures, cuisines and languages locally or through the media or internet.
My family/loved ones are overseas – I miss them so much	Try and keep touch using new communications technologies. If you do have to visit, take a single extended break rather than many shorter breaks.
I want to be sure of some sunshine	Sun can be experienced within Europe travelling on the train or ferry/car. Long-haul flights are unnecessary.
I have to travel for my job	Do you? Could the work be done by teleconferencing or the phone/email?

The simplest option to reducing emissions from travel is to stop or severely limit our flying, long-haul flights in particular. Figure 8.8 gives the CO_2 emissions for a return trip to a number of popular destinations. (I have used the emissions factors for short- and long-haul flights from the Defra website.)

If we are to halt our own flights and influence others to reduce theirs we need to understand and address why we want to travel such long distances.

Often our holidays make up the most cherished events in our lives. The climate conversation groups, which I describe in the next chapter, provide a structured forum for small groups of people to discuss how they might practically go about reducing their greenhouse gas emissions. One of the meetings is given over to transport. These meetings invariably discuss the difficulty people have in cutting back on holiday and business travel. The groups usually consist of navel-gazy, green-minded folk. In the meetings I have attended, with a hint of apology we all admit we have a problem in cutting back on our travel. Table 8.1 shows five common difficulties and some of the strategies that are mentioned to avert them.

All of us, mindful of the greenhouse gas emissions from flying, had developed ways of reducing our flights. Box 8.2 shows the approaches taken by Duncan.

A lot of the things that you hanker for from your holiday can be obtained locally. Dependable sunny weather can never be assured in the UK – but many other must-haves could be accessed in the UK. Windsurfing provides the same sort of sensory stimulation as skiing but can be experienced along the coast and in clay pits dotted around the country, see www.ukwindsurfing.com/links/clubs/. Though it sounds bizarre, a trip around Leicester, Wembley or Southall, especially during Diwali, offers all the culinary opportunities and colour you might get from a trip to India, but with better hygiene.

Many of us enjoy swimming outdoors. Though it's not possible to guarantee good weather, it's perfectly feasible to swim outdoors in the UK, sometimes in nearly idyllic scenery. Here are two websites with suggested locations: www.outdoorswimmingsociety.com and www.river-swimming.co.uk. The latter has Ordnance Survey grid references which you can use Google Earth to take a look at.

Box 8.2 *Travelling and reducing your emissions*

Duncan loves travelling and learning about different countries, but he also wants to reduce his emissions from flying. After university he spent a year in central America teaching English. He likes the idea of really immersing himself in any country he visits, learning enough of the language to have simple conversations.

He now works for a local authority. His employer allows staff to carry over leave from one year to the next; he's using this facility to accumulate leave so he can take a three-month sabbatical from work. He plans to travel, perhaps overland, to the Far East, or maybe sail to the US as a crew member. 'I had no idea you could do that', I say. He explains you need to have passed a few basic sailing courses first, but there are a lot of well-off people who only have a limited amount of time to sail and need others to bring their boats back home. He's obviously getting a lot of enjoyment and excitement from simply planning these trips. I remember I used to feel like this too, when I first started travelling independently, but now my own rushed and hastily arranged trips leave me feeling jaded.

He has decided to restrict his long-haul flights to a maximum of one every two years. But in actual fact he has not flown long haul for some years. Recently he has mainly holidayed in Europe and the UK. Last year he went to Spain – he flew one way and returned by train/coach. Both legs cost around £100. 'Actually the overland trip was a little cheaper as I didn't have to pay the extortionate fare to Stansted. The journey back was slow; it consisted of a five-hour train journey, an overnight sleeper and a night coach. Travelling over land, so long as you plan it (using websites like Seat61) and book it in advance, doesn't need to cost any more than flying and might even be cheaper, but it does take more time. You have to make the journey itself part of the holiday, breaking the trip in cities you're interested in visiting.'

Flights that cannot be avoided

The hardest flights to avoid are the big family set-piece events: weddings, major birthdays and anniversaries – giving rise to what George Monbiot calls 'love miles'. As we get wealthier, expectations of our families keep rising. When my parents first emigrated to the UK in the late 1960s they did not return to India for seven years. I didn't meet my grandparents until I was eight years old. In that time my parents missed the weddings of all their siblings, something that would be considered insulting today. Now relatives are invited to fly over for a simple birthday party; and sometimes they come too. Greater wealth means greater obligation to attend.

I have no answer for this. If we are going to reduce our emissions by 80 per cent over the next 40 years, we're going to have to learn to do without. One of the biggest challenges for the economical environmentalist is learning to be satisfied with staying closer to home most of the time. It means treating the occasional long-distance flight as a privilege to be cherished and carefully planned. If we desire to stay in touch we need to replace many short-duration visits with few long-duration visits. Sadly, trends in employment and schooling are making such extended vacations harder, not easier.

Reducing emissions from work trips

> *Why should we move tons of material and use gallons of gasoline to transport two kilos of brain?* (Eckart Wintzen, developer of the Eyecatcher videoconferencing technology)

In 2006, 13 per cent of international trips were for business. According to the DfT *National Travel Survey*, business also accounts for 15 per cent of domestic journeys over 50 miles.[12] Because business travel is commonly during peak times and business passengers pay premium prices for their seats, the impact of business on congestion and airline finances is higher than the share of traffic.

The evidence on whether investment in better telecommunications like videoconferencing (VC), conference calls and webcasting can reduce the need for travel is mixed. Companies that have introduced teleconferencing have typically managed to reduce business travel by 10–30 per cent.[13] However, teleconferencing is unsuited to many types of meetings, such as kick-off meetings for a new project. At the aggregate level there is no evidence that business travel has fallen as telecommunications have improved. Over the last year I have worked for two 'multi-continent SMEs'. The smaller employed a dozen people and had offices in the UK and China; the larger employed fewer than 200 staff and had offices in every continent. Such businesses successfully integrated *excellent use of telecommunications and targeted use of internal travel.* But there is no inevitability to firms successfully using telecommunications technologies. There are many examples of videoconferencing facilities lying idle while staff carry on flying. One company that has made it work is BT. A staff survey suggested on average each VC avoided travel costs of £95 per person, half avoided three hours of travel or more, and they improved staff's quality of life by reducing the stress of travel.

Webinars can be excellent way of remotely listening into, or participating in a conference. Once you log onto the site you can see slides in a window on your computer and perhaps see the speaker in another. If you are interested in seeing an example of what's on offer take a look at http://tiny.cc/NwKmU – an excellent presentation which synchronizes sound, slides and the image of the speaker, the ecological economist Peter Victor, speaking in Canada about his new book *Managing Without Growth.*

If you are in a position of authority within your organization try and reduce your business travel and influence others to do the same. We can only displace travel when we invest in, and use, telecommunications. Members of the Food Climate Research Network had a lively discussion of their experiences of using VC technologies.[14] These were mixed. Broadly you get what you pay for. The cheapest technologies, like Skype, use the internet to convey sound and picture over standard ISDN lines. My own experience with my far-flung family is that we spend half our time out of the range of the pin-hole camera, but it's a cheap way of keeping in touch. The next level up makes use of better cameras and plasma screens – the kit is made by companies like Tandberg – and costs several thousand pounds per unit. If money is no object than Cisco's Telepresence, which costs US$250,000 for the conference suite and US$10,000 per month to hire the bandwidth, is the Rolls-Royce option – with multiple plasma screens to link many locations together.

One member of the network had been invited to address a number of international conferences (on climate change) over the last year. She tried to participate remotely to avoid the long-haul flights. One conference organizer allowed her to play a pre-recorded mp3 file over her Powerpoint presentation since they could not afford full VC facilities. This worked well but the normal interactive question-and-answer session was not possible. Two other conferences refused to accommodate her even though she offered to research the feasibility. They declined, perhaps fearful the technology would fail, perhaps to avoid alienating the fee-paying attendees.

Box 8.3 *Work is an activity not a place*

Paul Dickinson is the energetic head of two teleconference businesses (and in his spare time runs the Carbon Disclosure Project, which publishes information on the CO_2 emissions of companies and public bodies). He is convinced that proper dedicated VC facilities could make much business travel redundant, if the existing telecoms companies didn't do such a brilliant job of underselling their own products. He estimates that an hour of flying emits the same amount of greenhouse gas emissions as 3.5 years of videoconferencing.

One of his businesses leases the Eyecatcher videophone which provides desktop videoconferencing for business use. The screen is designed so you are more or less forced to position your face so the camera centres on your eyes, greatly improving the quality of the communication. The units cost around US$200 per month to lease plus the cost of the communication line. His other company, www.eyenetwork.com, allows people to access VC facilities by the hour across 3000 locations around the world. Bookings are over the internet – but again they're not cheap, costing at least £80 per hour plus the booking fee: worthwhile if it avoids a long-haul flight once you factor in time saved; but not really priced to have a natter with your grandma on her birthday.

I asked Paul: 'Why so much?' It was essentially the cost of the kit, and the cost of the real estate in London. If the production runs were 100,000 the purchase price would come down to £600; as it was they were an order of magnitude higher.

Emissions from hotels and holiday activities

The hospitality industry is a significant emitter of greenhouse gas emissions. On holiday we get to use energy in ways we wouldn't at home; making more use of air conditioning, swimming pools, jacuzzis, saunas and regular laundry. The carbon emissions add up.

Public-sector buildings like public swimming pools and other leisure facilities are required to display their energy ratings (Display Energy Certificates), which is essentially an energy performance certificate for a non-residential building. This is not the case for the UK's private-sector leisure facilities. So there is no easy way of finding out the actual environmental performance of different hotels and eateries. The Carbon Trust does provide training – but in my conversations with smaller B&Bs there was little awareness of energy management.

If you wish to vet your accommodation and activities before you get there your options are either to go for an obviously low-carbon option like camping, or staying in a yurt, or otherwise be guided by green travel websites.

There are two broad types of such websites. The first type identifies and promotes businesses that are firmly targeted at the green holidaymaker market, such as www.greentraveller.co.uk/ and my own favourite, www.eco-escape.org/, which features the contact details for many low-carbon places to stay and enjoy yourself around the UK. How else could you readily find out about a new activity centre in Wales that houses people in wood cabins made by local artisans and is heated by ground source heat pumps. The accommodation featured covers the entire spectrum of prices from modest lodges like Tyf Eco Hotel in Wales for £16 per night to plush hotels in London for more than £1000 a night.

The other type of website encourages more conventional hotels and leisure facilities to clean up their acts. The Green Tourism Business Scheme is a not-for-profit organization based in Perth, Scotland, which has since 1997 provided a quality assurance scheme for hotels, B&Bs and tourist attractions. The grading is based on 60 measures covering energy, water, waste, purchasing and travel. Hotels are assessed every two years and receive either a bronze, silver or gold status. I was a little sceptical about whether this was just greenwash but I cycled over to see the Cavendish, London's only hotel with a Gold award. There is no getting away from the fact it's a four-star Mayfair hotel – guests are more likely to roll up in their Rolls-Royce than on a Brompton (as I did) – but the deputy manager was both enthusiastic and knowledgeable about the sustainability agenda. The management staff had been working their way through suggestions made by their auditors. This included an excellent waste management policy, sending all their wastes to recycling or anaerobic digestion facilities, using low-energy LED bulbs where they felt lighting had to be kept always on, and using motion-sensing switches in other communal areas. But they were not prepared to make sacrifices that would detract from the 'consumer experience', for instance scrapping their over-packaged designer toiletries. This isn't exactly low-carbon living, but it's lower than it might have been.

Leisure facilities are major energy users. It amazes me how feckless many businesses are with their energy use. We stayed at one place in Devon which kept an abnormally hot outside jacuzzi on all year round without a cover; the sauna was so poorly insulated the draught from the edge of the door was uncomfortable. The manager told me the jacuzzi used to have a cover but a customer had complained his unsupervised children were unable to lift the lid off – so they did away with it. He explained they didn't want to get sued! Unsurprisingly the energy bill for the ten cottages was £30,000 a year, even though occupancy rates were low in winter. No one from the Carbon Trust or local authority had ever contacted the cottages – though whether anyone could remedy such appalling management is questionable. Not surprisingly the properties were for sale as the absent owner couldn't make the business work financially.

In case you own a swimming pool or wish to have some ammunition to nag someone who does, here are a few titbits of information. The cost of heating a 100m² outdoor pool to 27°C is around £1800 a year (average for the US). In swimming pools, evaporation accounts for 70 per cent of heat loss; radiation to the night sky can lose 20 per cent. In daylight hours a well-illuminated pool will pick up heat – but at night it's essential to cover the pool – the payback period for a pool cover is just six months. A wind of 7mph triples heat loss – so make sure there's a decent wall/hedge to slow the air flow over the water. For indoor pools, a quarter of the energy use is to ventilate the pool; so invest in

---

Box 8.4 *Eco-dilemma: Is it OK to heli-ski?*

The manager of a heli-skiing business argues that his holidays 'give people the awareness of the things we should be protecting' (*Guardian*, March 2007).

There is no way to pretend that skiing is good for the environment, except perhaps in comparison to the delusional proprietor quoted above. But about 1.2 million people from the UK go skiing every winter. It can be a faddish sport with equipment, gear, resorts, even entire countries falling in and out of fashion.

Skiing is vulnerable to climate change, with many lower-altitude resorts finding their seasons shrinking in duration, and also a major source of CO_2 emissions, not just through flying to the resort but also road travel from the airport, heating of chalets, waste and emissions from the operation of ski lifts and snow blowers. The upmarket Austrian resort of Lech has been striving to reduce those emissions within its control.[15] This has included discouraging the use of private cars within the resort by investing in ten free ski buses, creation of an extensive district heating system fired by local wood chip (the chalets were already built to high energy-efficiency standards). There has also been investment in upgrading and electrifying the ski lifts. Ski lifts are an intrinsically efficient way of lifting people up slopes (the weight of the chairs descending balances the rising lifts so the only work done is in lifting the people and their skis).But only 10 per cent of guests use public transport to get to Lech despite there being shuttle buses from the nearby airports.

So what can skiers do to reduce their emissions? First, take the train to get to the resort and avoid driving in the village itself. Hire your equipment at the resort to save the cost, hassle and material use of purchasing your own equipment. Use the local ski buses if they exist. They reduce congestion and improve air quality, as well as reducing emissions. The ski club of Great Britain website (www.skiclub.co.uk/skiclub/resorts/greenresorts/default.aspx) has a green resort guide to help inform you of the eco-friendliness of the resort, in terms of green power use, green building policy and traffic reduction.

good heat recovery when you are expelling damp air. If you are feeling really capital rich, invest in a solar collector – the payback period is around three years, much better than for solar hot water. Maintain the temperature of the water as cool as you feel comfortable; the cost of heating a pool increases by between 5 and 25 per cent for every degree centigrade increase.

A well-insulated sauna is not very expensive to operate. A 6kW sauna costs just 60p an hour; once it's reached the desired temperature the heating need drops significantly. I read that the new infrared saunas are much more energy efficient than the normal electric-element ones.

If you're a skier and an environmentalist you might be feeling guilt for all sorts of reasons about your hobby. My take on the various issues is given in Box 8.4.

My Emissions from Travelling

I travelled a lot last year … and the year before … and the year before that too. It hasn't always been like that, and it's with bewilderment I recall that when I was a teenager I seldom travelled more than 2000 miles a year. School and back was five miles and we'd go to Birmingham or Manchester once or twice a year and holiday somewhere in the UK. We flew on holiday just twice during my childhood – once to India when I was 16 and once to the US when I was 18.

In 2007 I holidayed on the west coast of the US at Easter, in Ireland in the summer and had a couple of weekend breaks in Antwerp, which we travelled to on the Eurostar, and Pitlochry in Scotland. I also got married and had a brief honeymoon late in the year – but more about that later. Altogether I clocked up 18,000 miles. But of course none of this matters because while in the US we drove around in a hired hybrid … and I offset my carbon. And all this travel was on top of the day-to-day travel already described in Chapter 4. And while we're in the confession box there were also a couple of business trips to Copenhagen and Edinburgh which were work so don't count.

Table 8.2 records the emissions and cost of each mode of travel. Even forgetting about carbon, there really is little need to fly to the Benelux countries or France any more. The trip to Antwerp cost just £59 and resulted in a mere 20kgCO_2 emissions, underlining just how carbon efficient and cheap train travel can be if you book ahead and root out the cheap fares. It costs almost half that much just to take the train to Stansted. Our car journeys were as low carbon as the train because there were four of us in the vehicle, and both my own car and the hybrid Honda we used in the US were low carbon.

Table 8.2 Distances, emissions and cost of my holiday travel in 2007 by mode

Mode	Distance (km)	CO_2 (kg)	Cost (£/person)
Car	3613	128	36*
Rail	910	35	77
Ferry	202	24	90
Plane	17,600	3712	677
Total	22,325	3899	880

Note: * Just the cost of petrol. The gasoline price in the US was about half that in the UK.

My travel emissions in 2007 were responsible for $3.9tCO_2$ – that's a lot of greenhouse gases in just over five weeks of holiday. For the rest of the book I'd been doing rather well on my emissions but that's all changed now. And it's nearly all down to the return flight to the US. Well at least I offset my carbon emissions, but more about this in the next chapter. Interestingly, this same facility has been extended to the chronically unfaithful by the pioneering new firm cheatneutral (www.cheatneutral.com).[16]

I have very mixed feelings about last year's holidays. Our trip to the US had been planned before I considered writing this book. It certainly felt incongruous stepping into a plane to spend two weeks skiing at Lake Tahoe, visiting national parks and Disneyland while working in the Office of Climate Change … but then all my colleagues were doing this too, and many of them feeling the same sense of unease. But we had a great time in the US, my wife's brother lives in California and I too have quite a lot of family there, who we got to meet for the first time in two years. Unconstrained by carbon worries, it's the type of holiday we'd like to repeat many times over. It fills me with sadness, a feeling that the world is going backwards, that this sort of $3.7tCO_2e$ blowout will become a thing of the past if we make a sincere attempt to hold emissions down. For my generation supersonic flight has become a thing of the past. Maybe for my children this kind of holiday with their children will go the same way.

Our determinedly high-minded, sustainable holiday in Ireland was definitely low carbon, the combination of ferry and car emitted scarcely 100kg per person. But it rained all the time and we had no family or friends to visit. So we stayed indoors quite a lot and watched videos. I realized it was important to research the destination more carefully: '… it rained in Ireland … no kidding? my friends remarked when I got back, incredulous I hadn't anticipated this.

Box 8.5 *A low-carbon wedding*

It was three weeks before the wedding. I pick up the phone to the distinctive click of an international line. After listening for a few minutes I mutter: 'Which bit didn't you understand?' I cup my hands over the mouthpiece and bang my head against the wall. 'It says on wedding website: "We don't want any presents. Please make donations to either of these charities." Do you think we wrote that because we secretly hankered after another bloody vase?' More hyperventilation at the other side of the world. I try and explain patiently, 'I'm 40 years old. I've been married once already. I've owned a house now for over 15 years. Take it from me, we've already got all the pots and pans, toasters, crockery and photo frames we need. And if you're planning to fly, would you be so kind as to offset your carbon emissions. We explain how on the website. ... Oh, you're not coming after all. How did you say you know my fiancée? ... I'll let her know. She'll be very disappointed about that ...'

We were both keen to keep our ceremony as environmentally friendly as possible. All communications were carried out by email, there were no vehicles, and our photographer and video man delivered in digital. Also there was no printed stationery – I created a website with information about the venue, foods options and the programme of events and everyone emailed their responses. I would have gladly got my clothes from Oxfam Bridal (www.oxfam.org.uk/shops/content/bridal.html) but they only do women's clothes so I bought a versatile new suit instead.

One of the most important sources of carbon would be the guests' transport emissions (more than ten guests attended from outside Europe) and hotel use. The wedding and reception was held in a central London club right next to a tube station. Rather embarrassingly the venue faced a Defra office – symbolically demonstrating our inability to separate work from play. We sourced our foods and alcohol locally and tried to select menus that avoided beef and lamb.

Slightly paranoid about my carbon emissions, I insisted on travelling to my wedding by tube, on the hottest day in September. This was going too far. The temperature in the underground was around 25°C and I sweltered in my suit; I got off a stop early frantically scouring the pharmacists to find some deodorant. 'Going to a wedding are we duck?' asked the shop assistant slightly inanely seeing my drooping buttonhole. 'Yes, mine', I growled back.

We both decided we wanted to honeymoon locally. So we drove to a spa hotel near Marlow (dropping off one of our international visitors at Heathrow en route). There were some fabulous upmarket restaurants in nearby Bray. We pressed our noses to the window and tried to spot Heston Blumenthal and tried to get a whiff of the food. Unfortunately to secure a table we would have had to book it sometime before our engagement. 'It was probably overrated', we remarked, tucking into a curry at the nearby Bombay Duck. We learnt to sail on a gravel pit lake, fell in the water more often than strictly necessary, then strolled around Windsor and Eton – beguiled at this wondrous place less than 30 miles from our home.

Big life events

Our big consumption splurges are holidays and life events like weddings. I lump the two together because they both involve international travel, hotels and nice food. We have already talked about international flights in the transport chapter.

Weddings are a major carbon blowout, Indian weddings doubly so. Both our families are part of the great Indian diaspora, surely one of the most fascinating mass movements of people (without killing and conquering anyone) ever. Our cousins and aunts and uncles are dispersed over four continents, and are financially able and willing to fly halfway round the world to attend a half-decent wedding. Despite these odds, we were determined to make the wedding as environmentally sustainable as practical. Box 8.5 shows how to get married on the environmental cheap, and retain good relations with your relations … sort of.

Actions for Next Year

Carefully planning long-haul flights

My plan was that after my flight to Los Angeles I would do the same as Duncan and halve my long-haul flying by flying once every two years. It would be better still if I saved up my holiday so we could stay away for at least three weeks. This would also dramatically reduce the cost of holidays by halving our flight costs.

At the start of 2008 my wife and I spoke about where we should holiday. We agreed we deserved a belated honeymoon. A friend of ours was getting married in January in Sri Lanka so it seemed a nice idea to visit India in the same trip to meet one another's families. Goa is not so far away as the west coast of the US so I would be able to reduce my emissions compared to last year.

Carefully planning long-haul flights (reprise)

But then a few months into the year my brother-in-law announced his plan to get married – in Goa – so we found ourselves flying once again to Panjim, screwing up all my carbon budgeting. What I can say in my favour is that I did actually turn down many, many flights I might have made … we received a torrent of wedding invitations and conferences invites, which I declined. And … the dog ate my homework. But now all our siblings are married, and most of our cousins too. So no more surprises.

But it was a great party.

Holidaying in western Europe in summer

It seems a shame to miss out on the lovely European summer. We felt the ferry and car combination had worked last year. The priority was to find a place with more reliable hot weather and less rain. We chose the Loire Valley. With just this basic bit of planning the holiday worked much better. It wasn't exactly hot but the clay pit lakes and the unheated swimming pool at our accommodation were warm enough to swim in. Falling out of our kayaks into the Loire was bracing rather than hypothermia-inducing. The food was great and we got to see loads of paintings, horses, chateaux and weapons which kept the factional interests in the family in a state of peace.

Stopping going on last-minute.com-style city breaks in far-flung countries

This was easy as I always found the stolen weekend away in Prague pretty pointless. A sort of trophy tourism, like visiting every London Underground station, just to say you'd done it.

Reducing emissions from skiing

Meaning skiing less often but for longer; not skiing at all was not on my agenda. I had got into the habit of going on two- or three-day ski trips with my brother and a German friend using Ryan Air's handily located network of airports whose names have no geographic bearing to any town with the same title. They often worked out fearsomely expensive once you factor in the cost of new tickets if you miss your flights (as we have done ... twice). It's people like me that cross-subsidize others to fly for £29.99. *Well Baby – this cash cow has decided to turn his udders off.*

In February three of the ski party decided to take to train to the Dolomites instead of the plane. It was great. We set off from Kings Cross at about 2.30pm and were on the slopes in Cortina less than 24 hours later. The time in the train wasn't wasted – we had a nice meal in Paris where we were given our first insight into how far sterling had collapsed. The train from Paris to Venice Mestre was a delight...not particularly fast, but it reminded my brother and I of the sleeper trains we used to catch when we lived in India. All of us had taken our laptops so we could work during the journey. The train fare was about twice the price of the airfare, partly because we had booked the tickets so late, and partly because the European leg of the trip was priced in Euros.

Overall my 2008 emissions were 50 per cent higher than those in 2007. Not good. Next year I promised I really would clamp down. And at the time of writing I haven't flown for a whole year. And no plans to in the foreseeable future.

Notes

1   World Tourism Organization (2007) *Tourism, Air Transport and Climate Change – Discussion Paper*.

2   Defra (2007) *Environmental Reporting: Defra's Greenhouse Gas Conversion Factors for Company Reporting*, www.defra.gov.uk/environment/business/reporting/pdf/ghg-cf-guidelines-annexes2008.pdf. See Annex 6 footnote 13 and bring your magnifying glass. Not exactly screaming out for attention.

3   Grassl, H. and Brockhagen, D. (2007) *Climate Forcing of Aviation Emissions in High Altitudes and Comparison of Metrics: An Update According to the Fourth Assessment Report, IPCC 2007*, www.mpimet.mpg.de/fileadmin/download/Grassl_Brockhagen.pdf (accessed June 2009).

4   Yes I found this hard to believe too. Look at Figure 2.8 in Chapter 2 for the underlying data. Emissions from holidays 4.8tCO_2 per household, equivalent to 9tCO_2 once you take account of radiative forcing factor of 1.9; richest 10 per cent emit 22tCO_2e per household.

5   Thompson Future Forum (2006) *Holiday 2016*, www.almendron.com/politica/pdf/2006/8777.pdf (accessed June 2009).

6   Department for Transport (2006) *Transport Statistics Bulletin – National Travel Survey 2006*, Office for National Statistics and Department for Transport, London, Table 5.6b.

7   VisitBritain, VisitScotland, Visit Wales and Northern Ireland Tourist Board (2008) *UK Tourist 2007*, www.tourismtrade.org.uk/Images/UK%20Tourist%202007_tcm12-43993.pdf (accessed June 2009).

8   UN World Tourism Organization (2007) see note 1.

9   QinetiQ (2008) *Aviation CO_2 Emissions Abatement Potential from Technology Innovation*, Report to Committee on Climate Change.

10 IPCC (1999) *Aviation and the Global Atmosphere: Special Report of the Intergovernmental Panel on Climate Change*, Cambridge University Press.

11 Defra (2008) *Guidelines to Defra's GHG Conversion Factors: Methodology Paper for Transport Emission Factors*, Defra, London.

12 Department for Transport (2006) *Transport Statistics Bulletin – National Travel Survey 2006*, Office for National Statistics and Department for Transport, London.

13 Cairns, S. (2008) 'Can teleconferencing reduce business travel?', Draft paper submitted for journal publication. Paper funded by the Rees Jeffreys Road Fund, TRL and UCL.

14 Garnett, T. (2008); Video Conferencing: FCRN Member Comments and Feedback; Food Climate Research Network, unpublished.

15 Tonge, V. (undated) *A Study of the Literature and Current Research into Responsible Tourism and the Sport of Skiing, Skier Motivation and Destination Choice and Ski Resort Destination Management Strategies*, International Centre for Responsible Tourism, www.icrtourism.org/Publications/LiteratureandCurrentResearch.pdf (accessed June 2009).

16 The website allows you to assuage your guilt and also counterbalance the heartbreak, pain and jealousy in the atmosphere arising from infidelity. The single, monogamous and others with no prospect of finding a partner can sign up to form part of cheatneutral's network of fidelity.

Carbon Offsetting, Communities and Social Change

Now

- It is possible to reduce your emissions substantially by making a number of focused changes. Not all of these can be done immediately. Investments in the fabric of the house or to personal transport need to be planned years ahead. You start from where you start, and the important thing is to set a reasonable and realistic goal. The website that accompanies this book has a detailed carbon calculator to help you audit your life. It will give you a report on your GHG emissions and help you test how much emissions you can save by modifying your purchases and behaviours.
- Offset your emissions only once you've done everything else. The best offset schemes are those that purchase carbon from the EU Emissions Trading Scheme, or which reduce emissions locally.

Soon

- You might find the support of like-minded people helpful. They can provide expertise, practical help and encouragement. Good networks include the carbon reduction action groups and Cambridge carbon footprint. Consider setting one up yourself if none exists locally. You'll be surprised how many others there are like you, living locally.
- Try to reduce energy and materials use in your community – local schools, local government and neighbourhood groups all depend on volunteers to steer and guide them. A lower-carbon life is a cheaper life. You may well find you need to work fewer hours to support yourself and have more time to contribute to local activities. This could be a more rewarding way of using your time than paid work.

Longer term

- The changes suggested in this book are profound and could reshape the economy. The credit crunch and the climate challenge could precipitate a more egalitarian, more localized and more sustainable society or it could send the world into chaos. It is for us to choose through our actions. Console yourself that what you are trying to achieve is important.

Introduction

No! Try not. Do. Or do not. There is no try.
(Yoda, in *Star Wars Episode V: The Empire Strikes Back*)

The previous chapters have talked about what we can do to reduce our greenhouse gas emissions cost-effectively. There is huge scope for motivated individuals to use energy much more efficiently and to save money too.

This chapter kicks off by adding up the numbers from the previous chapters to see whether I have managed to achieve my goal of reducing my emissions by 40 per cent. After this, we look at carbon offsetting schemes to see whether using our Visa card really absolves us of our carbon overindulgence.

The bulk of the chapter looks more broadly. Even if every motivated and well-informed environmentalist reduces their emissions, it's not enough; so too must their neighbours, family and friends. We go on consider how we can work with others to reduce the emissions within our communities. This chapter also discusses the implications of the earlier chapters' recommendations on society more broadly.

Total CO$_2$ Emissions Reductions from the Actions Taken

Justin, what were you thinking? How can you fly to Jamaica if you're trying to live ethically? (Professor Tim 'climate coach' Jackson's measured and detached reaction on hearing about Justin 'ethical man' Rowlatt's gratuitous flight to Jamaica)

I deliberately stopped myself from bringing all my data together until the year had ended. Better to withhold the information from myself. As Schrödinger noticed with his incarcerated cat, the very act of observation can taint the experiment. I knew it was likely to be very close and a binge drink or a diet over Christmas could easily tip it one way or the other.

Table 9.1 brings together my scores in the carbon hexathlon. I have considered 2007 as the baseline and 2008 as the year being assessed. The table uses the deliberately oblique term 'soon' because I haven't yet installed the external insulation, nor have I sold my car, consciously deciding to wait for prices in the second-hand car market to rise off the floor. The last column in the table reminds us of the change that contributes the most to the change in emissions.

Table 9.1 Reduction in personal CO_2 emissions from the changes described in this book ($kgCO_2e/yr$)

	2007	Soon	Reduction	Percentage reduction	Main changes
Food	2400	1200	1200	50%	No beef, reduced dairy
Transport	1600	800	800	50%	Sold car
Heating house*	3100	1200	1900	61%	Uses SAP assumptions
Electricity	900	500	400	44%	Lighting, laptop
Goods/waste	1000	600	400	40%	Few new goods
Holidays	2500	3300	−700	−28%	Flew twice, to India and France
Total	11,500	7600	3900	34%	

Note: * Assumes the house is heated to the SAP2005 standard, rather than my own more modest heating needs.

Overall my emissions have fallen by 34 per cent. This is just a little short of the 40 per cent cut called for by the Committee on Climate Change by 2020. My emissions fell under every heading, except my holidays. My absurd decision to fly twice to India in 2008 counteracted all my other good work. As an analyst working in government I had ignored the cardinal rule for setting a new government target – *manage the baseline*. It's much easier to appear good by selecting an atrocious year to compare against. But instead I used 2007 as my reference point even though I had already begun making tentative attempts to cut back (turning down an opportunity to go to the US to my cousin's wedding, and choosing to honeymoon 40 miles away). I'd have fired myself if I was still in government.

This is of course a pathetic attempt to excuse my actions – I was never extraordinarily renditioned onto the plane. Much as I would like to blame my brother-in-law for sneakily organizing his wedding in India at short notice just to spite me, I have to accept I went of my own volition. Last year flights accounted for 40 per cent of my total emissions *even including all my purchases*. If I had not made these I could have smugly attested to hitting the targets for 2020 within a year. Next year I will fly less.

Otherwise I have a good story to tell. And it's been surprisingly easy. I will have saved money from my dietary changes; replacing beef and dairy with artificial meats and soya saves money, as does replacing air-freighted foods with canned. Selling my car will save me up to £3000 a year, by far my biggest financial saving. Energy costs have come down in line with carbon reductions.

I will have spent £21,500 installing the energy-efficiency measures in our Victorian terrace house – a few per cent of the value of the house. If I'd draught-proofed instead of double-glazing the windows, the cost would have been just £14,000 but the emissions would be 300kgCO$_2$ per year higher.

But whether spending money on improving the house is a cost, an investment or consumption depends on the way you look at it. My house was built in 1870. For the past 140 years a dozen families have viewed my home as their home. These previous inhabitants installed phone lines, electricity cables, TV antennae, gas networks and internal toilets for their successors to enjoy. Maybe this house will be there for others to enjoy in another 140 years; improving its energy efficiency is our generation's contribution to the house's development. This stops being a purely economic issue, and becomes one of legacy.

How different does life seem? Not very, is the honest answer – but maybe that's because I haven't really cut back on my travel yet. I have grown to like soya and other meat substitutes just as much as meat itself. Using the train instead of the car to go to Birmingham saves both time and, believe it or not, money too. Making the home more energy efficient has been time consuming and an unnecessary faff, but has, for the most part, worked out well. But there is a lot more that needs to be done by public authorities to help meet the capital costs, and vet suitable contractors.

Buying our Way Out of Climate Change Emissions

If you want to go beyond simply reducing your personal emissions and neutralize them entirely, or you want to assuage your guilt for flying, you can always buy emissions credits from the carbon markets.

The idea behind carbon offsetting is simple enough. There are two parties: *a company* looking for finances to fund a greenhouse gas-reducing project and *you* wanting a cheap way of neutralizing your emissions. The company needs capital. Why not pay to provide these projects with the resources they need? The atmosphere doesn't care whether the avoided carbon is from your chimney or the company's. If it can reduce its emissions more cheaply than you surely this is the quintessential opportunity for the economical environmentalist seeking a win–win outcome.

There is a bewildering range of carbon offsets on the market. Carbon offsetting has its own arcane language. Carbon saving, like any currency, is denominated according to the region that manufactures it and the sector it is made in. The terminology is largely unknown even to climate change policy-makers: CERs, ERUs, EUA and VERs are some of the currencies in circulation just now. These have all been created on what is known as the *compliance market*, which means savings created by government regulation. The other option is to buy carbon from carbon-reducing projects set up by companies voluntarily, which is unimaginatively known as the *voluntary market*.

The problem with buying carbon off the market is the problem all fledgling currencies have: are they really as valuable as they purport to be, or are you buying tin pretending to be silver? The voluntary market includes lots of flaky afforestation projects which are hard to monitor, and aren't truly permanent, so the carbon they claim to store might end up in the atmosphere a few years after the forester has gone. But the voluntary markets also include good renewables and energy-efficiency projects. At our wedding we recommended guests offset their flights through Native Energy. It invested in renewable energy projects in Native Indian land in the US. Nonetheless the voluntary market, slightly unfairly, is often regarded as a PR exercise to let rich Westerners – including senior environmental figures – assuage their guilt for jetting to Kyoto, Bali and Poznan. This is borne out by the low traded volumes, the low prices and the near-contempt in which many environmentalists hold the market.

The compliance market is generally regarded as being better policed and more likely to deliver additional carbon benefits. You can buy into projects in Russia, India or China which are policed using rules set out in the Kyoto Protocol. The other option is to retire carbon from carbon markets in countries which have agreed to put a national limit on their CO_2 emissions, like countries in Europe. The concept has some major PR issues but, trust me, the idea is sound. This is a perfectly valid way of reducing the countries' emissions to below what they would have been, but if you do this it won't be possible to point to a carbon-reducing project and put up a placard saying you paid for it. Instead retiring carbon works through more esoteric means, increasing the cost of carbon dioxide within the EU Emission Trading Scheme and encouraging the uptake of low-carbon substitutes.

There are two practical issues and one ethical issue to consider when you think about whether carbon offsetting is for you. The first practical concern is one of additionality: does your money actually mean any extra carbon will be abated? Much ink has been spilled on this one. Paying a Chinese coal mine to get heat and power from its methane instead of letting it pour into the atmosphere is obviously a good thing, but if we bag the credit for funding it aren't we simply subsidizing what many people would regard as a simple commercial opportunity, *they could and should have done it anyway without a few extra pounds from a rich Westerner*. It's like paying a sports journalist's salary for attending the world cup final. A more subtle issue is that in the bizarre world of climate negotiations and industrial lobbying, if rich Western countries are prepared to pay Chinese and Indian firms to undertake the lowest cost abatement measures – like installing equipment to collect and destroy accidental

Table 9.2 Different types of projects funded by the compliance and voluntary markets

Project type	Compliance market	Voluntary market
	(%)	(%)
Industrial gases (HFCs)	32	20
Renewable energy	29	33
Forestry	0.2	36
Energy efficiency	12	5
Methane mitigation	20	3
Transport	0.1	
Fuel switch	7	
Other		7
Total in 2007 (MtCO$_2$)	2700[a]	75[b]
Price (US$/tCO$_2$e)	15–30	2–15

Notes: [a] Annual contract volumes from Kyoto and EU markets; [b] Point Carbon estimate of Europe and US voluntary offset purchases.
Source: Tyndall Centre (2008);[1] prices and totals from Point Carbon (2008)[2]

emissions of HFCs from factories – we might actually delay the Chinese and Indian government from developing regulations to mandate these cheap and self-evidently worthwhile changes; regulations companies in the West have been living with more years. Trading regimes could perversely incentivize Indian and Chinese governments to *not* introduce these regulations.

The second practical issue is whether the purported carbon saving really occurs. This issue has dogged afforestation projects from their very start – the caricature goes like this: tree planting is financed by Western environmentalists, investigative journalist finds a plot of land where a poor, disgruntled farmer has cut down the newly planted trees and replaced them with their indigenous cassava (or maybe poppy crop), journalist feigns indignation and Western do-gooder is made to seem naïve. Unfortunately this type of story has been played out all too often, and some of the extremely cheap carbon you might be offered by your airline company doesn't just seem too cheap to be true; it is too cheap to be true.

The ethical issue is that offsetting programmes are essentially transactions between rich people emitting 10 tonnes each, purchasing carbon from poor people emitting 1 tonne each. Instead of buying our way out of our commitments we should be using our climate change budgets over the next two decades to finance the technology and infrastructure to make 90 per cent cuts.

Box 9.1 *Idiot's guide to carbon offsetting*

You would think paying someone not to pump a tonne of carbon dioxide into the atmosphere would be straightforward product to buy. Not like investing in a wind turbine where you have neighbours and neighbourhoods, wind speeds and electricity tariffs to worry about. But like with most things in life, you pay for quality, or in the case of carbon offsets – you pay for certainty. There are around 100 carbon offset providers listed on the website www.carboncatalog.org/. The price of carbon offsetting ranges from £1 and £27 per tonne of avoided carbon dioxide. Why the difference? Loosely, the more you pay the more likely it is the money will actually save some carbon. The cheapest offsets invest in tree-planting projects in developing countries, while the most expensive remove EU carbon dioxide allowances from the market. These are the things you might want to look out for:

- Additionality: would the project have occurred anyway because it was already economically viable, or because the government would soon have made it compulsory?
- Permanence: does the project truly stop energy being used or does it just temporarily store carbon as do most forestry projects?
- Checking: is a trusted third party making sure the carbon saving is really taking place?
- Other benefits: does the project provide any other benefits, for instance improvement in biodiversity, development, technological advancement or improvements in water or air quality?

Many projects that claim to reduce emissions fail some or all these tests. Projects that reduce methane emissions from cattle, coal mines or landfill sites, or that reduce HFCs from industrial manufacturing fail the additionality test; afforestation fails the permanence test. Renewable energy projects typically score better, as do some energy-efficiency projects, but often the extra US$20/tCO$_2$ is icing on the cake, rather than the deal-maker. The UK's renewables obligation subsidy is worth something like US$75/tCO$_2$ and is what really drives the investment.

 For households seeking to access the compliance market the most reliable way of really making a difference is by retiring EU emissions trading allowances through organizations like sandbag (www.sandbag.org.uk) or carbon retirement (www.carbonretirement.com) which to my mind are the most pukka ways of offsetting emissions.

Environmentalists call for a personal carbon allowance to encourage people to rein in their emissions, but evidence of that effect on people's behaviour is patchy

There's a lot of enthusiasm for personal carbon allowances among environmentalists. These apply the idea of tradable permits to private citizens so each person is allocated say 5 tonnes of CO_2 per year. If they want to consume more they have to buy carbon allowances from someone else or from the regular carbon market. This idea has been espoused by people like David Fleming and also for a couple of nanoseconds by ministers at Defra. To operationalize it, records have to be kept on how much gas, electricity, petrol/diesel and perhaps air fuel people use in a year – this would then be converted into the tonnes of carbon dioxide.

But what would be the consequences in terms of different sections of our society? Figure 9.1 shows how much households with different incomes spend on fuel and transport. Not too surprisingly rich people spend a high proportion of their income on *nice-to-have* discretionary items rather than *must-have* items needed to stay alive. The figures show that on average the poorest fifth of households spend over 6 per cent of their incomes on warmth and power; the best-paid households pay 3.5 per cent of their income. The poor spend little on foreign holidays; the richest 10 per cent of households spend ten times more. So a personal carbon allowance would mean the rich would have to buy the poor's carbon allowances. So the personal carbon allowance would be a vehicle for social change transferring income from the rich to the poor.

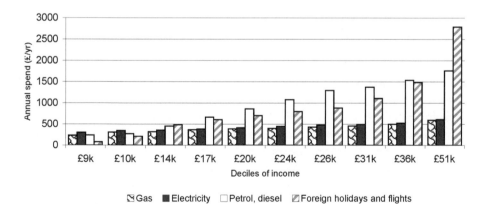

Figure 9.1 Domestic spending on energy for different household income bands, 2007

Source: Underlying data from ONS (2007) *Expenditure and Food Survey*

But the other side of the story is that the job of allocating and monitoring allowances is fiendishly difficult and intrusive. Does an urban-dwelling young man who works in an office get the same carbon allowance as a rural pensioner who is at home all day and needs to drive several miles to the local post office? Don't people who use electricity to heat their homes already pay for their carbon emissions because electricity generators participate in the EU's carbon market? How should you treat business travel with a brief holiday tagged on? Scarier still, if carbon could be bought for as little as £10–15 per tonne, might the rich feel unconflicted about flying as often and as far as they liked? A little bit of guilt is useful in dissuading them, because the modest increase in price from purchasing a tonne or so of carbon won't. When I worked in Defra the only argument we could find to support carbon rationing was a psychological one: that people would seek to maintain their consumption within their carbon budget to be good citizens *even though they could well afford to pay the extra costs*. But there was little evidence of this.

The underlying problem with personal carbon allowances is that they are not really equipped to deal with the problem we currently face. As a society we need to reduce our emissions to around 1 tonne per person. But it's not politically feasible, maybe not even technically possible, to live off so little just now without drastic changes to our lifestyles. Some people think this is precisely what needs to be done – but not enough to win an election. So far more than 1 tonne of carbon will be allocated to people for the foreseeable future. Introducing such a *too-generous* personal carbon allowance might actually lull individuals into thinking the problem is sorted, when in fact the tradable allowance system is doing nothing to actually change behaviours or develop and deploy new technologies.

There is one type of offsetting that I think it's quite legitimate to claim credit for. I'll call it 'community offset' and it involves helping others in your community reduce their emissions. You may have family or friends in need of financial support or physical help to install energy-efficient light bulbs or draught-proofing in their homes. This is real carbon being saved at very low cost. It can also be aid in kind. So, for instance, if you're planning to change your fridge and the old one still works, put some thought into how you can extend its life – perhaps by giving it away to someone with an old inefficient fridge. Replacing someone else's old G-rated fridge with your A-rated one would save $300 kgCO_2$ per year, so you can buy a smaller A++ fridge. The same logic could be applied to a car. Paying for the decommissioning of old and energy-inefficient kit within your own country is a great way of saving carbon and also reducing the need for investment in new electrical generation capacity.

Working through your community

This section is about local activities to reduce emissions in your community. Unlike trying to do this stuff professionally or at the national level, it's very easy to get into and you do not need to be particularly practical or knowledgeable to make a contribution. The appeal of working with others locally or through local institutions is you leverage in not just your own carbon savings, but also those of others, or those from local public services. Once you look around you see there are many people, still a minority but a reasonable chunk of people, who care about climate change very deeply.

The London borough I live in has three voluntary organizations solely concerned with local climate change issues, two local authority forums on environment/sustainable development, two transition town groups, and local branches of national environmental and development NGOs that campaign on climate change. There are also several green businesses including a farmers' market, several car-share clubs and even a social networking centre which provides office space and informal meeting rooms to social enterprises. So no one wanting to be involved with climate change activities locally need ever be short of things to do. There is actually the opposite danger of too much diffuse action – of too many people wanting to help, but struggling to do something that makes a real difference. How does an economical environmentalist best deploy his time to greatest carbon effect?

I have fairly arbitrarily identified five sorts of activity that might make a difference:

1   raising awareness;
2   support those trying to live a lower-carbon lifestyle;
3   provide low-carbon services;
4   local lobbying; and
5   traditional civic duties.

There are also some movements that try to do several of these in one go.

There's a number of means to raise awareness about reducing our greenhouse gas emissions. The commonest approaches are organizing speaker meetings with national figures or local advisers like recycling officers or Energy Saving Trust personnel. Other approaches include communal screenings of environmental movies followed by discussion afterwards: favourites include *Who Killed the Electric Car?*, an inquest into GM's deliberate sabotage of its own electric vehicle programme; *The End of Suburbia*, a reminder of the American dream's dependency on cheap oil; *An Inconvenient Truth*, Al Gore's assessment of the state of the climate science; and on a more positive note *The Power of Community*, an uplifting film detailing how Cuba sustained itself through an enforced shortage of oil after the fall of the USSR. There are also options for experiencing low-carbon lifestyles.

One of the big challenges facing people trying to reduce their emissions is remaining motivated. All of us have felt like George Monbiot when he wrote: 'When I take the bus, as I sometimes must, from Oxford to Cambridge, I arrive feeling almost suicidal.' It sometimes feels like town planners, public transport operators and shops are conspiring to make the life of the carbon conscious more difficult. Wouldn't I be happier if I could be like other people I know: fully aware of climate change, perhaps even professional environmentalists, yet cheerfully adrift in their private behaviour.

Luckily several locally based groups exist solely to motivate and support people trying to reduce their emissions. Carbon Reduction Action Groups (www.carbonrationing.org.uk) is a network for groups of people who set themselves carbon allowances which they reduce year by year. Groups are typically small enough to fit into a living room. The website has information to allow you to calculate your own emissions and inform you of local groups. The groups develop their own protocols for how much CO_2 each person is allowed to emit (ranging from a very unrealistic 2 tonnes per person in Glasgow, to the Dallas-style 8.4 tonnes) and the penalty for exceeding the limit – typically around £50 per tonne. There are around 30 groups in the UK. Another support initiative, the Low Carbon CO_2mmunity, based in Shropshire, uses a more top-down approach using funding from central and regional government to blitz businesses and homes to install low-carbon technologies.

My own favourite movement is Cambridge Carbon Footprint. This is based around five weekly sessions in which a group of four to ten people discuss and play games to motivate them into reducing their emissions. There are plenty of books to borrow, and gadgets like energy meters to try out.

The *Transition Town* movement set up by Rob Hopkins has a much more counterculture feel to it. It has developed its own slightly earnest, slightly-Maoist idioms for its programme of actions – *Energy Descent Plans*, *Honour the Elders* and the *Great Unleashing*. Its objectives are to create much more self-contained communities that have successfully weaned themselves off scarce fossil fuels and dramatically reduced their greenhouse gas emissions. The actual programme of work is more Women's Institute than Baader-Meinhof with movie screenings, advice on growing your own food and lots of commit-tees. There are now in excess of 120 transition towns around the world, and the first transition town in England, Totnes in Devon, has a small office. The website is at www.transitiontowns.org.

There are some NGO groups which provide local services to reduce emis-sions. These are often run by local volunteers. In earlier chapters I have already described the volunteer-run Freecycle network, an email-based service that helps the local re-use of goods; there are now over a million subscribers to

---

Box 9.2 *Shared commitment to reducing emissions – Cambridge Carbon Footprint*

The idea of developing a sense of shared purpose lies behind the Cambridge Carbon Footprint. This network was set up three years ago by Andy and Rosemary on the way back from the Centre for Alternative Technology in Wales. Rosemary, a trained psychotherapist, conscious of the powerlessness many of us feel in the face of climate change, developed a course to help people understand and adjust their attitudes to food, transport, heating and consumption. One meeting starts by asking us to describe the most enjoyable meal we could recall. Our recollections were not of fois-gras or Ritz teas but boisterous family Christmases with nondescript food, or fairground hot dogs on our first date. The foodie events that make us most happy are often more about who we eat with, rather than the haute-cuisine-ness of the meal.

The sessions last for about an hour and a half; participants play games to get them to apply the course material, in a quasi-real life setting. We were encouraged to think what we could accomplish immediately and in the longer term. Many of the participants go on to facilitate courses with their own friends or neighbours, or to run stalls using the carbon calculator software to get people thinking about their own footprint.

I helped run one at a local eco-weekend and we had an interesting range of carbon emissions ranging from around 80 tonnes per year for an ex-pat American who flew back to New England several times a year to around 2 tonnes from a retired lady living off state pension. Many of the academics in Cambridge where the software was first trialled had massively bloated carbon emissions arising from the conference trips with a few days of holiday tagged on at the end.

---

the emails in the UK alone. Certified Farmers' Markets is an organization that helps individuals and local entrepreneurs establish markets for local farmers' to retail their produce. Their website is www.farmersmarkets.net/. It is established as a subscription-based not-for-profit organization that provides practical help and sets standards (no coffee sales allowed, but locally sourced hot dogs are fine). At our own farmers' market I had a fascinating conversation with the fisherman about the John Dory he had caught earlier that day. It was the ugliest looking fish we'd ever seen and the kids were convinced it was a sea monster.

The Old Home, Super Homes network set up by the Sustainable Energy Academy consists of around 20 old homes that have been retrofitted with energy-efficiency and renewable technologies to reduce their energy use by 60 per cent or more. These homes have open days several time a year, and appreciate offers from volunteers to act as guides. The website is www. sustainable-energyacademy.org.uk/.

Local government is responsible for organizing and delivering many local services. These include waste collection and disposal, social housing, planning, schools, local buses and roads. You can influence local emissions by lobbying local councillors, attending local democratic processes like planning committees or conservation zones, or responding to local consultations. Local people are also represented on the boards of hospitals and primary health trusts.

Most local authorities regard reducing climate change emissions as one of their key roles. Local emissions of greenhouse gases are one of the national performance indicators by which national government judges the local authority. A fair bit of money hinges on this assessment. But this doesn't always filter down to the staff at the working level, and you might have to remind them of this. Many development control staff will continue to cheerfully turn down planning applications for energy improving measures, or the park authorities will continue to outlaw cycling because they don't understand how their decisions prevent people from reducing their emissions.

The large public institutions are major sources of greenhouse gases locally. A secondary school with 1200 children will have a gas and electricity bill of £100,000 and emit in excess of $500tCO_2$. The government has been pouring billions into updating the quality of secondary school buildings through its Building Schools for the Future programme. The quango set up to administer the programme, Partnerships for Schools (www.partnershipsforschools.org. uk/), has produced guidance material on sustainable design. Ofsted has given thought to how sustainability can be brought into the curriculum, purchasing and even the school diet.[3] But the actions of an energetic school governor can be important in converting good intentions into practical reality.

Public swimming pools are huge users of energy – and they offer scope for combined heat and power, not just the facility itself but neighbouring houses and offices too. Hospitals are under the control of NHS Trusts and if your CV manages to contain the requisite great-and-good markings you're welcome to try for a place. The NHS emits a massive $18MtCO_2/yr$,[4] so there is real scope for reduction.

Personal Emissions Reductions and the Macro-Economy

They will beat their swords into ploughshares and their spears into pruning hooks. Nation will not take up sword against nation, nor will they train for war any more. (Micah 4:3)

Imagine if we lived in a country where everyone had implemented the types of changes suggested in this book. The notion of radically restructuring the economy to shift it to another purpose is not a new one. The quote from the Bible talks about retooling a war economy so that people can enjoy the benefits of the peace dividend. But the Bible, while great at defining the policy goal, is less effusive on delivery.

In order to work, a modern country still needs a viable macro-economy. This means high levels of employment, investment funded either by savings or borrowing, reliable tax receipts, and world-class companies to produce export goods so we can pay for our imports. If everyone implemented low-carbon consumption, would the country remain economically viable?

A Green New Deal,[5] produced by a group of environmentalists, draws its inspiration from the profound interventions made by Franklin D. Roosevelt's administration in recovering from the Great Depression. It talks about the simultaneous threats posed by the credit crunch, peak oil and climate change, and proposes a range of policies to reduce fossil fuel use and relocalize and humanize financial flows within national boundaries. Its specific recommendations are a £50 billion investment in energy efficiency (and micro-renewables), raising energy taxes, cutting interest rates, breaking up the banks and restricting international capital flows. Most policymakers would agree with the majority of these, though the notion of breaking up banks, and reintroducing capital controls probably remains controversial. But, more importantly, what is missing from the report is whether and how the UK could pull it off. Turning swords into ploughshares might not be simple metallurgy but alchemy.

A low-carbon economy is likely to be a smaller economy

We are intensely relaxed about people getting filthy rich ... as long as they pay their taxes. (Peter Mandelson, 1998 speech to US computer executives)

I'm optimistic that we are actually seeing the opportunity of a generation being created in this. (Peter Mandelson)

Peter Mandelson's first quote reflected the views of many senior policymakers ten years ago – *what was the harm in wealth generation if it trickled down and created incentives for businesses to excel?* But this view has been discredited now. We have discovered the banks which created a great many *filthy rich* through paying their executives excessive bonuses are being bailed out from the taxes paid by people on ordinary wages. This must surely be one of the most dramatic and blatant transfers of wealth from ordinary people to the wealthy in many decades. The second quote better captures the present mood; it was actually made with reference to Northern Ireland but it reflects politicians' message that reducing our greenhouse gas emissions is fiendishly complicated but achievable.

I am not so sure; and I think if we go on underplaying the dislocation we risk being unprepared for the dramatic changes and, to present sensibilities, deterioration in lifestyles we will have to undergo.

The mantra shouldn't be 'Waste not; want not' it should be 'Spend less; suffer less'

This book advocates making changes that simultaneously reduce our emissions and save money. This can be a self-defeating combination. Why? Think what you will do with the money you save? If you fund a foreign holiday it will negate the carbon savings. If you save the money as shares or in a deposit account bank, the saved money is made available to others in the economy. In both cases your financial rectitude becomes someone else's consumption opportunity. The most innocuous way of saving of all – paying off your mortgage – reduces your future outgoings, and increases future consumption possibilities.

It's no good simply becoming more efficient at using carbon – you need to make sure you use the money saved to buy labour-intensive, rather than energy-intensive, goods. Certainly there is some scope for savings to be ploughed into paintings, antiques and cranial head massages. The happiness from shopping is short lived. Ultimately I hope we rediscover what makes us happy; people are happiest when they are with their friends and close family.

There is a lot of research confirming the rebound effect. Improved energy efficiency, especially among the fuel-poor, only generates modest energy savings because the improved efficiency is used to maintain homes to warmer temperatures. A recent evaluation of the government's programme to install energy-efficiency measures into fuel-poor homes found that energy use fell by just 1 per cent rather than the 30 per cent their models predicted[6] – reality is often a disappointing place for economists. The researchers found several reasons for the discrepancy: there were faults in the installation of the loft and cavity insulation; people chose to keep their homes warmer. But just as important was that people were often just stuck in their old habits: for instance, not using the heating controls properly and opening the windows when it got too hot, or turning on an electric fire because they liked the radiant heat even though the room was already at a comfortable temperature.

Installing energy-efficiency measures doesn't overcome these behavioural hurdles. What we need are policy tools that encourage installing energy efficiency, and also behavioural change. We are of course talking about energy taxes. Economists have long argued that government should raise more of its income from taxing social problems like pollution and excessive energy use, rather than social virtues like working (income tax) and employing people (national insurance contributions). Most economists advocate setting the level of carbon/energy tax at the level of the 'externality'.

In the UK we have a modest energy tax – the climate change levy – set at near 0.5p/kWh. Half of our CO_2 emissions occur in industries that are part of the EU's Emissions Trading Scheme (EU-ETS). This means that these industries also face a carbon price set within in the EU's carbon market; at one stage this peaked at 0.5p/kWh electricity, but has fallen since then because the economic downturn means there are far more carbon allowances in the market than industry needs at present. However, households are largely insulated from both of these instruments. Domestic electricity and gas customers pay no climate change levy, and domestic gas use is outside the EU-ETS. This is because two government policies, *fuel poverty* and *climate, change* are sparring against one another and climate change is having its ass kicked.

And it's worse still. As we have seen in earlier chapters there is a constant annual improvement in the average SAP rating in homes, and the energy performance of the stock of fridges and lighting. So energy costs are falling! No wonder we are lazy about turning lights and heating off; for the majority of people who are in work it costs almost nothing to leave them on and it's getting cheaper as we upgrade the efficiency of the devices.

Another approach to head off the fuel-poverty concerns, yet still encourage people to be less profligate with their energy use, is to create a household energy tax that increases in line with the *saving the average UK household makes every year from energy efficiency.* So, for instance, if the energy efficiency improves by 2 per cent a year, and the average energy bill is £1000 per house, the household energy tax would be charged per unit of gas consumed and would rise by £20 a year. Part of the proceeds of this tax could be set aside to install new gas boilers, draught-proofing and insulation for those who can't afford to do it themselves. This rising energy tax creates a strong and increasing incentive to install energy-efficiency measures and moderate consumption by using heating controls better.

The industrial mix in our economy will be radically different

Many of the suggestions in this book, if adopted by large numbers of people, would have a profound effect on the structure of the economy. A bigger question confronting the economical environmentalist is how industry and the workforce will adapt to the new challenges. This book identifies luxury cars, short-haul flights, air-freighted foods, dairy products, beef and sheep meat as climate disasters. It is difficult to see these industries surviving as they are now if Western countries reduce their emissions by 80 per cent over the next generation. Other sectors will grow in their place – renewables, retrofitting of energy efficiency, adoption of hybrid and electrical vehicles. And there will be shifts in use of one type of industry to another: the substitution of timber for steel and brick in construction, the move from plastic and paper distribution of information to electronic networks. It also means less production: buying fewer new consumer electronics and textiles and making them last longer.

What kind of dislocation will this have on our economy? How will the scaling-back of energy-hungry sectors work? How will workers adapt to the different roles and perhaps different working patterns? Who will fund the investment needed to retool industry? Less production is likely to mean less work: how will people react to less pay?

Barack Obama has agreed to billions of dollars in support of the US auto producers, seemingly in exchange for retooling their factories to make more fuel-efficient vehicles. Over the course of the recession government is going to play a huge role by loaning money to failing businesses and by being the customer for the major new public works programmes.

The transition will be painful and the dislocation difficult for people

A few years ago I applied for a job as an economist in the Department of Trade and Industry. In the interview I made an unfashionable plea that government should intervene to rescue Rover's Longbridge plant, near my then home in Birmingham. The faces of the HM Treasury and DTI economists dropped and they began citing mantras of *picking winners*, *level playing field* and *state aid*. At the time tampering in the market was seen as deviant behaviour in Whitehall. But we all knew even then that communities do not fully recover from the loss of a large employer. I know a proud 50-year-old man, who lost his job in the docks two decades earlier, and whose only paid work since has been to peel potatoes at a fish-and-chip shop, and do occasional stints as a lollipop man. Such drops in wages and status have been replicated for so many people in so many former steel, coal and dock towns.

But the intellectual mood has changed and propping up failing businesses is quite fashionable. In the UK, Jaguar Land Rover is asking for assistance. The downturn in the economy has demolished the demand for its products. The company employs 16,000 people in the UK and, according to the industry, five times this figure through the supply chain. These are seen as high-quality jobs – well paid and demanding of expensively acquired engineering skills.

Companies like Jaguar Land Rover face huge difficulties not just with the immediate threat of the credit crunch but the oncoming climate crunch ahead. Can a company producing the Jaguar XJ (global sales around 20,000, cheapest model a mere £45,000 and emissions from the *most* fuel-efficient model 209gCO$_2$/km) develop a luxury vehicle compatible with our emissions reduction targets? Will it invent the next Tesla?

Or will the marque stop being tolerated by consumers and instead be perceived as an environmental expense that we should no longer bear? This is a profoundly important issue. The switch to a low-carbon economy is going to have its casualties. And many environmentalists hope that Jaguar will be one of them. Tata, the Indian owners of Jaguar Land Rover, bought the company hoping to sell Jaguar Land Rover vehicles to wealthy customers in Asia. How things have changed. When I lived in India in the 1970s the only choice car buyers could exercise was what colour Ambassador to buy. No doubt Ratan Tata thought he was doing a service by extending the range of vehicles available to wealthy Asians. But can we really conceive of a world in which the 2 billion people in India and China are elbowing their way up the corporate ladders to afford the lifestyles these goods represent?

One insight into a world with dramatically lower fossil fuel consumption can be seen in Cuba

With the collapse of the USSR in 1990–1991, Cuba lost access to its allies and most important trading partners. Almost overnight the economy shrank by 30 per cent and trade fell by 80 per cent. Soviet oil imports imploded, dropping 90 per cent. Before, Cuba had been so flush with cheap Soviet oil it used to re-export some for profit. Cuba was also dependent on the USSR and Eastern Europe for many foodstuffs. The US State Department, with its infinite ability to bear a grudge, strengthened its embargo on Cuba, so Cuba – a mere 90 miles from Florida – found itself politically isolated, hungry and short of power.

Figure 9.2 shows how per capita emissions for Cuba and its next-door neighbour Jamaica have developed. Per capita CO$_2$ emissions for the two countries were roughly the same in 1990 but by 2003 those of Cuba were 45 per cent less. But despite this, on many indicators of development Cuba has been a success story: its life expectancy at 77 years is five years longer than that of Jamaica and is in the top third globally. In 2005, 95 per cent of its children had five years of primary education or more, again in the top third of the world.

Beyond this blur of numbers some profound and far-reaching changes took place. The country managed to hold itself together by simultaneously implementing many energy-saving technologies and putting up with great hardship.[7] Private cars were largely replaced by buses and high-occupancy

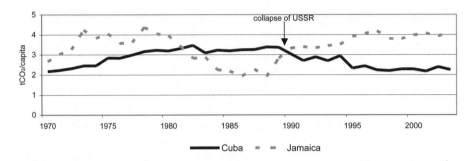

Figure 9.2 Per capita CO$_2$ emissions for Cuba and Jamaica

Source: World Bank, World Development Indicators

taxis and the import of large numbers of bicycles. Food consumption collapsed by around a third – the average Cuban lost 12kg in weight in the early 1990s. People had to learn how to grow food in cities using permaculture techniques taught by Australians; the state-run collective farms were unable to expand food production. But deaths caused by diabetes, heart disease and stroke have all dropped significantly. Electricity blackouts became the norm. But government reacted, banning the import of fridges and air-conditioning units to cut electricity use. More recently, power has become more reliable because of a switch to renewables, especially biomass, and oil imports from Venezuela. The US already so hate Chavez, that country's head of state, he need not worry about further reprisals.

The economy, measured in terms of GDP, is smaller; the population is ageing and growth is low. The socialist ownership of land proved to be chronically ineffective at producing sufficient food, encouraging the private production of food. But the country has maintained health and education services, and crime is lower than in other countries in the region. So life with less oil is possible, but the change is traumatic.

We need to appeal to people's hearts, not their wallets, if they are to reduce emissions

> Because I'm tired of it ... year after year ... of choosing between the lesser of two who cares ... of setting the bar so low I can hardly look at it.
>
> (Leo McGarry, *West Wing*)

> Bartlet: *Vitamin C, Vitamin D. Is it possible I'm taking something called euthanasia?*
> Sam: *Echinacea?* (banter between Sam and President Bartlet, *West Wing*)

I have chosen the above two quotes to remind us that the changes we need to make to reduce our emissions quickly will need a radical departure for business, not just business as usual. In the first quote Leo explains why he backed the maverick (though not by Sarah Palin standards) presidential candidate, Bartlett, instead of the blow-dried-looking John Hoynes. In the second quote we are reminded there are only a few letters difference between a poison and a panacea.

If we are to reduce our emissions by four-fifths within the next 30 years it won't be enough to replace a Jaguar with a Prius, allowing car companies the luxury of simply retooling. The changes will probably need to be more profound – choosing to live close enough to where you need to be so you can walk or cycle. If many of us do this there will have to be a correspondingly smaller car industry.

At present business doesn't get it. WWF's interesting report on environmental behaviour contrasts the current 'marketing approach' where *eco-goods* are a device to target a particular stratum of consumers with the 'just say no' approach the planet really needs.[8]

Public policy is stuck in a similar rut too. So much analysis is about fixing prices and honing incentives. A legitimate criticism made against economics is that is treats consumers as though we are walking and talking computers constantly weighing up the best deal, while in reality many of us cannot recall their annual energy bill to even the nearest £100. If we are going to get large numbers of people, and not just environmentalists, to restrain their consumption and aspirations for consumption we need to appeal to their base motivations. How do we make low consumption something they feel compelled to do?

This will seem an odd line of reasoning for an economical environmentalist, but the real challenge is making most people feel the moral dimension to climate change. The scientific and economic cases have already been made by the IPCC and economists like Nick Stern. But these arguments either leave people feeling cold or helpless. It is either a far-off threat, something to be unconcerned about just now; or so awesome and scary that nothing can be done. We need to make people feel the urge to make the necessary changes, *because they are both the rationale and the good thing to do*. So much of the policy effort goes into appeals to the wallet instead of the heart. Religious writers never release books with titles like *The Business Case for Belief in God*, or *Prayer: A No-Regrets Path to Heaven*. Why does the environmental movement so often contort its message into faux-business-speak: 'the triple bottom line', 'environmental auditing', 'greening GDP'. The religious unapologetically and without further elaboration can declare that Faith alone is the motivation directing what they do and how they are. How do we make low-carbon lifestyles equally motivating?

The increasingly shrill cries from the scientific community warn us we have only a handful of years to wean ourselves off our fossil fuel habit. Many climate scientists see a holocaust of suffering ahead for our children and our grandchildren. But just because the physical manifestation of this horror is the rising of gaseous concentration levels, instead of the erection of concentration camps, the stored up misery is no less real. Many people will be killed and rendered homeless, perhaps stateless if entire countries' ecologies collapse. We cannot go on as we are. How do we convert the fearful threat of runaway climate change into an imperative to switch to low-carbon consumption?

I haven't got any answer as to how to engender this shift. But I hope this book has helped to show that the personal changes – while sometimes awkward, sometimes odd, sometimes boring – are not unachievable.

I offer no apologies for saying I am scared for the future, and I want my children and their children to have as good a shot at a happy life as I had. This, rather than economics, needs to be our justification for change.

Notes

1   Estrada, M., Corbera, E. and Brown, K. (2008) *How Do Regulated and Voluntary Carbon Offset Schemes Compare?*, Tyndall Centre, www.tyndall.ac.uk/publications/working_papers/twp116.pdf (accessed June 2009).

2   Røine, K., Tvinnereim, E. and Hasselknippe, H. (eds) (2008) *Carbon 2008 – Post-2012 is Now*, Point Carbon, www.pointcarbon.com/polopoly_fs/1.912721!Carbon_2008_dfgrt.pdf (accessed June 2009).

3   Ofsted (2008) *Schools and Sustainability: A Climate for Change*.

4   Stockholm Environment Institute (2008) *NHS England Carbon Emissions: Carbon Footprinting Report*.

5   The Green New Deal Group (2008) *A Green New Deal*, www.neweconomics.org/gen/greennewdealneededforuk210708.aspx (accessed June 2009).

6   Hong, S., Oreszczyn, T. and Ridley, I. (2006) 'The impact of energy efficient refurbishment on the space heating fuel consumption in English dwellings', *Energy and Buildings*, vol 38, pp1171–1181.

7   Deere, C.D. (1991) 'Cuba's struggle for self-sufficiency: Aftermath of the collapse of Cuba's special economic relations with Eastern Europe', *Monthly Review*, July–August.

8   WWF-UK (2008) *Weathercocks and Signposts*, wwf.org.uk/what_we_do/campaigning/strategies_for_change/.

LIMERICK
COUNTY LIBRARY

List of Abbreviations

AR4	Fourth Assessment Report (of the IPCC)
ASHP	air source heat pump
BERR	Department for Business, Enterprise and Regulatory Reform (responsible for UK energy policy till October 2008)
BRE	Building Research Establishment
CBI	Confederation of British Industry
CER	Certified Emission Reduction
CFCs	chlorofluorocarbons
CFL	compact fluorescent light bulb
CHP	combined heat and power
CLG	UK department of Communities and Local Government
CNG	compressed natural gas
CO_2	carbon dioxide
COP	coefficient of performance
DECC	UK Department of Energy & Climate Change (formed October 2008)
Defra	UK Department for Environment, Food and Rural Affairs (responsible for climate change policy till October 2008)
DfT	UK Department for Transport
DOE	US Department of Energy
EPC	Energy Performance Certificate
EPR	European Power Reactor (French designed nuclear power plant)
ERU	Emission Reduction Unit
EST	Energy Saving Trust
ETS	EU's Emissions Trading Scheme
EUA	European Union Allowance
GDP	gross domestic product
GHG	greenhouse gas
GSHP	ground source heat pump
HCFC	hydrochlorofluorocarbons
HFC	hydrofluorocarbons
HGV	heavy goods vehicle
HMRC	UK Her Majesty's Revenue and Customs
HMT	Her Majesty's Treasury
ICES	International Council for the Exploration of the Sea
ICT	information and communications technologies
IEA	International Energy Agency
ILO	International Labour Organization
IPCC	Intergovernmental Panel on Climate Change
JAL	Japan Airlines
LCD	liquid crystal display
LED	light emitting diode (light bulb)
LGV	light goods vehicle
LPG	liquefied petroleum gas

MDF	medium-density fibre board
NGO	non-governmental organization
NHS	National Health Service
NO_x	nitrous oxides
OECD	Organisation for Economic Co-operation and Development
Ofgem	UK Office of Gas and Electricity Markets
ONS	UK Office for National Statistics
OPEC	Organization of the Petroleum Exporting Countries
PFI	private finance initiative
ppm	parts per million
PV	photovoltaic
RDC	regional distribution centre
RFI	radiative forcing index
RO(C)	renewable obligation (certificate)
RPI	retail price index
RSI	repetitive strain injury
SAP	Standard Assessment Procedure
SME	small and medium-sized enterprises (firms that employ fewer than 250 staff)
SO_x	oxides of sulphur
SSB	spawning stock biomass (of fish)
TAC	total allowable catch
TAR	Third Assessment Report (of the IPCC)
TRV	thermostatic radiator valve
TSO	The Stationery Office
UNCTAD	United Nations Conference on Trade and Development
UNEP	United Nations Environment Programme
UNFCCC	United Nations Framework Convention on Climate Change (of which the Kyoto agreement was a protocol signed in 1997)
U-value	heat transfer coefficient
VAT	value added tax
VC	videoconference
VER	Verified Emission Reduction
WMO	UN World Meteorological Office

Units and SI prefixes

ACH	air changes per hour
tCO_2e	tonne of carbon dioxide equivalent
$kgCO_2$	kilograms of carbon dioxide
kWe	kilowatt electric
kWh	unit of energy; one kilowatt-hour is equivalent of leaving a 100W light bulb on for ten hours
kWp	kilowatt peak
L	litre
mph	miles per hour
MW	Megawatt, unit of power; approximately the electrical power needed for 1000 homes
psi	pounds per square inch
rpm	revolutions per minute
m	milli, thousandth (10^{-3})
k	kilo, thousand (10^3)
M	mega, million (10^6)
G	giga, billion (10^9)
T	tera, trillion (10^{12})

Index